LETTERS OF A POET DYING

LETTERS OF A POET DYING

The Selected Correspondence of Frank Stanford

Edited and with an introduction by

A. P. WALTON

THE UNIVERSITY OF ARKANSAS PRESS
FAYETTEVILLE | 2026

978-1-68226-295-5 (cloth)
978-1-68226-296-2 (paperback)
978-1-61075-859-8 (electronic)

30 29 28 27 26 5 4 3 2 1

Manufactured in the United States of America

Designed by William Clift

The cover photograph, taken by Ginny Stanford in 1973, shows Frank Stanford at the entrance of the theater where he screened 16 mm films—at 8 Center Street, Eureka Springs, Arkansas.

♾ The paper used in this publication meets the minimum requirements of the American National Standard for Permanence of Paper for Printed Library Materials Z39.48-1984.

LIBRARY OF CONGRESS CATALOGING-IN-PUBLICATION DATA

Names: Stanford, Frank, 1948–1978 author | Walton, A. P. editor
Title: Letters of a poet dying : the selected correspondence of Frank Stanford / edited and with an introduction by A. P. Walton.
Description: Fayetteville : The University of Arkansas Press, 2026. | Includes bibliographical references and index.
Identifiers: LCCN 2026006337 (print) | LCCN 2026006338 (ebook) | ISBN 9781682262955 cloth | ISBN 9781682262962 paperback | ISBN 9781610758598 ebook
Subjects: LCSH: Stanford, Frank, 1948–1978 | Poets, American—20th century | LCGFT: Personal correspondence
Classification: LCC PS3569.T3316 Z48 2026 (print) | LCC PS3569.T3316 (ebook)
LC record available at https://lccn.loc.gov/2026006337
LC ebook record available at https://lccn.loc.gov/2026006338

For Irv Broughton, Eleanor Hamilton, William L. Fox, Cheryl E. Ross,
Bill Willett, James Babij, Ralph Adamo, and Ginny Stanford,
living legends.

CONTENTS

V. Spider Creek and the White River: Busch, 1973

VI. Rocky Branch and Beaver Lake: Rogers, 1973–75

VIII. The Music of the Soul: New Orleans and Fayetteville, 1978

In your sleep, in your dreams, I am wrestling the angel of death.

—FRANK STANFORD

INTRODUCTION

I had to create to exist.
—FRANK STANFORD

NEARLY HALF A CENTURY HAS PASSED since Frank Stanford's death at age twenty-nine on June 3, 1978, and for many of the years therein, the poet's legacy languished or hung on by bare threads. Poets and friends and acquaintances of Stanford's sometimes recalled the cultish qualities of his work. Younger readers and poets of the new century, myself included, also often experienced Stanford as an awakening, but more clearly delineated—regarding Stanford less as an outsider artist being tenuously sustained than as a bolt of uncontainable heat lightning, a bona fide maestro and undeniable iconoclast, and, chiefly, a poet irrevocably deserving of, and destined for, literary canonization.

How could there exist such a bifurcation between a poet's creative powers and his muted position in American poetry—with its many milieus of seemingly endless poets and largely propelled by a pay-to-play contest and blurb-fueled culture? At least, that was the question I often pondered.

As time goes on, though, Stanford continues to ascend. Much of his poetry was out of print for decades prior to the publication of a collected poems in 2015. Multiple books (collectively containing many hundreds of Stanford's poems) are in print today, and poets with a discriminating eye for vivid and large-scale or expansive poetry, especially young poets with passion and enough taste for rebellion, invariably find their way to Stanford. And Frank Stanford is not merely a poet's poet or a poet's poet's poet either. Readers seldom interested in poetry are routinely sucked into his creative macrocosm through his narrative legerdemain and instantly distinguishable voice.

Nearly half a century. I think of Arthur Rimbaud, whose last poems were written for *Les Illuminations* as a teen circa 1874 but not published until 1886, unbeknownst to him—and whose legacy was advanced with assistance from other poets (Paul Verlaine, Stéphane Mallarmé, et al.)—but whose star did not reach noteworthy heights until the twentieth century. Or Herman Melville, who experienced temperate success with *Typee* (1846) and *Omoo* (1847) but whose *Moby-Dick* (1851) was, like Rimbaud's work, not successful until the next century. In *Sexus*, Henry Miller proffers that, unlike for a genius painter, it can take centuries for a writer to be accepted, noting that it took

Melville maybe seventy years. In Stanford's 15,434-line epic, *The Battlefield Where the Moon Says I Love You* (1977), he writes, "call me Death I'm tired of Ishmael" (line 3450), and the poem follows in the lineage of Melville's stratospheric range.

We are not nearing the end of Frank Stanford's story but, rather, are merely beginning to understand just who this person was and the work he left behind. This book helps to tell the poet's fuller story.

WHO WAS STANFORD, AND WHAT MOVED him—and what is his story that these letters tell? He was a Southern poet with a distinctly Southern voice whose spirited imagination was not limited to his own tangible South. He spent nearly his entire brief life in the relatively confined radius of the Mississippi Delta, Memphis, and northern Arkansas, so to many he has seemed a localized poet of a specific geographical region and the product of particular eras—namely, the Civil Rights era of the 1950s and 1960s and the new American poetry era that thrived in the little magazines of the 1960s and 1970s. However, as these letters show, that world was only Stanford's corporeal world. Really, he is a world poet with vast spatial and temporal reach. Never mind that Stanford never finished college—like a scholar, he read widely and voraciously, especially English, French, Italian, and South American poets. The letters indicate readings across ancient Greek and Latin texts, varied texts in and from French (from Symbolist and Surrealist works to numerous film texts), a broad range of English poets (Old, Middle, and Modern English), Russian poets, classic American literature, adventure literature, historic epics, lieder, Eastern philosophy, multiple holy texts, various dramatic works and screenplays, mythological and folklore texts, poetry in translation from a range of languages, and so on—as well as Southern literature, poetry published across small literary magazines, the then-current poetry anthologies and single-author books, and hundreds of unpublished manuscripts of contemporaries. Writing and books were his passions; in his June 1972 patient history from the Arkansas State Hospital (the state's psychiatric hospital, where he was admitted after he and his first wife separated), under "What are the patient's chief sources of satisfaction and of disappointment?," the doctor, or perhaps social worker, wrote, "Cares only for books—his writing," and under "How does the patient spend his (her) spare time?," the answer was "Writing. (All the time!)" Stanford's deep passions across painting, music, and cinema were also broad—and historical and global in scope. In a February 1972 letter to Eleanor Bender, founding editor of the poetry magazine *Open Places*, Stanford laments the conservative Southern poetics of New Criticism and the perceived hegemony of writing programs—"Eleanor—I feel like I'm living in occupied territory!"; a month later, he quotes Middle French poet François Villon to poet Alan Dugan: "En mon païs suis en terre loingtaine" (In my own country I'm in a distant land). Stanford's own poetics were similarly less limiting.

The story that *Letters of a Poet Dying* tells is a scarcely believable, beautiful, and profoundly tragic story of genius, madness, passion, originality, creativity, love, and death. Stanford's is a classically romantic story of a toweringly prolific artist, a brilliant enfant terrible, and a "Huckleberry Rimbaud" whose life and death were even more dramatic than the Symbolist poet's. Stanford's immutable, unceasing obsession with death is reminiscent of William Blake and Emily Dickinson. However, his preoccupation with death is only an underlying thread; these visceral letters are driven by energy, rich emotion, and a connectable human element as they deliver the story of a born poet finding his way in life, love, writing, and publishing.

The classicism and romanticism so central to Stanford's work and very being could rattle readers who've idealized him as a cult writer—the poet whose whip-tight lines are virilely propelled by stark or violent images and lean, aggressive verbs and nouns. At Stanford's core, though, he is a full-on Romantic a century and a half removed from Keats, Shelley, Blake, Byron, De Quincey, Lamb, and Coleridge, as well as from Beethoven, Mahler, Schubert, Delius, and Wagner—all discussed in the letters. To poet Richard Eberhart in late December 1972, Stanford notes, "Ever since I was six, I've always carried a copy of one of the Romantic poets whenever I made a journey." The reader will hit on Stanford's own romanticism too, as he is at ease baring his deeply felt passions, aesthetic sentiments, and innermost feelings to distant pen pals such as Bender, poet David Walker, and Dugan—the former two of whom he never met; he met Dugan in November 1970 and again in August 1972, but their friendship thrived on the page in rich missives.

Stanford's soulful inner world ran galaxies deep—he appears to have regarded this life as a bare blip, a world between worlds. To Bender, he writes, "In some past life, I believe I must have roamed the seas. There is recollection of some cold, isolated island and ancient wood," while in the same letter, written three weeks before his twenty-fourth birthday, he adds, "I have never feared Death. I've always thought—rather I've never thought of living past 24 years old." Multiple people close to Stanford have recalled that he mentioned not planning to live past thirty, and in *The Battlefield*, the twelve-year-old poet-hero, Francis Gildart (named for Stanford's given names), notes, "I should have been / as though I had not been I should have been carried from the womb / to the grave" (8617–19), "just another bastard childhood is not worth living no matter what you hear" (9846), and "I who will be dead before one word is read a suicide note which is sung too late" (13272). In an existence marked by often fleeting encounters and such portended evanescence, Stanford sought out permanence, transcendence. "Really, I visualize the dead as well as the living," he wrote in an essay, "With the Approach of the Oak the Axeman Quakes." "I visualize *you* whom I will never know." Death was more his temporal link to perpetuity than a terminus, and his final dated letter, penned the day he died, indeed describes the commencement of a spiritual journey. Vast spatiotemporal reach was inherent in Stanford's perceptions of life and death; all of existence was both temporally and spatially interconnected. In *It Wasn't a Dream: It Was a Flood*—a 1975 short film about Stanford directed by Irv Broughton and shot mostly by Broughton and Stanford—Stanford says, "When I look at the bark of a tree, I might look at my arm. I might think of a spider floating along in fall or a shooting star, a constellation, or a mathematical formula, chess being played. Everything flows like that, I think."

A sense of desperation pervades some letters, especially in Stanford's early twenties, as in the period leading into the failure of his marriage to Linda Mencin. Stanford was an adoptee, and learning in 1968 of his adoption by his mother had been a traumatic, transformative event for him. He was similarly traumatized by the loss of his and Linda's aborted child (whom Stanford named Avalon, after the island from Arthurian legend) in fall 1970, his and Cheryl Campbell's miscarried (male) child in summer 1971, and likely others. Linda told me, in 2008, that Stanford had wanted her to have the baby ("Can you imagine? Rosemary's baby," she said), while Cheryl told me, in 2023, that Frank had felt that it wasn't the right time for them to have a child upon learning in June 1971 that she was pregnant (as finances were limited and he was also involved with Linda)—though Cheryl nonetheless miscarried within days, probably while still in the first trimester. In any case, it is perhaps no coincidence that one of the roughest patches of Stanford's life came less than a year later, in 1972—his most prolific epistolary year—as his marriage to Linda crumbled. To Bender in July 1972, he wrote, "At night . . . I would dream of the aborted children. Little fleets of coffins sailing into my solitary harbor. Would I ever return home on my horse with a dead child not in my lap. Would they ever live." Stanford's allusion to Goethe's "Der Erlkönig" (via Schubert's lied) conveys the agony and agita with which he realized that he had in some sense replicated the transgressions of his biological parents, whom he never met. In these early years of correspondence, Stanford seeks out mentors who might encourage him or offer glimmers of hope. Such reaching is clear in letters to established poets such as Allen Ginsberg and Dugan and to editors such as Bender. Stanford's 1969–74 letters are more commonly handwritten and in times of distress are scarcely legible. By his late twenties, in 1975, when he summons the "gumption" to write to another prominent literary figure he respects, poet William Stafford, Stanford's tone is seasoned and measured.

Stanford's most relaxed, longest-running correspondences are with his publisher Irv Broughton, his friend/mentor Alan Dugan, and poet John McKernan. Stanford and McKernan met at the University of Arkansas in Fayetteville in the late 1960s and, after crossing paths again at the Hollins Conference on Creative Writing and Cinema in Virginia in June 1970—where, incidentally, Stanford met Broughton—corresponded every year from 1970 to 1978. Stanford liked that McKernan was neither a Southern poet of the Fugitives / Southern Agrarians / New Criticism variety nor a schmoozing, status-driven poet-editor. Stanford also appreciated that McKernan's skinny, stapled-wraps magazine, *The Little Review*, was a straightforward publication uncorrupted by fluff, often spotlighting just a smattering of poets per issue. Broughton and McKernan published dozens of Stanford's poems in the 1970s in their respective magazines, the *Mill Mountain Review* (in 1970, 1971, and 1975) and *The Little Review* (in 1971, 1974, and 1975)—including most of Stanford's 1975 book *Arkansas Bench Stone* in the latter; in return, Stanford published McKernan's first book, *Walking Along the Missouri River*, and Broughton's early book *The Blessing of the Fleet* through his own press, Lost Roads, in 1977. In one of our conversations, in December 2008, McKernan proclaimed a monumental valuation of Stanford's poetic greatness—when prompted, he agreed to go on the record with simply: "Stanford is the best poet of his generation. Period."

It is clear from length, frequency, and content of correspondence to Broughton, Dugan, McKernan, editor Michael Cuddihy, and Walker that Stanford thought especially highly of them. In an unpublished elegy titled "why did frank stanford commit suicide," Dugan wrote that Stanford "wrote too much," and in a March 2008 phone call with me, Walker likewise uttered that Stanford "wrote way too much." This view is one I've never shared, especially considering, for example, that Stanford revered Stafford, who, from 1950 to 1993 alone, produced twenty thousand pages of daily writings. And Stanford's letters, like his poetry, read as nothing less than fully charged and inspired.

STANFORD'S WORLD IS A MASCULINE ONE, and as publishing poets and editors in the 1970s were more commonly men, most of Stanford's correspondents are as well. But in *It Wasn't a Dream: It Was a Flood*, Stanford states an interest in depicting strong female characters in his storytelling. Speaking slowly, deliberately, he says, "Like Strindberg and Faulkner and Lawrence and Bergman and Ophüls and Renoir, I'm interested in writing about women. It might have no contemporary significance. My point of view might not go along with anything current, but I've known some fine and great, powerful, and beautiful women, and I would like to write about them." Indeed, several of these writers and filmmakers incorporated strong female characters or leads into their work. In a 1981 essay titled "Remembering," novelist Joan Williams, a long-time Stanford family friend, wrote that Frank and his second wife Ginny (together with Broughton) had visited her in Mississippi in the early 1970s for an interview "while doing a documentary on women writers." When Cuddihy, founding editor of the journal *Ironwood*, sent Stanford his contributor's copies of *Ironwood* issue 4 (1974), an issue featuring twenty-eight male poets and nine female poets, Stanford responded that overall the poems by women impressed him the most. Eileen Myles has rightly contended (in a review of Stanford's selected poems, *The Light the Dead See*) that

Stanford's world is *a man's world*—"The word I can't avoid is masculinity"—but that world is panoptic, egalitarian, and geared toward change.

Stanford's closest loves were strong women—often artists in their own right, including Cheryl Campbell née Crites, a multi-instrumentalist; Ginny Stanford née Crouch, a painter and photographer; and C.D. Wright, a poet. Mencin was a politically focused social worker whose work Stanford also admired. Stanford met Ginny Crouch in March 1973 and expresses his pride in her artistry and technical proficiency across numerous letters; to Broughton in June 1973, Stanford describes her as "a great artist," adding, "You *must* see how she sees all my characters, images, and so on," and in a December 1974 letter to McKernan, he notes that he is more interested in Ginny's work just then than his own. He was similarly taken with Wright's talents as poet. From a November 1976 letter to Cuddihy: "I can't wait to lay ten of CDWright's poems on you. I think she is the most powerful poet I've read since Ai." Indeed, through Stanford, Broughton's little Mill Mountain Press—which published all Stanford chapbooks that appeared during his life (and copublished, with Lost Roads, *The Battlefield*)—published Wright's first book, *Alla Breve Loving*, in 1976, and after founding Lost Roads Publishers, the first title Stanford published, as Lost Roads No. 1, was Wright's next book, *Room Rented by a Single Woman*.

Still, Stanford was routinely, often humorously, and certainly intentionally what we would now refer to as politically incorrect—arguably in a manner that could seem jolty or outmoded to twenty-first-century sensibilities. Stanford suspected, after learning of his adoption, that he was multiracial, and he deeply identified with Black culture and civil rights in the South ("I use to ride the freedom rider buses often," he wrote to Eberhart); grew up with Black children in the levee camps along levees that his adoptive father, A. F. Stanford, engineered and built; and was close, longtime friends with members of Fayetteville's African American community such as Jimbo Reynolds, Sherman Morgan, and Claude Ricks. Stanford believed in the human condition's shared experiences and struggles regardless of race, gender, and geographical or cultural differences and, so, took subversive pleasure in verbalizing the unspeakable and the taboo ("*épater les bourgeois*"—to shock the middle classes—per a January 1973 letter to his grandmother) by demarcating our many differences within the "universality" (as he refers to it in his April 1974 letter to Walker) to which he so fervently adhered. Our embattled world was, to Stanford, a "battlefield" where the moon, like some higher power, forgives all of our flaws and trespasses and says, "I love you."

FRANK STANFORD'S LETTERS ARE VERY OFTEN written in a full-speed, stream-of-consciousness style, as he oscillates between multiple concurrent thoughts. This fast-and-loose quality is especially evident at, for example, the end of the circa September

15, 1972, letter to Stanford's close friend Bill Willett and toward the closings of his June 21, 1971, letter and October 16, 1972, letter to Dugan, when various thoughts are being presented simultaneously. A 1980 Lost Roads Publishers brochure describes *The Battlefield*, Stanford's magnum opus, as: "Told from the point of view of a twelve-year-old clairvoyant as if *Huckleberry Finn* had been written by Andre Breton." And Breton was, aptly, a favorite of Stanford's; Breton's first Surrealist manifesto (1924), with suggestions for automatic writing—for writing quickly, without rereading—as well as his tip, "Keep reminding yourself that literature is one of the saddest roads that leads to everything" (trans. Richard Seaver and Helen R. Lane), seem particularly relevant to Stanford's style.

Stanford was an imaginative virtuoso, especially in conjuring original, arresting images and in spinning a story. He throws away stunning lines in letters and postcards, and he writes with energy and passion—with blood and tears on the page and words ablaze. What the correspondence in this book adds to and illuminates in Stanford's poetry is the depth of emotion, distress, frustration, excitement, joy, and compassion that often existed beneath that raw vitality so present in his work.

With such intensity, spirit, and passion comes speed, which commonly leads to imperfection, error, and illegibility. Many letters include marginalia and insertions. As sample letter images throughout the book often show, some of Stanford's scrawl can be difficult to decipher; scribal errors and typos sometimes run rampant. Stanford's December 26, 1974, letter to Dugan refers to Ginny's parents having given him, for Christmas, a two-volume collection of " 'poetry in manuscript,' only 1,500 copies printed." The edition is the lavishly published, slipcased set (priced steeply at seventy-five dollars upon publication in 1973) *Autograph Poetry in the English Language: Facsimiles of Original Manuscripts from the Fourteenth to the Twentieth Century*, edited by P. J. Croft, which presented reproductions of "poets' own manuscripts"—including many of Stanford's favorite Romantic poets. Croft's introduction notes that a writer's handwriting typically matures and settles by their mid-twenties and that variations in a matured cursive are the result mostly of fluctuations in mood or conditions. But since most of Stanford's letters were written in his early to mid-twenties and very often with significant fluctuations in mood or conditions, his handwriting moved through numerous phases—including all-caps block lettering, a sort of irregular caps / sentence case blend, and (especially in fall 1972 and 1974 letters) a cursive written with a fountain pen. In times of distress and desperation—particularly in May–June 1972 and May–June 1978—a marginally legible quality seeps into his handwriting. He and Linda separated either at the close of April (per his hospital record) or in mid-May 1972 (per Linda's divorce filing), and he wrote to Bender that he had been jailed multiple times; in late May, he was firing off hysterical letters to Dugan that were barely more decipherable than scribble. The letters' content—alcohol, incarceration, madness, and burned manuscripts—is dramatic, emotionally charged, and eschatological. His handwriting in them is quite messy. On June 1, Dugan wrote to Stanford: "Read this carefully: I think that you are a genius and a beautiful poet. It pisses the shit out of me that you have destroyed some of your own work." Down the page, Dugan's wife, Judith Shahn, added, "Has Dugan told you that he *cannot read your handwriting?*" noting that she had to "translate" Stanford's letters for her husband: "The last four recent ones, which we tried to make out were (from the legibility alone) virtually incoherent." Those four letters are likely Stanford's May 15 and 16, May 21 and 22, May 26, and May 27 letters (that much of the May 26 letter is in Middle French surely didn't help), though all six of his May 1972 letters to Dugan are messily scribbled.

Some letters stand out in this collection. The utter desperation of the "May Day" and other May 1972 letters, mostly to Dugan, is striking. The sweeping romantic fervor throughout the letters to Campbell is palpable. Others also catch the eye, including the June 28, 1971, letter to Bender (in which Stanford lists much of his recent, "wandering" reading); the October 16, 1972, letter to Dugan (perhaps the apex of Stanford's surrealist epistolary writing), and the December 30, 1974, letter to Cuddihy (in which Stanford contemplates spacetime). Naturally, Stanford's two June 1978 letters to Ginny Stanford and C. D. Wright—his final two letters just prior to the resolute suicide whereby he entered a bedroom of his Fayetteville house and shot himself three times near the heart with a .22-caliber revolver—stand out as well for their emotional solemnity and sincerity, as the reader will experience in time. An argument I would proffer is that Stanford's manner of suicide (three gunshots) was symbolic and deliberate—a decided allusion to the film perhaps most influential on him: Jean Cocteau's *Le Sang d'un poète* (*The Blood of a Poet*). In the film, the poet shoots himself in the temple with a revolver, and a laurel wreath appears on his head; the sound effect of the gun firing is then repeated—thrice—and the words "*Toujours la gloire!*" ("*Glory Forever!*") are uttered slowly, intensely, in voice-over. Upon a final (fifth) firing, the poet is reborn, effectively—his eyes reopen. It isn't possible to shoot oneself three times in the temple, so Stanford shot, I premise, at the heart instead. (The influence on Stanford of European filmmakers and poets who died young, such as filmmaker Jean Vigo, who died of tuberculosis at twenty-nine, and poet Sergei Yesenin, who died by suicide at thirty, is also clear.) Chillingly, Stanford writes in *The Battlefield*, "a person might of thought three shots were fired" (2507). At any rate, for Stanford, the end goal was the journey to follow. In his last dated letter to Ginny and C. D., written June 3, 1978, the day of his death, Stanford writes, "I feel like an explorer, embarking on a journey I have been charting and studying for many years. I know something of death, so do not be afraid or terrified or lonely. The living spirit, now, is my concern." Rebirth was absolutely Stanford's intention.

MORE THAN A HALF CENTURY HAS passed since many of Stanford's letters and postcards were sent out into the world, and many of his missives are lost—some unfound or temporarily misplaced, others gone forever. Like detective work, research of correspondence consists of strikeout after strikeout and many blind alleys. Editors of magazines that published Stanford's work and I certainly worked to find materials, often without success. Anthony Sobin of *The Ark River Review*—which published Stanford's poetry in 1974 and 1976 issues—found only typescripts and markups of Stanford's poems and a contributor's note that was accidentally omitted from the latter issue: "FRANK STANFORD is a hero of the Iowa Review as well as the Ark. He is a land surveyor and lives in the Arkansas backwoods." Correspondence from Stanford to other magazines—including *FIELD*, *The Iowa Review*, *The Nation*, *The New York Quarterly*, *Road Apple Review*, *Out There*, and *West Coast Review*—as well as to editors and writers such as Celia Gilbert, Thomas Lux, Leon Stokesbury, Alberta T. Turner, and Joan Williams, and the bulk of the correspondence to Charles Plymell and David Walker, is likewise missing, at least at this time. Reader, I tried to locate correspondence from Stanford to Richard Howard, Robert Bly, John Berryman (for which I traveled to Minnesota, haplessly), and others. In a December 2025 phone call, Stanford's high school (Subiaco-era) girlfriend, the former Camille Corder, told me that she and Stanford exchanged letters—and that his (which would be the earliest surviving letters) were exquisite—but that they're no longer extant; Camille's mother discarded writings by her early boyfriends. Ezra and Matthew Bowen, sons of Williams, to whom Stanford sent poems and a short story over the years, looked through their mother's possessions for correspondence but found only Stanford's Bible—gifted to him on May 14, 1961, the day of his confirmation at All Saints' Episcopal Church in Memphis, and handed down to Ezra and Matthew by Dorothy Stanford, Frank's mother, in August 1964 during Williams's visit with her sons to the Stanfords' home in Mountain Home, Arkansas, while researching her second novel. And so on it goes. As of the mid-2020s, many individuals central to Stanford's story or body of letters have passed—including people with whom I spoke or corresponded, such as Lux, McKernan, Stokesbury, Walker, and Wright, as well as Fr. Nicholas Fuhrmann, John Stoss, John Wood, and Stanford's sister, Ruth Rogers. Each of those individuals was helpful to me in my research.

The research contained many hits too, though. Among the more incredible, bizarre finds is the July 1970 letter to poet Charles Plymell. Poet David Ray's wife Judy was able to discern from her notes that a letter from Stanford to Plymell existed in Ray's papers at the University of Chicago—written on the versos of a letter from Plymell to Ray; Plymell had flipped Stanford's letter over and written to Ray on the backs of the pages. Stanford's letters to Eleanor Bender (now Hamilton) at the State Historical Society of Missouri were also a find. And John McKernan painstakingly combed through four tall filing cabinets, finding years of Stanford letters and manuscripts. After searching fruitlessly for Cheryl Campbell for many years, I was fortunate somewhat late in my research, in 2023, to find and connect with her (now Cher Ross), and she also recovered (after much searching) important letters that Frank wrote to her in 1972 and 1973, a sampling of which is included herein. And James McWilliams, author of *The Life and Poetry of Frank Stanford* (2025), helped fill in several crucial gaps in my collection. More of Stanford's correspondence will surface in time, but we can be glad for materials that have emerged thus far.

Amid various transcription- and research-related tasks, a significant fact slipped by both Cheryl and me for more than a year of working with Stanford's July 5, 1972, letter to her: that its signature appeared to be written in blood. When I noticed the signature's variance from the letter and first suspected the presence of blood, Cheryl was dubious, but as we began corresponding with scientists and conservators about having the signature tested, Cheryl realized that another, subsequent page that she had not at first connected to the letter actually appeared to be a postscript to it. Following discussions with conservation scientist Daniel P. Kirby (and in consultation with Richard Newman, head of scientific research at the Museum of Fine Arts, Boston), samples from both the signature and subsequent page were taken in spring 2025 by Whidbey Island–based paper conservator Emily Derse of Conservation Studio of Seattle. Kirby tested the samples for blood in Massachusetts; the analytical method employed by Kirby was peptide mass fingerprinting, a technique involving protein digestion and analysis by matrix-assisted laser desorption/ionization (MALDI). The results from both the signature and postscript page were verified to contain hemoglobin consistent with human blood.

The words in Stanford's letters are an offering that he left to us, and the cross section in this book—only a modest portion of the total uncovered thus far—is substantial. Again, Frank Stanford published in small circles and has been relatively little known for roughly a half century. That these letters have survived obscurity for so long is a small miracle; they offer a clear window into the mind, soul, genius, originality, and creativity of one of the most gifted, prodigious, dynamic, visionary, and anguished poets of the twentieth century.

MANY DECISIONS MUST BE MADE IN selecting letters for a book gathering an author's letters for the first time. The 162 pieces of correspondence herein represent well fewer than half of the total number of surviving letters, postcards, and book inscriptions of Stanford's that have already surfaced. So, how should correspondence be chosen for a relatively compact selection? *Letters of a Poet Dying* was compiled according to various criteria. I sought to include a large variety of Stanford's strongest letters that offer a glimpse into his psyche; give a picture of his varied interests, intellectual range, and virtuosic technical abilities; and deliver the central story—of a young poet finding his way in the world while exploring his preoccupation with death. Attempts were made for the number of letters appearing in each chapter to be roughly representative of that time period's share of Stanford's total correspondence, and attempts were also made to incorporate a sizable range of recipients and to have the total number of letters included for each recipient be roughly representative of that correspondent's share of Stanford's total correspondence. A large number of Stanford's letters to women recipients are, by happenstance, lost, so many of the extant letters to women have been included. Preference was occasionally given to great letters that called for little annotating, and for space reasons, some very lengthy letters or some letters that called for an unusually large amount of annotation were excluded—especially since I've annotated thoroughly so that Stanford's encyclopedic range, little-known biography (which has often been misconstrued), and countless obscure references reach a range of audiences. On the whole, it was important to me to maintain the general narrative thread, whether through the letters selected or through scholarship, so I strove to integrate correspondence from most seasons of all years, without significant chronological gaps; to that point, letters with clear dating or that I could, through research, confidently date (or circa date) were frequently given preference over correspondence that I have not yet been able to place chronologically. Also, letter fragments have been excluded, and for all letters herein, no material from the date or salutation through the signature or postscript has been cut. Typically, the odd outlier letter that strayed greatly from the book's central story or letters that didn't help to propel that story were excluded, so, for example, while occasional repetition across adjacent or near-adjacent letters exists, attempts were generally made to avoid excessive repetition of subject matter, and correspondence with editors or collaborators about publications or projects that didn't end up materializing were usually excluded.

Other decisions must be made in editing a poet's letters. Should there be typesetting uniformity in letter formatting (block, indented, etc.)? How to date undated correspondence? Should marginalia and insertions be printed as such or inserted into the text's body? How to transcribe and present largely illegible handwriting? To what degree should profuse misspellings and typos be corrected? And so on.

To tackle this process, I asked two primary questions: (1) What would Frank Stanford have wished? and (2) How can I maximize readability for audiences while also maintaining fidelity? On one hand, underlining for emphasis and underlining or all caps for titles of publications (book and journals or magazines) have been presented as italics. Stanford often forgot to open or close quotes and parentheses. When the punctuation's intended placement is clear, quotes and parentheses have been bookended; in other cases, explanatory endnotes have been added, or Stanford's writing has been left untouched. Similarly, Stanford typically placed his commas and periods within his quotation marks but sometimes didn't, and other times still, his handwriting renders their placement unclear; his positioning of such punctuation has generally been retained, but in unclear instances, the comma or period has been placed within the quotation marks. On the other hand, some items have been presented as they appear in Stanford's original communication when they add color or flavor, such as some use of all caps. As Stanford's handwriting and even his typing are frequently messy, many of his blatant errors and typos have been corrected for readability's sake, but other misspellings, such as misspellings of individuals' names and titles of creative works and misspellings with multiple instances, have often been retained, typically with "[*sic*]" and/or an added endnote providing the correct spelling, and marginalia and insertions have been reproduced in line, enclosed in curly brackets, with as much fidelity as possible when and where feasible, with endnotes included for marginalia to indicate the writing's position on Stanford's page (e.g., "*left side, right facing*"). Stanford's strike-throughs have been preserved when his crossed-out text is readable. Double hyphens have been changed to dashes. All addresses atop letters—whether in letterhead, stamped, or handwritten (left, center, or right)—are presented in the top left with zip code on the same lines as the state, and all signatures (whether left, center, or right) are presented in the bottom right. In endnotes, poem titles are usually formatted in title case (i.e., with the initial letters of major words capitalized), as Stanford's capitalization of titles was sometimes inconsistent, but titles of poems that are clearly part of Stanford's collection of early poems, *St. Francis and the Wolf: Some Poems 1957–1964*—which, Stanford insisted, were typically unrevised in adulthood—are presented in all lowercase, as Stanford commonly presented them. When no date is included atop Stanford's letter but the letter is specifically dated herein, the date has usually been taken from the envelope's postmark, while other approximate or circa dating has been achieved through research. If poetry enclosed with letters is previously unpublished or otherwise especially relevant, it is occasionally included herein. Where relevant, Stanford's volume in which a poem was first collected in book form is included in parentheses following the poem's title in quotes (and notably, Stanford's manuscripts *Automatic Co-Pilot*, *Flour the Dead Man Brings to the Wedding*, *The Last Panther in the Ozarks*, *Plain Songs*, *Smoking Grapevine*, and *Wounds* were either collected or first published posthumously in *What About This: Collected Poems of Frank Stanford*). In endnotes, any uncredited translations are my own. References to line numbers in *The Battlefield Where the Moon Says I Love You* are to the third edition (2026).

As for the title, it could just as well have announced letters of a poet *living*—what a paradox that Stanford was, concurrently, so vibrantly alive and on the precipice over the abyss for so long. This is a poet who was dying not merely for some minutes or weeks but, rather, was on a mission toward his death for many years and expected to not live past his relative youth. Stanford's course toward death was charted early. Dorothy Stanford, Ruth Rogers, and Bill Willett have been consistent that Frank's discovery (or realization), in 1968, of his adoption by Dorothy changed his outlook metamorphically. There are 190-odd instances of "death," "die," "died," and "dying" throughout this book—hundreds more across Stanford's full correspondence and poetry. This is a book of letters by a poet who titled a book *Crib Death*; *Letters of a Poet Dying* isn't far off. The title bypasses assumptions that Stanford's death was solely some sudden decision after his relationships came to a head; it lifts the burden from Ginny Stanford and the late C. D. Wright, hopefully offering them a belated reprieve, and suggests something larger, more metaphysical.

I REMEMBER WHEN I FIRST LEARNED of Frank Stanford, as one does. As a young poet, I traveled to Providence, Rhode Island—meeting Forrest Gander, who invited me to a reading that evening. There, I met C. D. Wright. Later, at a local bar, Wright asked about my poetic interests and suggested that I might be drawn to a poet named Frank Stanford. I read snippets and later relayed back that I hadn't been blown away but remained interested, asking what I should read. She said: *The Battlefield Where the Moon Says I Love You*. So, I read the poem and was immediately won over. When I told her some months later, "It really knocked me down," she guffawed. To my eye, Stanford's rightful place in the highest echelons of the American literary pantheon was clear. I have been researching Stanford since 2008 and authored a graduate thesis on him at Lund University in 2015, and recently I coedited the third edition of *The Battlefield Where the Moon Says I Love You* as well; all of my prior Stanford research, however, has effectively equated to preparation for editing this book.

Letters of a Poet Dying: The Selected Correspondence of Frank Stanford is the culmination of thousands of hours of sleuthing, transcribing, research, and editing over years—thousands of emails and internet searches, thousands of files, and tens of thousands of pages of material. A great many individuals helped make the work possible. I am grateful to everyone mentioned in the acknowledgments section—and especially for the trust and support shown to me by Irv Broughton and by Ginny Stanford, the late C. D. Wright, and Forrest Gander. Without their help and the help of countless others, this book would not have been possible.

A. P. WALTON

LETTERS OF A POET DYING

Frank Stanford with Allen Ginsberg and friends at Christ of the Ozarks near Eureka Springs, Arkansas, on Sunday, May 4, 1969. *Left to right:* Sandra Wood, John Wood, Frank Stanford, Allen Ginsberg, Peter Orlovsky, Lynnice Butler, and Jack Butler. *Photographer: James Whitehead.*

I.

STUDENT LIFE

Fayetteville, 1969–70

Frank Stanford graduated from Subiaco Academy, a Benedictine preparatory school in the Ouachita Mountains of western Arkansas, in May 1966 and, in the fall, matriculated at the University of Arkansas in Fayetteville—first in the College of Business before switching to the College of Arts & Sciences in fall 1967. Stanford studied primarily English and philosophy while also developing his poetry. In 1968, around his twentieth birthday, he learned, or fully realized, that he had been adopted by his mother, Dorothy, which reportedly instigated a metamorphic change in his disposition and general outlook; he underwent a period of forlornness and introspection but also decided to pursue the path he wished—that of being a poet. In spring 1969, at the invitation of professor James Whitehead, Stanford joined the graduate poetry workshop as an undergraduate, studying alongside poets Leon Stokesbury, Jack Butler, Larry Johnson, John S. Morris, Phyllis Franklin Morris (then Phyllis Glass), John Wood, et al. In fall 1969, he met Linda Mencin, a recent graduate. In summer 1970, he attended the Hollins Conference on Creative Writing and Cinema, where he met his future publisher, Irv Broughton, and R. S. Gwynn landed Stanford a job with Kemp, Christner and Associates as a chainman/rodman on Gwynn's land surveying crew, training Stanford in the rudiments of surveying.

To Allen Ginsberg: November 10, 1969

Nov. 10
#20 UARK Courts
Fayetteville, Ark.

Dear Allen and Peter,[1]

Come back to Arkansas. Imagine you have been about everywhere since you left last spring. How is your farm? Did you get many Woodstock people stopping at your place? Hope you had a good harvest.[2] Wrote poems, read poems all summer. That is what I'm doing now. The Ozarks are red and the snakes are going to sleep. Sounds like something Bly would ~~say~~.[3] Write not say. How has the long poem progressed? The one about all the states?[4] Are you writing, Peter? You are both mentioned in this book I read the other day *American Poetry Since 1945*. {(Stephan Stepanchev)}[5] There are around nine pages about Allen. I've been reading a lot of City Lights books and European translations the past month. Especially Lamantia, Prevert, McClure, Snyder {(not City Lights)}, you, Corso, Michaux, and Parra (Williams translation) (you translated in that), *Neruda*, Artaud, *Vallejo*, Machado, Alberti, and *Jean Follain*.[6] Donald Justice was just here for 10 days and W. D. Snodgrass is here now.[7] What a difference! They both teach at Syracuse, though. ~~Justice and Snodgrass both liked my poems, but~~

Charles Plymell wrote me a letter about my poems that made me feel great.[8] I sent "Gospel Bird" to *Poetry*.[9] Haven't heard yet. You both probably think I am a shit hook for not writing, but after you left all the goddamn poets said they were going to write you a letter. I felt that my letter would just be another bother for you. This is for real though. Looked at *Wales Visitation* and it looked like the hills around here.[10]

I just saw Midnight Cowboy and Easy Rider last week.[11] They were great. Do you know Hopper?

I have a place rented for this summer, only $10 a month on top of a mountain. No running water or bathroom. Really going to like it. It is a long walk from school though (sold my car).

Tim Leary is going to be here sometime before long and debate this gov't. drug doctor. Read a little of his new book the other day.[12] Also read your biography. *A. G. in America*.[13] What do you think about it. ~~Tell~~ Peter! I heard that country and western song you sung to me (Lamb something) on the radio the other day. Truth man. The academic road is really washing out. Justice and Snodgrass both liked my poems, but I just mean the academic scene is getting all fucked up. I want to just leave this place and camp out sometimes. I'm a lot better friends with Whitehead this year and understanding a man with all these kids and responsibilities helps me out a little.[14] I don't want to go that route though.

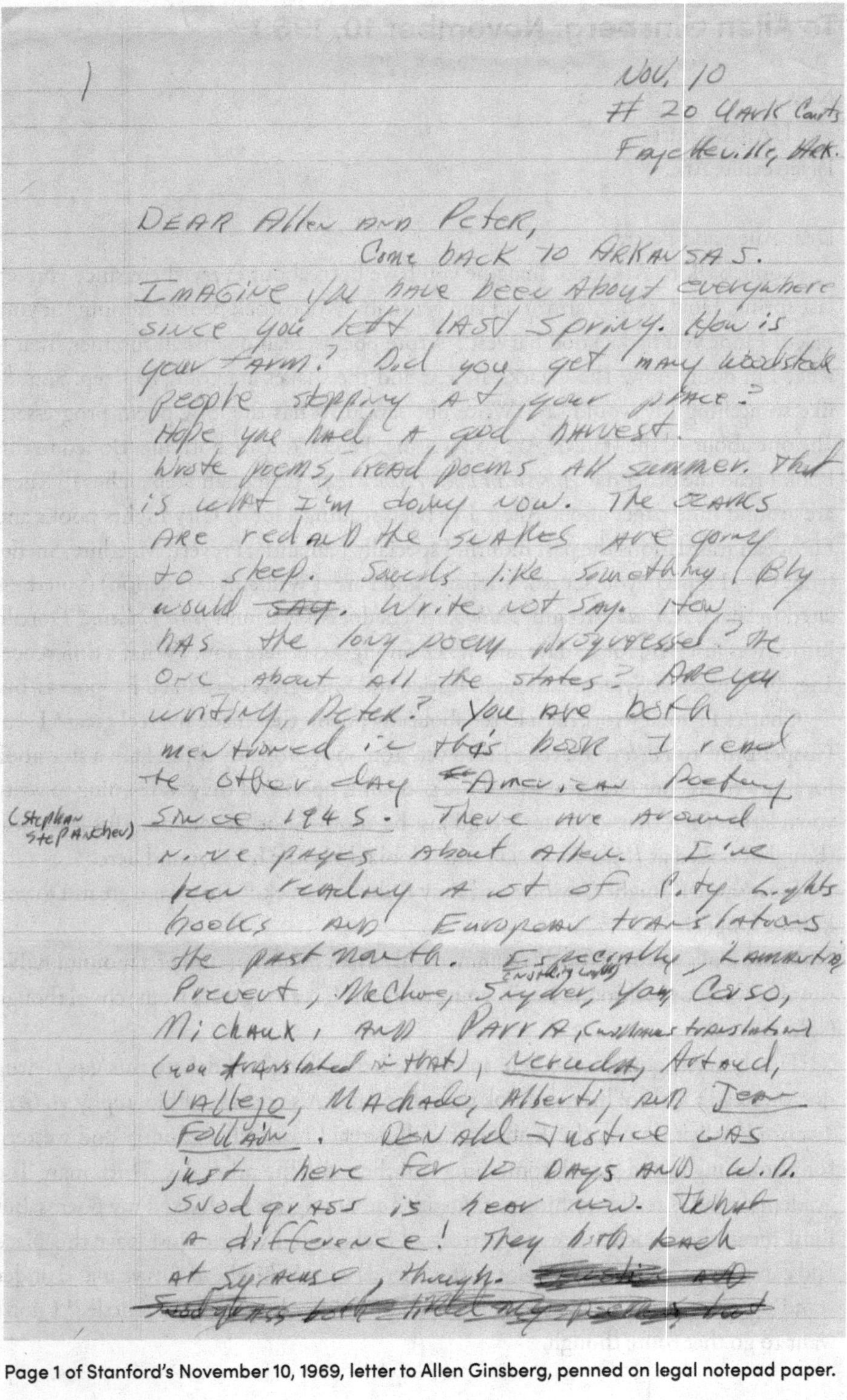

1

Nov. 10
20 Clark Courts
Fayetteville, Ark.

Dear Allen and Peter,
Come back to Arkansas.
Imagine you have been about everywhere since you left last spring. How is your farm? Did you get many Woodstock people stopping at your place? Hope you had a good harvest.
Wrote poems, read poems all summer. That is what I'm doing now. The ozarks are red and the snakes are going to sleep. Sounds like something Bly would ~~say~~. Write not say. How has the long poem progressed? The one about all the states? Are you writing, Peter? You are both mentioned in this book I read the other day American Poetry Since 1945. (Stephan Stepanchev) There are around nine pages about Allen. I've been reading a lot of City Lights books and European translations the past month. Especially, Lamantia, Prevert, McClure, Snyder (Earth House Hold), [illegible] Corso, Michaux, and Parra (Williams translation) (you translated in that), Neruda, Artaud, Vallejo, Machado, Alberti, and Jean Follain. Donald Justice was just here for 10 days and W.D. Snodgrass is here now. What a difference! They both teach at Syracuse, though. ~~Justice and Snodgrass both liked my poems, but~~

Page 1 of Stanford's November 10, 1969, letter to Allen Ginsberg, penned on legal notepad paper.

Been writing a lot of surreal stuff lately (not imitating American surrealists like Bly and Wright,[15] but trying for what Neruda and Vallejo do). {I read Ferdinand Alquie's *The Phil. of Surrealism*}[16] Talked about surrealism with Justice and he asked me about my images, if they were meant to be surreal. I really didn't know how to start so I ~~quoted~~ {paraphrased} this passage from Breton's *Nadja*. Nadja is glancing "along the buildings. Do you see down there, that window? It is black, like all the others. Keep looking at it. In a minute it will light up. It will be red. The minute passes. The window lights up. It has, in fact, red curtain[s]."[17]

When you aren't busy I hope you will read the poems. The two rough drafts are example of 15 or so long narratives I have that are uncompleted. They might be short stories instead, I hope not. After reading and discussing Pound, Duncan, Olson with John Wood, I *am* pumping the rhythm, with breaths + pauses.[18] The II part of the "Outhouse" (still too rough) is about hauling the dead spades out of the shit hole. The III part tries to get funny again (grim) it is about Jimmy teaching me how to jack off. There are *other* poems about the albino, too. Hope you all won't take as long as I did in letting me hear from you.

Love,
Frank

P.S. Peter! be sure and let me hear from you. Did you plant the tomatoes the way we talked about?

PEACE the 15th and forever.[19]

Notes

1. Peter Orlovsky (1933–2010), poet and lifelong partner of Allen Ginsberg (1926–97).
2. In 1968, Ginsberg had bought a farm in Cherry Valley, New York, roughly one hundred miles north of Bethel, where the Woodstock festival took place in August 1969.
3. Robert Bly (1926–2021), poet/translator associated with the Deep Image school of writing, particularly with a focus on concrete, as opposed to abstract, imagery.
4. Ginsberg's *The Fall of America: Poems of These States 1965–1971* (1972).
5. *Marginalia: left side, upright.* Stephen Stepanchev's *American Poetry Since 1945* (1965).
6. Philip Lamantia (1927–2005), Jacques Prévert (1900–1977), Michael McClure (1932–2020), Gary Snyder (b. 1930), Ginsberg, Gregory Corso (1930–2001), Henri Michaux (1899–1984), Nicanor Parra (1914–2018), Pablo Neruda (1904–73), Antonin Artaud (1896–1948), César Vallejo (1892–1938), Antonio Machado (1875–1939), Rafael Alberti (1902–99), and Jean Follain (1903–71), poets. A US edition of translations from

Parra's books *Poemas y antipoemas* (1954) and *Versos de salón* (1962) was published as *Poems and Antipoems* (1967), ed. Miller Williams; Ginsberg translated one Parra poem and cotranslated (with Lawrence Ferlinghetti) another one for the book.

7. W. D. Snodgrass (1926–2009) visited the University of Arkansas campus for ten days in November 1969.
8. Charles Plymell (b. 1935), poet and contemporary of Ginsberg; see note 9 below.
9. Having corresponded with Ginsberg for several years, MFA student John Wood (1947–2022) helped to facilitate Ginsberg's visit to Fayetteville in May 1969. Wood's journal entry for May 2, 1969, notes that Ginsberg had met and quickly "[taken] a liking to" Stanford. A few months later, on September 25, Ginsberg wrote to Wood, "I've forgotten name of poet with dungarees—dark glasses but I liked his poetry. If he has copies he can send to *Charles Plymell*," who "would appreciate them" as "there's something akin in their poesy." Following an exchange, Ginsberg wrote to Wood on October 9: "Frank's poems always seem slightly electric—curious what he'll make of Plymell's poesy. Stanford might try sending it out to Poetry or Evergreen or anywhere wherever it interests him if it interests him to publish some; it's readable." John Wood, "With Allen in Arkansas: An Ozark Diary," *American Poetry Review* 41, no. 5 (September/October 2012): 47, 49. (Minor corrections have been made to these quotations based on this editor's access to the originals.)
10. "Wales Visitation," a poem in Ginsberg's book *Planet News: 1961–1967* (1968). The poem describes the idyllic hills, mountains, and other landscape features around Tintern Abbey, the twelfth-to-thirteenth-century Cistercian abbey near Tintern, Monmouthshire, in Wales featured in William Wordsworth's poem "Lines Composed a Few Miles Above Tintern Abbey" (1798).
11. *Midnight Cowboy* (1969), dir. John Schlesinger, and *Easy Rider* (1969), dir. Dennis Hopper.
12. *new book*: likely either *The Politics of Ecstasy* (1968) or *High Priest* (1968) by Timothy Leary (1920–96), author and psychologist popular in the 1960s counterculture movement.
13. Jane Kramer's *Allen Ginsberg in America* (1969).
14. James Whitehead (1936–2003), poet and cofounder of the University of Arkansas's MFA program. Having been impressed with Stanford's writing, Whitehead had invited him to join the graduate poetry workshop as an undergraduate, starting in spring 1969.
15. James Wright (1927–80), poet. Stanford's mentions of "Wright" prior to 1976 refer to James Wright.
16. *Marginalia: left side, right facing*. Ferdinand Alquié's *The Philosophy of Surrealism*, trans. Bernard Waldrop (1965).
17. From André Breton's 1928 Surrealist novel, *Nadja*, trans. Richard Howard (Grove, 1960), 83: "Nadja's eyes now sweep over the surrounding houses. 'Do you see that window up there? It's black, like all the rest. Look hard. In a minute it will light up. It will be red.' The minute passes. The window lights up. There are, as a matter of fact, red curtains."

18. Ezra Pound (1885–1972), Robert Duncan (1919–88), and Charles Olson (1910–70), American poets.
19. The Moratorium to End the War in Vietnam, a series of demonstrations nationwide, with more than fifteen million people marching, took place on October 15, 1969; the Second Moratorium to End the War in Vietnam (a.k.a. the Moratorium March), which Stanford and Linda Mencin (b. 1948) attended with Stanford's friend Charles "Big Time" Sonny Morris (1948–2014) and two others, took place in Washington, DC, a month later, on November 15.

To Allen Ginsberg: November 23, 1969

Nov. 23

Dear Allen and Peter,

I was in Washington last week and everything was beautiful. I got gassed, but I didn't get hit.[20]

Today, my Howl and Kaddish records finally came in.[21] I've been so busy lately, it has been terrible; writing all these goddamn papers.[22] Saw a poster said you were appearing the 22 for this guy. T. Leary was supposed to have been here this week but he didn't make it.

What is all this pollution,[23] Agnew,[24] Mitchell, Song My,[25] etc. stuff going on. It is all insane. Saw D. Dellinger, A. Hoffman, and J. Roubin, but I didn't get close enough to meet them.[26]

Poetry rejected my poem.[27] I'm going to send it off again somewhere else. I didn't feel as bad as I thought I would.

I've got to go to class so I'll say goodbye. Please write soon.

Love,
Frank

P.S. Do you know where I can get a copy of Howl?[28]

New Poems:

MacCulduff[29]	complete
The Outhouse	Part I
Mad Dogs	Part I
5 short poems[30]	

Blood

I've seen them
Dip warm cornbread from dinner
In their afternoon milk,
Taste it,
Then tell the maid to take it away.

In postures better than mine
They lean back,
Sure of antimacassars,
And hum "My Creole Belle."

Sophisticated Lady

She plays with the collies
And thinks she is
The best one in the room.
She is.
She watches the people
As if they were clowns
Skating in a smoking frozen forest.

The first time,
Her breasts were like
Two collie pups
Nuzzling their soft noses
Into my hands.
Her soft eyes are treacherous.

Notes

20. See note 19 above.
21. *Allen Ginsberg Reads "Howl" and Other Poems* (1959) and *Allen Ginsberg Reads "Kaddish": A 20th Century American Ecstatic Narrative Poem* (1966).
22. In fall 1969, Stanford was taking Elementary French, Greek Philosophy, an American literature survey course, an English literature course, and the graduate poetry workshop (but he didn't receive a passing grade in any of them).

23. Air pollution was thick across the US in fall 1969, especially in some major cities, and was a topic of public concern.
24. Spiro Agnew, Richard Nixon's vice president, was a vocal opponent of the anti–Vietnam War protests of 1968–69 and delivered a series of anti-progressive speeches in October and November 1969, including a live national address on November 13.
25. The Mỹ Lai Massacre (or Song My Massacre, variant of Sơn Mỹ Massacre), the murder by US soldiers of South Vietnamese civilians on March 16, 1968. "Mitchell" refers to David Mitchell, a sergeant and squad leader accused (and later acquitted) of shooting people at Mỹ Lai. The massacre instigated international outrage following reporting about it on November 12 and 13, 1969.
26. David Dellinger (1915–2004), Abbie Hoffman (1936–89), and Jerry Rubin (1938–94), three members of the Chicago Seven charged with inciting the anti–Vietnam War riots at the 1968 Democratic National Convention, protests for which Ginsberg had been a part of. (Both Ginsberg and Leary would testify as defense witnesses at the trial of the Chicago Seven in December 1969.) The three activists attended the Second Moratorium to End the War in Vietnam in November 1969, where Dellinger also spoke.
27. "The Gospel Bird"; see note 9 above.
28. *Howl and Other Poems* (1956), Ginsberg's first book—number four in City Lights' Pocket Poets Series.
29. I.e., "The Hole"—an early version of "The Albino" (*The Singing Knives*)—whose character MacCulduff is presumably based on David McElduff, a worker for levee engineer Albert Franklin (A. F.) Stanford (1884–1963), or Frank Sr., Stanford's adoptive father.
30. Stanford enclosed twenty-two poems with the November 10 and November 23 letters to Ginsberg, including "The Pump," "Living," "Civil Rights at the Inverness Ice House," "The Gospel Bird," "The Minnow," "The Outhouse," and "Mad Dogs" (a variant of "The Brake"); "Blood" and "Sophisticated Lady," heretofore unpublished, are presented here from the included poems.

To Charles Plymell: July 13, 1970

Monday, July 13

Dear Charles, Pam, and Liz,[31]

Received your letter of the 10th, today. And yes, Jim has the material from Johns Hopkins and he doesn't think anything additional will be needed.[32] He has never been turned down by the English Dept. Chairman before, so I think everything is going to be set up, shortly. Jim talked with them before he left for Washington State to do a conference. (This is the state of Washington, although he might be at W.S.U.[33] I don't know.) He left Sunday, the 12th, and will be back Sunday, the 19th. Monday, the 20th, we are both going up and see the people, then get your stuff together. This will be finished sometime in the middle of the week. As soon as things are confirmed, we will call you and mail all forms. Please don't get discouraged if Jim hasn't sent you a letter, but he is doing all the necessary talking and I am writing the letters. (He wants you here as much as I do. He might have written you the Friday or Saturday before he left without me knowing, as I was out of town fishing. ((I caught 25 crappie.))) He has a backlog of stuff to do and he's in the same shape you are about his novel.[34] He *MUST* finish it by the middle of August, then take it to his editor in N.Y. I'm going with him, and we might just take you up on that extra bed and space.[35] About something for Pam: Jim has three *good* friends in the Language Dept. One in classics, one in German, and one in French. He knows the first two the best though, dedicating his book to Mark Doyle in the German Dept.[36] We'll see about that as soon as he returns, too. I know she could get a job in the library though, especially if that is what she wants to go into.

Goddamn man! Ray is something.[37] Gone back and read some of his poems in magazines and also the 3 anthologies. (A Poetry Reading Against the Vietnam War, Where is Vietnam, New Poets of England and America.)[38] Shit man! He *is* good. Somebody is pulling in the net. When I was down deep in the pond, I would see you, Bly, or Ray, maybe Wright, swimming around. Sometimes, sunning in the shallows, eating mosquitoes, I would hear a huge tail hit the water as he sucked in nymphflies off the willows, this must have been Neruda or Vellejo,[39] I thought I saw Bly wreck a trotline once, and you had a whole belly full of crawdads. I believe Ray is a flathead cat that nobody can catch. I almost got caught once, but I saw how Neruda shook his gills. I saw how it was done. My mother wasn't a fish, but I am. Man, somebody is pulling in the net. That is why I'm getting to know people and know of them, people I have the deepest admiration for. Whoever it is, pulling in the net, we'll bust his strings, but we'll see each other. They'll never make a landing; the fish are too big. I'm still a minnow, so I'll just swim through the hole. Man, that would be some anthology! That would be a *book*! Did you get to meet Bly or Wright? Wish I could give my poems to them and let them read them if I come to N.Y. I hope I could meet some of these poets. I know you are enjoying their company and imaginations.

Well, this is too long. Let you know about things as soon as we know.

As ever,
Frank

P.S. I'm getting David Ray's books. He's good! Some-*thang*!

Notes

31. Pamela Beach Plymell (b. 1947), publisher and Charles Plymell's wife, and Elizabeth Plymell, Charles and Pamela's daughter.
32. James "Jim" Whitehead.
33. Washington State University in Pullman, Washington.
34. *Joiner* (1971) by Whitehead.
35. After receiving an MA from Johns Hopkins University in 1970, Plymell moved with his family to New York.
36. Mark Doyle, professor in the University of Arkansas's foreign languages department.
37. David Ray (1932–2024), poet.
38. *A Poetry Reading Against the Vietnam War* (1966), ed. Robert Bly and David Ray; *Where Is Vietnam? American Poets Respond: An Anthology of New Work by 87 Poets* (1967), ed. Walter Lowenfels; and *New Poets of England and America: Second Selection* (1962), ed. Donald Hall and Robert Pack.
39. César Vallejo.

Frank Stanford and Linda Mencin at their Mount Sequoyah cabin in Fayetteville.

II.

ATOP MOUNT SEQUOYAH—AND ON LINDELL AVENUE

Fayetteville, 1970–72

In 1970, Stanford and Linda Mencin moved in together, living in a cabin, or log home, at 115 Skyline Drive on Mount Sequoyah, a hill in Fayetteville. Stanford's last semester at the University of Arkansas was fall 1970—he took the graduate fiction workshop and studied the literature of China and Japan; he never earned a degree. In early November 1970, poet Alan Dugan visited Arkansas's writing program; Stanford and Dugan commenced a correspondence and friendship. Stanford also met Cheryl Campbell, who in late February or March 1971 moved into his small apartment, a writing studio, on Lindell Avenue; Stanford thus maintained, for several months, a double life, moving between Linda at the cabin and Cheryl, who often typed his poems for him, at his studio. Stanford also began sending out his work and publishing. Following his and Cheryl's split in summer 1971, he married Linda on August 21. Irv Broughton worked to publish Stanford's first book via his small press, Mill Mountain Press. From fall 1971 through the following spring, Stanford typed up many of his early drafts and juvenilia and started showing his major epic, THE BATTLEFIELD WHERE THE MOON SAYS I LOVE YOU*—then a long poem in progress excerpted from his collection of early writings,* ST. FRANCIS AND THE WOLF: SOME POEMS 1957–1964*—to other poets and editors.*

To John McKernan: October 6, 1970

10/6/70

Dear John,

My friends are amazed with *Multitudes*. Needless to say, so am I. Leon Stokesbury and Sam Gwynn think they are great, which was my first impression at Hollins and still is.[40] Where have you sent the book? For what you have done and from what you told me you wanted to do with the book, I certainly believe it is the most publishable manuscript I know of. Of all the new young poets that will be published this season, we all know that only a few of the books we need. Personally, I need to have *Multitudes*, rather than a lot of other things.

There are about 6 or 7 all three of us agree on that we don't like. And about 4 we would revise, but it is certainly a grand accomplishment to sustain the kind of motion you have generated in the book. This is the truth, once the book was in a person's hands it couldn't be taken away. We had to read over one another's shoulders.

If I had the power, I would like to publish your book. Well, hell!

I need some info urgently. What is James Wright's address? We gonna get him down here, but I got to have his address. Also, tell me some good review or mag you know of in N. York or anywhere. I have some good poems I want to sell. No money. Isn't there a new thing out in N.Y. called N.Y. Quarterly or something like that?[41]

You send some *Multitudes* to

Irv. Broughton
Mill Mountain Review
Box 2212
Roanoke, VA. 24009

Send $1.00 get a copy of last issue.[42]

Well, write me soon.

As ever,
Frank

Notes

40. Leon Stokesbury (1945–2018) and R. S. Gwynn (b. 1948), poets and graduate students in the MFA program at Arkansas in the late 1960s–early 1970s. In October 1970, Stokesbury,

Gwynn, and Stanford were all taking a course titled Film Survey, and Stanford was working on Gwynn's small surveying crew. *Hollins*: the Hollins Conference; see note 59 below.

41. *The New York Quarterly*, founded in 1969.

42. *Mill Mountain Review* 1, no. 2 (1970), which included five poems by Stanford.

To Irv Broughton: February 10, 1971

Feb 10

Dear Irv,

I started this sequence called *Wounds* early in the fall. I sent you {(here)} eleven out of the fifty, random selection.[43] Then {later that fall}, I did about fifty poems and *forced* them together under the title *Naegling*.[44] I sent {(here)} you eleven, (including all I sent you in black manuscript and a few {(more)} others,) randomly selected.[45] (Actually I sent {(am sending)} the poems that were typed.) I believe the idea of two sequences like this sounds pretentious and calculated. That is why I broke it up and sent you some of the *Naegling* poems {autonomous} for the pamphlet.

I want to know what you think. These are not for the pamphlet. What do you think about *Wounds*?

As ever,
Frank

P.S. I believe the *Naegling* poems should be split up and can stand on their own—some of them—the ones that are good, but I believe I could or should continue the Wounds sequence. What about it?

(I need these back—only typed copies)

The Snake Doctors (4 poems)

X 1 page
X 1 page
X 2 pages
X 1 page

Irv, these last poems, the best, return to lonesome + mysterious past of the first eight poems. Some of them are brutal, some of them ebullient, some of [them] melancholy, but not the same loneliness of the second eight poems.

Since 1966 I have written many poems. The ratio of *quantity* and *quality* is not impressive, but that makes no difference as long as you can clean up the shit and dispose of it. The practice was good. I was writing good shitty poems. When I started in with the writing program, I started affecting bad shitty poems. When I realized this, I was frightened. It haunted me like a nightmare. For a long time I eluded it by going into the deep regions of a different poetry, then I confronted it, and I was victorious. I was compelled to write so much. I knew, back then, I needed to be in good form, if and when the *good* poem came. Then, I couldn't wait around for the perfect poem to come ~~through~~ {to} an occidental sensibility. Now, I write more than most I know, but the good poems have really increased, while the bad ones have almost gone away.

		10 good ones plus 10 good unfinished ones
Example:	between Jan 69–Jan 70	100 bad poems
	between Jan 70–Jan 71	25 " "
		20 good ones
		plus 30 good unfinished ones

I've tried to meditate in stillness and inactivity, far away from creative acts spending time quiescent, inert as an artist, and it is painful. You don't read much, you just write—write—and finally a poem comes. I don't like this, neither do I like automatic writing, but I do think there is something in the discipline of the Japanese {*Sumye*} painters that goes much further down than what the Surrealists did.[46] *Now*, I know if I control the centrifugal + the centripetal, Parmenides, Heraclitus {Boo!}, Valéry and Rimbaud, all those tensions, the impurity of Neruda, the purity of Jiminez, the self-consciousness of Mallarmé, the gregariousness of Apollinaire, the shyness of Laforgue, fuck fuck.[47]

I mean I want my fists to break open like ripe fruit.[48] What I have said has nothing to do with a poem. These theories only delude and echo, driving you insane and impotent or at best sterile, as a poet. We can analyze, but the paradigms + conclusions we *produce* are worthless. It cannot be explained away (nor can it be created by exegesis) demonstrated. Who said artistic conventions and the deception of the theories created one or the other is only a method of spiritual deficit-financing?[49] Yes. But it's not that either, it is a shoe or an oar. Any bright young man can be taught to be artful (they tried it on me). It is impossible to *teach taste*, but you *can* teach most anybody caution. It is the lesser ones who are "artful," they learn by rote—a trade as it were. They can never step falsely, never speak out of a carefully synthesized character.

The Dishevelled! K. Rexroth.[50]

Oh, by the way, the only reason I have given you some "statistics" let us say, is that recently I have gone over manuscripts and filed stuff away, so I know.

I like this Seidman guy. Haven't got his book, though.[51] Who do you like now—young + old.

I'm through translating + collaborating shit.

What is happening at Hollins? I heard rumors. Is John Currier still around? I liked him.[52] There is some girl I screwed, but can't remember her name. I believe she tried to write. Seen any good films? When are you going to send me some poems dammit. This is the way I am. Just send me some and say, "look, but don't touch, these poems are finished," and I will read them. I don't have to do all that editing you know. I just like to read the poems. So what if some fucking poem only has one eye, it was a pretty one.

I've been harboring fugitives from the law. One of my best friends is a hillbilly from Mountain Home, Ark. and all his family, except him, are convicts.[53]

One of his brothers was wanted for attempted murder and he hid out with me a few years back. He is the only man I know who quit the army "I quit" on a note and busted the fuck out of a captain. Stole a bunch of boobytraps and tried to get people with them. He was slinging hash until they found out he had syphilis. When I was in the eighth grade we use to park on the square and listen to him yell out of the courthouse jail window "Tarzan!" He rigged up the commode and flooded the whole fucking courthouse.

Since I never see anyone worthwhile, I have to indulge in these kinds of letters.

If you want to read something great get Horace Gregory's translation of Ovid's Metamorphoses. Read the deal on Pythagoras in "The Philosopher." It is near the back.[54]

Well, poems will be there tomorrow. Take it easy,

As ever,
Frank

These poems aren't blunt, they aren't clubs. They aren't javelins that pierce right through. No they are not a dull sword or a sword that will sever a head they go half way through and hold on a barb.

Notes

43. *Wounds*, a manuscript of Stanford's that has survived as twelve three-line poems; see *What About This: Collected Poems of Frank Stanford*, ed. Michael Wiegers (Copper Canyon, 2015), 433–35.

44. *Nægling* (as Stanford notes in a January 22, 1971, letter to Broughton, "The *a* and the *e* in Naegling is a ligature"), an unpublished manuscript of Stanford's, named for the sword that Beowulf uses against the dragon—and that breaks, failing him—in

Beowulf (line 2680). Sources of all letters herein, including letters quoted in endnotes, are listed in the "Correspondence, Poetry, and Image Sources" section.

45. The "black manuscript" reference here is unclear (perhaps the folder was black); Stanford enclosed ten poems from *Nægling* with his January 22 letter.
46. Automatic writing—a manner of writing in which, theoretically, the writing flows forth unconsciously. The tactic was central to Surrealism, as written about in André Breton's two Surrealist manifestoes (1924 and 1930), in which he defined Surrealism as "psychic automatism in its pure state." *Manifestoes of Surrealism*, trans. Richard Seaver and Helen R. Lane (University of Michigan Press, 2001), 26. Japanese sumi-e painting uses predominantly black ink in a simplified style, sometimes combined with poetry.
47. Parmenides (ca. 515 BC–fifth century BC), pre-Socratic Greek philosopher; Heraclitus (ca. 540–ca. 480 BC), pre-Socratic Greek philosopher; Paul Valéry (1871–1945), French poet; Arthur Rimbaud (1854–91), French poet; Pablo Neruda, Chilean poet; Juan Ramón Jiménez (1881–1958), Spanish poet; Stéphane Mallarmé (1842–98), French poet; Guillaume Apollinaire (1880–1918), French poet; and Jules Laforgue (1860–87), Franco-Uruguayan poet.
48. Cf. similar language in Frank Stanford, *The Battlefield Where the Moon Says I Love You*, 3rd ed., ed. James McWilliams and A. P. Walton (University of Arkansas Press, 2026), lines 1498 and 2603 (hereafter cited as *The Battlefield*).
49. From Kenneth Rexroth's introduction to *Selected Poems*, by D.H. Lawrence (Viking, 1947), 16: "The sonnet and quatrain are like the national debt, devices for postponing the day of reckoning indefinitely. All artistic conventions are a method of spiritual deficit-financing. If they were abandoned, the entire credit structure of Poets, Ltd. would be thrown into hopeless confusion. . . . Lawrence's free verse . . . can be analysed, but the paradigms produced by the analysis are worthless. It cannot be explained away, demonstrated in a mathematical sense."
50. Stanford loosely quotes from Rexroth's introduction to *Selected Poems* by Lawrence (1885–1930) here. Rexroth writes:

> Any bright young man can be taught to be artful. It is impossible to teach taste, but you can teach most anybody caution. It is always the lesser artists who are artful, they must learn their trade by rote. They must be careful never to make a false step, never to speak out of a carefully synthesized character. The greatest poetry is nobly dishevelled. At least, it never shows the scars of taking care. "Would he had blotted a thousand lines," said Ben Jonson of Shakespeare. Which thousand? Lawrence was always mislaying those manuscript books of poetry and writing around the world for them . . . simply because he forgot. (18)

Notably, in his ca. September 15, 1972, letter to Bill Willett (b. 1947), Stanford writes of having misplaced and lost manuscripts.

51. Hugh Seidman (1940–2023), whose book *Collecting Evidence* (1970) won the Yale Series of Younger Poets prize in 1969.
52. John Currier, a former graduate student in creative writing at Hollins College.
53. Edward Leon Willett and Benny Willett, brothers of Bill Willett, both spent time in prison.
54. Ovid's *The Metamorphoses*, trans. Horace Gregory (Viking, 1958). "The Philosopher" is a section within *The Metamorphoses*'s final book, book 15.

To *The Massachusetts Review*: March 1, 1971

March 1, 1971

Dear Editor,

There were so many names and poets on your staff—I wasn't sure who to address this to. A linguist and teacher, who has helped me out some, gave me a Kotex box full of reviews and quarterlies before he went to Spain and told me to read them and send off some poems to the ones I liked the best.[55] He put an x on the ones that {(he thinks)} wouldn't accept my poems. Yours had an x on it. I like your review. I don't know if you will like my work or not, but I would appreciate what comments any of you might have. They said it is a bad idea to submit only one poem, but I think a long narrative sets better by itself.[56] If you are interested in these characters—they appear and will appear in some other published work of mine.[57]

Where you are—you might know if this Pasolini has made any new films.[58] The friend I mentioned above gave me the money to attend a writing and cinema conference and I saw some of his work that I liked alot.[59] I didn't go to many of the workshops—because they showed films all day and I would never get the chance to see them again.[60] I liked Kurosawa, Bunuel, Mamoulian, Truffaut, Bergman, Rossellini, and all the old Russian films.[61] I did go to Richard Wilbur's group and he liked my poems.[62] He talked about one for 45 minutes.[63] He told me he burned down a flop house in California, once. It's funny though—I have an uncle who is shell shot (shock) from WWII and they are alike.[64] I also met a man who toured Dylan Thomas around for a month, before he died. (Not the one that wrote the book.[65]) The man would get drunk and start crying when he talked about him.

Whenever my friend goes to a different country—he sends me a book or two with some translations and asks me to help with them. He sent a book by Follain when he was in France.[66] I also like the Spanish poets and some of the Greek poets and the stories [he] tells about them. There is also a beautiful Russian poet—Yesenin—I like.[67]

Well, excuse me for indulging in a long letter, but I don't associate with the writers here much and the only poets I see are the ones who come here for a week and I like to hear from other poets. I'm looking forward to seeing Hecht this spring.[68] If any of you could spare a letter—I would appreciate it. Thank you. (Do any of you have any new books coming out?)

B: Born Greenville Mississippi. Twenty-one years old.[69] Undergraduate University of Arkansas (Phil. French. English[70]) Sat in on workshops for four sem. Miller Williams is here now.[71] Had poems accepted in a few quarterlies (not yet out). Recently, first published poem "The Gospel Bird" came out in *New American Review #11*.[72] Also, Don Allen accepted 135 of a 300 line poem I'm working on for *Evergreen*. I only sent 135 lines.[73] When Alan Dugan was here he took back some poetry for *Poetry* and wants me to send him some more.[74] I don't know if they will like it or not. A man in New York wrote for something for an anthology—(Miller Williams isn't pushing anything of mine in his for Random House[75]). And had two offers for book which I have turned down—I'm broke but I'm not ready. If you have a suggestion about who to send this poem to if you don't like it—I would appreciate it.

Frank Stanford

Notes

55. Plausibly poet James J. McAuley (1936–2021)—an MFA student who had taught collegiately since 1968—who drove Stanford, Kathy Walton, and others from Fayetteville to the Hollins Conference. Otherwise, possibly Ben Kimpel (1915–83), linguist and professor at the University of Arkansas who traveled in France in 1968 and in various European countries in 1970.
56. Stanford submitted his poem "Tapsticks," which was accepted in spring 1971 and published in the Autumn 1972 issue. An earlier version of "Tapsticks" appeared in *Tansy* 4 in 1971.
57. "Tapsticks" includes appearances by Stanford characters Baby Gauge, Jimmy, and Born In The Camp With Six Toes; Stanford's original submission included Melvin in place of Jimmy.
58. Pier Paolo Pasolini, Italian filmmaker and poet.
59. The Hollins Conference on Creative Writing and Cinema at Hollins College in Virginia, June 15–27, 1970—a large conference with 254 attendees (mostly students), poetry and fiction workshops, and over 250 film screenings. Poetry workshops were led by James Dickey (1923–97), George Garrett, James Whitehead, Richard Wilbur (1921–2017), et al.; fiction workshops were led by Fred Chappell (1936–2024),

William Harrison (1933–2013), Richard Yates (1926–92), et al.; film seminars were led by Thomas R. Atkins (b. 1939), R. H. W. Dillard (1937–2023), John G. Fisher, Larry McMurtry (1936–2021), et al.; readers, speakers, and panelists included Ralph Ellison (1913–94), Shelby Foote (1916–2005), Samuel Goldwyn Jr., and Frederick Wiseman; and students and other attendees included poet/dramatist John Biguenet (b. 1949), publisher/writer Irv Broughton, poet/novelist Jack Butler (b. 1944), poet Larry Johnson (b. 1945), poet/editor John McKernan, and Frank Stanford. Among the films screened were *The Gospel According to St. Matthew* (1964), dir. Pier Paolo Pasolini; *Les Mistons* (1957), dir. François Truffaut; and *Hour of the Wolf* (1968), dir. Ingmar Bergman, and film seminars included Fisher's session "Movies and Contemporary Issues: War, Race, Sex" and Harry Antrim's session "Soviet Films of the 1920's." Stanford and Broughton met at the conference.

60. Atkins wrote in a 1970 *Film News* article that fifty-seven feature-length films and nearly two hundred short films were screened at Hollins.
61. Akira Kurosawa, Luis Buñuel, Rouben Mamoulian, François Truffaut, Ingmar Bergman, Roberto Rossellini, filmmakers.
62. Richard Wilbur, poet.
63. Larry Johnson, who attended Wilbur's workshop—on the conference's first day, June 15, 1970—noted, in a November 30, 2023, email to this editor, that the poem discussed was Stanford's "The Picture Show Next Door to the Stamp Store in Downtown Memphis" and that Wilbur liked the poem and responded well to the "orange triangles" image (lines 29–32); Johnson clarified that the poem was discussed for probably twenty to thirty minutes and that "45 minutes" is embellishment.
64. Presumably Stanford's uncle Robert Lloyd Gilbert (1921–2004), who fought in the Battle of the Bulge in World War II and later served as a sponsor for Stanford's baptism (along with A. F. Stanford) in Greenville, Mississippi, in September 1948; see Stanford's December 26, 1974, letter to Dugan below, par. 3.
65. Presumably *Dylan Thomas in America: An Intimate Journal* (1955) by John Malcolm Brinnin.
66. Jean Follain, French poet.
67. Sergei Yesenin (1895–1925), Russian poet.
68. Anthony Hecht (1923–2004), poet.
69. Stanford was born on August 1, 1948, in southeast Mississippi (not Greenville); he was twenty-two years old (not twenty-one) in March 1971. Stanford was beginning to circulate a mythology that he was born in 1949. Possibly the first such instance in print was on the contents page of *Preview: Eight Poets* (University of Arkansas) (1971), printed in late May 1971 ("*Frank Stanford* born 1949 in Greenville, Mississippi"). (Notably, the contributor's note for his *New American Review* appearance—in 1971 but accepted in 1970 [see note 72 below]—states, correctly, "b. 1948." *New American Review*, no. 11 [1971]: 239.) He continued the ruse throughout his life.

70. In addition to numerous English courses at the University of Arkansas, Stanford took five philosophy courses—Reflective Thinking, Introduction to Philosophy (honors), Ethics (honors), Existentialism, and Greek Philosophy (twice)—and Elementary French (twice).
71. Miller Williams (1930–2015), poet, translator, and University of Arkansas professor.
72. *New American Review*, no. 11, published Stanford's poem "The Gospel Bird" in 1971. *Tansy* 1 had published Stanford's poems "Early Times in a Mississippi Liquor Store" and "The Hole" in spring 1970, and *Mill Mountain Review* 1, no. 2 published five Stanford poems later in 1970, though *New American Review* had purchased "The Gospel Bird" in June 1970.
73. Stanford is referring to "The Outhouse." The rough, partial draft that Stanford sent to Ginsberg in November 1969 is sixty-seven lines; Stanford evidently continued expanding the poem.
74. Stanford's work never appeared in *Evergreen Review* or *Poetry*.
75. *Contemporary Poetry in America* (1973), ed. Miller Williams, contained poetry by ninety-six poets, many discussed herein—including Ralph Adamo (b. 1948), John Berryman (1914–72), Alan Dugan (1923–2003), Richard Eberhart (1904–2005), Lawrence Ferlinghetti (1919–2021), Allen Ginsberg, Anthony Hecht, Donald Justice (1925–2004), W. S. Merwin (1927–2019), William Stafford (1914–93), James Whitehead, Richard Wilbur, Miller Williams, and James Wright.

To *kayak*: March 15, 1971

March 15, 1971

Dear Editor,[76]

You haven't ever heard of me and I don't know what to write except what is below.

B: Born 1949 Greenville, Mississippi.[77] Undergraduate at Univ. of Ark. I sat in on workshops for a couple of years, but I don't have anything to do much with people in *creative* writing. They laughed at my poems. Last spring Solotaroff came down here and took a poem back to New York with him. He published it in *NAR* #11.[78] Also, Don Allen accepted 135 lines of a long poem called *The Outhouse* for *Evergreen*. Also, Alan Dugan came down here and took back some of my poems for *Poetry*. That is how I have submitted, but some poets told me to send you some poems. I don't know if you will like my poems or not. Anyway—would you send a copy of your magazine. They are hard to get here. I haven't really made any submissions, so I don't know what else

Stanford MARCH 1, 1971

DEAR EDITOR,

THERE WERE SO MANY NAMES AND POETS ON YOUR STAFF-- I WASN'T SURE WHO TO ADDRESS THIS TO. A LINGUIST AND TEACHER, WHO HAS HELPED ME OUT SOME, GAVE ME A KOTEX BOX FULL OF REVIEWS AND QUARTERLIES BEFORE HE WENT TO SPAIN AND TOLD ME TO READ THEM AND SEND OFF SOME POEMS TO THE ONES I LIKED THE BEST. HE PUT AN X ON THE ONES THAT (HE THINKS) WOULDN'T ACCEPT MY POEMS. YOURS HAD AN X ON IT. I LIKE YOUR REVIEW. I DON'T KNOW IF YOU WILL LIKE MY WORK OR NOT, BUT I WOULD APPRECIATE WHAT COMMENTS ANY OF YOU MIGHT HAVE. THEY SAID IT IS A BAD IDEA TO SUBMIT ONLY ONE POEM, BUT I THINK A LONG NARRATIVE SETS BETTER BY ITSELF. IF YOU ARE INTERESTED IN THESE CHARACTERS -- THEY APPEAR AND WILL APPEAR IN SOME OTHER PUBLISHED WORK OF MINE.

WHERE YOU ARE-- YOU MIGHT KNOW IF THIS PASOLINI HAS MADE ANY NEW FILMS. THE FRIEND I MENTIONED ABOVE GAVE ME THE MONEY TO ATTEND A WRITING AND CINEMA CONFERRENCE AND I SAW SOME OF HIS WORK THAT I LIKED ALOT. I DIDN'T GO TO MANY OF THE WORKSHOPS --BECAUSE THEY SHOWED FILMS ALL DAY AND I WOULD NEVER GET THE CHANCE TO SEE THEM AGAIN. I LIKED KUROSAWA, BUNUEL, MAMOULIAN, TRUFFAUT, BERGMAN, ROSSELLINI, AND ALL THE OLD RUSSIAN FILMS. I DID GO TO RICHARD WILBUR'S GROUP AND HE LIKED MY POEMS. HE TALKED ABOUT ONE FOR 45 MINUTES. HE TOLD ME HE BURNED DOWN A FLOP HOUSE IN CALIFORNIA, ONCE. IT'S FUNNY THOUGH-- I HAVE AN UNCLE WHO IS SHELL SHOT (SHOCK) FROM WW II AND THEY ARE ALIKE. I ALSO MET A MAN WHO TOURED DYLAN THOMAS AROUND FOR A MONTH, BEFORE HE DIED. (NOT THE ONE THAT WROTE THE BOOK.) THE MAN WOULD GET DRUNK AND START CRYING WHEN HE TALKED ABOUT HIM.

OVER

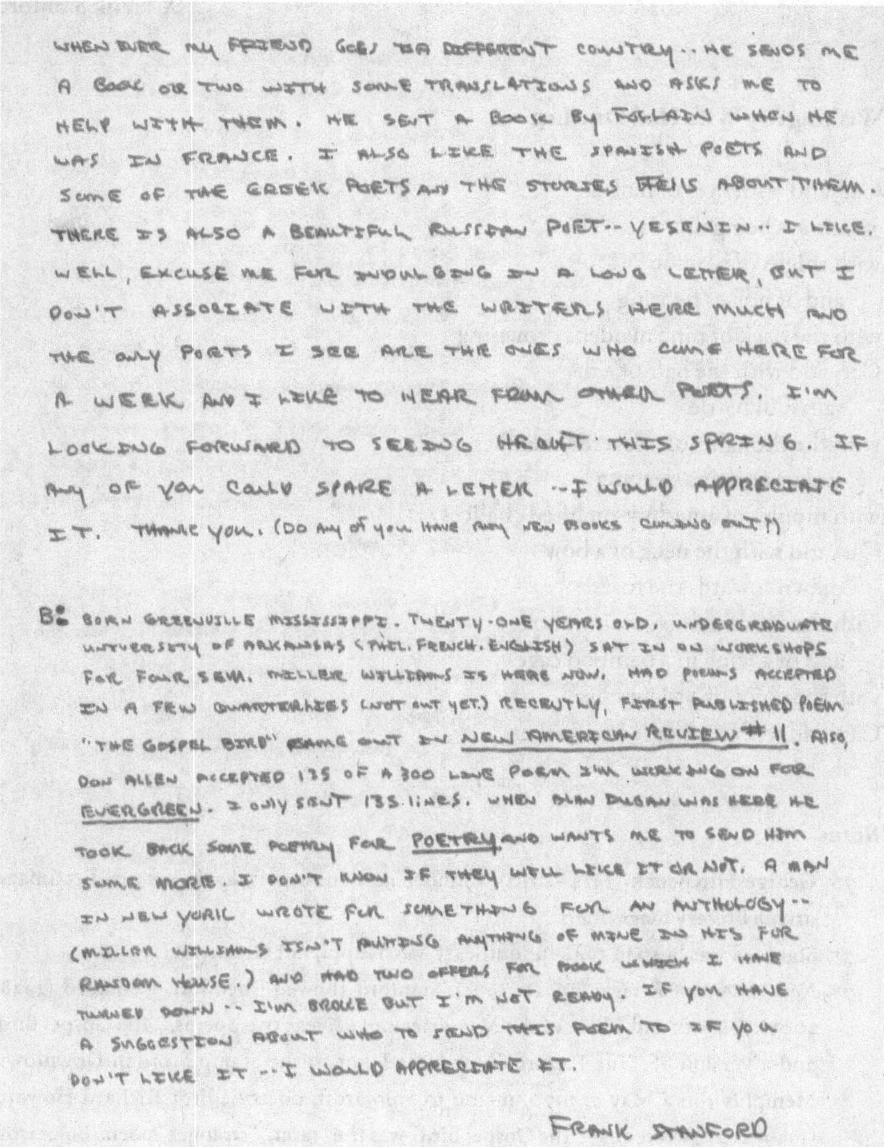

WHEN EVER MY FRIEND GOES TO A DIFFERENT COUNTRY.. HE SENDS ME A BOOK OR TWO WITH SOME TRANSLATIONS AND ASKS ME TO HELP WITH THEM. HE SENT A BOOK BY FOLLAIN WHEN HE WAS IN FRANCE. I ALSO LIKE THE SPANISH POETS AND SOME OF THE GREEK POETS AND THE STORIES [illegible] ABOUT THEM. THERE IS ALSO A BEAUTIFUL RUSSIAN POET-- YESENIN.. I LIKE. WELL, EXCUSE ME FOR INDULGING IN A LONG LETTER, BUT I DON'T ASSOCIATE WITH THE WRITERS HERE MUCH AND THE ONLY POETS I SEE ARE THE ONES WHO COME HERE FOR A WEEK AND I LIKE TO HEAR FROM OTHER POETS. I'M LOOKING FORWARD TO SEEING HRAULT THIS SPRING. IF ANY OF YOU COULD SPARE A LETTER --I WOULD APPRECIATE IT. THANK YOU. (DO ANY OF YOU HAVE ANY NEW BOOKS COMING OUT?)

B: BORN GREENVILLE MISSISSIPPI. TWENTY-ONE YEARS OLD. UNDERGRADUATE UNIVERSITY OF ARKANSAS (PHIL. FRENCH. ENGLISH) SAT IN ON WORKSHOPS FOR FOUR SEM. MILLER WILLIAMS IS HERE NOW. HAD POEMS ACCEPTED IN A FEW QUARTERLIES (NOT OUT YET.) RECENTLY, FIRST PUBLISHED POEM "THE GOSPEL BIRD" CAME OUT IN NEW AMERICAN REVIEW #11. ALSO, DON ALLEN ACCEPTED 135 OF A 300 LINE POEM I'M WORKING ON FOR EVERGREEN. I ONLY SENT 135 lines. WHEN ALAN DUGAN WAS HERE HE TOOK BACK SOME POETRY FOR POETRY AND WANTS ME TO SEND HIM SOME MORE. I DON'T KNOW IF THEY WILL LIKE IT OR NOT. A MAN IN NEW YORK WROTE FOR SOMETHING FOR AN ANTHOLOGY-- (MILLER WILLIAMS ISN'T PUTTING ANYTHING OF MINE IN HIS FOR RANDOM HOUSE.) AND HAD TWO OFFERS FOR BOOK WHICH I HAVE TURNED DOWN -- I'M BROKE BUT I'M NOT READY. IF YOU HAVE A SUGGESTION ABOUT WHO TO SEND THIS POEM TO IF YOU DON'T LIKE IT --I WOULD APPRECIATE IT.

FRANK STANFORD

Here and previous: Stanford's two-page March 1, 1971, cover letter to *The Massachusetts Review*, which published his poem "Tapsticks" in its Autumn 1972 issue. Stanford's handwriting moved through various iterations. In 1971 and for much of 1972, all-caps block lettering—with lowercase letters incorporated sporadically and at random—was his standard.

to say—except, Charles Plymell is putting some of my poems in an anthology.[79] Maybe I send you too many poems?[80]

X Frank Stanford

Wishing My Wife Had One Leg

Caryatid with eyes of nails
    always being driven
with thighs of a canoe
    and of horses fighting
with the back of nine maidens drowning
Caryatid with the hair of a flag
    raised in battle
with the thoughts of a severed member
    and of orphans sleeping
with nipples of amethyst on lifted chalices
Caryatid with the neck of a bow
    drawn towards the forest
with the sex of a ship coming about
    and of a wing in a bamboo cage
with the voice of a silent chisel
Caryatid with the heart of a feather

Notes

76. George Hitchcock (1914–2010), founder and editor of *kayak*, a surrealist/image-driven literary magazine.
77. Stanford was born in 1948 in southeast Mississippi, not Greenville.
78. *New American Review*, no. 11 (1971). Stanford showed Theodore Solotaroff (1928–2008), founder and editor of the *New American Review*, two poems, "The Gospel Bird" and a version of "The Picture Show Next Door to the Stamp Store in Downtown Memphis"; in a May 7, 1970, memo to Solotaroff, poetry editor Richard Howard (1929–2022) wrote that "The Gospel Bird" was the "rarer," "stranger" poem. Solotaroff bought the poem for sixty dollars on June 12, 1970.
79. A letter from Plymell to Stanford, postmarked December 10, 1970, notes, "Ray Bremser . . . myself + Reed Fry are putting together an anthology of poets we dig. Can you give me copies of half a dozen or so of your poems that you like best?" The project apparently stalled out.

80. The only Stanford poem in the *kayak* archives at University at Buffalo is "Wishing My Wife Had One Leg," which includes an editorial notation indicating that the poem was accepted on March 25, 1971. The poem was published in *kayak*, no. 26 (1971).

To *Open Places*: March 26, 1971

Dear Editor:[81]

I refer you to my letter of the 25th of this month, in which I sent you four poems. The carbon of "Becoming the Unicorn" has an error in the second line. It should be "my" not "m." Sorry. {I'm not good on a T.W.}[82]

Frank Stanford
Box 1333 U. of A.
Fayetteville,
Arkansas
72701

Bequeath[83]

An arm that nailed sixteen dollars
  to a mast and lost all hands
An arm that wrote its name
  in blood on a mirror
An arm that pulled the knife thrown by a friend
  out of its back
An arm hung from a roof of spears
  in Heorot
An arm that holds the reins of the horse
  with eight legs and rides always
An arm that laid Enkidu and Gilgamesh
  low
An arm like salt thrown over my shoulder
An arm that will haul down the black sails
  and hoist Karsavina
An arm that means nothing to me
  and everything to some
An arm that was the last to make a move
  the first to land a blow

An arm that has been tied into a knot like a poem
with one hand without the use of cord
and can never be undone
An arm that is bound to come around me at night
like a harp around its strings
black arm of Pythagoras

Notes

81. Eleanor Bender, founder and editor of *Open Places*, a poetry magazine.
82. *Marginalia: left side, left facing. T.W.*: typewriter.
83. This typescript copy was included with Stanford's March 25, 1971, letter (evidently lost) to *Open Places*; this March 26 correspondence is merely a note card. On April 25, Bender replied, "I am delighted with these poems and I have decided to go all out and publish all four. They are 'Bequeath,' 'Strappado,' 'Becoming the Unicorn,' and 'Narcissus.' "

To John McKernan: April 11, 1971

Easter Sunday

Dear John,

All along I thought you had a version of "The Pump" that I am using now, but today it hit me that you had the wrong one. The one you have is a revision of the original, but the revision is incorrect in two lines and a whole quatrain is bad. The original, included here, is better. Sorry! Probably too late. I hope not. If you have already set it up, don't go to any trouble on my account.[84] I have included three other poems if you want to use them.

In the green folder I have included ten poems in chronological order. 1966–1970. I don't include but one short poem, of which I have many, and I don't include any long poems, of which I have many. {or any new ones}[85] I would appreciate it if you could show them to Dickey.[86] I talked to him a lot at Hollins. About work, his novel into film,[87] karate, but I didn't get a chance to show him any poems. I don't know if he remembers me or not. I told him Peckinpah should do it and F. Wiseman and D. Slavitt agreed.[88] I wasn't deferring to him like a lot were so he could remember that. He might not like me, I don't know, but he is one poet I need to tell me what he thinks one way or the other. I was at Ark when he came a few years ago, but not in any Writing Program.

Anyway, sorry for the error and favor. Will be hearing from me soon. My number is 501 521-4706. You can call me collect. Let me know if he has already gone or what he says.

Also, what *you* think!

Best Regards,
Frank Stanford

He probably won't like them.

{You have original →}[89] "Living" published in different form {(revised)}[90]
You have "The Pump"
"Gospel Bird" *NAR* #11[91]
Rest OK except for one in *kayak*[92]

[The ten poems enclosed included the following cover letter.]

TEN POEMS 1966–1970[93]

Frank Stanford
Box 1333 Univ. of Ark.
Fayetteville, Arkansas 72701

Mr. Dickey,
I would appreciate it if you would read these. We talked at Hollins last summer, but I didn't show you any poems.

Frank Stanford

Notes

84. The version of Stanford's poem "The Pump" that appeared in *The Little Review* 2, no. 2, issue 4 (1971), varies from *The Singing Knives*' version; most notably, the second quatrain is different, and the book version incorporates Jimmy.
85. *Marginalia: right side, upright.*
86. James Dickey, Southern poet and *Esquire*'s poetry editor from 1970 to 1977.
87. Dickey's novel *Deliverance* (1970) was adapted into the film *Deliverance* (1972), dir. John Boorman.
88. Sam Peckinpah, filmmaker; Frederick Wiseman, filmmaker; and David R. Slavitt (1935–2025), poet / film critic.

89. *Marginalia: left side, upright.*

90. Stanford's poem "Living," *Mill Mountain Review* 1, no. 2 (1970).

91. See note 72 above.

92. "Wishing My Wife Had One Leg," *kayak*, no. 26 (1971).

93. The ten poems included are: "Living," "The Pump," "Elegy for My Father," "Tapsticks," "Wishing My Wife Had One Leg," "Narcissus to Achilles," "Transcendence of Janus," "The Gospel Bird," "The Albino," and "If I Should Wake."

To Alan Dugan: April 27, 1971

April 27

Dear Alan,

I guess you didn't get my first letter or didn't feel like answering it. I know you have to have your own time. I didn't know if you were still interested or not.[94] To repeat: you and your work mean very much to me. I am not being obeisant and I hope you don't think another letter is presumptuous.

What has happened to you since November that you care to talk about? Are you planning on staying where you are? You said something about a new book, but I can't remember what. I can remember the new poems you read.

If I seemed fucked up while you were here, this is the reason. Either the day before or the day after your arrival, Linda, my girlfriend found out she was pregnant.[95] If you recall, she acted funny herself, and was very shy around you. Well, we talked about it and she decided she wanted an abortion—even the doctors thought a child would be harmful. She got a legal abortion. {Here!} No one knew about it. It ended up costing about $1,000.00. She had a few complications, but she is fine mentally + physically now.[96]

To get the money I couldn't go to school second term. I have two jobs now and we have payed the damn bill completely off. I don't know how, though. Anyway, she invites you and your wife to visit us for as long as you want in the cabin. It is nice now and in the early + late summer. If you would like to stay here in solitude, we could stay at this other place.[97] We wouldn't tell anyone you would be here. I think you might like it. You have an invitation.

Another apology: my friend and old roommate who is head of the Black Americans for Democracy,[98] B.A.D., told me to tell you that they were sorry not many black people attended your reading, but they were holding a special crises meeting that night. Also, usually there are just as many or more blacks at my {Linda's} house (when I did have parties) but they won't come to one if Whitehead or any of the English dept. people are there. Also, I met that S.O.B. Jesse Hill Ford last summer.[99] He made me sick.

After you left I thought about what you said, then Mishima killed himself.[100] That did it for me. I think I quit "indulging in a romanticism" as you say. Since then, I have just stayed here alone with Linda. I've done a lot of writing. I saw Jim one time after you left. I have yet to see Miller Williams. I don't associate with anybody you met here but Stoss and Butler, occasionally.[101] The people I thought were my friends did me in. Let's just say this. I'm not as naive as I was when you were here. It is a long + back stabbing + fucked up story. However, recently, I have met a few people who I would like to be friends with. I haven't seen any of the writers that have visited here or been to any workshops. I don't pay any fealty or kiss M. Williams ass, so I'm not considered. Anthony Hecht is coming here the 6th. Nobody told me when you ~~have~~ {had} to turn work in, but they wouldn't let me anyway. I like Hecht.

My land surveying job is v. good. I saw a pair of bobcats for the first time in a long time. Also saw a wolf and almost got snake bit. We have been doing this job 40 miles on a gravel + dirt road back in the mountains. This farm happens to be in the path of a Confederate hold-out, lead mine, and retreat. Have you ever heard of the legend of the silver bullets. Well, this is the mine that they ran out of lead and hit silver. I talked to two brothers, 80–89 years old, and they told me some tales about it.[102]

Also, I have been going out to the lake to take care of Linda's father. He is a retired ace pilot and an alcoholic.[103]

I've had some good luck. A few editors + poets have written me letters asking to see my work. Some poems coming out in *kayak*, *West Coast Review*, *Open Places*, and I'm almost finished with the poem for *Evergreen*. I'll send it to you first. The men at *Partisan R.* + *Chicago R.* have had my poems for 3 months.

Well, this letter is all about me. I hope you will answer it if you have time. I haven't read any of those books in the N.B.A. yet.[104] This bookstore is slow. Neither have I read Wright's or Ignatow's *Collected.*[105] But I can always be thrilled by the last two poets who I like. I read Howard's *Findings.*[106] Only liked a few poems. The poet that screws me up because of his publicity and the way he was when I met him was {is} Dickey. I still like some of his poetry. I have about 10 good questions about your poems and in another letter I'll try to begin with some of them. To me—as Borges is to a S.S., your poems are to the poem.[107] I don't know if you agree with that or not. I don't know much about Borges, except a guy who has been after me to make a pamphlet, went to New York and met him. He even showed him some poems of mine and got me a autographed book. So.

I hope we can always be friends. You and your work mean alot to me. You helped me a lot while you were here. The best to you always.

With regards,
~~Frank~~ Stanford

Poems enclosed[108]

Could you ask the editor of *Shank Painter* to send me a few copies?[109] I really liked the poems in it.

Notes

94. On November 13, 1970, at the University of Arkansas, Dugan inscribed Stanford's copy of his *Collected Poems* (1969), "Let's keep in touch, Frank: I like your work. Alan."
95. Linda Mencin, Stanford's wife from August 1971 to October 1972; Frank and Linda lived together at 115 Skyline Drive, a log home on Mount Sequoyah—though, at the time of this letter, Frank was also living with Cheryl Campbell in his writing studio on Lindell Avenue, about two miles away.

    In this book, Linda Mencin Bond (née Mencin and Stanford) and Ginny Stanford (née Crouch) are referred to as being, respectively, Stanford's first and second wives. Notably, in a December 18, 1972, letter to Cheryl Campbell, Stanford states that his marriage to Linda was his "second" marriage—"the first one was annulled," he writes; regardless, to date no pre-Linda marriage or annulment records for Stanford have been found.
96. Per an interview of Linda Mencin Bond by this editor conducted primarily between January and July 2014, Linda had become pregnant unexpectedly; her ob-gyn performed a dilation and curettage (D&C). Linda believed that Frank had wanted to marry her and have the baby—which, she noted, he named Avalon.
97. Stanford may be referring to his Lindell Avenue studio.
98. James Seawood (1947–2014), who lived above Stanford and Bill Willett ca. 1967–68 at 221 Buchanan Avenue (a north-south street that formerly ran between Dickson Street and Fairview Street) in Fayetteville.
99. Jesse Hill Ford (1928–96), Southern author who problematized the Caucasian-favoring justice system in his works; Ford spoke at the Hollins Conference. On November 16, 1970, Ford shot and killed a Black soldier on his (Ford's) property; ironically, on July 2, 1971, Ford was acquitted by a jury of eleven white men and one Black man.
100. Yukio Mishima (1925–70), Japanese author; Mishima committed seppuku on November 25, 1970.
101. John Stoss (1940–2024), poet, and Jack Butler. Stoss and Butler attended Arkansas's MFA program in creative writing.
102. Per the chapter "The Mysterious Silver Bullets" in *Lost Treasures of Arkansas Waterways: Hidden Mines, Buried Fortunes, and Civil War Artifacts* by W. C. Jameson, the legend of the silver bullets is as follows: In the late nineteenth century, a Kentuckian, Tobe Inmon, settled in the Moccasin Creek Valley, north of Dover, Arkansas. In 1903, Inmon paid a Dover physician, Benjamin Martin, for services with thirty rifle bullets that, he stated, he had made himself from lead dug from a nearby mine. Upon Martin's closer examination later, the bullets were determined to be made

nearly entirely of silver. Inmon had left Arkansas, and Martin spent years searching for the mine, losing his house and career in the process. The legend was revived in 1951, when a Cherokee man, Lawrence Mankiller, sold a nugget of high-grade silver in Fort Smith, Arkansas, stating that he had found it in a mine shaft in the Moccasin Creek Valley, but like Inmon, Mankiller subsequently disappeared. The exact location of the purported mine apparently remains a mystery.

103. Lt. Adolph Mencin (1916–98), US Navy ace who retired to a home on Beaver Lake in Rogers, Arkansas, in 1968.
104. *N.B.A.*: National Book Award.
105. James Wright's *Collected Poems* (1971) and, probably, David Ignatow's *Poems: 1934–1969* (1970).
106. Richard Howard's *Findings* (1971).
107. Argentine writer Jorge Luis Borges (1899–1986) was antifascist, anti-Nazi, and anti-Schutzstaffel, so Stanford is asserting that Dugan's poems are antipoems; see Parra's *Poems and Antipoems* (1967).
108. Stanford enclosed twenty poems (some with dates) in "more or less" chronological order, including: "The Blood Brothers" (1964), "Living" (1966), "The Gospel Bird" (1969), "Transcendence of Janus" (1970), and "The Snake Doctors"—which, he noted on a poem list enclosed, he had "been working on . . . a long time." He also included notes explaining his selection and revision processes.
109. *Shankpainter: A Magazine of the Fine Arts Work Center in Provincetown.*

To Eleanor Bender: Circa Late April or May 1971

Dear Eleanor Bender,

Your letter of April 25 has reached me here. Needless to say, I am glad you want to use all four poems. I got a copy of *Open Places* and I read it. A fine issue. I read your magazine in the library.

Enclosed is a short poem that is said to be my best short one by other poets. Because of its length + lack of title, other than "Poem," I always never sent it out. I didn't think anyone would want to publish it.[110] Could you?

You asked about contributors' notes. Here is all I want to say:

B: 21 born Greenville, Mississippi. Live on Sequoyah Mountain in Fayetteville, Arkansas. First published poem in *New American Review #11*. [Since then, 40 poems accepted at magazines.][111]

I hope to be hearing from you and seeing the next issue of *Open Places*.

Regards,
~~Frank~~ Stanford

Notes

110. Stanford's poem "Poem" ("When the rain hits the snake in the head,").
111. Brackets Stanford's.

To John McKernan: May 10, 1971

May 10

Dear John,

Tonight is the full moon. This is a note asking if you would select the best from some poems of mine if you have time. I need to know. Instead of a book now, I've decided to make a pamphlet. I'll probably do two. Also, got a letter from Paul Carroll who wants to read my poems for possible inclusion in a new *The Young American Poets*.[112] I don't know who recommended me. Probably Howard or Dugan. If you say yes, I'll send a few poems your way. 5 poems accepted in *Open Places* and 15 in *West Coast Review*. Got letter from Dugan and David Ray. I'll tell Carroll about your poems. The 24th will be the new moon. Best to your wife.

Best,
Frank

Notes

112. *The Young American Poets* (1968), an anthology edited by Paul Carroll with introduction by James Dickey (no editions were published subsequent to this letter).

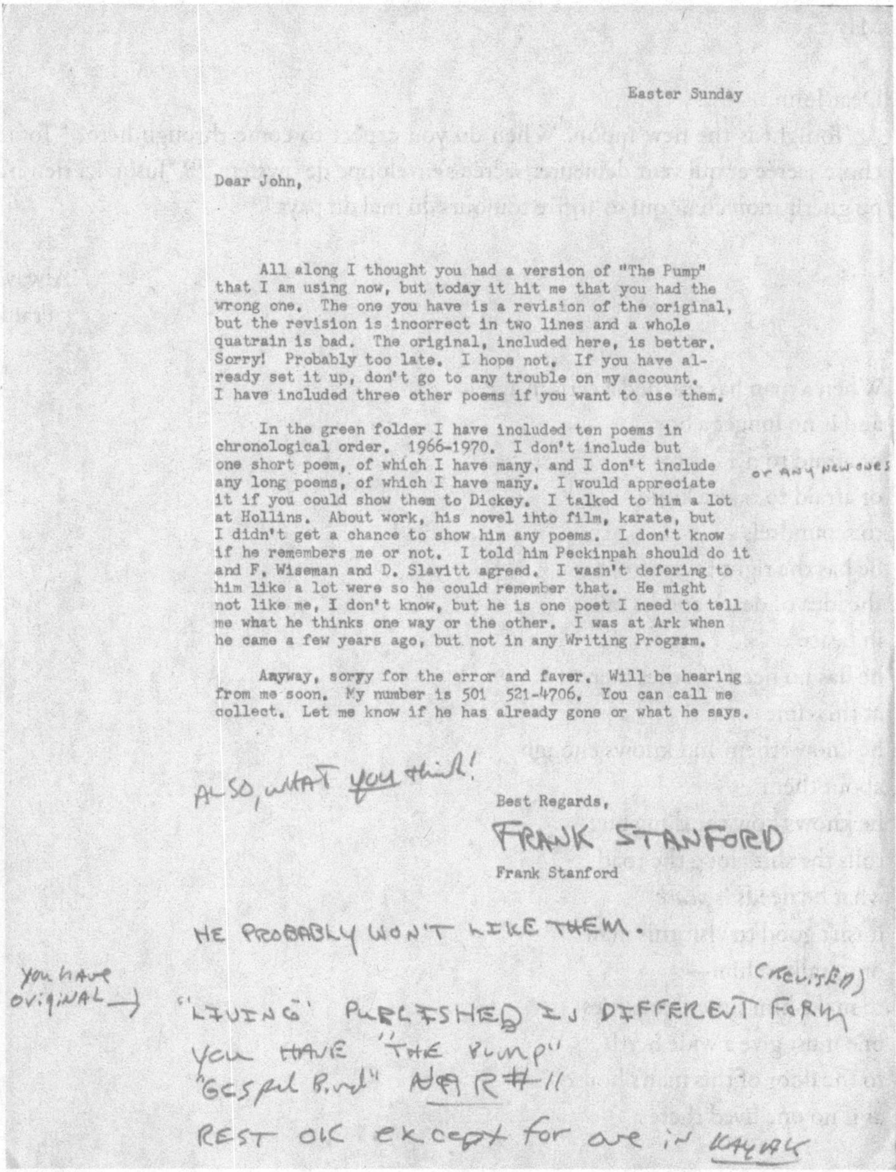

Easter Sunday

Dear John,

All along I thought you had a version of "The Pump" that I am using now, but today it hit me that you had the wrong one. The one you have is a revision of the original, but the revision is incorrect in two lines and a whole quatrain is bad. The original, included here, is better. Sorry! Probably too late. I hope not. If you have already set it up, don't go to any trouble on my account. I have included three other poems if you want to use them.

In the green folder I have included ten poems in chronological order. 1966-1970. I don't include but one short poem, of which I have many, and I don't include any long poems, of which I have many. I would appreciate it if you could show them to Dickey. I talked to him a lot at Hollins. About work, his novel ihto film, karate, but I didn't get a chance to show him any poems. I don't know if he remembers me or not. I told him Peckinpah should do it and F. Wiseman and D. Slavitt agreed. I wasn't defering to him like a lot were so he could remember that. He might not like me, I don't know, but he is one poet I need to tell me what he thinks one way or the other. I was at Ark when he came a few years ago, but not in any Writing Program.

OR ANY NEW ONES

Anyway, sorry for the error and faver. Will be hearing from me soon. My number is 501 521-4706. You can call me collect. Let me know if he has already gone or what he says.

ALSO, WHAT *you* think!

Best Regards,

FRANK STANFORD

Frank Stanford

HE PROBABLY WON'T LIKE THEM.

you have original →

"LIVING" PUBLISHED IN DIFFERENT FORM (REVISED)

YOU HAVE "THE PUMP"

"Gospel Bird" NAR #11

REST OK except for one in KAYAK

One of Stanford's earliest typed letters—to John McKernan, early in their eight-year-long correspondence—with Stanford's manuscript additions and marginalia. In a March 1971 note to Eleanor Bender, Stanford noted, "I'm not good on a T.W." He soon developed the requisite skills, though, his progress accelerated by the sizable project he undertook between fall 1971 and spring 1972 of typing up much of his juvenilia and other early manuscripts.

To John McKernan: May 24, 1971

May 24

Dear John,

Tonight is the new moon. When do you expect to come through here? "Toute chose sacrée et qui veut demeurer sacrée s'enveloppe de mystère."[113] "Jusqu'ici rien n'a pu guérir mon cœur qui so[u]ffre toujours du mal du pays."[114]

Always,
Frank

When a man has reached a certain age
and is no longer a boy
or afraid to die
or afraid to take a knife
to scoundrels
he has the right to confront
the idea of death and its sails
in peace
he has no need of other men
at this time
he knows them and knows enough
about them
he knows how the dung bug
rolls the shit along the road
what he needs is *peace*
it isn't good to visit this man
or to talk to him—
to make him suffer banalities
one must give a wide berth
to the door of this man's house
as if no one lived there

after Meng-tse[115]

(You are about the only person I would enjoy seeing. I like you. I hope we'll always be friends.)

Notes

113. The opening sentence of Stéphane Mallarmé's 1862 manifesto "Hérésies artistiques: L'art pour tous" (Artistic heresy: Art for all): "All things sacred that wish to remain sacred are enveloped in mystery."

114. Likely by French poet/novelist Arsène Houssaye (1815–96): "So far nothing has been able to cure my heart, which still suffers from homesickness." (The line is frequently attributed to French poet Gérard de Nerval [1808–55], but Nerval scholar Michel Brix believes it was actually composed by Houssaye and passed off by him as having been written by Nerval. Email to editor, December 10, 2021.)

115. Meng-tzu, or Mencius (ca. 371–ca. 289 BC), Chinese philosopher. A translation of the Meng-tzu version of this poem appears in Miguel Serrano's *C. G. Jung and Hermann Hesse: A Record of Two Friendships*, trans. Frank MacShane (1966); see Stanford's June 28, 1971, letter to Bender below, par. 2.

To Alan Dugan: June 21, 1971

June 21, 1971[116]

Dear Alan,

Thank you for your letters and the help with my poems. I took your advice. You are right.

It looks like today is summer and the new moon is tomorrow. All I can say is: I feel good. I hope you do too.

If you don't mind, I'd like to ask you a few questions. I know a great many people must write you asking questions and sending manuscripts—and being one of the best living poets you need your own time, but I would like to see any of your new work. You mentioned that you had about twenty poems that would be published in the fall. I surely would like to know some of the magazines that they will appear in. Also, do you have any plans for a book soon? If you have any extra copies of your new works, I wouldn't show it to anyone, but I wouldn't blame you for not sending it.

I get up every morning about 4:00 and everything is fine. I read over what I wrote the night before and whenever I use the T.W. the squirrels go nuts. I can call them with my mouth and they will come right up to the desk—they love to listen to the T.W. though. If I go downstairs, they will follow me and get up on the bottom ledge. I have to be at work at 7:00 usually, the rest are late and I sit in the truck and sometimes get some good things down. The guys I work with are good souls and they think I'm Indian or something because every time I called, the rain has come. Once—I was fucking around—dancing out in the woods and I told them some B.S. and right after we left the place, there were tornadoes. They could give a shit that I'm a writer, but they respect the other. The job *is* money and outside.

I haven't seen anyone here since you left, except this girl who they don't know I see. According to her, most of them hate my guts.[117] They talk all night on what's wrong with me + my poems. You see, everyone of them was dead wrong about me in the beginning, so they're trying to take the slack out now. I was their prisoner + shine boy for awhile, because I didn't want to hurt their feelings. The more + more I let them know about myself + past—they got fucked up. It was the opposite from what they thought. They took too much credit for what my parents did. I told them about how I had to learn the *black* way which is near the Socratic method, when I was a kid. When I started telling them the truth about my life, they would get up + walk out. I told them how my mother + I would clean fish + she would explain the paradoxes in Kafka + Life, etc. She had all the great books—those old dk. blue books with the gold trim in dynamite boxes in camp.[118] By the time I got to high school I had read most of the stuff you have to for a masters—I didn't know shit about it. Some of the books: Don Q., Melville's, Conrad's, Twain's, and a lot of the poetry I knew like the back of my hand. When I told them about reading Stevenson and Marx and Boccaccio and Keats and Turgenev and all those fucking Russians out in the woods with my mother, they really got fucked up. They condescended to those old Blue Books, even. I remember now: "The Book League of America"[119] Do you? Also, I read just about all of Dickens when I was very young, which I don't regret. Now some of the authors mother would tell me to read—I wouldn't. I'd read comic books instead. After the jobs were over + the levee was done, we'd go back to Memphis to the big house and my daddy would teach me elementary phil. + history + geography.

Then, when I went to the Benedictine monastery to school—that is where I learned a lot.[120] There wasn't anything else to do.

I had my mind set on being a writer way before I met the likes of these bastards here.

I have been reading your poetry alot and for me there are many of them that are just as good or better than some of your famous ones. I know at least two dozen that you never hear much about, ~~but I~~ that I think are some of the best. I will send you a list and maybe you might have something to say.

Do you remember my friend *Willett* the hillbilly. They took him into the Army and I'm getting him out on a C.O.[121] Right before he went in—his brothers + himself got jumped up in the 101 woods in Mo. and he got stabbed. It didn't kill him. It made him so mad, he beat the shit out of the other guy.[122]

About my poems: *The Massachusetts Review* and the *Chicago R.* took some. Enclosed is a poem you haven't seen, that *The Nation* took.[123] I sent one of my best poems—you haven't seen—to *Poetry*. It is called *The Singing Knives*. When I type it up again I'll send it to you. It's old.

I sent a copy of this mag. they told me to be editor of—I just got the $ + stamps + printed what they gave me. I don't know shit about being an editor and I don't care.—to the *New Yorker* and told them to read Butler's and Stoss's work.[124] They took a poem by Butler.[125] (Butler went nuts a month ago—I like him + poems—but we never see each other. He confessed to a stabbing murder he didn't do—they sent him to the loony farm.)[126] He thinks he is Shakspeare [*sic*] sometimes—he's crazy. I like him.

Have you ever heard of a novelist, Joan Williams?[127] She grew up in Memphis. Her old man sold dynamite and he + my old man cooked up an idea how to blow ditches (which was safer) because when they dug them men (blacks) were always getting killed. The idea worked—he made a million selling powder—use to light it with his cig. Anyway she went to school at Bard—wrote—came back to Memphis—was introduced to Faulkner.[128] He was v. impressed with her work. Personally sent it to Harper's—they rejected—so he says "no use wasting postage" and sent it to his agent. He titled it and it was an Atlantic First back in the late fifties, became the novel "The Morning and the Evening" was pretty well known at the time.[129] She was the *only* young writer that Faulkner was interested in. They had a long standing relationship which nobody knows about.[130] Blotner in Va. who is doing his biography has it all screwed up.[131] She wrote her second novel a few years ago at our house.[132] Most of the details she got from my mother.[133] My ole man + mother are main characters.[134] Penn Warren reviewed it in Life.[135] (I don't like Tate + Ransom + that crew, though.)[136] Her new book is about she + Faulkner.[137] She wrote it just to get things straight I guess. Faulkner is Jeff Almoner.[138] She was about the last one to see him not drunk before he died. "The Wintering" (I have to go to work now.) She wants me to come to Memphis to see her. She is moving away from Conn. {She was married to Cath. Drinker Bowan's son, but just divorced him.[139] She is almost 40.}[140]

I didn't get to meet Hecht. That SOB Miller Williams. I did hear him read. I like many of his poems.

This poem enclosed is about myself I guess. If you wrote one like it you would probably end it:

"I know shit from Shinola."

Always my best to you I hope I can be your student one of these years,

FRANK

Notes

116. This letter exists, in Dugan's papers, both in manuscript and typescript versions (the latter not by Stanford, as the typist was confused over "dk." [typing "(?)" there] in par. 5 and misread Stanford's spelling of "Almoner" in par. 12); only the manuscript version is signed. This transcription is primarily of the manuscript version. Prior to

June 1972, nearly the only (known) typed Stanford correspondence is from April–June 1971; as Frank and Cheryl were living together on Lindell Avenue (part-time, it appears, as he was also living with Linda) from ca. late February / early March to ca. June or early July 1971 and as Cheryl was typing up his poems for publications, she likely typed some April–June 1971 letters as well.

117. Probably Cheryl Campell, the likely typist of this letter's typescript version, who knew at least a couple of people involved, however peripherally, with Fayetteville's literary community (such as Fred McCuistion and Big Time Sonny Morris). Otherwise, ostensibly Kathy Walton, an MFA student with whom Stanford had a sporadic intrigue between 1969 and 1971 and who had lived at 115 Skyline Drive prior to Linda and Frank's living there. James McWilliams, *The Life and Poetry of Frank Stanford* (University of Arkansas Press, 2025), 232.
118. *dk. blue*: dark blue.
119. A mail-order book club, 1930–1950s. Editions included Cervantes's *Don Quixote*; Melville's *Moby-Dick*; Conrad's *Chance*; Twain's *A Connecticut Yankee in King Arthur's Court* and *The Adventures of Tom Sawyer* (under Twain's birth name, Samuel L. Clemens, for the latter); several books of Stevenson's works; tales from Boccaccio's *The Decameron*; *Fathers and Sons* and other well-known works by Turgenev; works by Chekhov, Andreyev, and Tolstoy; and several books of Dickens's works.
120. Subiaco Academy, Subiaco, Arkansas.
121. *C.O.*: conscientious objector. Stanford wrote a letter of support to Willett's commanding officer, re: Willett's request for a C.O., on May 5, 1971.
122. Willett noted in a June 10, 2023, text to this editor, that this clash occurred at an establishment known as the G & G Lounge, located on Highway 101 northeast of Gamaliel, Arkansas, across the state line in Missouri; Willett's brother Edward Leon was with him.
123. *The Nation* published Stanford's poem "Belladonna" on October 4, 1971.
124. *this mag.*: presumably *Preview: Eight Poets*, which Stanford edited. Butler and Stoss were two of the eight poets Stanford published.
125. *The New Yorker* accepted Butler's poem "Subplot" (published in September 1972) on June 1, 1971.
126. On April 12, 1971, a University of Arkansas student, Pauline Storment, was stabbed to death; Butler confessed and, after being deemed not of sound mind, passed a brief stint at the Arkansas State Hospital. The murder remains a cold case in Fayetteville.
127. Joan Williams (1928–2004), writer whose father was a professional colleague and friend of A. F. Stanford. Stanford's poem "Women Singing When Their Husbands Are Gone" (*Ladies From Hell*) is dedicated to Williams.
128. William Faulkner (1897–1962), author.

129. Williams's short story "The Morning and the Evening" was published in *The Atlantic Monthly* in January 1953; Williams developed the story into her first novel, *The Morning and the Evening* (1961).

130. See Lisa C. Hickman's *William Faulkner and Joan Williams: The Romance of Two Writers* (McFarland, 2006).

131. Joseph Blotner's *Faulkner: A Biography* (1974).

132. Williams's *Old Powder Man* (1966).

133. Williams's remembrance of Stanford, "Remembering" (first published in *Ironwood* 9, no. 1, issue 17 [Spring 1981], collected in *Remembering: Joan Williams' Uncollected Pieces* [2015]), describes her experience of researching *Old Powder Man* via conversations with Dorothy Stanford in Mountain Home, Arkansas, in summer 1964.

134. In the novel, Will Carrothers (levee engineer) and Martha Carrothers (Will's wife, who works at the levee) are fictional depictions of A. F. and Dorothy Stanford; as well, in the novel's early pages, Henry "Poppa," Cally, Frank "Son," and Cecilia Wynn bear some clear likenesses to the Stanfords—i.e., to A. F., Dorothy, Frank, and Frank's sister, Ruth (1949–2019), respectively.

135. Robert Penn Warren's "Death of a Salesman—Southern Style: *Old Powder Man* by Joan Williams" in *Life*, May 20, 1966.

136. Allen Tate (1899–1979) and John Crowe Ransom (1888–1974), poets and members (alongside Warren [1905–89]) of the Fugitives, a group of poets noted for editing and publishing *The Fugitive*—a magazine published at Vanderbilt University from 1922 to 1925—whose Southern poetics emphasized formalism and Southern regionalism and centered on a conservative fundamentalism, controlled verse, and occasional ironic affectation. All three also contributed to the Southern Agrarians' 1930 manifesto propounding antimodern ideas, and Ransom later led the New Criticism—an academic movement in the 1940s and 1950s (following his 1941 book, *The New Criticism*) that, like the Fugitive movement, focused on formalism and on controlled readings of poems as systems of symbols and metaphors, insisting à la T. S. Eliot on an "impersonal" poetry. T.S. Eliot, "Tradition and the Individual Talent," in *The Sacred Wood: Essays on Poetry and Criticism*, 7th ed. (Methuen, 1950), 53, 59; and John Crowe Ransom, *The New Criticism* (New Directions, 1941), 151–52, 156–57, 246, 290.

137. Williams's novel *The Wintering* (1971).

138. Jeffrey Almoner, the fictional double for Faulkner in *The Wintering*.

139. Ezra Bowen (1927–96), son of biographer Catherine Drinker Bowen (1897–1973).

140. *Marginalia: left side, right facing.*

To Eleanor Bender: June 28, 1971

June 28, 1971

Dear Eleanor,

Your kind letter of June 10th has reached me here. Of course, I am glad you like my writing. And I congratulate you on your first effort as an agent.[141]

No, I haven't read the poets you mentioned. The bookstores here don't have much. The last book of poems I read was by a Russian. I liked them very much. My reading has really been wandering: *Byron In Italy*,[142] Mishima, Chesterton, *Memoirs From The House Of The Dead*,[143] Melville, some Symbolist work,[144] *Don Quixote*, the Bible and the Koran, a record of the friendship of Hesse and Jung,[145] Wolfe,[146] *The Decameron*, a lot of Keats and Shelley, Drayton and Marlowe, Webster,[147] d. h. Lawrence, Conrad, Hoffmann,[148] Sophocles, the life of Sir Richard Burton,[149] *With Lawrence In Arabia* by Lowell Thomas,[150] Whitman and Twain, here and there some Poe, Kafka, and Hawthorne, texts on Japanese swords, North American Indian Mythology[151]—during the Fall and Winter all I read was mythology—especially northern and celtic, volumes of all these new film texts,[152] *Confessions Of An English Opium-Eater*,[153] some boxing history books, D. G. Rossetti,[154] and Faulkner. Most of these I had already read, but ever since I quit school I've been going back and re-reading what my mother and I read out of dynamite boxes in the levee camps. Do you remember the old blue books with gold trim, called The Book League Of America? Well, I believe they had just about every book written—at least my mother did. Those were good times. Some of Stevenson I could recite.[155] Sometimes it seemed as if students were talking about old friends when they chattered about some of these books. I leave my windows open at night and the lightning bugs come in. Sometimes a dozen of them. I get up at about 4:00 every morning and the squirrel will come to the ledge. He wants me to use the typewriter because he likes to chirp with it. I have to be at work at 7:00. If the others are late, I sit in the truck and dream.

You asked me about publishing. Since you last heard from me, *The Massachusetts Review*, *The Chicago Review*, *The Nation*, and some others have taken poems. The editor of *the nation* got me a scholarship to a poetry festival, but I doubt if I will be able to attend. I need to write back so some other person could have a chance.[156] Also, an opportunity to go to a film conference, but I only want to see films and this will be mostly criticism. I have had three offers for a book, but I didn't want to at the time and I'm glad I didn't. However, an editor in Virginia who won a National Arts Endowment is going to make a pamphlet of 22 of my poems. I selected them. The first poem in it I wrote in 64—the last one 70.[157] Every poem in it is forthcoming in various magazines. I had thoughts about writing for a very long time but I didn't decide I wanted to be one until I went to this Benedictine School after my father died. That was the last two years of High School. A monk, Fr. Nicholas, weeded my reading and gave me modern and contemporary works to read.[158] He warned me about Writing Programs. I wish I had taken his advice. Even my Freshman English teacher, himself a writer, warned me.

My brief and unhappy career as a creative writer brings no fond memories. I have seen a lot of people die in all manner of ways but the way they do it in the literary business I think is the most horrible. They had me tied up by the feet and they were ready to slit my throat, but I got away and I ran a long time until I quit. Of course, I'm going to finish college, but I have to watch out. I'm still a little bat shy—I hope you understand.[159] Some of them gave me A's and some of them F's in Creative Writing.[160] I didn't mind that. I was really a fool though. People would say "I'll give you 15.00 for that poem." or give me that image, or could I have that. Pretty soon, they weren't asking. And since I wasn't enrolled in Workshops anymore, they thought they could use just about anything they wanted.[161] I still didn't care. I felt sorry for them. They thought they knew all about me, but they didn't know a thing. Then, if I happened to be at a party, I could expect a condescending lecture. I thought something was really wrong with me because I never was interested in what they were saying. It all sounded meretricious. So different from listening all day at some people I knew. Some of the people in Phil, Lang, and Music, I could listen to all day. I have always liked being alone and liked privacy. Everybody started analyzing me. This girl I knew says they talk about me all the time and they all have me figured out. I wish they'd tell my mother. She would like to know. So would my girl friend. I haven't seen any of them in about a year. The last time about was when they asked me to give a party for Dugan. Me and him like one another from the start. The sycophants started bugging Alan, they started making fun of my sister and her husband,[162] they started telling my next door neighbors who are black what kind of music to sing in their next record, so it all let loose. I had been cutting some dead timber out back. So I got the chainsaw started up and ran them out. I also used the shotgun. Then the lovely dancers came. (I use to live in a house with six girls and they were all musicians and dancers) They always came at midnight and we would dance. Ever since, I've been happy. Well, not always happy—or I couldn't be a poet—but what was bothering me about the others went away and hasn't come back as long as I stay away. The dance teacher here use to be famous. She is old now. Eleanor King is her name. She is retiring—but only to go to New Mexico to teach indian dances.[163] It is getting light and the squirrel loves this, but I need to read something this letter has excited me with. Lazarillo.[164] I have a new translation.[165] I've read it in Spanish or tried to a long time ago. If I read over this letter I won't mail it. So please excuse all the spelling and grammer [*sic*]. I beg your pardon. Your letter was charming.

I correspond with a couple of Pulitzer Prize winners who like my writing and who help me with it.[166] There are so many things I have to learn yet. They have said something about that Yale Prize, so I haven't been interested in doing a book until I'm ready to try my luck at that. (I have been coaxed into that) Personally, I need the money. I'd like to go to the Yuc. Pen. in Mexico, so the next person or house that offers I might take it.[167]

However, I still think I'm too young to be publishing anything besides a pamphlet. There are a lot of older writers who have been at it a long time who should publish books. I'm not in any hurry. I would like people to read my poems first hand though and not in other people's versions of them.

I will send you a manuscript of the 22 poems as soon as I make up my mind as to which long poem to include. I've been working on a half a dozen of them for a long time now—they say they are my best work. I want to use one called "The Snake Doctors".[168] I got a letter from Paul Carroll about work for his new anthology. He sent it in care of the English Dept. so I'm lucky to even get it. They throw most of my mail away and if I do get it, it has been opened like his was. It is over a month old. When I type his up, I'll send you one. I hope you find a patron for your magazine. I am

respectfully yours
Frank Stanford

PS If you would like some good reading and also like to know exactly many things on my mind, please read the *introduction* to DH Lawrence's poetry by RexRoth.[169] Also, The Argentine Writer and His Tradition, an essay in *Labyrinths* by Borges.[170]

Notes

141. In Bender's June 10, 1971, letter to Stanford, she begins, "I am really very astonished by your poetry," accepts "Poem" for publication, and notes that matters are "up in the air" for *Open Places* but that an issue including Stanford's poetry is forthcoming. Bender had sold the manuscript for the first book of poems by Rosmarie Waldrop (b. 1935) to editor Nan A. Talese at Random House; explaining this to Stanford, she asked him what his publishing plans were, noting that she would be interested in seeing his manuscript and helping him publish it. She then suggested the poetry of Zbigniew Herbert (1924–98) and Vasko Popa (1922–91).

142. Peter Quennell's *Byron in Italy* (1941).

143. Fyodor Dostoevsky's *Memoirs from the House of the Dead*, trans. Jessie Coulson (1956)—originally published in Russian as *Zapiski iz Myortvogo doma* (1860–62).

144. See, e.g., Stanford's May 24, 1971, letter to McKernan above re: Mallarmé.

145. Serrano's *C. G. Jung and Hermann Hesse.*

146. Thomas Wolfe (1900–1938), author.
147. John Webster (ca. 1580–ca. 1632), English dramatist.
148. E. T. A. Hoffmann (1776–1822), German Romantic author, composer, and artist.
149. Presumably Isabel Burton's *The Life of Captain Sir Richard F. Burton* (1893), a two-volume biography (as opposed to Thomas Wright's *The Life of Sir Richard Burton* [1906], also a two-volume biography); cf. *The Battlefield*, lines 5896–98.
150. Lowell Thomas's *With Lawrence in Arabia* (1924).
151. Cottie Burland's *North American Indian Mythology* (1965).
152. Stanford may be referring to late 1960s / early 1970s books of screenplays published by the Orion Press—e.g., Jean Cocteau's *Two Screenplays: "The Blood of a Poet," "The Testament of Orpheus"* (1968) and Luis Buñuel's *Three Screenplays: "Viridiana," "The Exterminating Angel," "Simon of the Desert"* (1969); Orion published similar books for Ingmar Bergman (in 1967), Federico Fellini (in 1970 and 1971), et al. Similar titles published by other presses include *Four Screenplays* by Carl Theodor Dreyer (1970) and *The Adventures of Antoine Doinel: 4 Autobiographical Screenplays* by François Truffaut (1971).
153. Thomas De Quincey's autobiography, *Confessions of an English Opium-Eater* (1821).
154. Dante Gabriel Rossetti (1828–82), English poet/painter.
155. Cf. *The Battlefield*, lines 364–71, where hero Francis Gildart recites Robert Louis Stevenson's novella *The Beach of Falesá*.
156. Allen Planz (1937–2010), *The Nation*'s poetry editor from 1969 to 1973, recommended Stanford to the National Poetry Festival's director, poet Robert Vas Dias (b. 1931), who offered Stanford a small scholarship that excluded transportation and housing.
157. "The Blood Brothers" is dated 1964 in *The Singing Knives*, whose first edition contained twenty-three (not twenty-two) poems; per correspondence, the book's closing poem, "The Snake Doctors," wasn't finalized until ca. August 1971.
158. Fr. Nicholas Fuhrmann, OSB (1929–2019), monk and Stanford's English teacher at Subiaco. Fuhrmann also officiated Stanford's wedding to Mencin and his funereal mass at Subiaco. Stanford's 406-line poem "The Snake Doctors" is dedicated to Fuhrmann.
159. *bat shy*: in baseball, often used in reference to a batter fearful of inside pitches but also to a catcher scared of being struck by a batter's bat mid-swing; see *The Battlefield*, lines 7046–51.
160. Apart from one undergraduate writing course taken in spring 1968, the creative writing courses that Stanford took at the University of Arkansas were all graduate workshops; he received an A in the spring 1969 poetry workshop, an F in the fall 1969 poetry workshop, and an F in the fall 1970 fiction workshop.
161. Stanford's last workshops were fall 1969 (poetry) and fall 1970 (fiction).
162. Stanford's sister, Ruth Rogers, and her husband, Larry Rogers.

163. Eleanor King (1906–91), dancer, choreographer, and Arkansas professor from 1952 to 1971; upon retiring, King moved to Santa Fe, New Mexico.
164. *La vida de Lazarillo de Tormes y de sus fortunas y adversidades* (*The Life of Lazarillo de Tormes: His Fortunes and Adversities*) (1554), an anonymous Spanish novella.
165. *new translation*: possibly W. S. Merwin's (Anchor Books, 1962), or else Michael Alpert's, *Two Spanish Picaresque Novels: "Lazarillo de Tormes," "The Swindler"* (Penguin Books, 1969).
166. Dugan and, feasibly, Howard.
167. Yucatán Peninsula.
168. In her August 5, 1971, response to this letter and *The Singing Knives* in manuscript (see Stanford's July 27, 1971, letter to Bender below), Bender applauds Stanford for his "admirable" hesitations about getting "swept away with the tide of things" but asserts that he "should publish a book of poems as soon as possible." She also notes, " 'The Snake Doctors' and 'The Outhouse' ought definitely to be included before you seriously try to publish the book."
169. *Selected Poems* (1947) by Lawrence, with a lengthy, manifesto-qualitied introduction (on Lawrence and on poetry/poetics) by poet Kenneth Rexroth (1905–82), in which Rexroth argues that Lawrence was a genuine and prophetic commoner, personal poet, profound Imagist, and effective poetic channeler simultaneously of hallucinatory, psychological, supernatural, metaphysical, mystical, and earthy experience. Rexroth outlines the paths of Lawrence's poetry across his romantic relationships—including his relationship with his wife Frieda Lawrence (1879–1956) and the "battlefield between love and hate that is so carefully mapped in certain of the poems." Introduction to *Selected Poems*, 13. See also notes 49 and 50 above.
170. Borges's essay "The Argentine Writer and Tradition," trans. James E. Irby, in *Labyrinths: Selected Stories & Other Writings* (1964).

To Alan Dugan: July 26, 1971

July 26, 1971

Dear Alan,

Here are just a few lines to see if you are feeling OK. This is the most melancholic part of the year for anyone no matter what their age—when they say the summer is almost over and you drift to so many things. You make up your own constellations so you can follow them.

Linda + I are going to get married Aug 21. I think things will be fine. I'm going back to school too. The *Partisan Review* liked the part of "The Snake Doctors" I sent and wants to see the rest. Enclosed poem is v. old, but I never sent it to you because I couldn't find all of it just the 1st + 2nd page. I know you didn't like "Caryatid" + "Bequeath"—I based them {(structure)} on this since I couldn't find the complete manuscript. Now, I threw the other two away + keep this one—I sent it to Hine.[171] Maybe I shouldn't try to use a poem I wrote 5 yrs. ago? I don't know.[172]

I read some more by Ibsen, Lawrence, Gide, Conrad, Dostoevsky, and Wilde.[173] Also, OE + MEng poetry that I like.[174]

I know you are busy. So I'll knock this off. Hope you + your family are well. Linda gives her best.

yours,
Frank

P.S. About that poem "Belladonna."[175] A long time ago I read where Goethe was riding back from a girl's house in the woods and he saw himself passing on a horse. That mystified me.[176]

Notes

171. Daryl Hine (1936–2012), *Poetry*'s editor from 1968 to 1978.

172. Per Stanford's June 21, 1971, letter to Dugan above, par. 10, and Dugan's July 30, 1971, letter, the poem Stanford is enclosing here is "The Singing Knives," a 126-line poem employing frequent anaphora, as both "Wishing My Wife Had One Leg" (presumably the "Caryatid" Stanford mentions) and "Bequeath" also do. (Dugan actually labeled the former "a beauty" in a May 19, 1971, letter.) Dugan replied that "The Singing Knives" was "magnificent."

173. Henrik Ibsen, D. H. Lawrence, André Gide, Joseph Conrad, Fyodor Dostoevsky, and Oscar Wilde—nineteenth-century and early twentieth-century authors, playwrights, and poets.

174. *OE + MEng*: Old English and Middle English.

175. See Stanford's June 21, 1971, letter to Dugan above, par. 10, and note 123 above.

176. From Johann Wolfgang von Goethe's autobiography (1811–33): "I now rode along . . . and here one of the most singular forebodings took possession of me. I saw, not with the eyes of the body, but with those of the mind, my own figure coming towards me, on horseback. . ." *The Autobiography of Goethe: Truth and Poetry, from My Own Life*, trans. John Oxenford (London, 1897), 433. Cf. *The Battlefield*, lines 8835–36. "Belladonna" was written about Cheryl Campbell (see Stanford's July 29, 1972, letter to Campbell below), so Stanford appears to be alluding here to his double life between Linda and Cheryl.

To Donald Justice: July 27, 1971

July 27, 1971

Dear Donald Justice,

I don't know if this will reach you. I hope so. I know you must be very busy. Whether you know it or not, in your brief visit here a few years ago, you helped me very much.[177] I don't know quite what to say, except I'll always remember you. I'm not trying to be obeisant or ask favors. I'm sure you get that. Just a note to say you + your poetry are in my thoughts often.

I haven't seen any of the other writers here in about a year. I'm not in their *circle* anymore. I didn't go in for what you warned me against: the neo-Fugitive-nouveau redneck local color—so I'm out.[178] I've been lucky in my work though—on my own. All goes well.

I wish you well always. Maybe our paths will cross again.

Yours,

Getting married Aug 21.

Frank Stanford

Notes

177. Justice visited the University of Arkansas in fall 1969; see Stanford's November 10, 1969, letter to Ginsberg above, par. 1.

178. See note 136 above.

To Eleanor Bender: July 27, 1971

July 27, 1971

Dear Eleanor,

Here is the manuscript I promised you. The title poem is at *Poetry*.[179] Sorry for the last boring letter, but I was a little drunk. If you want to show this to Random House you can. My best to you. I'm in a hurry with some new writing.

yours,
Frank

Mt. Sequoyah
Fayetteville

Notes

179. See Stanford's July 26, 1971, letter to Dugan above, par. 2, and note 172 above; with this note, Stanford is sending the manuscript for *The Singing Knives*.

To Irv Broughton: July 31, 1971

July 31, 1971

Dear Irv,

Here are six poems for George's issue. Use what you want. I like all six. They don't say "For G.G." But they are and he'll know.[180]

Could you please send me copies of some of the sketches you are having made of me? Linda wants to approve. I know your time is rushed. I will have "The Snake Doctors" to you by the weekend.[181] Tomorrow is my birthday: 22.[182]

yours,
Frank

E: 6 poems
+
Ex. copy of ". . . Singing Knives"

Notes

180. *Mill Mountain Review* 1, no. 4 (1971), published "as a tribute to George Garrett" (5), included six poems by Stanford: "Planning the Disappearance of Those Who Have Gone," "The Bandits," "Bergman the Burning Ship," "Bend Sinister," "The Mother of Yánnis Rítsos," and "The Men."
181. To this editor (in a June 28, 2023, interview), Irv Broughton noted that Stanford dictated "The Snake Doctors" to him by phone for addition to *The Singing Knives*. Both Irv and Frank laughed hysterically through section 4 ("Chainsaw") re: the guitar player's hand being cut off (line 218) and the speaker singing to it (lines 254 and 310), culminating in uncontrollable laughter at lines 316–17: "I took it to the palm reader / I said 'Sister, read this.' " Broughton added that to him, line 317 is one of the "craziest, funniest, stupidest lines in literature." Stanford sent another, post-call note on August 20, 1971, clarifying some lines in section 5.
182. Stanford turned twenty-three years old (not twenty-two) on August 1, 1971.

To Donald Justice: October 19, 1971

October 19, 1971

Dear Mr. Justice,

I hope you don't mind if I send you these poems I wrote a few years back. I would appreciate your advice on something that is troubling me about them. I have alot of old poems I wrote when I was younger. Should I go back and revise them? Should I leave them intact as early poems? Or, should I just forget about them? A man in Washington wants to use about 20 of them in his magazine, if I leave them as they are. He thinks they are worthwhile; and it would screw the purpose up if I revised them. The ones I sent you no one has seen. Are they any good? I've also taken the liberty of enclosing two "after" poems that will give you an idea of my ineptitude at translation. I'm not sure of the two more recent poems. I would have sent you some new poems, but I sent them out before I knew you were an editor. Not too long ago, I saw the film "Le Sang d'un poete," and I've been messed up ever since. Do you remember when Cocteau says, "When he plays the game of cards, he cheats by taking from his childhood that which he should draw from within himself."[183] This bothers me more with the poems I've written in the last few years. It is all like a sea anchor: if you take it out from under the water, about the only thing you can do with it is catch butterflies, or tell the direction of the wind. I don't know if I'm stealing the aces from a dead child, or not; but I know if I wrote about other things it would be artificial.[184] I have a new long poem called "The Knife Fight" I'll send you, soon. Hope you will have time to look at these.

yours,
Frank Stanford

Notes

183. When Jean Cocteau's film *Le Sang d'un poète* (*The Blood of a Poet*) debuted in Paris at the Théâtre du Vieux-Colombier cinema in January 1932, Cocteau introduced it with a talk, which included: "I can tell you that the snow ball fight is the poet's childhood, and that when he plays the game of cards with his Glory, with his Destiny, he cheats by taking from his childhood that which he should draw from within himself." *The Blood of a Poet: A Film by Jean Cocteau*, trans. Lily Pons (Bodley, 1949), 51.
184. Stanford reproduces the Cocteau quotation in a November 10, 1971, letter to Bender, adding, "I didn't like going back to [the *St. Francis and the Wolf* poems] as a source—why not let them die a happy death, for better or worse, by being published. . . . I confess the source of some of my poems are my childhood poems, but it is time to let them be."

To George Hitchcock: November 30, 1971

November 30, 1971

Dear Mr. Hitchcock,

Some of the places have been taking poems that I wrote as far back as 1957. Here is a long one I wrote in 1959.*[185] Donald Justice is going to publish some I did along about then, but they are fairly short.[186] A person told me no one had guts to publish a long poem like this—that's not true though; I just don't think they have the space or money. You might not think it is any good, anyway. I'd like to hear what you think. I'm not going to ever revise the real old ones—so they have told me. I've got another one twice as long as this: d 1960.[187]

Yours,
Frank Stanford

*unrevised

I have never submitted this poem.
The only revisions were in the spelling.

F.S.

The title I gave to the collection of old poems comes from the last line of this one.[188]

[Included is a copy of Stanford's certificate for receiving "the fourth prize" on April 14, 1958, in a poetry contest for students in Memphis and Shelby County Schools—atop which Stanford has written:]

A dubious achievement, but my first recognition. The poem that won this is already accepted.[189]

Notes

185. Stanford is sending his 355-line poem "the mind reader," which he maintained—per his contributor's note in the Fall 1972 issue of *West Coast Poetry Review* (which published the poem) and his letters—had been written in 1959.
186. Justice published Stanford's "the buried sword" (1962), "keeping the lord's night watch" (1962), "the actresses of night" (1961), and "the paramour" (1961) in *The Iowa Review*'s Summer 1972 issue.
187. Assuming that Stanford is not referring to "the books" (460 lines), his second-longest published poem, he is likely referring here to *The Battlefield Where the Moon*

Says I Love You—a "short version" of which had been drafted ca. 1960; see note 206 below.

188. I.e., *St. Francis and the Wolf: Some Poems 1957–1964*. The closing (lines 353–55) of "the mind reader" reads:

> I'll have such a crew in the gospel ship
> me and my dreams
> like Saint Francis and the wolf
> (Frank Stanford, *Hidden Water: From the Frank Stanford Archives* [Third Man Books, 2015], 11)

189. Per a *Memphis Press-Scimitar* article ("Poetry Contest Winners Are Announced," April 14, 1958, 10), Stanford received this certificate (see Stanford, *What About This*, x) for his poem "the sphinx"—inspired by the Egyptian pyramids, though which publication may have later accepted the poem isn't known.

To Donald Justice: Late January or Early February 1972

[On the cover of *Open Places*, issue 11, January 1972—which published Stanford's poems "Strappado," "Poem," "Becoming the Unicorn," and "Narcissus to Achilles":]

Mr. Justice:
Would you mind turning to my poems inside.

F.S.

[On page 20, beginning under "Strappado," in which "wings" is misprinted as "winds," and continuing onto page 21 above/around the other three printed poems:][190]

Here are some of the poems you like. When one reads Emily,[191] and many of the Oriental poets, this is what happens. I'm glad you liked "Strappado." It is the most orchestrated poem I've written; that is to say, of the poems here. I don't use forms, which I gave up a long time ago. I built this poem like a ship; from the laying of the keel to the lines and compass, I built it. I hope it floats. It has *nothing* to do with Merwin, whatsoever.[192] I'd never read a book of his when I wrote it. I had read somebody else's translations of a few Follain pieces.[193] This poem is, for me, like a dream of a chess game, when you can't, or you don't know how to play or move. The rough lumber for this was: Plato's cave: what did the infants feel before they were bound and chained.[194] Mozart's *Die Zauberflöte* + the reversal, the use of two Italian words, instead of German. If you know the opera, you know what I mean. Ger. Nat'l. Opera, etc.[195] Also, I'd read a few poems by Trakl.[196] My own little libretto for "Strappado" aria can be found in the poem "Holy Night" that appears in October 1971 issue of West Coast Review.

Do you know that Baudelaire line: "I felt the wing of the wind of madness pass over me"? Well, that was in my head at the time too; and, as you can see: the printer made an ironic error.[197]

F.S.

[To the side of "Becoming the Unicorn":]

This poem shouldn't be punctuated.

Notes

190. Below the four poems published in the issue, Stanford has dated the poems' compositions: 1969 ("Strappado" and "Poem") and 1970 ("Becoming the Unicorn" and "Narcissus to Achilles"). The four poems appeared in *The Singing Knives* shortly after this issue's publication. The misprint in line 5 of "Strappado" (see images of this letter later in the chapter) necessitated the insertion of an erratum slip into the binding. Bender had also accepted "Bequeath" in April 1971 but noted—in her November 8, 1971, letter—that she wanted to publish it in a future issue alongside other poems Stanford might submit.
191. Emily Dickinson, presumably.
192. W. S. Merwin, poet.
193. Stanford's poem "The Intruder" (*The Singing Knives*) is an imitation of W. S. Merwin's translation of Jean Follain's poem "Exil" ("Exile"), as translated and published in Follain's *Transparence of the World: Poems* (1969).
194. A reference to Plato's allegory of the cave—from his dialogue *Republic*, book 7, beginning at 514a. In the allegory, prisoners "with their necks and legs fettered" who have lived in a cave "since childhood, fixed in the same place" are unaware of reality or that a better life exists. Plato, *Republic*, trans. G. M. A. Grube, rev. C. D. C. Reeve, in *Compete Works*, ed. John M. Cooper (Hackett, 1997), 1132. Cf. *The Battlefield*, line 11945.
195. Wolfgang Amadeus Mozart's *Die Zauberflöte* (*The Magic Flute*), a 1791 opera. The opera contains a number of character reversals: The seemingly virtuous Queen of the Night and her three ladies-in-waiting turn wicked, while the seemingly wicked Sarastro and three priests are, it becomes clear, actually virtuous. Stanford is also alluding to the two arias sung by the Queen of the Night, the opera's main character. Italian music bore ineluctable influence across German culture in the late eighteenth century—a trend that *Die Zauberflöte*'s success helped to abate; the notion of the *Deutsche Nationaloper* (German national opera) was that German opera should achieve its own

style as opposed to being overly reliant on foreign cultural influence. However, the Queen of the Night's two arias—"O zittre nicht, mein lieber Sohn" (*Oh, don't tremble, my dear son*) in act 1 (before the character's reversal) and "Der Hölle Rache kocht in meinem Herzen" (*Hell's vengeance boils in my heart*) in act 2 (after the character's reversal)—are both composed in the Italian (opera seria) style, requiring a high (*coloratura soprano*) voice. The two Italian words in "Strappado" suggesting a character "reversal" are *fantoccini* (a guileless show of puppets operated by strings) and *strappado* (the suspension of an individual by ropes for the purpose of torture) in the title.

196. Georg Trakl (1887–1914), Austrian poet.

197. The convoluted irony of the misprint in "Strappado" is that, in this letter's concluding paragraph, Stanford is also inverting the "wind of the wing" line by Charles Baudelaire. Baudelaire's line, from section 109 of *Intimate Journals*, reads: "Now I suffer continually from vertigo, and today, 23rd of January, 1862, I have received a singular warning[.] I have felt the wind of the wing of madness pass over me." *Intimate Journals*, trans. Christopher Isherwood (Beacon, 1957), 56.

To Eleanor Bender: February 1, 1972

February 1, 1972

Dear Eleanor,

As I am writing, it will be almost impossible for me to write a decent letter for a month, or so.

It is strange that the same days I wrote those last two letters—or thought about writing them—I received your letters later in the day, the same day![198]

Don't worry about the errors the printer made: I'm the last person on earth to worry about those kind of details! I don't believe the printer *knew* the line from Baudelaire was in the back of my head: "I felt the *wind* of the *wing* of madness pass over me." Really though, it was mostly Plato: what did the infants feel, see, and think, before they were bound; and Mozart's Die Zauberflöte, even to the point of substituting two Italian words, rather than the German: 1st Ger. Nat'l. Opera, etc.[199] I've never laid a keel like I have for this poem. It's the most orchestrated! I liked the magazine!

You are correct on the last 4 or 5 lines of "the girl cousins."[200] About the Felleni element:[201] *maybe* in some later poems, but impossible in the early ones, since I'd never heard of them when I wrote them. That is not to say they share the same shadow.

I really don't have any publishing plans.[202] If Dugan ever wants to submit them for the Yale thing he can. I appreciate your interest + *Random House*. I've got four manuscripts of old poems I want to get typed up. Here is an idea:

1. Mill Mountain Press—a pamphlet called *The Singing Knives*: 23 selected poems written during the last 7 years. Most of these recently published in magazines. 1964–1971

2. A manuscript in the memory of Yukio Mishima, childhood idol, but having nothing to do with him. 23 short poems, including the Bergman poem—I call the short collection *Naegling*. Most of the poems published in little magazines. 15 of them in *West Coast Review*.[203] 196[illegible]–71[204]

3. Mill Mountain Review #5—a whole slew of poems I wrote during the years 1957–1964. These are the *childhood poems*; not *about* childhood! About 40 poems—I guess—in this manuscript, which is very long; I call it *St. Francis and the Wolf*.[205] One of the poems is over 125 pages long and I don't mean two or three words to a line.[206]

4. A manuscript I have to type up—I'm still not finished typing the above—of poems, about 2 dozen, I wrote while I went to school at the monastery. 1964–1966. No title

5. A manuscript of long poems 1969–71. Untitled.

6. A manuscript of new poems, about 40: these last two books are really what I'm interested in—but what with all this goddamn typing!

Eleanor, the year or so I associated with people in a writ. program was odd. They wrote 6 poems a year and worried about the business of selling them. It takes *all* of my time just to go through my drawers and type them up. I've got so many new things I'm working with: poems, films + screenplays, S.S.,[207] etc. If I decide to publish a book with a big house, I will do it for the money, so I'll have a little more free time to write. This is the first time I've ever been specific about *what* I want to do. You are the only person who has asked me.

The way it is with these films I have in mind: I wanted to make them 4 or 5 years ago, but I never had the opportunity. I'm glad you said that you were a little suspicious of Bog??? Last Picture Show.[208] I feel the same way about MacMurtry.[209] I don't see how he can go around lecturing about the history of Cadillacs and cowboys, and still think he can [make] me believe him as a novelist.[210] Since Warren and his bunch,—especially in the South—writing has become such a bureaucracy; it is a lot like the superfluous technology we now have, and still don't, or can't, do much good with it. Since most new writers were created in his own image of poet-critic, it is almost an impossible situation for me.[211] They know *I know* them for what they are. Consequently, I'm a threat; not just for that reason, but because I know what I'm writing about. All this sort [of] crap makes me sick. I wonder if Faulkner knew that the same people who took over the banks, would one day have sons running writing programs + journals, etc. I admire artists like Bergman + Faulkner very much. Eleanor—I feel like I'm living in occupied territory! Maybe sometime in the future I'll have my say? The country will return to the hands of the country.

The fire needs another stick of wood, so I'll close; and put this in the mailbox when I go out. Don't worry, if you don't hear from me for awhile; I'll only be heaving at "the loins of thinking." Durrell's line.[212]

Love,
Frank

Notes

198. The Bender letters to which Stanford is referring are missing or lost.
199. *Die Zauberflöte* would be a candidate for one of the earliest operas of the *Deutsche Nationaloper.*
200. A poem in *St. Francis and the Wolf.* It appears that Bender may have suggested that Stanford cut the 4–5 lines that (originally, or else for a time) closed "the girl cousins," as he did so.
201. Federico Fellini, Italian filmmaker.
202. Stanford appears to be referring back to Bender's June 10, 1971, letter; see note 141 above.
203. Stanford's poem "Bergman the Burning Ship" was published (alongside fourteen other poems) in *West Coast Review* in October 1971 as being "from *Naegling.*" This poem and "The Nocturnal Ships of the Past" were added to *The Singing Knives* beginning with the 1979 edition, "as was the poet's intention," per C. D. Wright's (uncredited) afterword to *The Singing Knives*, by Frank Stanford (Lost Roads, 1979), n.p. (Cf. a notation in Stanford's ca. 1971 handwriting atop a typescript of "The Nocturnal Ships of the Past," dated 1971, in the Ginny Crouch Stanford Collection of Frank Stanford, Yale Collection of American Literature, Beinecke Rare Book & Manuscript Library: "If you want one more to make an even 24, use this." [See note 157 above.])
204. Stanford's handwriting here is unclear (the digit could perhaps be a 4, 5, 8, or 9); in a February 8, 1972, letter to Broughton, Stanford notes that *Nægling* was finished in "1970–1971."
205. The manuscript's full name is *St. Francis and the Wolf: Some Poems 1957–1964.*
206. This statement and others Stanford makes across correspondence serve as indicators of the development of his epic, *The Battlefield Where the Moon Says I Love You*, over time. As Stanford notes in his April 1, 1974, letter to David Walker, "'[T]he battlefield where the moon says I love you' . . . comes from . . . St. Francis and the Wolf: Some Poems 1957–1964." In a May 10, 1972, letter to Dugan, Stanford notes that "the mind reader" (composed "in 59") preceded "a short version of" *The Battlefield* that he drafted "the following year," probably 1960, before diving deeper into the poem's composition in 1964 (a date he mentions across the letters). He typed up the handwritten

1964 poem in early 1972 (possibly having started in late 1971), revising and expanding it by compiling other 1964 (or *St. Francis*–era) poems with it. In February 1972, Stanford refers or alludes to *The Battlefield* as being "over 125 pages long" in this letter, 150 pages and "over 5000 lines long" in a February 8 letter to Broughton, and more than 200 pages and 8,000 lines long in his February 28 and March 1 letters to Broughton and Dugan, respectively (though he was only to page 160 in his typing/compiling work at that point), even as he also claimed in the letter to Dugan that "the manuscript goes on forever." By May 1972, approximately 300 pages (of the full "500"-page epic) had been typed up (see Stanford's May 15, 1972, letter to Solotaroff and ca. late May 1972 letter to Bender)—or 291 pages (per Stanford's typescript), to be precise; this is almost certainly the typescript version Stanford is referring to in an early October 1972 letter to Dugan when he writes, "[Broughton] is going to publish that 12,000 line thing in its entirety." Then, in late May, Stanford burned all of his early (presumably largely handwritten) manuscripts (whether typed up or still unused—see his May 26 and 27, 1972, letters to Dugan and his July 18, 1974, letter to Cuddihy). Later, in fall 1972 and early 1973, he further worked on the poem—with additional writing (or rewriting of fire-lost material) and typing and perhaps additional revising. Per a March 4, 2008, email from Ginny Stanford to this editor, Stanford was still somewhat finalizing the poem in Eureka Springs when she met him in early March 1973, though he may not have worked on the poem much more after that.

In the early October 1972 letter to Dugan mentioned above, Stanford notes that Broughton said that the poem "will be the—or one of the—longest poems published in this country. Is that correct? I don't know." After that, he added several thousand lines to the typed poem. At 15,434 lines, *The Battlefield Where the Moon Says I Love You* is indeed one of the longest singularly composed poems in American literature.

207. *S.S.*: short stories.

208. *The Last Picture Show* (1971), dir. Peter Bogdanovich.

209. Larry McMurtry, cowriter (with Bogdanovich) of *The Last Picture Show*.

210. At the Hollins Conference, McMurtry—author of *Horseman, Pass By* (1961), the novel on which Martin Ritt's film *Hud* (1963) was based—taught a seminar titled "The Western: Cowboys and Cadillacs," presumably related to, or after, his chapter "Cowboys, Movies, Myths, and Cadillacs: Realism in the Western," in W. R. Robinson, ed., *Man and the Movies*. With assistance from George Garrett (Louisiana State University Press, 1967).

211. See notes 136 above and 221 below re: the Fugitives, the Southern Agrarians, and the New Criticism—three Southern movements in which Warren, Ransom, and Tate participated centrally.

212. From Lawrence Durrell's 1957 novel *Justine* (from *The Alexandria Quartet*): "All night long you can hear the rush of blood in the cerebral arteries. The loins of thinking. It starts you going back along the cogs of historical action, cause and effect." *The Alexandria Quartet* (Faber and Faber, 1970), 117.

OPEN PLACES

MR. JUSTICE;

would you mind turning to my poems inside.

F.S.

11

75c

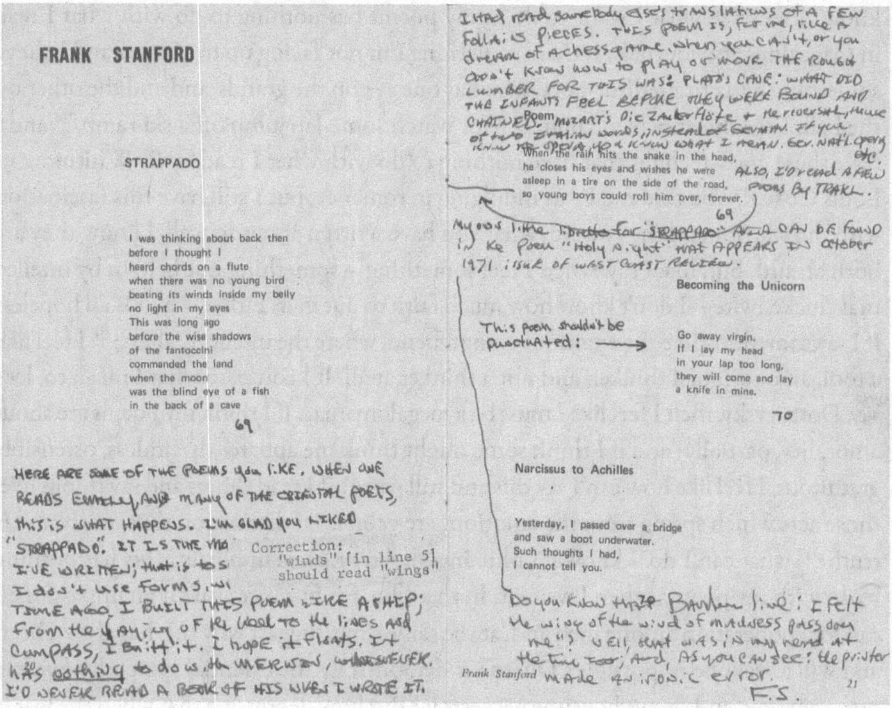

FRANK STANFORD

STRAPPADO

I was thinking about back then
before I thought I
heard chords on a flute
when there was no young bird
beating its winds inside my belly
no light in my eyes
This was long ago
before the wise shadows
of the fantoccini
commanded the land
when the moon
was the blind eye of a fish
in the back of a cave

69

HERE ARE SOME OF THE POEMS you LIKE, WHEN ONE READS EMILY, AND MANY OF THE ORIENTAL POETS, this is WHAT HAPPENS. I'M GLAD YOU LIKED "STRAPPADO". IT IS THE MO[…] I'VE WRITTEN; that is to s[…] I don't use forms, wi[…] TIME AGO I BUILT THIS POEM LIKE A SHIP; from the laying of the keel to the lines and compass, I built it. I hope it floats. It has nothing to do with MERWIN, whatsoever. I'D NEVER READ A BOOK OF HIS WHEN I WROTE IT.

Correction:
"winds" [in line 5]
should read "wings"

20

I HAD read somebody else's translations of a few Follain pieces. This poem is, for me, like a dream of a chess game, when you can't, or you don't know how to play or move. The rough lumber for this was: Plato's Cave: what did the infants feel before they were bound and chained. Mozart's Die Zauberflöte + the reversal, here of two Italian words, instead of German. If you know the opera you know what I mean. Ger. nat'l. opera etc.

Poem

When the rain hits the snake in the head,
he closes his eyes and wishes he were
asleep in a tire on the side of the road,
so young boys could roll him over, forever.

ALSO, I'D read A FEW POEMS BY TRAKL.

69

My own little ~~libretto for "STRAPPADO"~~ AREA CAN BE found in the poem "Holy Night" that APPEARS IN October 1971 issue of WEST COAST REVIEW.

Becoming the Unicorn

This poem shouldn't be punctuated: →

Go away virgin.
If I lay my head
in your lap too long,
they will come and lay
a knife in mine.

70

Narcissus to Achilles

Yesterday, I passed over a bridge
and saw a boot underwater.
Such thoughts I had,
I cannot tell you.

Do you know that Barker line: "I felt the wing of the wind of madness pass over me"? Well, that was in my mind at the time, too; and, as you can see: the printer made an ironic error.

F.S.

Frank Stanford

21

Here and previous: Stanford's late January or early February 1972 letter to Donald Justice—who published four of Stanford's poems in the Summer 1972 issue of *The Iowa Review*—written on the cover and pages 20–21 of issue 11 of *Open Places*, edited by Eleanor Bender and published in January 1972.

To Alan Dugan: February 14, 1972

Dear Alan,

You probably think I'm falling off fool for writing such straight sounding letters. I'll mail—one of these days—a letter like I feel, a letter crazy as hell like the last one I got from you, but you'd think I was pulling your leg. I don't give a shit about alot of the literary goings on I hear about, which makes me feel, maybe, like something is wrong with me. Is it pretentious, or puerile, to feel this way? I'm being honest with you. I don't know! I feel like what I want to do in my poems has nothing to do with what I read in magazines and journals. Is there something I'm not facing up to? How can I believe something by a critic-editor-poet, who has one eye on the grandstand and the other on the ball. I see this movie 7 Samurai,[213] or watch some Jap jump off a ski ramp,[214] and I have these crazy feelings that have nothing to do with what I read by R. Whitmore or Louis Coxe.[215] You told me I was indulging in romance, but I still have this fascination with the warrior and the coward, what you have written about so well. I know they are both absurd, but, like I say, when I feel something—something not held in by intellectual chickenwire—I don't know how much faith to put in it. Either way, it is all hopeless. If I say something like the emotions comprehend, where the intellect falters;[216] I feel like a fool, an unoriginal thinker, and not a thinker at all. If I compare what I mean to, let's say, Dostoevsky, then I feel like I must be a megalomaniac. If I think my poems are about amorality, partially; and if I think some might think me apparently aimless, ostensibly gratuitous, I feel like how can I say this and still write? If I read things and say things like: those acts which spring from the emotions are valid acts; that action thus motivated is truth;[217] what can I do. I know it's phil. incompetent, and simplistic. This has nothing to do with my poetry, when I write it. In that film, for instance; isn't it an impassioned call for cooperation among men and, at the same time, suggest why this has always been and will always be impossible? Doesn't it demonstrate the essential sympathy *binding* men together, and shows how war perverts it? But how depressing that when the war is over, the villagers and samurai are not friends. All this tragedy; the strategy of tragedy. This chatter and poetry has nothing to do with one another. In one I am awake, the other asleep. Once I read a poem + commentary by Cocteau: "the poet is unskilled when he speaks, as he is awoken from sleep in which he composes his work."[218] I can't remember the rest; shit like: like a medium speaking out of a trance; the poet's work detests and devours him; etc. I don't want to sound so fantastic about it all. Like you, I have great contempt for the rules; and I despise the neurosis of aesthetic deceptions, so I'm crazy.

All I wanted to say in this letter was: when Claude and Annie went to the funeral in Miss, the white undertaker had her sister sitting up, contorted, on a piece of plywood, supported by concrete blocks, in the garage. She was so fucked up she couldn't attend the services. You probably think I'm fucked up with my "association" with Blacks. This is the way I've always been: most of my life was not spent with white people. My experience, I took for granted. I was actually in high school before it dawned on me I was probably one of the only white boys in the world, who had done what I'd done. This was in 63, when my father died. He told me this. I knew I was a poet. (Please don't laugh at what I'm saying) He saved this land for all people. He woke up in the middle of the night with visions of floods. All farmers white + Black + rich + poor knew him. He didn't hang around with white people, either. He'd rather live in a tent. I want to do the same for the land and the people. I know what *can* and will happen here if certain things don't take place. This, at the moment, is a letter from occupied territory: I say piss on the neo-Fugatives [*sic*]; piss on Sterling Sillaphant + Jesse Hill Ford phoney goddamn scalawags;[219] piss on The Southern Review[220]—fraternity "good old boys" banker sons, football players, intellectually phoney hillbilly music, exploiters of the truth, the Black man, the white. There. I know all this, but none of it enters my mind when I write my poems. I have no stand when I write.[221] I write about what I know; what is the truth. I know this other stuff is counterfeit; but they will always have the power. Fuck.

Enclosed is a clipping of what my black friend is doing, when we aren't drunk. (Claude Ricks.) Some letters from women my mother sent me. A coin that came out of a dead man's, a prisoner's, ass at the penitentiary. A picture of me and two buddies. I'm still running around with the monks; boxing some. We told the inmates they could drill a hole in their money and sell it to the free world, especially up north, and make more; but the officials wouldn't allow them to do it. Claude's house is shot at, again, "Ain't no niggers doing it" he told me: they kicked his kids out of school.

Linda is doing great in her job. The cannery is finished; now she's helping plant gardens for the spring.[222] I'm getting a job driving a milk truck; rural delivery. The film I am making at the monastery will take about 8 months and cost 3 or 4 thousand dollars.[223] No one has ever done anything like it before. After this one, I'll let these two guys film a couple of my poems—if I have say so. I'm choreographing a ballet! Ha ha. A monk will dance! I'll be sending you a big manuscript, soon as it's all typed. Then, later on: some new stuff. Linda sends her love. The grandstand can go to hell, my other eye is on the memory of Babe Ruth.

yours,
Frank

Notes

213. *Seven Samurai* (1954), dir. Akira Kurosawa.

214. Japan swept the gold, silver, and bronze medals of the men's normal hill individual ski jumping event on February 6, 1972, at the 1972 Winter Olympics, held from February 3 to 13, 1972, in Sapporo, Japan.

215. Reed Whittemore (1919–2012) and Louis O. Coxe (1918–93), poet-critics.

216. From the discussion of *Seven Samurai* in the chapter "1946–1971" in Donald Richie's *Japanese Cinema: Film Style and National Character* (Anchor Books, 1971), 232: "Only those acts which spring from emotion are valid acts; that action thus motivated is itself truth. This truth . . . is one which is shared with Zen and with the haiku, as well as the films of Ozu and Kurosawa—the emotions comprehend where the intellect falters."

217. See quotation (which Stanford has slightly modified) in note 216 above.

218. From Cocteau's January 1932 introduction of *Le Sang d'un poète* in Paris: "I will tell you that the poet is very unskilled when he speaks, as he is awoken from the sleep in which he composes his works. It is like a medium speaking out of a trance. The poet's work detests and devours him. There isn't room for both the poet and his work. The work profits from the poet. Only after his death can the poet profit from the work. And anyway, the public prefer dead poets and they are right. A poet who isn't dead is an anachronism." Jean Cocteau, "Postscript" to *The Blood of a Poet*, in *Two Screenplays: "The Blood of a Poet," "The Testament of Orpheus,"* trans. Carol Martin-Sperry (Penguin, 1969), 67. In *Le Sang d'un poète*, the poet shoots himself with a gun, and a laurel wreath appears on his head; the firing of the gun is then repeated—thrice—and the author utters the words "*Toujours la gloire!*" ("*Glory forever!*"). Upon a final (fifth) firing, the poet is reborn and his eyes reopen.

219. Stirling Silliphant, screenwriter of *In the Heat of the Night* (1967), dir. Norman Jewison. Re: Ford, see note 99 above.

220. *The Southern Review*: a literary quarterly established by Warren and published at Louisiana State University, focusing on the New Criticism.

221. An allusion to the Southern Agrarian authors' manifesto—the essay collection *I'll Take My Stand: The South and the Agrarian Tradition* (1930). Many of the book's twelve authors were connected to Vanderbilt University, and the conservative, pro-agrarian movement—focused on critiques of industrialism and modernity—had evolved from the Fugitives (see note 136 above); Ransom, Warren, and Tate, as well as Arkansas poet John Gould Fletcher (1886–1950), contributed to the collection.

222. Linda Mencin Bond (Linda Stanford, as of this letter's writing) worked for the War on Poverty in Fayetteville from 1969 to 1973, "helping poor people grow vegetable gardens and can their fruits and vegetables at the home cannery" that she had installed for them (per a January–July 2014 interview of her by this editor).

223. Stanford's early 1972 film—about a fourteen-year-old poet and "his visions and dreams" (see Stanford's July 10, 1972, letter to Bender below, par. 3), filmed at Subiaco and based on manuscripts Stanford wrote while a student there—was never completed; per a July 21, 1972, letter from Stanford to Broughton, it appears that Stanford burned the footage ca. late May 1972.

To Irv Broughton: February 18, 1972

February 18, 1972

Dear Irv,

Thanks for the call last night, rather: early this morning, here. I'm trying to lay off the booze, but last night was one of those evenings. Sorry I was incoherent, if not suborbital. You sound good + clear + broke. Once again, I'm encouraged that I will see the little bunch of poems in print; soon, I hope.

Remember to watch Cocteau's "La Belle et la Bête," tonight. (Too late.)[224] He is one of my guardian angels. Have you seen: "Les Parents terribles," "Orphée," "Le testament d'Orphée?" (And of course: "Le Sang d'un poete.")[225]

Alot of American artists say: "Don't spend your time looking+reading these crazy men. Look at America. This is where we should start from." It is this kind of condescending flatulence and insecurity that is leading all America downhill.

The very people who are admonishing we poets to forget Europe, S.A.,[226] god only knows where else, in favor of America, are the same people who turned their backs on Whitman years ago; and now they, forgiven, are overreaching the other way. They point [out], godly so, that folks to the South and Europe were looking at Whitman, when they wrote their best. This is true; but I feel that Americans are all paranoid and insecure now, and so they form these stupid little clichés of ways of writing poetry. Myself, I believe all artists are in heaven, where everything is fine. They are invisible. There is none of this fodder vying fodder. Since I refuse to listen to America's neuroses—just the animals + voices—these other whisperings are voices from hell. My mind is clear: artists of all persuasion and nationalities appeal to me. I am in heaven with these artists. I may descend into hell occasionally, but no longer than Dante![227]

Americans, in trying to rediscover their own past + traditions, thus themselves, are overreacting: camping, hiking, farm poetry. How completely ridiculous + absurd + artificial. These Americans are reacting this way, because their suburban + urban backyards were full of dog poop + so small—so small. Since my backyard was infinite, anything and everything can and did happen. I won't go along with this phoney rediscovery movement in poetry, other arts the Indian, blues, country, Jesus. It has always been this way, and I don't truck much with those who are exploiting it in the arts at present, Merwin included.

I will continue my own way. My poetry has nothing to do with the hist. of literature, schools, magazines, etc. A few quotes to help me on my way. "The poet is unskilled when he speaks, as he is awoken from sleep in which he composes his work." (Apathetic, cross, keen, malleable, wanting to go back to sleep, to his poems.) "It is like a medium speaking out of a trance. The poet's work detests and devours him. There isn't room for both the poet and his work."[228] The tragedy of poets is that they must live beyond the means of the era. If they live in the means, they mean nothing. They are bureaucrats and the heads of associations. This is not poetry; this is power + organization. Beckett, Ionesco, Neruda, Yeats, Kafka, Joyce, Faulkner, Poe, Rimbaud, all knew this. They were poets, like Dostoevsky.[229] The most absurd position is to write about that absurdity.

This is why I am poet.

Poets of all persuasions, so far, have liked my work. That means I'm writing poetry, and not following orders.

A man who dozes, his mouth half open, in front of a wood fire, lets slip some secrets from that night of the human body that is called soul, over which he is no longer master. The sentry of his mouth has fallen into a deep and imprudent sleep, and words escape that do not know the password.[230] Some more paraphrases of Jean Cocteau: film {(poetry)} has nothing to do with dreams except that it borrows the vigorous illogicality of dreams, their way of giving during the night. A kind of freshness to the falsehoods of the day that is dulled by routine.[231] (My dreams + days were never dull, however.)

It is *realistic*, yes, not *surrealistic*.[232] (The interest in my work comes, what arouses the readers, from its isolation when compared with other works. My poems can't be classified as subliminal, dreams, un-conscious, automatic, etc. It's fun to talk about all that, though. Ha Ha. I, deliberately, avoid these conscious+calculated+intentional manifestations of the unconscious. I can do this without being aware of it I've been doing it so long now. I avoid this in favor of a kind of half-sleep where I wander through insane reality—a labyrinth + cruel + real.)[233] If realistic means a detailed living painting of the intrigues of the universe, that is *personal* to every artist and is totally unrelated to what we are used to *accepting* as reality.

We disobey dead rules, paying homage to all past, present, future, who wish to remain free. It brings into play a form of logic that reason does not recognize.[234] Enough. Don't lose this letter.

yours,
Frank

Je congnois vision et sommes
Je congnois tout fors que moy mesmes.
Villon[235]

Notes

224. Cocteau's *La Belle et la Bête* (*Beauty and the Beast*; 1946) played on television at 9:30 p.m. Central time on Monday, February 21, 1972; as Stanford's letter is dated Friday, February 18, he is assuming here that his letter will reach Broughton on Monday.

225. *Les Parents terribles*, *Orphée* (*Orpheus*), *Le testament d'Orphée* (*The Testament of Orpheus*), and *Le Sang d'un poète*—1948, 1950, 1960, and 1932 films, respectively, dir. Jean Cocteau.

226. Presumably, South America.

227. See Dante Alighieri's *Inferno*, from *The Divine Comedy* (ca. 1308–21).

228. See note 218 above.

229. Samuel Beckett, Eugène Ionesco, W. B. Yeats, Franz Kafka, James Joyce, Edgar Allan Poe, and Fyodor Dostoevsky—nineteenth- and twentieth-century authors, playwrights, and poets.

230. This paragraph's first two sentences ("A man who dozes" through "the password") are Cocteau's words (paragraphs 1–2—with slight modification of "called the soul" to "called soul") from his "Preface" to *Le testament d'Orphée* (*The Testament of Orpheus*), as translated by Carol Martin-Sperry. *Two Screenplays*, 73.

231. "This film has nothing to do with dreams except that it borrows the rigorous illogicality of dreams, their way of giving during the night, a kind of freshness to the falsehoods of the day that is dulled by routine." Jean Cocteau, "Preface" to *The Testament of Orpheus*, in *Two Screenplays*, par. 5.

232. ". . . the day that is dulled by routine. In addition, it is realistic." Cocteau, "Preface" to *The Testament of Orpheus*, par. 5. See note 234 below.

233. Some of this parenthetical aside is paraphrased from the opening paragraph of Cocteau's 1946 "Preface" to *Le Sang d'un poète* (*The Blood of a Poet*), which reads: "It is often said that *The Blood of a Poet* is a surrealist film. However, surrealism did not exist when I first thought of it. On the contrary, the interest that it still arouses probably comes from its isolation from the works with which it is classified. . . . At the time of *The Blood of a Poet*, I was the only one of this minority to avoid the deliberate manifestations of the unconscious in favor of a kind of half-sleep through which I wandered as though in a labyrinth." Jean Cocteau, preface to *The Blood of a Poet*, in *Two Screenplays*, 3.

234. In the previous paragraph and here, Stanford is returning to Cocteau's preface to *The Testament of Orpheus* (par. 5): "In addition, it is realistic, if realism means a detailed painting of the intrigues of a universe that is personal to every artist and is totally unrelated to what we are used to accepting as reality. The film disobeys dead rules, paying homage to all who wish to remain free. It brings into play a form of logic that reason does not recognize. In short, it is Cartesian by means of anti-Cartesianism." "Preface" to *The Testament of Orpheus*, 73.

235. "Je congnois visïon et somme" and "Je congnois tout fors que moy mesmes," lines 21 and 24, respectively, of François Villon's poem, "Je congnois tout fors que moy mesmes" ("Everything But Myself"). As translated by David Georgi: "I know open eyes from sleeping" and "I know everything but myself." Villon, *Poems*, trans. David Georgi (Northwestern University Press, 2013), 182–83. The lines appear in *The Battlefield*, amid the conversation between Francis and Sylvester about guerillas/gorillas, as parts of lines 3585 and 3635, respectively.

To Irv Broughton: February 28, 1972

February 28, 1972

Dear Irv,

Here are some of the old poems from *St. Francis and the Wolf* that Donald Justice took. More or less, they are all this good or bad. The longer ones are better than "S.K."[236] I repeat: when will *MMR V* be ready;[237] and how much space can you give me? The poems are ready to send to you, except the 8,000 line one that I'm re-typing.[238] I'll send it somewhere else. Let me hear, soon.

yours,
Frank

Who will even read a poem
200 pages long?

Notes

236. Either "The Singing Knives" (poem) or *The Singing Knives* (book).
237. Re: *Mill Mountain Review* 2, no. 1 (the magazine's intended fifth issue), see Stanford's June 22 or 29, 1975, letter to Broughton below and note 892 below.
238. See note 206 above; in early 1972, Stanford typed up a long 1964 poem, compiling other 1964 (or *St. Francis*–era) poems with it and revising along the way in creating *The Battlefield*—expanding the work from fewer than five thousand lines to nearly twelve thousand lines in winter and spring 1972 while typing it from its early manuscript draft version. (He later added nearly thirty-five hundred lines to the typescript, in late 1972 and early 1973.)

To Alan Dugan: March 1, 1972

March 1, 1972

Dear Alan,

Just got through reading 6 plays of Strindberg, that I hadn't read before.[239] I'm crouching down with my feet in the chair like a monkey. Once you get the hang of it, it's easy on your legs and back. You've seen pictures of V.C. prisoners and country people![240]

Last night, and the night before, I saw two old movies I like from way back: "Odd Man Out" and "The Informer."[241]

At the moment, I'm re-reading your last letter dated Aug 11—mailed Oct 25—the one with the note from Kunitz.[242] I guess the Kennedy bunch wanted to be monarchs.

Listening to Saint-Saens Cello Concerto by Rostropovich.[243]

I'm writing more than ever. I don't know where it is coming from. All the time I'm in a daze; like an 18 hr. slow and easy orgasm (with some torture added for good measure). I put out like a ship, then, when it's over I'm depressed and want to get drunk. I wish art was rewarding *as sex*!

Everything is absurd like Beckett writes.[244] I went to the monastery to box. A couple of monks and a priest named Nicholas, and I went drinking in the woods.[245] They are all kind of fat + stout Germans, so I said "Let's go buy a big fish from the (forget his name)"—an old man who lives alone in a hut on the lake and takes fish for a trifling livelihood. I don't remember his name, but we've bought fish from him many times. A monk, Brother Louie, says "Didn't you know he was dead."[246] They found him and some fish three days dead floating alone out in the lakes. The monks found him. They buried him in the monastery cemetary [*sic*].[247]

If I wrote in blood, then maybe I'd take more care in my letters. There are 39 poems sitting in a bushel apple basket, but I'm not going to send them until I finish typing 40.[248] I'm on page 160—the manuscript goes on forever, but at page 200 I'm quitting.[249] Then, I can, at last go to something new. Poetry talk: bullshit. Who cares.

yours,
Frank

Don't write me until I send you this manuscript.

"En mon païs suis en terre loingtaine"
F. Montcorbier[250]

Notes

239. Presumably August Strindberg's *Six Plays of Strindberg: "The Father," "Miss Julie," "The Stronger," "Easter," "A Dream Play," "The Ghost Sonata"* (1955).

240. *V.C.*: Việt Cộng.

241. *Odd Man Out* (1947), dir. Carol Reed, and *The Informer* (1935), dir. John Ford.

242. Stanley Kunitz (1905–2006), poet. The postmark on the envelope for Dugan's August 11, 1971, letter to Stanford appears to be October 26, 1971; atop the August 11 letter,

Dugan wrote, on October 24, that he had forgotten to mail the letter, which begins "I enclose 2 of your poems and a letter from Stanley Kunitz" regarding the two poems and proceeds into a mocking discussion of how prolific the Kennedy family is in procreating. In Kunitz's August 9 note to Dugan (enclosed with Dugan's letter), Kunitz writes of Stanford, "This poet is obsessive, romantic, redundant—but he's for real, + a rare one. What can we do for him?" In marginalia dated October 25 on his August 11 letter, Dugan adds, "I agree with Kunitz's phrase 'but he's for real, + a rare one.' The first phrase I disagree with."

243. Cello Concerto No. 1, op. 33, an 1872 concerto by Camille Saint-Saëns, performed by Mstislav Rostropovich, cellist.

244. From the introduction of Albert Camus's 1951 essay, *L'Homme révolté*: "I proclaim that I believe in nothing and that everything is absurd." *The Rebel: An Essay on Man in Revolt*, trans. Anthony Bower (Vintage International, 1991), 10. Camus's writings shaped the criticism of Martin Esslin (1918–2002), which analyzed Samuel Beckett's play *Waiting for Godot* (1952) and other works.

245. Fr. Nicholas Fuhrmann.

246. Br. Louis M. Fuhrmann, OSB (1930–2012), known as Brother Louie, Father Nicholas's first cousin.

247. In an October 31 and November 1, 1972, letter to Dugan, Stanford notes, "I also have the free loan of a cabin on the lake (river). The monks own it, and that fisherman I told you about lived there until he died." The cabin, owned by Subiaco Abbey, is a small structure about fifteen miles east of Subiaco on Lake Dardanelle, a reservoir on the Arkansas River; the waterside nearby served as a shooting location for *It Wasn't a Dream: It Was a Flood* (1975), a dreamlike documentary about, and co-shot by, Stanford, filmed in Arkansas and Mississippi and directed by Broughton.

248. The forty-poem manuscript Stanford is referring to here is *St. Francis and the Wolf: Some Poems 1957–1964*, of which *The Battlefield Where the Moon Says I Love You* was evidently, at this point in time, a part; see note 249 below.

249. Poem "40" (in the previous sentence) is *The Battlefield*—the manuscript that "[went] on forever," of which Stanford was on page 160 of 200 (or more) in typing up here. (See the postscript note in Stanford's February 28, 1972, letter to Broughton above.) Of the forty (or possibly more) poems from *St. Francis and the Wolf* that Stanford typed up in winter 1972, he sent thirty—including his long poem "the books" but excluding *The Battlefield* ("the long son-of-a-bitch")—to Dugan on March 3, 1972, with a brief covering letter. On March 23, Dugan replied, "I have your *Saint Francis and the Wolf* + will return it shortly—I'm half way through. You do my heart good. Never forget that you're a true poet." While Stanford's mention of "the manuscript" in this sentence refers to *The Battlefield*, his mention of "this manuscript" below the signature appears, in light of his March 3 note to Dugan, to refer to *St. Francis and the Wolf*.

250. François de Montcorbier, putatively the actual name of Middle French poet François Villon (1431–after 1463). The quote, translated by Galway Kinnell as "In my own country I'm in a distant land," is of line 3 of Villon's ballade beginning "Je meurs de seuf auprès de la fontaine" ("I die of thirst beside the fountain"). *The Poems of François Villon*, trans. Galway Kinnell (University Press of New England, 1982), 176–77.

To Alan Dugan: May 9, 1972

May Day

Dear Alan,

Sometimes, it makes me want to shit, or kill myself, too, this bloodsucking poetry. When I think of all that it cost me when I was a kid, I want to vomit. Ever since 1964, I've *tried* to quit writing, but I never could. I don't believe in that literary malarkey about living to write, or writing to live.[251] In fact, I only like art, or what is said about art, when I can't tell it from life. When I read your letter, my first impression was to call you up, but I'd only bother you. You are the only one alive I feel I can talk to. {(my life is crazy)}[252] The rest bore me; I mean, oh, I don't know! If you killed yourself, I would keep writing, but I would write without any hope for what I was doing.[253] I'd rather have you like what I write, than ~~I would~~ someplace like *New Yorker* or *Poetry* publish it. I'm crazy. With me, not to publish a book is my way of throwing the gauntlet down. I'm an outcast, but no one would pick it up anyway. You sound as if your life on this earth has been a torture; well, I for one, want to hear your screams! Whenever I get down (and I've almost killed myself a dozen times since childhood) I listen to Beethoven's Ninth—I mean, I *really* listen to it.[254] Fuck words, anyway. Right now I'll give you two of the best lines ever written since Dylan Thomas:[255]

"When the Lord was a man of war and sailed out
through the sky at night with all the stars"[256]

That is poetry and you wrote it. That's not Dickey shit, Merwin shit, Bly shit, Ginsberg shit; that is poetry. Why? Because it came to my head just now, like Browning or Rossetti or Swinburne.[257] Don't get me wrong; I admire a portion of the above, but none of them are human beings, since they only come across with one kind of poetry. I suspect the stylized + public personality already. {No one can be one way all the time—a lie.}[258] I have lost faith in poets, but not poetry. You are better than them, but you must not quit writing. I can understand how what you did in the past makes you sick, simply because it was *done in the past*, so it is, that what words you want to use now seem meaningless.

Forget everything. There is a silence that overcomes the racket. "(Your) visions are not casual but final: there's no place to go but on . . ."[259] [I didn't look that up.][260]

Since around the 1st of March I've been holding down a 80 hr. a week job, which has certainly helped my insomnia + drinking. I come home out of the weeds at sundown and pass out. My time has become really valuable, again. Did you get that Gug. Fellow.? Hope so. I'm saving half of what I make for my film. The other night, this Black guy and I got thrown in jail. Enclosed is my only lit. notice, since the fourth grade.[261]

yours,
Frank

(Does your wife have a mailable portfolio, or anything? What kind of work does she do?)

Notes

251. This claim conflicts with epistolary statements Stanford made to Bill Willett and Eleanor Bender in July 1972. To Bender, e.g., Stanford writes, "You have heard it said about others: a born writer, he lives to write. Well, I tell you for the past year it has been antipodal for me. . . . I had to create to exist." See Stanford's July 10, 1972, letter to Bender below, par. 4.
252. *Marginalia: right side, left facing.*
253. In Dugan's March 23, 1972, letter to Stanford, he writes, "I'm just out of near-suicidal block against writing—everything I write seems to be a lie."
254. Symphony No. 9 in D Minor, op. 125, Beethoven's 1824 symphony.
255. Dylan Thomas (1914–53), Welsh poet.
256. Lines 1–2 of "The Life and Death of the Cantata System" from Alan Dugan's *Poems 2* (1963). *Poems Seven: New and Complete Poetry* (Seven Stories, 2001), 110.
257. Robert Browning (1812–89), Dante Gabriel Rossetti, and Algernon Charles Swinburne (1837–1909), English poets.
258. *Marginalia: left side, left facing.*
259. From the last stanza of "Against a Sickness: To the Female Double Principle God" from Alan Dugan's *Poems 3* (1967)—correctly:

    My visions
    are not causal but final:
    there's no place to go to
    but on. . . .
    (*Poems Seven*, 135)

260. Brackets Stanford's.

261. To the left of his signature, Stanford has pasted a newspaper clipping that reads: "A 22-year-old man was treated for acute alcoholism." The sentence—from the Friday, April 28, 1972, edition of the *Northwest Arkansas Times*—is taken from a brief article on p. 2, "Twelve Drug-Related Cases Treated Here During Week," noting the "record high" drug-related cases treated at Washington General Hospital over the previous week. No patient names are listed, but the adjacent column (in an article on the University of Arkansas's Honors Day, held that day, "Honors Day Convocation Held Today at UA") mentions Stokesbury receiving the John Gould Fletcher Award for "outstanding achievement in literature," and the day's paper included the *Times Cookbook* supplement, which, incidentally, included recipes contributed by both Frank and Linda Stanford, 115 Skyline Drive, Fayetteville—for pumpkin bread and brownies, respectively.

To Theodore Solotaroff: May 15, 1972

May 15, 1972

Dear Mr. Solotaroff,

It would be better if I could begin this other than I am (going to). I intended on sending all 500 pages, but several things have so recently happened to me, making it an impossibility to type one more letter of the last 20 sections. (About 200 more pages.)[262] Oh, it's finished alright. It's been done for a very long time, but, at this moment, writing seems to be like why Gauguin painted the strange white bird in "Where Do We Come From? What Are We? Where Are We Going?"[263] (I forgot. "The two {naked} hi yallows eating melon" aren't in what I send along, now.[264]) I'm afraid this letter will efface this *frame* of mind you'll need to read it.

The other day, I just stopped where I did, so I could get a new T.W. ribbon. As far as the style—how what happens in the story changes it—it was a good place to halt. Several days later, my wife and I left one another. Today, I found out I have a rare skin disease. Where all my hide has to be burned off by ultraviolet lights.[265] Also, the doctor gave me a V.D. test.[266] (? as yet.) I've tried to push down on a key, but when I do, it feels like I'm giving myself blood tests of the heart. *They* won't let me see her. I can't explain it, here. Sorry to bother.

Alan Dugan, the only other writer I correspond with, is the only person to read this. (Never submitted or published any of it.) I sent him a carbon, uncorrected, unrevised, last week. Today, in his letter, he writes "It should be published as is, as soon as possible."[267] I'm not trying to promote myself; it's just a good feeling from his letter. Hope you don't resent me repeating it. I know you are the editor.

The Battlefield Where the Moon Says I the character, who is twelve years old, is, very simply, a mind reader.[268] But what would seem a blessing by most, is nothing but a curse. Since he always knows what it is you are thinking, he is always in pain. This is the long story he tells himself, while he is floating down the river on his raft, the boat he has bound himself to.[269] This is what he does to rid the so-called gift, or "powah",[270] from his mind: he rigs up a Chinese torture out of a molasses bucket with a hole in the bottom of it.[271] When I wrote it, I didn't mean for him to tell it in a frenzy; I didn't mean that at all. Even when the others push the drive inn screen over with the bulldozer, I never intended the voice to draw attention to itself.[272] I wanted it all low key, like a child huddled under a piano, telling a story to himself. The only breaks in the voice are when the muscles have their spasms, as they do from cold water, or a prolonged *period* of weeping. I never intended to make wisecracks, or to be funny—no more funnier than Beowulf.

You might not think it worth your while; I don't know. If you don't like any of this, then I doubt if you'd like the last 20 parts (almost chapters), where capitals, quotation marks begin to appear. There are even white spaces for commas and periods.

Now, I suppose I could go back and revise it, and make it into an easily read book, but that's not why I wrote it the way I did. (I'm not saying I won't cut some of it.)

I'm sorry I don't feel like being a conversationalist, but I'm just too goddam miserable.

The best to you. I'll abide by what you say.

yours,
Frank Stanford

P.S. Tell Mr. Howard: I'll have forty poems to you as soon as I can. Maybe I can mail them tomorrow; I have a few days off from my job: 80 hrs. a week.

Apologies for the shoddy condition of the MS. No money for a typist. No time to re-do it, myself. I was correcting typos, when the bottom fell out at 110.

It might be that Mr. Howard would be interested.[273]

Notes

262. Stanford is sending to Solotaroff roughly 300 pages (likely 291 typescript pages) of *The Battlefield Where the Moon Says I Love You*.

263. *D'où venons-nous? Que sommes-nous? Où allons-nous?* (*Where Do We Come From? What Are We? Where Are We Going?*), an 1897–98 painting by Paul Gauguin (which he considered his magnum opus) that was to be his final painting before committing suicide. In a February 1898 letter, Gauguin wrote that the old woman in the lower-left corner is "nearing death" and "appears to accept everything, to resign herself to her thoughts" and that the "strange white bird" at her feet "represents the futility of words." Gauguin to Monfreid, February 1898, in *The Letters of Paul Gauguin to Georges Daniel de Monfreid*, trans. Ruth Pielkovo (Dodd, Mead, 1922), 95.

264. See Stanford, *The Battlefield*, lines 13119–23:

> I even sent off and got some pictures by Gauguin
> Baby Gauge and Melvin thought they was high yellows eating watermelons
> but I said his name and said the name of his pictures
> Tahitian Women Eating Mango Blossoms
> Spirit Of The Dead and so on

Stanford used the latter painting, *Manaò tupapaú (Spirit of the Dead Watching)* (1892), as the cover for *Constant Stranger* (1976).

265. According to skin disease expert Dr. Thomas Bieber, possibly a disorder such as lichen planus or psoriasis. Email to editor, September 18, 2023.

266. *V.D.*: venereal disease (STD).

267. Stanford sent roughly 300 carbon typescript pages (or, again, presumably 291 pages, to be precise) of *The Battlefield* to Dugan on May 10, 1972, writing, "I commend this orphan to you. F.S." On May 12, Dugan replied, "Received your blockbuster of a ms. and am reading it: it's wonderful, so far, and I think that it should be published as it is in a small edition of books: it could sleep for a number of years and then explode" and noted (re: Stanford's May 9 question), "yes I won a Guggenheim." He mentioned that he planned to hire a typist to type many of his handwritten poem drafts "for a book to be called either *Poems 4* or *Failed's Book of Quits*," and he noted, "I still think you should publish. You have too much good stuff to let it sit around."

268. Francis Gildart, the twelve-year-old clairvoyant poet-hero of *The Battlefield*. In the May 10, 1972, letter to Dugan, Stanford writes, "The character is endowed with the gift of second sight at birth. What would seem to most a blessing, is, in fact, a curse." Cf. Stanford's poem "the mind reader."

269. See Stanford, *The Battlefield*, lines 135–38, 8652–53, 9747–48, 12083, 12974, and 15326.

270. *"powah"*: power. See Stanford, *The Battlefield*, lines 1712–13.

271. See Stanford, *The Battlefield*, lines 9747–49, 10907, and 11323–24.

272. See Stanford, *The Battlefield*, lines 8328–31 and 11922–27.

273. Solotaroff may have shown the typescript to Howard; see Stanford's April 1, 1974, letter to Walker below, par. 13.

To Alan Dugan: May 15 and 16, 1972

May 15, 1972

Dear Alan,

Poetry takes its toll. It just took my wife. Rather, it took me and, while I wasn't looking, it took my wife.

I've only made life miserable for, what use to be, my sweet girl. I drove her crazy. I doubt if we'll ever get back. We're through with feeling sorry for one another. For a few months it was lovely. I should of taken your advice, I knew it then, and she knows it now.[274] She has grown up. I commend her, my love, my little wife, to the middle class, my sweet Linda. I was her lover, her brother, her father, her husband, and her friend. Now, I only hurt her.

Last spring, I broke her heart. I had to do something, so I married her. Were we ever in love! I'll write a book about it. We took on all comers and we cowed the most. I miss her, but it's better for her not to suffer, to live a happy life. I was going to leave her, but she would have killed herself, so I drove her away like a doe I didn't want to shoot.

Don't worry about me; I'll make it. I have a mad love for loneliness, but I don't want to hurt anyone. Really I don't.

I'm so glad you are back with it. That helps me out. Steer clear of the booze awhile, and love your wife, and be happy, and write your book. What do you have to do to get one of those Guggenheim things? How long will you be abroad?

Failed's Book of Quits is just about the best title I've heard. Wish you could call it *Poems 4: Failed's Book of Quits*, or V.V. I almost read it as Failure's Book of Quitter's Fits, or something![275]

I feel good that you liked the manuscript. Maybe I'll send some work out to publishing places; I don't know where.

Spoon music: two spoons in one hand.[276]

I'm either going to stay here; go work with the monks a while (just until I get horny); go to Mississippi and work on my uncle's farm; or just—shit, I don't know. Say, give me a stratoutt [*sic*] answer to this question: should I finish school? When? Where? I'll go now. Make your poems, and get your wife to send me some pictures of her work.

yours,
Frank

May 16

If my poems to you slow up for a while, I hope you'll understand. I don't feel as easy as I did last night, but I'm going to in a minute; I'm going to try to write. You see, I can't work for a week on account of this unusual skin disease. The doctor has to burn all my old hide off with ultraviolet lights. (What an irony—shedding skin like a snake.) I don't have any control of my mind—feelings just come and go. But I'm going to be alright.

I have some new work I want to work on. After I get it typed, do you think that Yale place would look at it,[277] or am I too young?

Notes

274. In Dugan's July 30, 1971, letter to Stanford, he wrote, "I suppose I should congratulate you and Linda (give her my love) about getting married, but I don't know," noting that he and Judith "Judy" Shahn (1929–2009) had gotten married "because of social pressure." He closed, "We both knew that the legal contract made a difference, but we couldn't state what the difference *was*. I still don't know, and I'm still married to the same woman, unlike most of my friends."
275. In Dugan's December 18, 1972, letter to Stanford, he again asked, "How about *Failed's Book of Quits* as a title?" Stanford returned the letter with annotations, including: "As I said last summer, *Failed's Book of Quits* is a great title. Yes. Yes. What do you think of these: Blue Yodels, Field Talk?"
276. In Dugan's May 12, 1972, letter to Stanford, he asked, "In spoon-music, are both spoons held in the same hand like castanets, or does each hand hold a spoon as in norteña stick music of north México?" See Stanford, *The Battlefield*, line 206 ("one of them was named Willie he had the spoons").
277. I.e., the Yale Younger Poets Prize.

To Irv Broughton: Circa Late May 1972

May Day

Irv,

Is there any way you can get your hands on $150.00? Don't go out on a limb, or jeopardize yourself, because I don't know when I can get it back. Otherwise, I'm going to jail.[278]

Don't try to call me, whatever the case may be. I can get my mail at this address, though.

115 Skyline
Mt. Sequoyah

I'm ducking + dodging, so no time to go crazy.

Soon as Solotaroff + Howard send back the 400 pages, I'll send to you.

yours,
Frank

Notes

278. Why Stanford would have gone to jail is unclear, but see his Circa Late May 1972 letter to Bender below, par. 1.

To Alan Dugan: May 26, 1972

May 26, 1972

Dear Alan,

I burned everything in the house. I was going to for the film, anyway. There is nothing of mine existing in this house. Don't send me my poems, or I'll burn them. There is no such thing as "The Battleground Where the Moon Says I Love You." I burned it—the whole thousand pages. A couple of weeks ago I sent a synopsis of the last 700 pages to Solotaroff; I sent him what you have, too. Somebody could make a screenplay out of it with the latter information, but I'll never touch it, or make a modern, sleek novel out of it. There is no one here the least bit interested in what I write, including my wife. So, fuer elise to poetry. Folles amours font les gens bestes. Car j'ay le plumail au vent,[279] or le suyve qui a attente, de ce me tais doresnavant. Et s'aucun m'interroge ou tente Comment d'amour j'ose mesdire ceste parolle le contente, Qui meurt, a ses loix de tout dire.[280]

Love,
Frank

Here are some typing scraps from some page in "... the Moon Says I..." You might have a few ideas, a few poems.[281]

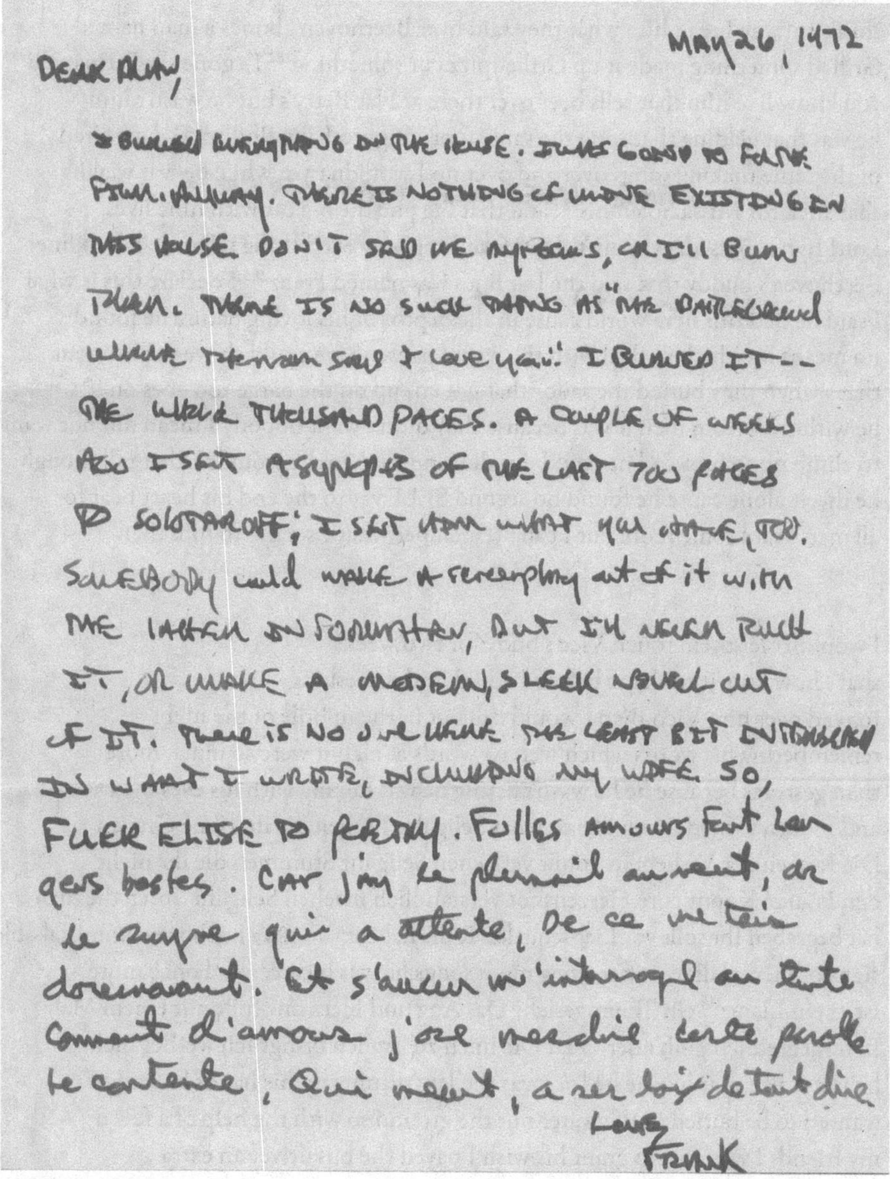

May 26, 1972

Dear Alan,

I burned everything in the house. I was going to leave them anyway. There is nothing of mine existing in this house. Don't send me any poems, or I'll burn them. There is no such thing as "the battleground where the woman says I love you." I burned it — the whole thousand pages. A couple of weeks ago I sent a synopsis of the last 700 pages to Solotaroff; I sent him what you have, too. Somebody could make a screenplay out of it with the latter information, but I'll never touch it, or make a modern, sleek novel out of it. There is no one here the least bit interested in what I write, including my wife. So, Fuer Elise to poetry. Folles amours font les gens bestes. Car j'ay le plumail au vent, or le suyve qui a attente, De ce me tais doresnavant. Et s'aucun m'interrogue ou tente comment d'amours j'ose mesdire cette parolle le contente, Qui meurt, a ses loix de tout dire

Love,
Frank

Page 1 of Stanford's May 26, 1972, letter to Alan Dugan. Beginning with "Folles amours," the last six lines consist of selected excerpts from François Villon's *Le testament* (1461).

I just had to find some words I finally I did I found them in a book about that deaf man Beethoven I found out lots about him I bet they'd quit playing his records on the radio in Greenville if they knew he had syphilis what'd you think anyway I read him what they said over Beethoven's bones a man named Grilled something made it up Grilledpizza or something[282] I's gone say Farinanelli[283] you know like him that sells beer over there at Flat Betty's but he wasn't him he was that gelding that sung the same four songs to King Philip[284] I'd get tired of the same fucking songs over and over no I wouldn't yea while he was waving that stick for Missa Solemnis[285] and that big one the big cat with nine lives Lord Byron passed away ain't that something how everything seems to fall in line Beethoven's buddy that said the last lines was named Franz[286] I declare this is what I said he fled this here world cause in the depths of his loving nature he found no means by which to deal with the world pause so we could shove the beat out that's when they buried the sailor that got cut up on the barge too goes on if he withdrew from men it was because they didn't want nobody I mean did not want to climb up to him and he could not descend to them he wouldn't that tall though he dwelt alone cause he found no second SELF yet to the end his heart beat for all men I said some more but I can't remember what I set fire to him then

*

I wouldn't let them touch Vico's body for two weeks
that's how long it took me before I could find something
to read over him Vico Bico I would call out in the middle of the night
remembering his words which weren't words at all but were so much more
than gestures because he he wasn't acting he was talking with his eyes
and mouth turned down like so what Selig ihr Tauben die ihr ohne Grauen
Die Klagen der Verliebten konnt verlachen Selig ihr Stummen die ihr nicht
den Frauen Konnt eure Herzensnot verstandlich machen Selig ihr Toten die man
hat begraben Ihr sollt vor Liebsequalen Ruhe haben[287] in 1897 he showed unmistakable
signs of mental illness after a few more songs he was incarcerated once more
Ist es ein Llang[288] ein Traumgesicht Das Aug und Herz mir fullt mit einem Mal
In unbegreiflich gluh'nder Qual Die mich zu Tranen bringt Ich weiBes nicht[289]
he put it like that like he he [*sic*] was the Jew turning up his hands he said he
wanted to be buried in the water not the ground so with the help of a few o
my friends I was able to grant his wish I payed the bus driver an extra
f[cut off]

*

fair so suffer the little children my ass sometimes on sundays they play
classical records for an hour it is usually brought to you by the local

music shop I was hoping they'd have something but it was already off the air
and the other station that don't come in good just had a baseball game I
tried to remember the words of one of those he taught me but I couldn't
all I could remember was Lady of Spain I adore you Lady of Spain I so I sung
that the people that was there looked at me kind of funny they wasn't at his
burial they was waiting for another one I thought he'd like it if I wore
one them altar boy robes so I stoll one and done it I had to bite down with
my teeth so I could sing but I sung Lady of Spain I
then I couldn't sing no more I had a catch in my throat so I whistled it[290]

Notes

279. Correctly: "Car j'ay mys le plumail au vent."

280. Stanford is quoting Villon's *Le testament* (1461). The first sentence of this Middle French passage is line 629—the fifth line of the "Double ballade"—translated by David Georgi as: "Love's folly turns men into beasts." Villon, *Poems*, 69. Then follow seven lines of octet 71—lines 721–23 and 725–28—translated by Georgi as:

 Let the hopeful still give chase;
 I have tossed my plume to the wind.
 Henceforth I'll say no more about it;
 . . . .
 And if someone should ask or wonder
 How I dare speak ill of Love,
 this old adage will have to do:
 a dying man can say what he likes.
 (Villon, *Poems*, 75, 77)

281. The text of three enclosed scraps (torn from separate sheets of paper) follows; none of these fragments were published in *The Battlefield*.

282. Franz Grillparzer (1791–1872), Austrian poet/dramatist who wrote the oration for Beethoven's March 29, 1827, funeral in Vienna. Grillparzer's long poem "Beethoven" describes the composer's arrival in the underworld and his encounters with other composers (Haydn, Mozart, et al.) and poets (Shakespeare, Dante, Tasso, Byron, et al.). Stanford may also be alluding to Lord Byron's famous January 12, 1821, entry in his diary: "Grillparzer—a devil of a name, to be sure, for posterity; but they *must* learn to pronounce it. . . . And *who is he*? I know him not; but *ages will*." *The Works of Lord Byron*, rev. ed., *Letters and Journals*, vol. 5, ed. Rowland E. Prothero (John Murray, 1901), 171.

283. Carlo Broschi Farinelli (1705–82), Italian castrato singer.

284. King Philip V of Spain (1683–1746) commissioned Farinelli to sing the same four songs every night.

285. *Missa solemnis*, op. 123, an 1823 mass by Beethoven.

286. Franz Gerhard Wegeler (1765–1848), German physician and Beethoven's close friend.

287. A quotation from "Selig ihr Blinden, die ihr nicht zu schauen" (Blessed are the blind, who cannot see), an October 4, 1890, song by late Romantic composer Hugo Wolf (1860–1903)—based on an anonymous Italian folk poem as translated into German by Paul Heyse. Stanford quotes lines 3–8 of the eight-line song (omitting punctuation and diacritics), translated by S. S. Prawer as:

> blessed are the deaf, who without shuddering
> can laugh at lovers' laments;
> blessed are the dumb, who cannot tell women
> of their heart's anguish;
> blessed are the dead in their graves—
> they are safe from the torments of love.
> (S. S. Prawer, ed. and trans., *The Penguin Book of Lieder*
> [Penguin Books, 1964], 121)

288. Correctly: "ein Klang."

289. A quotation from "Fühlt meine Seele das ersehnte Licht" (Does my soul feel the longed-for light), a March 25, 1897, song by Hugo Wolf—based on a sonnet by Michelangelo (poem 76) as translated into German by Walter Robert-Tornow. Stanford quotes lines 5–8 of the song, translated by Prawer as:

> Is it a sound, a dream-vision
> which suddenly fills my eyes and my heart
> with inconceivable, searing pain
> that makes me weep? I do not know.
> (*The Penguin Book of Lieder*, 133)

290. "Lady of Spain," a 1931 song by Tolchard Evans with lyrics by Erell Reaves (a pseudonym for Stanley J. Damerell, Robert Joseph Hargreaves, and Henry Tilsley). Cf. *The Battlefield*, lines 14290–91 and 15317.

To Alan Dugan: May 27, 1972

May 27

Dear Alan,

Here are two more rejected ones. The longer is the Johnny Keats one. There are ~~four~~ {six} more out, and as soon as they return, I'll send them.

A few nights ago I burned everything I had, about 10,000 pages, except for the rest of "The Battlefield Where the Moon Says I." I'm insane right now. The book of new poems I can re-write; doing it now. It was just regiments and regiments of wounded soldier-children crying out for mercy. I had to put them to sleep. I commend them back to their source. Now I am equal with other young poets; no longer do I have the reservoir of expressed + written feelings to rely on. I must do it now.

I haven't seen anyone. Linda calls, but I don't feel like talking. I've never felt like this.

As I re-read this, after getting it rejected, I went back to my copy of *Keats*, that I stole from the Abbey library.[291] I read all his letters; of course his poems.

This torn page is how I feel.[292] Now, I can't send you the new book. I'll send you it a poem at a time, as I re-do it.

Frank

I ~~had~~ {have} so much I wanted to say to you last night, but today it has vanished.

Notes

291. I.e., Subiaco Abbey's library.
292. Enclosed is page 64 torn from *The Complete Poetry and Selected Prose of John Keats*, ed. Harold Edgar Briggs (Modern Library, 1951)—Keats's second, revised preface to *Endymion* (1818), which begins, "Knowing within myself the manner in which this Poem has been produced, it is not without a feeling of regret that I make it public." Keats notes that "the reader . . . must soon perceive great inexperience, immaturity, and every error denoting a feverish attempt, rather than a deed accomplished" and adds, "It is just that this youngster should die away. . . . The imagination of a boy is healthy, and the mature imagination of a man is healthy; but there is a space of life between, in which the soul is in a ferment, the character undecided, the way of life uncertain, the ambition thick-sighted."

To Eleanor Bender: Circa Late May 1972

May Something

Dear Eleanor,

Since I last wrote, in fact, during the last 10 days, my life has almost put itself out. You say, and it has happened. My wife has gone insane; I've been in jail 3 times; her parents and the doctor won't let me see her; I got fired from my job for hitting the boss; I've drunk all my earnings up and I'm about to be evicted; my mother is in the hospital; a woman's husband says he is going to kill me. There is more. I've always feared an unravelling of the baldachin, and I've held something out: a bottle, some good drafts, a few bucks, and your interest in getting my poems done as a book. I don't know if you feel the same way, or not.

There is nothing left. Some people have tried to come and get me, but I've still got them afraid of me. I'm not going to any nut house.

I can't sleep. I have nightmares when I do. I'd rather box 15 rounds, then fall asleep. I feel like a fool. I'm getting out of here. I'm writing you, now. If you are still interested in seeing about 100 poems, including 300 pages of a 500 page long piece, let me know. Write anyway.

I love you for your letters,
but I'm crazy.

yours,
Frank

To William L. Fox: Circa June 1, 1972

Dear Mr. Bill Fox,

I've heard about you, but I'm writing you now on matters of business. Last year, D. Walker accepted 3 new poems of mine for *EDGE*.[293] This winter he accepted parts of the enclosed long poem. (And the short one.) Some other national magazines are publishing old work of mine, as far back as 1957. At the moment, I'm 22.[294] I know this is unusual, but I'd like to follow through with what Long + Walker suggest.[295] The other editors + poets publishing poems {unrevised} from my *St. Francis and the Wolf 1957–1964* have said they're sticking their necks out.[296] I was under the impression *EDGE* was going to use this, maybe you don't want to anymore.

yours,
Frank Stanford

[Stanford has enclosed a letter to himself from David Walker dated May 27, 1972, suggesting that Stanford write to Fox "about the possibility—which Don Long mentioned—of our doing a special supplement of your work (new & old?)." At the bottom, Stanford has written in:]

Mr. Fox,

There is so much that has
happened to me in the
last 3 weeks, I just
can't explain here.
Tomorrow, I'm being
committed to a mental hospital.[297]
Sorry I can't fill you in. I
can't fill myself in.

yours,
Frank Stanford

Notes

293. David Walker; *Edge*, a literary journal published from 1971 to 1976 in Christchurch, New Zealand.
294. Stanford was twenty-three years old (not twenty-two) in June 1972.
295. *Long*: D. S. Long (b. 1950), *Edge*'s editor.
296. I.e., *St. Francis and the Wolf: Some Poems 1957–1964*.
297. Stanford was admitted to inpatient status at the Arkansas State Hospital on June 2, 1972.

Postcard image of Subiaco Abbey, looking across the Inner Court Garden to the Cloister Walk and to the towers of St. Benedict Church (where, in 1978, Stanford's funeral procession was held). Stanford spent portions of spring and summer and all of fall 1972 at Subiaco and used this postcard several times—including in correspondence to Alan Dugan and William L. Fox in June and to Eleanor Bender and Cheryl Campbell in July.

III.

WAYFARING

Little Rock, Subiaco, New England, New York, and Subiaco Redux, 1972

As Stanford's marriage to Linda fell apart, he spent eleven days at the Arkansas State Hospital, the state psychiatric hospital, in Little Rock and then passed much of June and July in Subiaco, where his mother lived and worked. In June and into early July, Stanford was suicidal, but he managed to reconnect with Cheryl Campbell—who had moved to Staten Island in late summer 1971 when he married Linda—on July 5, just before Linda filed for divorce on July 7. This reconnection buoyed him and his psychic state, shifting his outlook radically. In August, Stanford traveled with Irv Broughton and James Babij, a film student, to New England, interviewing and filming well-established poets—John Crowe Ransom and Richard Eberhart first, followed (after Babij returned west) by Richard Wilbur and Malcolm Cowley—and Stanford visited Dugan on Cape Cod. Stanford then lived for several weeks with Cheryl on Staten Island before leaving on September 15; moving on to Washington, DC, briefly; and then returning to Arkansas on September 18. He spent fall 1972 at Subiaco, and his divorce from Linda was finalized on October 18.

To Irv Broughton: Early June 1972

Dear Irv,

Sorry I haven't kept in touch. I no longer live in Fayetteville in the log cabin. My temporary address is: Coury House, Subiaco Abbey, Subiaco, Arkansas.[298] For awhile I worked there with the monks. I am not there now.[299] I'm in Little Rock, where I've been committed to the state mental institution.[300] I have very few rights here. I only wish I had one: the right to leave, but I am contained here, until a team of doctors say I can go. Irv, this is so humiliating for someone like myself. Strange though, I only feel for all the poor, unfortunate, suffering creatures around me. I can't begin to describe their plight. The only thing I have here with me is a copy of Lawrence's *Complete Poetry*.[301] I see things, feel things so much like him. I feel so ashamed to be in a place like this. It must have been more than women, whiskey, and song. Except for about 50 things I have out in the mail, all my manuscripts are burned. I burned them, all 10,000 pages. All my poems, stories, essays, novels (nascent), plays, everything. Nothing is left. Nothing. I'm ready to rise from my ashes, though. I'm ready to spread my wings, and have perpetual intercourse with the living, the becoming, and oh what a strange, dark progeny will I have. Have alone. I don't know what I'll do, when I get out of here. I'm not going back to Fayetteville. Perhaps to school somewhere. Linda is so worried about me, bless her heart, but she doesn't understand. Now, at this "hard time," I need a woman deep as the night herself. I need to be happy + carefree once again. I need to quit playing every role. I am a whole repertory company unto myself. I want to laugh with no worries. I want to make love with nothing but the moon on my mind. I want to be in love again. This poet might as well do himself in, if he can't let the bullcalf blood of his blindfold art bellow in the waters of the night running through his body like a silent fire. Come all you Queens of Hearts and meet the Ace of Sorrows. He's here today, he's gone tomorrow. As always your friend,

Frank

P.S. Are there any film conferences this summer? Something like that would help me.

Notes

298. *Coury House*: Subiaco Abbey's guest lodge, of which Dorothy Stanford was caretaker.
299. It appears clear that Stanford was at Subiaco between living in Fayetteville and being in Little Rock, though the amount of interim time passed at Subiaco was no more than a few days; the return address and postmark on the envelope for the May 27 letter to Dugan indicate that Stanford was still in Fayetteville then.

300. Stanford was admitted on June 2, 1972, and released on June 12.

301. *The Complete Poems of D. H. Lawrence*, ed. Vivian de Sola Pinto and Warren Roberts, 2 vols. (Viking, 1964, published in paperback in 1971). On the verso of this letter, Stanford has written out Lawrence's thirty-nine-line poem "Restlessness" ("RESTLESSNESS by DHL") sans stanza breaks, which includes the lines: "I will escape from the hollow room," "I will go out to the night," "I will catch in my eyes' quick net / The faces of all the women as they go past," "I can . . . always offer myself to one mistress, who always receives," and "But oh, it is not enough, it is all no good." *Complete Poems*, 179–80.

To Alan Dugan: June 16, 1972

[Postcard of view looking across Inner Court Garden to Cloister Walk and towers of St. Benedict Church, Subiaco Abbey (see image at the beginning of this chapter).]

Alan Dugan
Box 97
Truro, Mass. 02666

Dear Alan,

Both of your kind letters reached me as soon as I was released.[302] Don't have any idea what Linda wrote you, but I didn't exactly commit myself, as such. She is *sore* afraid of me.[303] The doctors, the jury, found me not guilty, although I still stand accused; society always gathers enough evidence. The doctors have hopes for my poetry! (And film plays). I'm no monk, but this monastery will do for awhile. I've given up the cabin in Fayetteville; have more regards for the several women there, I love, to ever see them again. Let them go their way, I'll go mine. Too many, too much to hurt. Not in contact with Linda. Wouldn't doubt her filing a divorce suit against me, soon; adultery would be the grounds. I'm no count. Whatever, I will endure; so will you. We'll keep in touch. Thanks to your wife, bless her heart.

Yours,
Frank
June 18[304]

Notes

302. I.e., Dugan's letters to Stanford dated June 1 (postmarked June 6) and June 8, 1972.

303. On June 4, 1972, Linda Stanford wrote to Dugan: "Frank asked me to tell you that he committed himself to the State Hospital last week. He'll be there for tests for at least ten days—and after that, we don't know what will happen. When I last saw him, he didn't want to live anymore and had destroyed all of his manuscripts. I spoke to him a few moments ago, and he seems to be better." Linda stated, "You are one of the very few people that Frank feels close to. Closer to you than anyone, because others can love him but not know him." Linda noted that her husband's "address now" was "Arkansas State Hospital / Unit 3 Lower / 4313 West Markham / Little Rock, Ar 72201." She added, "When he can leave the hospital, he wants to work for awhile at the monastery," noting that Coury House would be his address there. She closed, "Thank you for helping to keep him alive." Dugan's June 8 letter to Stanford began, "I have Linda's letter transmitting your message that you committed yourself to the Arkansas State Hospital. I'm glad you did because your action itself indicates a desire for survival and sane inter-personal relations and productivity."

304. Assuming that the postcard's Subiaco postmark (the afternoon of June 16—a Friday) is correct, this date is incorrect.

To William L. Fox: June 19, 1972

[Postcard of view looking across Inner Court Garden to Cloister Walk and towers of St. Benedict Church, Subiaco Abbey.]

William Fox
1103 Strand Place
Reno, Nevada 89503

Dear Bill,

Let me say I'm touched by your kind letter. When I wrote you, I was a wanted man. Free at last. Released from the Hospital with these words, "We can help you with the Dionysiac madness which flows from drink but we wouldn't dare tamper with that other, 'Divine Madness', as Plato says, which is particular to your orphic genius."[305] They went on, "We look forward to your work, your future." Anyday, I'm expecting to be sued for divorce; adultery, etc. I've left my cabin on the mountain in Fayetteville for good; just too many lovely women to hurt and contend with. I'm no monk (count either), but I'm here for now. The good brothers have given me a place to stay in return for work in the fields. As you said, we'll let time and poetry take care of itself. I'll be keeping in touch—a manuscript, etc., so you don't worry. "Je reviens a mes loups a mes facons de sentir/ La belle la violee/ Avec eux et le vent j'ai tout ce qu'il me faut/ Ou les arbres volent/ L'enfant aux yeux d'eau pour boire en prison/ Furieux sur le perron du chateau de la violence/ La chevalier Mene par les anges terribles. . . ."[306]

I remain
Frank

Notes

305. Dionysia, an ancient Greek festival in honor of Dionysus (or Bacchus), the god of (among other things) wine, insanity, and ritual madness. "Divine Madness" comes from Plato's dialogue *Phaedrus* 256b: "After death, when they have grown wings and become weightless, they have won the first of three rounds in these, the true Olympic Contests. There is no greater good than this that either human self-control or divine madness can offer a man." *Phaedrus*, trans. Alexander Nehamas and Paul Woodruff, in *Complete Works*, 533.

306. Stanford is oscillating in a symmetrical pattern (1-2-3-2-1) here across three André Breton poems (and is modifying two of Breton's lines). Stanford's words translate to: "I come back to my wolves my ways of feeling / The beautiful violated / With them and the wind I have everything I need / Where the trees fly / The child with eyes full of water to drink in prisons / Furious on the steps of the castle of violence / The knight led by terrible angels. . . ."

Stanford's first three lines are lines 31, 72 (partial), and 66 of Breton's seventy-eight-line poem "Pleine marge" ("Full Margin") (1940). Then follows line 25 of Breton's untitled poem beginning "A ta place je me méfierais du chevalier de paille" from his 1934 book *L'air de l'eau* (The air of the water). Stanford then modifies "Ma femme" ("My wife") to "L'enfant" ("The child") in line 58 of Breton's sixty-line poem "L'Union libre" ("Free Union") (1931). Stanford then shifts back to the *L'air de l'eau* poem, quoting line 17. He closes by returning full circle to "Pleine marge," modifying line 60 by changing "Joachim de Fiore" to "La chevalier" ("The knight"). In the translation above, lines 1–3, 5, and 7 are, apart from the modifications in lines 5 and 7, from André Breton, *Selections*, ed. Mark Polizzotti (University of California Press, 2003), 91, 108–10. "Pleine marge" was translated by Mark Polizzotti, "L'Union libre" by David Antin. Translations from *L'air de l'eau* (lines 4 and 6) are the editor's.

Re: "L'Union libre," cf. Stanford's poem "Wishing My Wife Had One Leg" (later published in *The Singing Knives*) in his March 15, 1971, letter to *kayak* above; Stanford refashions Breton's poem into an ode or homage to caryatids.

To Alan Dugan: Circa July 3 or 4, 1972

My Dear Friend,[307]

It is raining and lightning, but I'll stay out. There are tornado warnings. On the tenth darkness will descend. The angel of Death

A dream. And so poetry a potion that resides
in the threat of the world, a dead girl I was in love with,
to you I drink to you I say
with this kiss I wed and die.

When you listen to Mahler's Das Trinklied vom Jammer der Erde, think of me.[308] I will always be with you as poetry has always been with me.

yours,
Frank

My love to your wife.

Many close to me, in love with me, have suffered, become victims, on my behalf. To go on alone would mean more casualties. I'm {not} giving up the battle. In your sleep, in your dreams, I am wrestling the angel of death. I have no wish to further myself in this world.

[On a separate page, the verso of the second page of a two-page letter to Dorothy Stanford, dated "Thursday 18" (probably May 18, 1972), from Emma Spriggs of West Memphis, Arkansas, Stanford has written:]

Dear Alan,

I made Mama Covoe out of this woman Emma. She is around 90 now. Read the black brackets.[309]

Frank

Notes

307. This letter's envelope is postmarked July 5, 1972 (morning), from Subiaco; the letter's circa dating here is based on cross analysis of Stanford's July 5 letter to Campbell (par. 2), his July 10 letter to Bender (par. 4), and his early July 1972 postcard to Dugan,

as well as of a July 3, 1972, article in the *Daily Courier-Democrat* of Russellville, Arkansas (twenty-five nautical miles from Subiaco, ten from the Lake Dardanelle cabin), noting that the holiday weekend (July 1–2) had experienced "heavy thunderstorms, hail, high wind and tornadoes" and that the "same type of weather" would continue through July 4. As Subiaco's post office was presumably open on Monday, July 3, this letter would appear to have likely been written late on July 3 or on July 4.

The letter and its enclosures are bundled, in Dugan's papers, with an August 12, 1972, letter from Linda Stanford to Dugan; see note 371 below.

Also enclosed is a page (pp. 145–46, front and back) torn from *The Penguin Book of Lieder* containing lyrics in German and English to Gustav Mahler's music—respectively, to part of *Des Knaben Wunderhorn* (*The Boy's Magic Horn*) and to "Das Trinklied vom Jammer der Erde" ("Drinking Song of the Earth's Misery"), the first movement of *Das Lied von der Erde* (*The Song of the Earth*), a 1912 vocal and orchestral symphony. The former includes lyrics to "Der Tamboursg'sell" ("The Drummer Boy"), a funeral march for an imprisoned drummer boy, in which the speaker closes:

> With a loud voice
> I take my leave of you.
> I take my leave of you!
> Good night! Good night!

Further enclosed is a small card containing "A Prayer of Saint Francis of Assisi," which begins, "Lord, make me an instrument of Your peace" and closes, "And it is in dying that we are born to eternal life."

308. The movement's refrain reads "Dunkel ist das Leben, ist der Tod" ("Life and death alike are dark"). Prawer, *The Penguin Book of Lieder*, 146.
309. *Mama Covoe*: Francis's first mother in *The Battlefield*. The words of Emma Spriggs (1893–1980—seventy-nine years old as of this letter) within black brackets in the letter read: "But we are pulling our stakes and folding our tents + moving on."

To Cheryl Campbell: July 5, 1972

July 5,[310]

Dear Cheryl,

I love you. I love you. As I read your blessed letter,[311] my body shivers as if there is snow all around me. My soul is yours. My body is yours. My mind is yours. Whatever there is to create, I create it for you. Forever. This letter, like a white bird bearing your spirit, comes to me on this day, which was to be my last.[312] Your reprieve is most sweet, beauty. Cheryl, la belle, la violée, la victime, la voyageuse "Aux hanches de lustre et de pennes de flèche."[313] You could cut me open I am so happy, and play my taut veins like the strings of a guitar. Because of you I live. I live for you. My blood sings. I could write this letter in its red joy. I am reading your letter and trying to write this one. Always, for all times, we have been, we will be lovers; I knew that, but I did not know you still loved me as I love you. As you give me your light once again, I am able to see. Each word is a seed that will blossom. You are like a thousand birds singing to me at once. How can I ever begin to answer your call as you answered mine? I am so in love I am sick. I'm as cold as the keel of a ghost ship off the coast of Iceland. I'm as hot as the tempered blade of Roland. I'm alone in the monastery, reading your letter, listening to Mahler: The Song of the Earth—Das Trinklied von Jammer der Erde.[314] A monk brought me your letter. I've read it all the way through, and I'm mad with joy. There is a place a few miles from here. I'll ride there as fast as I can, alone, on a gentle spirited mare, and read this again, beside the lake. Tell the friends you live with: I am riding a horse from a monastery, shouting your name. Cheryl, Cheryl. I love you, I must say farewell to the "Kingdom of Melancholy, Hopelessness," where I have ruled, alone, the weary king. Everything you say is good + right. Your dark hair is a dream. When the night arrives, it is you with your fingers consoling your dark hair. When the moon rises, it is you Selene, drawing the sheets from your bed. And you caress me, Endymion, as I sleep.[315] When the night is gone, and I awake, it is you letting down your dark hair, oh Cheryl of light that travels like a lovely ship a million years through my soul. I love you. There are so many answers, variations on your beautiful songs. I want to hear your music once more. Forever. Are you really saying we will be lovers again? Will I hold your waist in my arms soon?

Beside the lake now. So happy in the midst of all the suffering I have caused, and guilty, too. The forces, the weakness, the pale master, Death, commands, have been waiting for me for so many months. That which made me betray you, wants my life, now. Through the winter and spring, Death says "Come with me." He lurks everywhere. "There is no one who loves you, now." I thought it so. The cage became a trap. I couldn't even pace + prowl. Kill or let go. What can one ever know about a beast who is wounded, captured, snared? Your letter has saved me from death. Here, at this very spot by the water, I took all of my clothes off, and set out to swim to my death, not more than a few days ago. I knew I was weak; knew I would drown. I set out from the solitary shore at darkness; I swam, and swam, saying, "Angel of death, you have won," but I kept on swimming. I don't know how many miles it was. What kept the muscles from giving out? You. You were all I thought of. You gave me the strength of Beowulf yes you did. I swam from dark until dawn, saying your name. When I was younger, I could swim long distances, but never this far. I sought out oblivion, as I thought our love was dead to this world. I brooded over writing you; I didn't want to be cruel, to bring up the past to make you suffer again. Rather than hurt you again, I *would* die.[316] I thought that madness wasn't all of the price I must pay for betraying you. Once more, on another night, I tried to swim into oblivion. Once again, you. Oh the ancient strokes of your eyelashes like a girl rowing a boat over the calm waters where her first lover has drowned. Your soul like a pool of echoes—dream I have dreamt. Cheryl, the spectre of the swan, the lily, and the mirror who pursues heat lightning in the spring to forget, who pours salt water into the wounds of the dead roses, the black roses, coming to life.

Is it true? Will we see one another again? Will we be as one, soon? If it is not so, don't spare me the truth! In torn chain mail, I kneel before you my lady. My helmet is under my arm, my head is bowed. Touch me with my sword, or strike off my head.

Cheryl I do not hate you. I love you.[317] What I hate is myself: the suffering I caused you. Whatever, I shall love you forever. Now, at this moment, if I try to think about it, what could have been, what was done, I *will* go mad. I weep from joy + sadness, my love. The wounds and zoos of society have made me violent. I will be gentle with you. I will touch you as gently as you touch your guitar, or your flute. I love you. You say you love me + want to see me, then we will know.[318] Pray tell me, my love, when can this be?

I swear by what's left of my blood,
I love you forever.[319]

FRANK

I am not mad. My only madness is longing for you. You.

There is a strange pony across the way. Our bodies are the same dark shade. Its mane like my hair, is a darker color than its body.

Death, pale and black
waits for me with the reins
of my hair in his hand.

There is a long journey on horseback. Then, a voyage in a ship. There are knives and roses, mountains on fire, snow that weeps, and a knight waiting out the nights for his lover. Write me Cheryl.

I love you.

Notes

310. This letter was returned, undelivered, and then enclosed with another, July 10, 1972, covering letter to Campbell. (Stanford had, he explained in the July 10 letter, written "New York instead of Staton Island [*sic*]" on this letter's original envelope.)

311. I.e., Campbell's July 1, 1972, letter to Stanford. Stanford had written a six-page letter to Cheryl from the Arkansas State Hospital on June 4 but didn't have her mailing address at the time; on June 28, from Subiaco, he wrote another, one-page covering letter and, having acquired Cheryl's address (in his June 4 letter, he notes that he had asked Linda to get it for him—likely through the Economic Opportunity Agency, where she worked for the War on Poverty and where Cheryl had worked, in a different office, in 1971), mailed the two letters together. (Stanford's covering letter is dated June 28; the envelope's postmark reads June 27, p.m.) Though Stanford had also followed the letters up with a postcard mailed on June 30, 1972, Cheryl's nine-page July 1 letter, penned on legal-size paper, was a reply to these two letters. In her letter, she describes her traumatic experience of her and Frank's 1971 relationship ending; explains about her move to New York (around the time of Frank's marriage to Linda); writes, "You are forgiven" and "I love you"; and closes, "I await *anxiously* your reply." She also enclosed an eighty-four-line love poem to Frank titled "Letter to Frank Stanford July 1, 1972."

312. See Stanford's Circa July 3 or 4, 1972, letter to Dugan above, mailed on the morning of July 5.

313. *la belle, la violée, la victime, la voyageuse*: the beautiful, the violated, the victim, the voyager. "La belle la violée" is part of line 72 of Breton's poem "Pleine marge" ("Full Margin"). See Stanford's June 19, 1972, postcard to Fox above. Stanford's quotation here is of line 45 of Breton's poem "L'Union libre" ("Free Union"); lines 44–45 read: "Ma femme aux hanches de nacelle / Aux hanches de lustre et de pennes de flèche," translated by David Antin as "My wife with the thighs of a skiff / That are lustrous and feathered like arrows." *Selections*, 90. See also note 306 above.

314. Correctly: "Das Trinklied vom Jammer der Erde"; see note 307 above.

315. Endymion, a handsome Greek king and/or shepherd as well as lover of Selene, a goddess personifying the moon, in Greek mythology—and in John Keats's poem *Endymion* (1818) (with "Cynthia" in place of Selene).

316. Stanford is referring to the emotional pain he caused Cheryl in the summer of 1971. To this editor, Cheryl "Cher" Ross (formerly Cheryl Campbell) explained that Frank unknowingly impregnated her ca. June 1971 and chose, upon being pressed by Linda, to be with her rather than Cheryl; upon Cheryl (and Frank) subsequently discovering that she was pregnant with her and Frank's (male) child, Frank stated that it wasn't the right time for them to have a child together. Within days, in early July, Cheryl had a miscarriage, followed by a D&C. Not long thereafter, in August, Cheryl moved to New York, and on August 21, Frank married Linda. Cf. Cheryl's words in note 359 below. Phone calls with editor, October 2 and December 9, 2023; and texts to editor, October 2 and December 8 and 17, 2023.

317. In her July 1, 1972, letter to Stanford, Cheryl writes, "I know you hate as well as love me + could kill me—faster than the flight of a wee sparrow."

318. In her July 1 letter, Cheryl writes, "I love you—+ want to see you—for then we will know what is next," adding, "I cannot come back to Arkansas immediately."

319. This letter is written in pencil, but the signature and postscript are written in blood.

To Eleanor Bender: July 10, 1972

July 10
Coury House
Subiaco Abbey
Subiaco, Arkansas

Dear Eleanor,

How was your trip to New England? Enjoyable and soothing I would like to think. Did you go to Maine and Vermont?[320] It has always been a dream of mine to go to the ocean. In some past life, I believe I must have roamed the seas. There is recollection of some cold, isolated island and ancient wood. Raw hands, use to the fins of fish and grip of the broad sword, seem to hold up the chin of some bold, weary woman as she looks out at the night sea over my shoulder. Strangely enough, the girl looks like a young Ingrid Thulin.[321]

Thank you for the copy of *Open Places*. Read through it in an open mood. The faces you introduced in previous issues seem to be moving as well as ever. However, I can see the difficulty in making selections—and you made some good ones—with another group of editors. It is my wish your magazine does not lose its own identity, which you created. If it is true that in the future the "board" intends to use fiction and long prose poems, perhaps I could submit what is left of some of my long poems.[322]

I don't know if you have returned from your vacation or not. There should be an illegible, desperate note addressed to you. I was able to get it off just before I was committed to the State Hospital.[323] It is a real sorrow: all that has come to pass in the last year, a tragic, labyrinthine tale of woe. Sometimes, my life and art become so complicated, so inextricable, it is hard, for the sake of others—their lives—to go on. For the time being, I have done my share of ruining the lives of several women. Oh, there was much happiness for awhile, but all was doomed. Last spring, I betrayed a woman who was Light to my Dark soul. Not intending to make poetry here, I believe there are souls, if they can meet, who are bound as day and night. The woman I speak of ruled the nights of my instinct. Call her Ishtar, Cybele, Eros, Isis, Selene, no just call her by name Cheryl.[324] And I was more than some Endymion. Do you recall the dark haired actress John Baptiste was in love with in Les Enfants du Paradis;[325] or the dark lady of death in Orphee;[326] or Rossetti's woman;[327] well it was as haunting and lovely as that. Far more. If my grammer [*sic*] breaks down, forgive. Anyway, when one lover betrays another, he is doomed to madness and death. He is able to make other women happy in their souls, bodies, and minds, but he is torn apart. He cannot be happy at the expense of another. My poor wife has suffered so much due to me. Sometimes all this life I have lived in the shadow of death is like a dream. I was I was not I; I did not write all I have written since I was a child. It would be much easier on others and myself if I could discover this I and make him and his work known. As you know I was making a film about a fourteen year old poet, his visions and dreams in a monastery. I was also putting together the typescript of a thousand page poem I wrote in 1964.[328] I had finished collecting (selecting) the un-revised poems for St. Francis and the Wolf: poems 57–64. While this past was being collated, the present was becoming new work. Since some have been responsive to both old and new, I was seeing if any of the stories, plays, and short novels would be good enough for someone to read. (As I said in my note to you, all but 300 pages of the long poem, and over a 100 poems—new and old—were burned. I had planned to burn all my manuscripts anyway—in the film—just as I did when I was coming along as a poet.)

If this lacks chronology, I'm sorry. My wife had to endure so much. There was me the animal in a cage, at best. At worse, gnawing at myself in a trap. Is that the way one knows a beast in the field. It was so damned Lawrentian. Other women, married, divorced, single, and so on. Pain. I had given up all hope of ever again seeing Cheryl. If ever, there is only one meeting of lovers like us. Forlorn, I had given up hope of reprieve. Death was always there, a pale master holding the reins of my horse. At night in the cabin, my [wife] asleep, I would dream of the aborted children.[329] Little fleets of coffins sailing into my solitary harbor. Would I ever return home on my horse with a dead child not in my lap. Would they ever live. (Listen to Schubert's Der Erlkonig)[330] Of course, I was drinking pretty much. I have never feared Death. I've always thought—rather I've never thought of living past 24 years old. The doctors in the hospital were amazed by the absence of any trace of a normal, long life.)[331] You have heard it said about others: a born writer, he lives to write. Well, I tell you for the past year it has been antipodal for me. What I had already created made me live. I had to create to exist. I was hoping to be born again through this. Hopeless. I reigned king in a kingdom of melancholy. After I burned my manuscripts, my wife had me committed. I'm free now. (There was some jails, drinking, violence, before.) Working here with the good monks. I asked her to divorce me and she is.[332] Thinking that love was not ever again to be found: I knew not where Cheryl was, I decided to wrestle the angel of death. The monks had an unusual boys camp here.[333] Boys from all over from all kinds of backgrounds. Rich and poor. It was their innocence and joy that kept me alive for two weeks. After they left there seemed to be nothing. One night after listening to Mahler's Song of the Earth, I went to the lake—rode a horse.[334] Wrote a poem, and swam off in the darkness into what I had hoped would be oblivion. I swam into oblivion for eight hours, until dawn. I don't know what made my body keep on, physically, but I knew where my strength came. I thought of Cheryl. I won some more bouts. A knife broke off in me, etc. Then, what happens. A monk walks in and hands me a letter from Cheryl. She is in New York. She loves me, forgives me, and we will get together as soon as possible.[335] I have to pay for law suits, divorces, etc., doctors.[336] That is why I'm taking sanctuary here. I'm doing my share of work. Much has been unsaid here, many people left out, etc. I am in love and want to live.

Once you said you'd like to see if RH would publish a book of mine.[337] At the time, I told you that a book wouldn't mean what it should to me. As I told you, I wanted to wait. If a book of mine could be published now it would mean much. (I would hope a little money, too.) The only poet to have seen the four manuscripts I have left is Dugan. (You've seen the Singing Knives)[338] He feels the old poems, especially the long one, should be published as is. This is what I'm asking: would you be willing to read my manuscripts? I would appreciate a reply. If you have any questions, please ask.

yours,
Frank

Notes

320. Bender and her children frequently spent their summers on Clark Island in Maine.
321. Ingrid Thulin (1926–2004), Swedish actor known for her frequent collaborations with Ingmar Bergman.
322. Bender had evidently sent to Stanford *Open Places*, nos. 12/13 (May 1972). Issue 10 (1971) had mentioned that Stephens College had begun financially backing *Open Places*; issues 10 and 12/13 noted intent to begin including fiction.
323. See Stanford's Circa Late May 1972 letter to Bender above.
324. Ishtar (a.k.a. Inanna), Mesopotamian goddess; Cybele, Anatolian goddess; Eros, Greek god; Isis, Egyptian goddess; Selene, Greek goddess; and Cheryl Campbell.
325. Stanford is mixing up the names of actor Jean-Louis Barrault (1910–94) and his character Baptiste Deburau, a mime and star of the Théâtre des Funambules in Marcel Carné's 1945 film, *Les Enfants du paradis* (*Children of Paradise*). Baptiste suffers in pursuit of Garance (played by Arletty), a dark-haired woman with whom several male characters are in love. A black cat that Frank and his second wife, Ginny, later had was named after Deburau (spelled as Debureau).

326. *Orphée* (*Orpheus*) (1950), dir. Jean Cocteau, in which the Princess (played by María Casares) is revealed to be Death (or deathlike).

327. Elizabeth Siddal (1829–62), poet/artists' model who became Dante Gabriel Rossetti's muse and wife (from 1860 until her death in 1862). Siddal had dark red hair. In an uncut interview of Stanford by Broughton (ca. 1972–74 but dated 1972–73 in the Frank Stanford Papers), Stanford explains that as a young child, at the levee camps, he sometimes dug graves for long-deceased women who had served as poets' muses. When asked what the woman in his imagination had looked like, Stanford replied, "The closest thing to what she looks like, I think, are the drawings of Elizabeth Siddal." Transcript, Frank Stanford Papers, Yale Collection of American Literature, Beinecke Rare Book & Manuscript Library. See mention of Siddal—and allusion to Jane Morris (1839–1914), wife of Rossetti's friend William Morris (1834–96)—in *The Battlefield*, lines 12228–29.

328. *The Battlefield Where the Moon Says I Love You*.

329. I.e., the unborn children conceived with Linda and, presumably, with Cheryl—though, as Stanford was aware, Cheryl actually miscarried and then immediately had a D&C, as Linda had also had for her abortion—as well as (at least) a third impregnation of an unspecified woman (which also led to an abortion); see Stanford's Circa Late September 1972 letter to Willett below.

330. "Erlkönig," op. 1, D. 328, an 1815 lied by Franz Schubert (adapting Goethe's 1782 poem "Der Erlkönig") about a father riding at night, holding his sick son; the child is menaced by a forest demon known as the Erlking (king of the alders), but the father doesn't detect the threat. By the time the father arrives home, the child is dead. Also cf. *The Battlefield*, lines 10650–52.

331. This closing parenthesis has no matching opening parenthesis.

332. Linda Stanford filed for divorce on July 7, 1972; the divorce was finalized on October 18, 1972.

333. Camp Subiaco, a two-week-long camp for boys ages seven to twelve (in the 1970s) held on Subiaco's campus each June since the early 1940s.

334. *Song of the Earth*: Mahler's symphony, *Das Lied von der Erde*. See notes 307 and 308 above.

335. Re: Stanford's description in this passage, cf. his July 5, 1972 letter to Campbell above, par. 2.

336. Linda Stanford's July 7 divorce filing argued that Frank, the defendant, "should be required to pay attorney's fees and Court costs incurred by plaintiff [Linda] in connection with this action."

337. *RH*: Random House.

338. See Stanford's July 27, 1971, letter to Bender above and note 168 above.

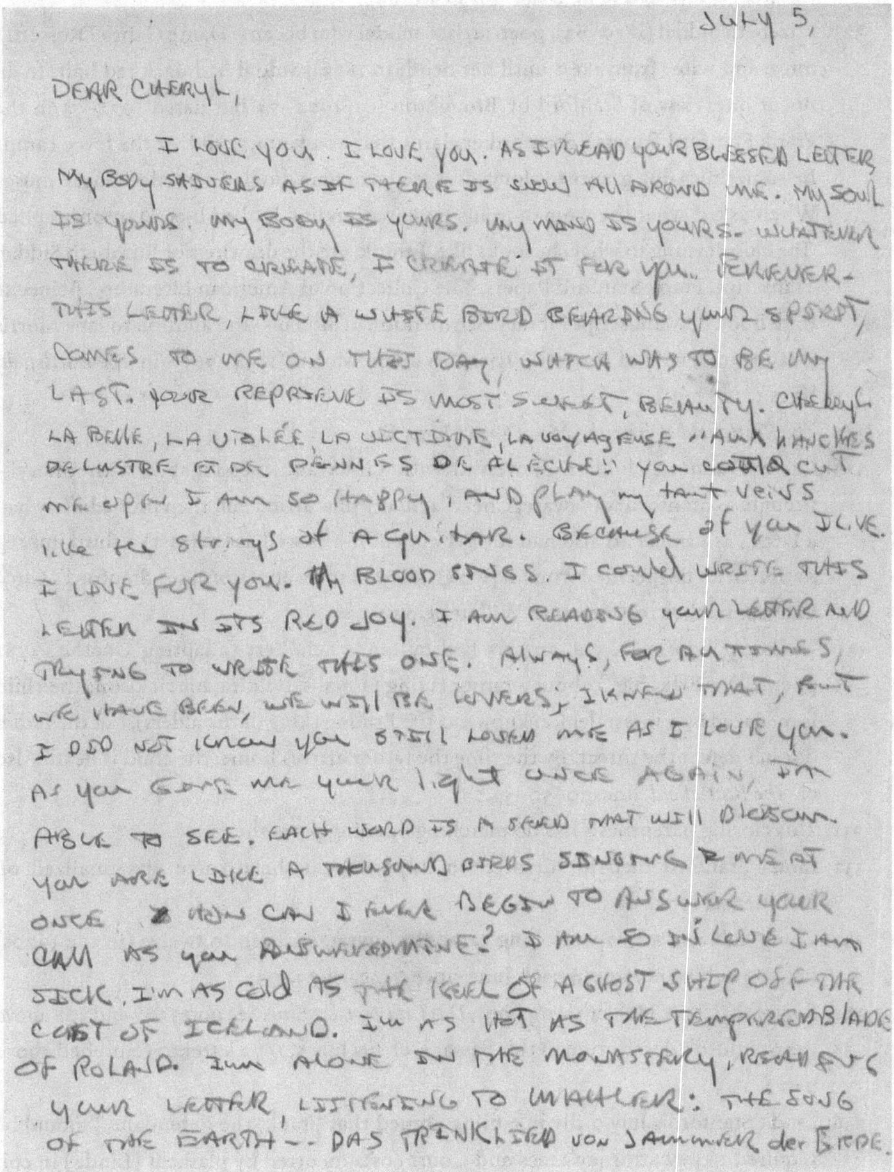

JULY 5,

DEAR CHERYL,

I LOVE YOU. I LOVE YOU. AS I READ YOUR BLESSED LETTER MY BODY SHUDDERS AS IF THERE IS SNOW ALL AROUND ME. MY SOUL IS YOURS. MY BODY IS YOURS. MY MIND IS YOURS. WHATEVER THERE IS TO CREATE, I CREATE IT FOR YOU. FOREVER—THIS LETTER, LIKE A WHITE BIRD BEARING YOUR SPIRIT, COMES TO ME ON THIS DAY, WHICH WAS TO BE MY LAST. YOUR REPRIEVE IS MOST SWEET, BEAUTY. CHERYL LA BELLE, LA VOILÉE, LA VICTIME, LA VOYAGEUSE "AUX HANCHES DE LUSTRE ET DE PENNES DE FLÈCHE!" YOU COULD CUT ME OPEN I AM SO HAPPY, AND play my taut veins like the strings of A GUITAR. BECAUSE of you I LIVE. I LIVE FOR YOU. MY BLOOD SINGS. I could WRITE THIS LETTER IN ITS RED JOY. I AM READING your LETTER AND TRYING TO WRITE THIS ONE. ALWAYS, FOR ALL TIMES, WE HAVE BEEN, WE WILL BE LOVERS; I KNEW THAT, BUT I DID NOT KNOW YOU STILL LOVED ME AS I LOVE YOU. AS YOU GAVE ME YOUR light ONCE AGAIN, I'M ABLE TO SEE. EACH WORD IS A SEED THAT WILL BLOSSOM. YOU ARE LIKE A THOUSAND BIRDS SINGING TO ME AT ONCE. HOW CAN I EVER BEGIN TO ANSWER YOUR CALL AS YOU ANSWERED MINE? I AM SO IN LOVE I AM SICK. I'M AS cold AS THE KEEL OF A GHOST SHIP OFF THE COAST OF ICELAND. I'M AS HOT AS THE TEMPERED BLADE OF ROLAND. I'M ALONE IN THE MONASTERY, READING YOUR LETTER, LISTENING TO MAHLER: THE SONG OF THE EARTH—DAS TRINKLIED VON JAMMER der ERDE.

Page 1 of Stanford's July 5, 1972, letter to Campbell. Stanford had been suicidal in the weeks leading up to this letter but writes in jubilation after having received Cheryl's July 1 letter in reply to letters he had sent her on June 28. He sometimes wrote letters in a roughly standard print, and this letter is an example of such penmanship. The letter is signed in blood, and the last, postscript page is written in blood.

To Alan Dugan: Early July 1972

[Postcard of northwest view of St. Benedict Church, Subiaco Abbey.]

Alan Dugan
Box 97
Truro, Massa 02666[339]

All of us wander through a kingdom of hopelessness and melancholy, having sympathy with death and oblivion, and empathy with life and its black roses. A year ago I betrayed the woman I love. I spoke of her last spring.[340] From then on my life was doomed. When Light and Dark are in love as we were, either two come through together, or the one who betrays the other seeks out his rendezvous with madness. The other day, a monk handed me a letter. It was from her. I was born again. She will be leaving N.Y. soon. We will go somewhere. She is no caryatid, she is a woman.[341] Naked, she would play the flute in the bed, while I wrote poems. Soon. After I wrote you that letter, I went out to swim into oblivion.[342] I swam from dark to dawn. I wrestled the angel of death and won. My body wasn't that powerful, it was Cheryl singing to my spirit. Make your book.

yours,
Frank

Notes

339. The postcard's stamp covers part of "Massachusetts," and the postmark's date is unclear.
340. Stanford's use of "last spring" here is not clear. He appears to be referring to his June 21, 1971, letter to Dugan above, par. 5. Otherwise, see his May 15 and 16, 1972, letter to Dugan above, par. 3, in which he wrote of breaking Linda's heart (i.e., by being with and impregnating Cheryl). Here, though, when he states that he "betrayed the woman I love," he means that he betrayed Cheryl by opting for Linda over her; see Cheryl Ross's words in note 359 below.
341. A veiled allusion to "Wishing My Wife Had One Leg"; see Stanford's March 15, 1971, letter to *kayak* above.
342. I.e., Stanford's Circa July 3 or 4, 1972, letter to Dugan above.

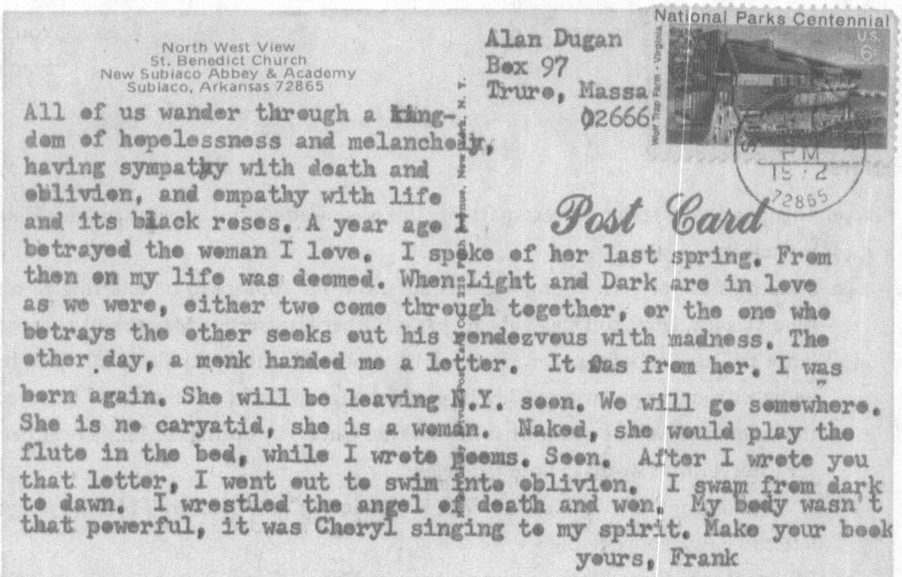

North West View
St. Benedict Church
New Subiaco Abbey & Academy
Subiaco, Arkansas 72865

Alan Dugan
Box 97
Truro, Massa
02666

Post Card

All of us wander through a king-
dom of hopelessness and melancholy,
having sympathy with death and
oblivion, and empathy with life
and its black roses. A year ago I
betrayed the woman I love. I spoke of her last spring. From
then on my life was doomed. When Light and Dark are in love
as we were, either two come through together, or the one who
betrays the other seeks out his rendezvous with madness. The
other day, a monk handed me a letter. It was from her. I was
born again. She will be leaving N.Y. soon. We will go somewhere.
She is no caryatid, she is a woman. Naked, she would play the
flute in the bed, while I wrote poems. Soon. After I wrote you
that letter, I went out to swim into oblivion. I swam from dark
to dawn. I wrestled the angel of death and won. My body wasn't
that powerful, it was Cheryl singing to my spirit. Make your book
yours, Frank

Stanford's early July 1972 postcard to Dugan. The postmark is not clear, but the content aligns with Stanford's July 10, 1972, letter to Bender. He often typed postcards, especially in June–July 1972 while in Subiaco before he traveled in August to New England with Irv Broughton and James Babij.

To Irv Broughton: Circa Mid-July 1972

[This letter is penned on the back of a business envelope that was sent from Broughton to Stanford; the postmark from Seattle is July 5, 1972.]

Type up a 10 page invocation + essay—as a screenpoem on death, and send it to Irv.

Irv,

Do you think death comes only for the poet, and not for all. Death is not over a book. Like the knight in 7th Seal, like Johan in Hour of the Wolf, Don Jaun [*sic*] in the Devil's Eye, Vogler in The Face, dreams have made being into becoming.[343] There is creation in death

"Sing the song of death, O sing it
for without the song of death, the song of life
becomes pointless and silly" DH. L[344]
"once dipped in dark oblivion, the soul
has peace, inward + lovely peace"[345]

"Never" the knight replies[346]

{The Poet is 14 years old walking alone through the forest + fog in the morning. Song of the Earth is playing. The boy is old + dark. His cape trails the ground. He knows death is 8 yrs. away. He is at peace. He aches like the field hand.}[347]

Notes

343. *The Seventh Seal* (1957); *Hour of the Wolf* (1968); *The Devil's Eye* (1960); and *The Magician* (or *The Face*) (1958)—all dir. Bergman. The notion of being vs. becoming is discussed by Stanford across various 1972 correspondence, and cf. *The Battlefield*, lines 12389–90 and 15329–30.

344. The opening stanza of "Song of Death," one of D.H. Lawrence's last poems:

Sing the song of death, O sing it!
for without the song of death, the song of life
becomes pointless and silly.
(*Complete Poems*, 723)

345. "But dipped, once dipped in dark oblivion / the soul has peace, inward and lovely peace"—the closing stanza to "The End, the Beginning," another of Lawrence's last poems. *Complete Poems*, 724.

346. In *The Seventh Seal*, Death asks the Knight, "Don't you ever stop asking questions?" to which the Knight replies, "No, I'll never stop."

347. *Marginalia: left side (side flap and seal flap), various facing.* Re: "Song of the Earth is playing," see note 307 above.

To Eleanor Bender: July 12, 1972

[Postcard of view looking across Inner Court Garden to Cloister Walk and towers of St. Benedict Church, Subiaco Abbey.]

Eleanor Bender
Open Places
Stephans College[348]
Columbia, Mo.

Dear Eleanor,

Last night, I put on a cassock, and rode a horse through the mountains. I'm taking sanctuary here, until John Law + courts + my wife, others leave me alone. Soon, the woman I love will be here. At present, she is in New York. Hope my desperate letter did you no harm. It's just that I have so much love to tell the world: the human condition as I see it, beauty + truth—yet I've hurt so many I love. Either a poet sings, or he moans like a wounded beast. If *they* could see it as I see it, like you know I see it. One day.

yours,
Frank

Notes

348. Correctly: "Stephens College." The postcard was forwarded to Bender in Spruce Head, Maine.

To Cheryl Campbell: July 15, 1972

[Postcard of a seashore and Isaiah 60:1.]

Cheryl Campbell
56 Harvard Avenue
Staton Island [*sic*]
New York

Dear Cheryl,

"There lies the world my Darling, full of wonder, and wistfulness, and strange. . . ."

D. H. Lawrence[349]

"Seule toutes les femmes de ce monde
Je les ai aimées pour t'aimer
Mon unique amour
[Cheryl] Glace de ténèbres
Miroir d'amour
Entre toutes les amants
Le jour et la nuit échangeant
Leurs promesses. . . ."

A. Breton[350]

When the night arrives
It is. . . .

Love
Frank

Notes

349. Line 9 of Lawrence's poem "Dreams Old and Nascent: *Old*" (variant—correctly with a comma after "world"; ellipsis added by Stanford). *Complete Poems*, 905.

350. Stanford is shifting here across three Breton poems (and is modifying several of Breton's lines). Stanford's words read:

Only all the women of this world
I loved them to love you

My only love
[Cheryl] Ice of darkness
Mirror of love
Above all lovers
Day and night exchange
their pledges. . . .

Stanford's first three lines are lines 308 (partial) and 310 of Breton's long poem "Fata morgana" (1940), with Stanford adding "Seule" ("Only") to begin his quotation (his second and third lines, together, make up line 310). Following "Cheryl" (brackets Stanford's), his fourth and fifth lines make up line 13 of Breton's untitled poem beginning "On me dit que là-bas les plages sont noires," from *L'air de l'eau*. Stanford's sixth line combines a refrain and line 53 (partial) from "Pleine marge" ("Full Margin"); his last two lines make up line 52 of "Pleine marge." All ellipses in this postcard are Stanford's. The translations of the quoted lines from "Full Margin" used above are from Breton, *Selections*, 107–9.

To Cheryl Campbell: July 19, 1972

[Postcard of view looking across Inner Court Garden to Cloister Walk and towers of St. Benedict Church, Subiaco Abbey.]

Cheryl Campbell
56 Harvard Avenue
Staton Island [*sic*], New York

Yesterday, I got in a canoe and made down the white river. I made a fire on an island, and made poems to you. Two eagles circled over a bluff, one calling the other. I was alone, but you were with me when the sun went down. How I wished you were in the sleeping bag, looking at the fire. The fog and the animals came out. I looked up at the stars and said your name. Do you remember that night on M. hill?[351] The horses prancing in the dew on the grass. My body is stronger. There is no need for drink. We have come through, you and I.

I love you forever,
Frank

Notes

351. Markham Hill, a treed hillside area with cabins and a meadow on the west side of Fayetteville where Frank and Cheryl met ca. January 1971. Stanford is referring to a night he and Cheryl spent in a shared sleeping bag under the stars, with horses playing around them, in spring 1971.

To William L. Fox: July 20, 1972

[Postcard of northwest view of St. Benedict Church, Subiaco Abbey.]

William Fox
1103 Strand Place
Reno, Nevada

Dear Bill,

Still taking sanctuary here; the law can't touch me. It is night. The stars and the bell tower are better than Dali or Chirico.[352] A monk is singing Scubert's *Einsamkeit*.[353] Soon, a woman from N.Y. will be passing through here and we'll travel somewhere together. Already, I've begun the screenplay again. I don't want to write it on "location." About biography. Well, you just type up a list of questions—I'll answer. About what's left of my manuscripts: the one I want you to have, I no longer have with me. My wife, whom I jilted and left, has it. *PLEASE* write her, impressing upon her your desire to see it: Linda Stanford c/o EOA 1100 N. College Fayetteville, Ark.

Be brief + firm, asking for St. Francis and the Wolf—about 50 poems. She might send some not in that MS. You'll be able to recognize, though, by typography.[354] Keep in touch.

Notes

352. Salvador Dalí (1904–89), Spanish Surrealist artist, and Giorgio de Chirico (1888–1978), Greek Italian artist and writer.
353. "Einsamkeit" ("Loneliness"), song twelve from Schubert's 1828 song cycle *Winterreise* (*Winter Journey*).
354. On August 12, 1972, Linda Stanford wrote to Fox: "I am sorry for the delay. I was hoping to be able to find what seems to be 'page 1' of the manuscript. It may be among the unnumbered pages. I don't know. Frank may have another copy."

To Irv Broughton: July 20, 1972

July 20, 1972

Dear Irv,

Believe it or not, I'm going to Staten Island to live with Cheryl. For how long, I couldn't tell you. Probably no more than nine months, then we'll move on to live somewhere else, maybe Seattle. I'm in love with her as much as I am death.

You said you'd be heading East the last of this month. I'd like to meet you whenever you make your lowest southern arc, and go north&work with you for awhile. If this is impossible, out of the question, I'll find another way up there. Whatever, let me know as soon as you get this.[355] It's remotely possible I might be able to suggest something about your cutting, when it's time for the knife.

In N.Y. I'll be able to see and hear enough beauty to last me a lifetime. (If I don't go crazy there like Lorca.)[356] If and when I ever make a film, either I'll have to learn every trick of the trade myself—digging up the money, or someone else will have to have faith in me with their crew and money. The reason Cocteau, Carne (Prevert), Bresson, Tati, etc. never did have to worry about being commercial, making money with their art, is because there was always someone to foot their bills.[357] They never went out and looked for an audience, betraying their art—however majestic and intolerable it was—, they said come here to the spectators with their fingers, never leaving their tents. No one knew what to make of them then, and most of your critics still don't. They created their own worlds. Don't forget Vigo, dead at 29.[358] Someday, with your help, maybe I can offer something worthwhile up. Read what Bullfinch says about Endymion.[359]

I'll have to go now. Tonight, a monk by the name of Wolfgang, really, and I are going to get drunk and listen to music. He's black—former dancer and opera singer.[360] If you can put up with me over the next few years, I believe I might be able to lift the veil, as Shelly says, from some of this beauty hidden in the world.[361] Love calls. So do the bells.

Be in touch,
Frank

What Dugan would like, Justice wouldn't. What Hecht would like, Ginsberg wouldn't. What Wright would like, Howard wouldn't. Etc. If you can find anything not trite in the 300 page fragment of juvenilia,[362] you can have it.

Notes

355. Stanford's letter arrived just in time. Broughton and James Babij's eastward trip in Broughton's green Oldsmobile Cutlass passed through Cheyenne, Wyoming, during its annual Cheyenne Frontier Days festival, July 22–30, 1972. The two traveled on to Subiaco, picking Stanford up and heading northeast.
356. When Spanish poet Federico García Lorca (1898–1936) traveled to New York in 1929, he was already nearly suicidal, but New York's urban decay, racism, and socioeconomic brokenness—alongside the stock market crash—deeply affected him. He wrote his influential collection *Poeta en Nueva York* (*Poet in New York*) in New York and returned to Spain within nine months of having arrived in the US.
357. Jean Cocteau, French writer/filmmaker; Marcel Carné, French filmmaker; Jacques Prévert, French poet/screenwriter; Robert Bresson, French filmmaker; and Jacques Tati, French filmmaker. Prévert wrote (or cowrote) screenplays for seven of Carné's films, including *Les Enfants du paradis*.
358. Jean Vigo, French filmmaker.
359. Endymion is discussed in two main areas of *Bulfinch's Mythology* (1867)—in book 1 (*The Age of Fable*), specifically—by Thomas Bulfinch: in a chapter devoted partially to Endymion (chapter 26) and in chapter 7. Which of the two chapters' passages Stanford is referring to isn't clear, but either could be read as relevant to his romantic pursuits as of mid-1972. If Stanford's reference is to chapter 26, he is suggesting that Bulfinch's descriptions of the classical Endymion as a youthful, romantic, and melancholic poet apply to him. If the reference is to chapter 7, he is drawing comparison between Bulfinch's analysis of the retelling in Keats's *Endymion* of the legends of the fisherman/sea-god Glaucus, the goddess/"enchantress" Circe, and the "beautiful maiden" Scylla from Greek mythology and Stanford's own romantic relationships with Linda and Cheryl—viz., with Stanford in the role of Glaucus, Linda as Circe, and Cheryl as Scylla. *Bulfinch's Mythology: "The Age of Fable," "The Age of Chivalry," "Legends of Charlemagne"* (Modern Library, n.d.), 54, 165–66.

   To this editor, Cheryl Ross notes:

   > Unbeknownst to me, Frank had been seeing Linda before I was with him. He told me she just would not accept that they had broken up. I did not know about her until one morning a screaming woman was banging on the door, yelling, "Frank, Frank! Frank Stanford, I know you're in there!"—quite dramatic. I think that happened late June 1971. Frank eventually had to choose. I declared my feelings but if he did not choose us, I was leaving. I did not demand. (Not my mutable nature.) She demanded. I am not certain that he declared to me his choice; he simply acquiesced. (Text to editor, December 17, 2023)

   It is also possible that Stanford is referring to both passages.

360. Fr. Wolfgang Mimms (1925–2008), the first African American monk to be ordained at Subiaco Abbey.

361. From Percy Bysshe Shelley's 1821 essay, "A Defence of Poetry": "Poetry lifts the veil from the hidden beauty of the world, and makes familiar objects be as if they were not familiar." *Shelley's Critical Prose*, ed. Bruce R. McElderry Jr. (University of Nebraska Press, 1967), 12.

362. I.e., *The Battlefield*, of which Stanford had sent a draft excerpt to Broughton earlier in July 1972.

To Cheryl Campbell: July 29, 1972

Saturday

BELLE[363]

The last two days I've spent by myself in the mountains. I took long rides + swims, and thought of you. I want to suck the plum from your belly, and take the pit of the ruby between my teeth.[364] [Last year, I showed someone a poem I'd written soon after I met you. It was published in *The Nation*. It was the first and only one about you that I ever showed a soul, though I wrote many to you; the name of it was: "Belladonna."][365] Your S.D. card came.[366] Why does the P.O. insist on delaying our letters? The eclipse was you. I lay my head back on the wet grass; the clouds, old friends of all shades, seemed to enquire as to the whereabouts of my lover. I could say nothing. There she is I thought. Like one of Byron's characters, I am gloomy—being madly in love with you with you not here. Oh what can I do. I fear these words are without full meaning, since your beautiful accompaniment is so far away. As if this pen was a dagger and the paper your flesh. I mustn't scar you with my unworthy words. How I do love you. Yes I love you. As you said, to say it is so good. Damnit! The post office will be closed. So I'll have to hurry, love. My editor should be here tomorrow; we'll leave Sunday or Monday. I don't intend to go in to doc.,[367] but if I help him, he'll help me. So dear, it will be a week at least, two weeks at the most, before I'll touch your eyes with mine. Must rush. What's this, another card from you! Beautiful. All I'll be bringing is myself, my love for you, my dreams, a suitcase, type W, and about $400.00 I've managed to earn since they let me go. Until then I am

yours. And so much in love with
you—I always have been
FRANK

I would rather come to N.Y. with your friends, as I would see you so soon. However, this editor is looping down all the way from Seattle. Knowing that I will be with you I give up a roar that will frighten a thousand fishermen. I'm mad with joy.

CHERYL CHERYL ————————————————

Notes

363. Stanford often addresses Campbell as "Belle" (Beauty) in their correspondence, sometimes signing off as "Bête" (Beast)—after Cocteau's 1946 film, *La Belle et la Bête*—a carryover from pet names they had used in 1971.
364. Cf. lines 10–11 of "Dante Gabriel Rossetti with His Head on the Virginal" (*Ladies From Hell*), which Stanford composed on a yacht belonging to poet Richard Eberhart in August 1972: "Salome gashes the sole of her drunken foot / on the ruby she danced from her belly." *What About This*, 130. Also cf. lines 88–89 of "Blue Yodel of the Desperado" (*Constant Stranger*), a 156-line poem (seemingly after Pier Paolo Pasolini's 422-line poem "Il pianto della scavatrice" ["The Cry of the Excavator"] [1956]) loosely narrating the New York and Washington, DC, parts of Stanford's August–September 1972 trip northeast, with Cheryl as the addressee: "I thought about how a ruby would look on you / A stud for your belly." Frank Stanford, *The Light the Dead See: Selected Poems of Frank Stanford*, ed. Leon Stokesbury (University of Arkansas Press, 1991), 66.
365. Brackets Stanford's. "Belladonna" is also presumably a play on Stanford's byname for Campbell.
366. *S.D.*: Special Delivery.
367. *doc.*: documentary films.

To Cheryl Campbell: August 6, 1972

[Postcard of rowboats in a New Hampshire millpond.]

Dartmouth or thereabouts
Sunday[368]

Cheryl Campbell
56 Harvard Ave.
Staten Island,
New York 10301

Belle,

I think of beauty I see death. I love you. Like the water, you are my death.[369] I miss you so much. Like night and day, our spell cannot be broken. I possess nothing. I love you. It's been so long since a good sleep, I don't know how I can still see through the camera. Up to Maine tomorrow, to film on a yacht. To see you—a life to see you, within the next week.

Love
Frank

Notes

368. Stanford mailed several postcards to Campbell on Monday, August 7, 1972, including this one, each postmarked in Hanover, New Hampshire.
369. Stanford reiterates this notion in an August 10, 1972, letter to Campbell, penned from Cape Rosier, Maine: "I don't know what the ocean is! . . . I came back to the ocean like an old lover. You are this water, my own death."

To Cheryl Campbell: August 7, 1972

[Postcard of the Dalton Covered Bridge in Warner, New Hampshire.]

Cheryl Campbell
56 Harvard Ave.
Staten Island,
New York 10301

Belle,

How will it be. Not one second has passed me by without cutting its throat since I saw you last. Pray for the hour of vanished lives. The stallion still has his head down. The water is like a quilt I want to turn back. Nothing is too soon. I want you, I love you.

Bête

To Alan Dugan: August 7, 1972

[Postcard of Ben Shahn's painting *The Red Stairway.*][370]

Dartmouth today
The coast of Maine Wednesday

Alan Dugan
Box 97
Truro, Mass.

Dear Alan,

As I said, I'm in love and on my way to N.Y.[371] Luck has it I have a ride + job on my way there: riding around, expenses paid, taking doc. footage of J. C. Ransom and Richard Eberhart. It's experience, and a way to N.Y. What the hell. I don't like the mixing with people though. Last night I slept in Eberhart's house and wrote a poem. The guy I'm working for has relations in Cape Cod, and he's invited me there for a couple day vacation. I won't bother you since I know you're writing your book. We might run into each other. Don't worry about me, just your poetry. We'll endure. This part of the world is like a dream for me. [My love?] to your wife.[372]

Always
Frank

Notes

370. Ben Shahn (1898–1969), artist and father of Judith Shahn, Dugan's wife.

371. On August 12, 1972, while Stanford was in Maine with Broughton, Babij, Eberhart, et al., Linda Stanford wrote to Dugan:

> Dear Alan,
>
> Frank left some of his manuscripts with me. He asked me to send you a copy of *Nægling*, and to re-type those poems which hadn't yet been included. But the unfastened poems are also unfinished, and I can't finish them. I'm enclosing them as he left them.
>
> I filed for a divorce last month, and I believe Frank left for New York soon afterward. I haven't heard from him since then and don't know how he is. He has some friends in New York who care for him.
>
> Thank you for your letter of June. I hope Frank will have some of your 'spiteful desire to live.' You and your wife, Judy, are rare and kind.
>
> Linda

Linda included her address—an apartment on N. Leverett Avenue in Fayetteville. (Dugan's June 8, 1972, letter to Stanford included, "Our colleague, Diane Wakowski, in responding to the recent rash of suicides and break-ups among us, stated the correct position; 'I have a spiteful desire to stay alive.'")

372. This postcard's stamp partially obscures the words conjectured here in brackets.

To Cheryl Campbell: August 11, 1972

My love,

Where are the horses breathing in the garden of the dead? Nightfall, omens, shoots, wedding reception given in honor of death, blue organdy and a straw hat, the dead actress of the fire place, all in one life. I fear this travelling-filming job has almost done me in. Not nearly as steady as I was when I left Arkansas. Didn't know I would go this long without seeing you. I'm holding on until Friday, when I'll be there.[373] Trying not to drink.

Do you remember how it was when we would lie down almost forever it seemed in one another's arms. And be so still, dreaming a deep sleep of peace, union, and solemnity, without sleeping. Was it a dream? No. It was *all* true. The first night like a shaft of light through the window of an old house. The dust coming together in the isolated corridor. I speak these words *so* slowly as I write them, if this contraption like a camera could be called. . . . You on your farm and I in my cabin.[374] I Must Not allow myself to think of these days, not here, at least until I see you. The energy that will come together when you and I meet is enough to wound the darkness. It is so crowded here, so unlike your soul. You must consider the possibility of my really being mad. Who can judge. A year without you—how did I breathe. I should have cut my heart out. The weeping the color of the dusk. The lament of the one who drank wine and grew silent. I dreamed you walking by, swimming in a river that was not there, innocent and evil. Your skin as I recall it smooth as a petal. The impossible fragrance of your body. Passion drowned in melancholia. Lonely as a shade of purple. My portrait, your foreboding eyes.

I love you
Frank

Notes

373. Stanford didn't actually arrive on Staten Island until August 21.

374. When Stanford first met Campbell ca. early 1971, she was living just south of Fayetteville in Greenland, Arkansas, on a farm where she had lived with her husband

Ritchie Campbell—before their nascent marriage failed ca. late 1970—taking care of cattle. Frank and Cheryl spent time at the farm before she moved into his Lindell Avenue studio some weeks later.

To Bill Willett: August 11, 1972

[Postcard of a windjammer on the coast of Maine.]

Bill Willett
Old Arkana Road
Mtn. Home, Arkansas

Dear Bill,

Spending the night on a 39' yacht.[375] Sailing all over. Met, at Eberhart's house, a Greek family with 3 daughters. Drinking at a shanty with fishermen, eating seafood and Canadian French women. Women staying here from Congo, Morocco, Greece, and Rumania. The ocean is a dream. Will be here about 6 days or so. Met on the Cape, spent the day with the 87 year old anarchist-farmer-philosopher Scott Nearing (ask Fred M. about him).[376] Also many others, including poet Daniel Hoffman, whose book on Poe just came out. (He had heard of me!)[377] All [is?] fine, but too cold. 38° last night!

Where will I put the stamp.[378] Did you get into law school?

Notes

375. Eberhart's yacht was a 1928 34' (not 39') Playboat named *Reve.*
376. Scott Nearing (1883–1983), progressive economist/philosopher (Nearing turned eighty-nine years old, not eighty-seven, on August 6, 1972), and Fred McCuistion (1940–2022), writer from Little Rock who had studied at the University of Arkansas with Stanford and was friends with him and Campbell. *the Cape*: Cape Rosier on Penobscot Bay; this postcard's postmark is from Harborside, Maine, on the west coast of Cape Rosier.
377. Poet/scholar Daniel Hoffman (1923–2013) served as a contributing editor for *The Hollins Critic*, which published Stanford's poem "Chimera" in April 1972; Hoffman's book of criticism *Poe Poe Poe Poe Poe Poe Poe* was published in January 1972.
378. This postcard's stamp partially obscures the word conjectured in brackets in the previous paragraph (and possibly other words) and could feasibly be covering a signature.

WINDJAMMER ON COAST OF MAINE

WINDJAMMER ON COAST OF MAINE

Dear Bill, spending the night on a 39' yacht. Sailing all over. met, at Eberhart's house a Greek family with 3 daughters. Drinking at a shanty with fishermen, eating sea food and Canadian French women. ~~women~~ they were from Congo, Morocco, Greece, and Rumania. The ocean is a dream. will be here about 6 days or so. Met on the cape, spent the day with the 87 year old anarchist-farmer-philosopher Scott Nearing (ask Fred M. about him.) and many others, including poet Daniel Hoffman, whose book on Poe just came out. (He had heard of me!) Fine, but too cold. 38° last night! where will I put the stamp. Did you get into law school?

ADDRESS

Bill Willett
Old Arkana Road
Mtn. Home, Arkansas

783—Published by Augustus D. Phillips & Son, Northeast Harbor, Me., U.S.A.

HARBORSIDE AUG 11 PM 1972

National Parks Centennial
Wolf Trap Farm, Virginia
6¢

Stanford's August 11, 1972, postcard to Bill Willett. Stanford sent several postcards to Willett in August and September 1972 on his travels in New England and New York. This one is postmarked from Harborside, Maine, on the west coast of Cape Rosier, where Stanford, Broughton, and Babij visited Richard Eberhart's cottage and spent time on his yacht.

To Richard Eberhart: Mid-August 1972

[Inscription in *The Singing Knives*.]

For Richard Eberhart

If someone had told me, a few years ago in high school, when I first read your poems, that someday I would be asked to help make a film about you and be a guest in your home, I would have thought them dreaming. Then again, I never thought any of the poems I've written during the last sixteen years would ever be read—certainly not by you, under these circumstances. We are, if I may say so, both like Lawrence, in that we have going a love affair with death. We court her like a mysterious woman, a dream. So, I'm honored to give you these few poems that have, by chance, not gone to ashes.

Faithfully
Frank Stanford

Undercliff[379]
Summer 72

Notes

379. A road along Weir Cove on Cape Rosier.

To James Babij: Mid-August 1972

[Inscription in *The Singing Knives*.]

Dear Jim,[380]

In the future, let's hope we can resolve some of these visions on film. I'll keep in touch. For now, let's hope the doc.'s work out. It's been good travelling + learning the camera from you + with you. I have complete faith in your eyes + the genre itself. Until then

Frank Stanford

Cape Cod
Summer 72

Notes

380. James Babij (b. 1942), who had met Broughton while a student at the University of Washington. Shortly after the Cape Cod portion of the trip, Babij left the group and began attending the film school of the University of California, Los Angeles (UCLA), where he made *The Singing Knives*—a now-lost (approximately ten-minute) 8 mm film adapting part of Stanford's poem "The Singing Knives." Babij is credited in *It Wasn't a Dream: It Was a Flood* as an additional cinematographer.

To Bill Willett: Late August 1972

[Postcard of *The Unicorn Rests in a Garden*, from *The Unicorn Tapestries*, Metropolitan Museum of Art.]

Billy Willett
Old Arkana Rd.
Mtn. Home, Arkansas

Dear Bill,

Arrived here on the 21st;[381] how uncanny, when I think of a year ago.[382] All is well. Don't know how long we'll stay here. Hope you made it, old friend. Saw Dugan on the Cape; got drunk with him. Also, later on, in Mass. and Conn., filmed Richard Wilbur + Malcolm Cowley.[383] Glad to be done with it. Next summer, let's build a silo to live in! Saw one, loved it.[384] Hello to your family. Wish I had Sonny's address.[385] Feel bad about not writing him. Where is he? Say hello to Fred, Jimbo, Claude, Sherman . . .[386] I boogied right on out of there, didn't I.

Notes

381. I.e., New York City; the precise August 1972 postmark on this postcard is unclear—the date could be the 23rd or later.
382. Stanford and Linda Mencin married on August 21, 1971; also, in a July 9, 1972, letter to Willett, Stanford writes, "Cheryl was my body soul and spirit mind all. We have always been lovers. Linda found out about us last Spring, but she just thought it was nothing. . . . On the day Linda and I were married, she left."
383. Malcolm Cowley, poet/critic.
384. Stanford appreciated Wilbur's writing studio, converted from a silo; though correspondence from Stanford to Wilbur has been lost, a November 30, 1973, letter

from Wilbur to Stanford includes a contact and suggestions for getting a silo built or converted.

385. Big Time Sonny Morris.
386. Fred McCuistion; Jimbo Reynolds (1911–87), bootblack and cook; Claude Ricks (1936–2019), Church of Christ minister; and Sherman Morgan (1914–2001), proprietor of Sherman's Tavern, formerly located at 312 E. Rock Street in Fayetteville—Stanford's friends.

To Bill Willett: Late August 1972

[Postcard of *The Unicorn Surrenders to a Maiden*, from *The Unicorn Tapestries*, Metropolitan Museum of Art.]

Bill Willett
Rt. 2
Old Arkana Rd.
Mtn. Home, Arkansas

Dear Bill,

That was a fine letter you wrote. Of course, don't despair if you don't get in this time.[387] Sounds like fate keeps a marked deck when she plays with your family. Give them all my best. What can I say about Cheryl and New York: just in love. Don't know how long I'll be here, though. Every night I drink a fifth of cheap Cold Duck, and listen to classical music. Cheryl is in a very good, original semi classical + new rock group. Sort of like "A Beautiful Day," but better.[388] Do their own songs mostly, but can also play others well. All the musicians are fine classical ones. You would really love walking around the various ethnic parts of the city, listening to their speech + music, eating and drinking in their hangouts. Cheryl and I went to Chinatown the other night. (When I drink Cold Duck, I read French poetry.) The Village has it all. (Sonny would go mad.) Been to some great museums + films, etc. Sat down—quite by chance—next to Hal Holbrook, the actor, at a Bergman film. Then guess who sits down in front of me, but the film critic Paulene Kael.[389] Met + talked. Have the address—given to me by a lady from New H.—of Al Pacino's girlfriend.[390] Supposed to go over + have drinks with them. C and I live in the 3rd floor of a huge old house, completely surrounded by trees. (Like the cabin.) Lot of room. Clive, the Jamaican dancer, was student of the great dancer Martha Graham + good friend.[391] He led off Bernstein's "*MASS*."[392] An "encore."

{Would like to meet her.
I like writing poems on the Staten Island Ferry.

Bless you.
Love,
Frank}[393]

Notes

387. I.e., to law school; see Stanford's August 11, 1972, postcard to Willett above, par. 2. To this editor, Willett noted that he (thankfully) wasn't accepted to law school. Text to editor, August 9, 2023.
388. It's a Beautiful Day, a classical-rock-jazz band. Cheryl noted, to this editor, that her band, whose name was Catseye Ramble, played jazz-rock of sorts and included classical guitar, cello, piano, flute, French horn (by Cheryl), drums, and vocals (by Cheryl and another band member).
389. Pauline Kael (1919–2001), film critic for *The New Yorker*; see note 412 below.
390. Presumably actor Jill Clayburgh, with whom Pacino lived uptown, on Broadway, in 1972.
391. Martha Graham (1894–1991), dancer/choreographer—and founder of the Martha Graham Dance Company. Clive Thompson (b. 1935), a Jamaican dancer who moved to New York in 1960 and studied and worked with Graham from 1960 to 1970, worked with the Alvin Ailey American Dance Theater for more than a decade. Thompson and his wife, dancer Elizabeth "Liz" Thompson, owned 56 Harvard Avenue on Staten Island, where they lived with their two young sons; Cheryl rented a third-floor room from the Thompsons.
392. *MASS: A Theatre Piece for Singers, Players and Dancers*, a 1971 musical theater work composed by Leonard Bernstein (1918–90) and choreographed by Alvin Ailey (1931–89), dancer/choreographer. Thompson was a cast member in *MASS*'s ensemble at the Metropolitan Opera House in New York from June 28 through July 22, 1972.
393. *Marginalia: right side, left facing.*

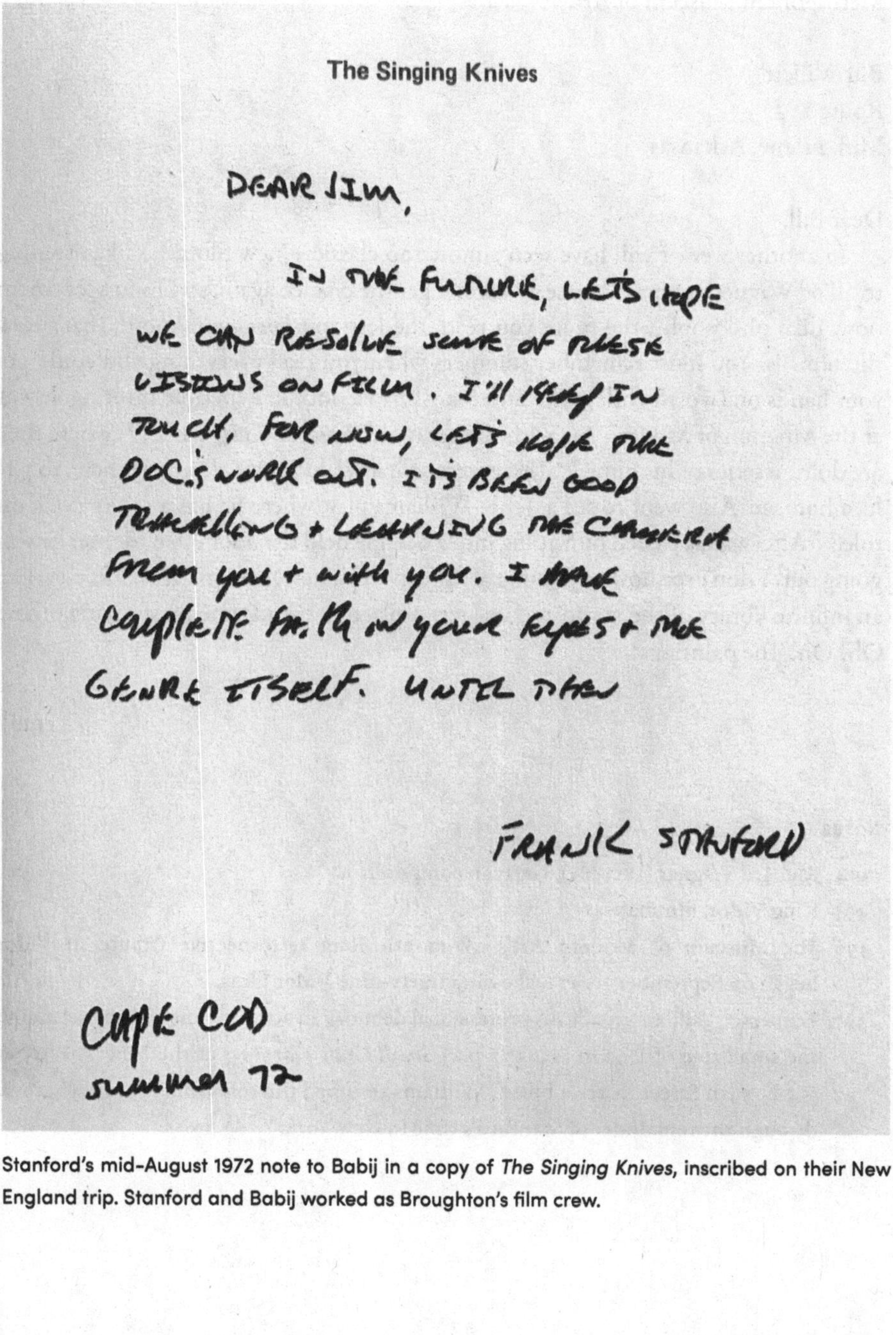

The Singing Knives

DEAR JIM,

IN THE FUTURE, LET'S HOPE WE CAN RESOLVE SOME OF THESE VISIONS ON FILM. I'LL KEEP IN TOUCH. FOR NOW, LET'S HOPE THE DOC.'S WORK OUT. IT'S BEEN GOOD TRAVELLING + LEARNING THE CAMERA FROM YOU + WITH YOU. I HAVE COMPLETE FAITH IN YOUR EYES + THE GENRE ITSELF. UNTIL THEN

FRANK STANFORD

CAPE COD
SUMMER 72

Stanford's mid-August 1972 note to Babij in a copy of *The Singing Knives*, inscribed on their New England trip. Stanford and Babij worked as Broughton's film crew.

To Bill Willett: September 13, 1972

[Postcard of *Saint George* from *The Belles Heures of Jean of France, Duc de Berry*, Metropolitan Museum of Art.]

Bill Willett
Route 2
Mtn. Home, Arkansas

Dear Bill,

In another week I will have seen almost 100 classic + new films. It's like listening to all of Wagner's operas at once.[394] I won't get the chance again, so I must view them now. Like philosophy, the more you read, the less you *know* you know. That's how "the film" is. You must remember summers when you read everything you could get your hands on (worthwhile). The other day I had a once in a lifetime meeting. It was at the Museum of Modern Art with the great old director King Vidor;[395] where they are doing a series of his films.[396] There were so many old stars + directors there, to pay him homage. Also went to see a Tenn. Williams play, where he has a minor walk on role.[397] Afterwards, passed him going into a bar. He held the door open for me; he was going out. I don't see how any young artist can work here, though. It is, this city, like an infinite library of the world and its arts. A place to spend time in, studying others. Oh! Oh! The paintings!

Frank

Notes

394. Richard Wagner (1813–83), German composer.
395. King Vidor, filmmaker.
396. The Museum of Modern Art's 2½-months-long retrospective tribute to Vidor began on September 1, 1972, showing thirty-nine Vidor films.
397. Tennessee Williams made his professional debut as an actor in June 1972 by assuming the small role of Doc in his 1972 play *Small Craft Warnings* at the New Theatre at 154 E. 54th Street. After a break, Williams resumed the role from August 30, 1972, through the remainder of Stanford's time in New York.

To Bill Willett: Circa September 15, 1972

Dear Bill,

I hadn't really intended to write a letter; I had selected postcards, eleven of them, bearing the likenesses of some of my favorite paintings, as seen in the multitude of museums, and typed out a little Coleridge–De Quincy–Lamb kind of essay on them.[398] Alas, I left them inside the pages of my newest manuscript—the first draft of which I sketched out on the trip, recalling the last year in Arkansas, and had begun a second draft of—when I lost it at some theatre, including my long series of cards to you.[399] Strange that all three manuscripts I've done since Fayetteville have all been lost: 1) the one I did in the hospital, lost by the P.O. 2) the other on the trip, blew out of Eberhart's yacht 3) this last one left in a picture show, where I'd just seen "The Virgin and the Gypsy" and "Elvira Madigan."[400] Anyway, I'd thrown in some lighter things, apart from the melancholic, which was, more or less, in the line of "still drinking wine in the picture shows, seeing about 5-or-6 films a day. Going to concerts, ballet, etc." Met the social organizer Saul Alinsky at a showing of "Ikiru."[401] Also, a coinsidental [*sic*] thing about asking for street directions at the Theosophical Society, and running into a girl that knew Linda. To go on, riding around in my underwear, drinking Cold Duck with this black Jamaican who lives here—not the dancer—: this is an ex taxi driver from Jamaica who likes country music, and fighting cocks. He speaks with a British accent. Went to a West Indian festival, etc. Claude, Jimbo, and Sherman would have really dug.[402] These are all the light things. However (riding in a half-hot M.G.[403]), most of what I wrote you was fairly serious. I was in a trance, when I jotted the ideas down on the Staten Island Ferry rides I have to take every day to get into the city, and was fairly filled with that inner hush when I typed them. At the moment, I'm not in that state of the poet's grace; I'm just drunk, so what I say, how I say it now, won't be like I had intended it. Imagine a diver, not a storyteller, telling about a recent and quite mysterious descent: I am speaking now, only of the 11 part essay, which was more like a painting by Blake or Rossetti, or a s. story Lawrence would write, and a saint would dream. I'll try to chant it in less than two pages; so it goes: as poet, I seek out the mystery of all women. Like a no account priest, I transubstantiate the body and spirit of their beauty, one into the other. This white bird of the dream flys from one woman to another, lighting whenever it will.[404] You gaze at the uncovered shoulder of this woman, or that one. You try to capture it. Like Byron, I long for the joy and misery of the chase. It takes seconds to find this mystery in some women; in others, years, sometimes several lifetimes. Once you have found it, the spell is broken. You seek another. The curse of the poet is: he can never see beauty and have it; it is one or another, unless you want to live a hellish life all your life, or are able to flirt easily. Oh yes, the spell will last a few days, but not for long; the mirror will crack and soak up all of anyone's beauty. So, what I am saying is: God bless the beauty in *all* women, in all things, wherever it hides like a wounded animal. The poet lives the present through the future by way of the past.[405] He remembers his dreams so that he will live them again, dream them again. I am saying when Linda + I were together, it was difficult to love. Now, she is beautiful. Now I love her. For I know we will never again be together. I *can be*, only now, the poet, who she loved. Already I am writing about her. She should be happy that we can care for one another, again. The innocence has come back to the two dream children. The "lovers of the moon" we are once more. Apart forever, we can endure. The first nights alone in Fayetteville I wrote her, telling her what I meant. She should never think that any woman is better than she. She is all women, as everywoman is. What the poet sees 👁, what the human being sees. I hope you understand. I am in love with beauty, for it is everywhere. Let her go her way, and I mine. Let us be happy always—and kind. For once, I can be kind to her. Let us all live. And now, I'll say this. I dreamed my old dream here. It's done. I've stayed too long with the dream. After five, no 3 or 4 days, it was gone; the spell was broken. It was time for my ship to journey. The dancer's wife wants to run away to Arkansas with me. No. I've already become enchanted with yet another girl, Diedre, a woman from England, who works in the museum. However, I know from my instinct to survive and write, I must not become so involved with their realities. Not for now, at least. [On the journey here, I almost did.][406] Diedre is a minister's daughter from the Lake Country in England.[407] She hates it there + here. And is, sorry to say, infatuated with the South, its violence, me, etc. She attributes things to me I really don't consider having. Maybe, I don't know. Anyway, I'm not going to become involved with either. [The English girl says she will support me + my writing, etc, but I'll never do that again. It doesn't give love a running chance. Do you understand?][408] I've got an invitation to go read my poems, if I had copies of them, in Boston. A place there is going to do another book. That makes 3 more in the gin. Diedré wants to quit her job and go, buy a car etc. If I was as cruel as she thinks, I'd go, but really I'm not that cruel, though Linda + Cheryl might think otherwise; including a few more. As you can see, I'm quite mad. Do you understand? So, Byron, what can you tell me now? When I'm not really looking for advice anyway, since I know I must set my own course in the stars. When I saw you, Cheryl was the brightest star, now another. Linda is a constellation all by her little self. Forgive me Lord.

Until, then. Let me know how you are doing my good friend, and is there news of Sonny, Jimbo, and Claude. My best to your family.

Frank

Notes

398. Samuel Taylor Coleridge (1772–1834), English poet and essayist; Thomas De Quincey (1785–1859), English essayist and writer; and Charles Lamb (1775–1834), English essayist and poet.

399. This letter is postmarked September 16, 1972, from Washington, DC, but was evidently penned in New York. Ca. September 14, Stanford had written a postcard to Willett, which he left in a manuscript book in a cinema (Murray Hill Theatre, it appears—see note 400 below). In an emotional thirty-five-hundred-word letter to Willett (whom she didn't know), dated September 17 and postmarked September 20, Cheryl explains about Stanford having left the book in the theater (and his having been upset that the cinema's staff hadn't been able to find it) and notes that he left her, unawares, on September 15 while she was at work. Cheryl and friend/housemate Liz Thompson managed to retrieve the book, which Stanford had said to be half-filled with manuscripts, from the theater; "Bill, a fantasy . . . ," Cheryl wrote (ellipsis in original)—the book contained only an apparent draft of the text of the ca. September 14 postcard, on the last page, as well as the postcard (but no poetry). Cheryl included the postcard with her letter to Willett. In comparing their content, it is clear that Stanford's letter to Willett is a rewrite of the ca. September 14 postcard.

Upon leaving 56 Harvard Avenue, Stanford left Cheryl a note:

> I think you know I must be alone for a while.
> How long it will take, I don't know.
> As you can see, I'm quite mad. Write + send my mail.
> Until then, love
>
> Frank.

The physical loneness didn't equate to epistolary loneness, though. On September 17, Stanford penned a letter to Cheryl, mailed on the afternoon of September 18 (postmarked in Russellville, Arkansas, likely en route to Subiaco—showing that he had returned to Arkansas posthaste), and several further letters between Frank and Cheryl were exchanged in October and early November.

Re: the loss of manuscripts, see note 50 above re: Rexroth's point about Lawrence having frequently misplaced his poetry manuscripts. Also cf. *The Battlefield*, lines 11419–21, with Francis noting that whatever writing he produces seems to vanish one way or another, "or I leave it at the pitchu / show or something shoot"—lines almost certainly typed in Stanford's spring 1972 work on the poem.

400. *The Virgin and the Gypsy* (1970), dir. Christopher Miles (adapting Lawrence's 1930 novella), and *Elvira Madigan* (1967), dir. Bo Widerberg. The two films screened at Cinema 5's Murray Hill Theatre at 3rd Avenue at 34th Street in Manhattan from September 13 to 20, 1972.

401. Saul Alinsky (1909–72), community activist / political writer, and *Ikiru* (1952), dir. Akira Kurosawa. *Ikiru* screened at the Elgin Cinema at 8th Avenue at 19th Street in Manhattan on September 11 and 12, 1972.

402. Brooklyn's West Indian–American Day Parade on September 4, 1972; roughly 150,000 people attended.

403. *M.G.*: MG, British sports car brand popular in the 1960s and 1970s.

404. From It's a Beautiful Day's signature song, "White Bird" (1969)—about a caged bird with glowing eyes that dreams of an aspen tree: "White bird must fly / Or she will die." Also cf. note 263 above and *The Battlefield*, lines 15204–7.

405. Cf. *The Battlefield*, lines 6538, 8717, 9138–41, and 12285.

406. Brackets Stanford's.

407. The Lake District, a scenic region in North West England.

408. Opening bracket Stanford's; closing bracket added.

To Bill Willett: Circa Late September 1972

[On the back of a page torn from *William Blake's Illustrations to "The Grave"* (Double Elephant Folio & Quarto, 1969).][409]

Dear Bill,

Death has always been my mistress. In a black cape in the dead of winter by the beach I have waited for her rendezvous. This woman I spoke to you of called Cheryl. We have always been lovers, in all times. When one lover betrays another, as I did her, there is only one ultimate price: death. She knows that. As a poet, Cheryl is my wife. As just another citizen, Linda is my wife. I've been unfaithful to both. As I am poet, I love all women. There is one in Fayetteville who you know {by acquaintance} {(but you don't know who I speak of)}, older than myself, a married woman with a family. No one knows about us. I will not tell you her name, as I promised never to do so: there is too much to lose, if others should find out. Anyway, it was brief and sweet. If this woman should one day come up to you and ask about me, tell her I loved her (I told her I didn't). She was another who had to have an abortion. At night, I dream of a fleet of coffins under sail, bearing the bodies of dead infants. To all the queens of sorrow I say good night. Death like a solitary beach I walk, like a ship I sail alone, like a horse I ride in the night: "that I might all forget the human race, and hating no one, love but only her."[410]

Give my love to Cheryl and Linda.

yours,
Frank

Notes

409. Specifically, this letter was written on the back of the book's page (unopened at publication) for *The Reunion of the Soul & the Body*, William Blake's twelfth and final

(published) drawing for his 1808 book illustrating Robert Blair's poem *The Grave* (1743). Willett next heard from Stanford around the close of 1972, after Stanford had arrived in Eureka Springs; they met at the New Orleans Hotel, and Stanford asked Willett if he still had this letter, which Willett affirmed. Stanford then handed Willett the book, told him to reinsert the page into it, and keep it. Though Billy the Jew in *The Battlefield* is modeled after Stanford's Jewish next-door neighbor (from childhood) in Memphis's Audubon Park neighborhood, Bill Phillips (b. 1948) (see lines 2846 and 14456), Billy's act of opening "the dusty book of Blake" (line 14478) could have also been inspired by this experience with Willett (with the two Billys being blended there).

410. From canto 4, stanza 177, lines 1587–88 of Byron's four-canto narrative poem, *Childe Harold's Pilgrimage*: "That I might all forget the human race, / And, hating no one, love but only her!"

To Irv Broughton: Late September 1972

Dear Irv,

Tried to get in touch with you several times. Guess you'd already left, but I'm sure this address is correct. Waited to hear if you were coming back up to shoot more film. In the other letter, I said I met a German cameraman who was vacationing in this country with some of his equipment: Eclair, Nagra, etc.[411] He would have done any filming in or around the East Coast for a ride, food, to the West Coast, where he was sailing a boat to Japan. I said all this before. Guess you ran out of money + drive. (He was in Cape Cod a couple of the same days we were.)

While I was in N.Y. I saw over 100 films, mostly old classics from every country. Met the great director King Vidor. Went to see two Bergman films, and to the left of me, and to the right of me were Hal Holbrook and Pauline Kael.[412] Tenn. Williams opened a door for me, as I was entering a bar. Lots of film people, critics, directors, actresses go to films—matinees. A rich English girl called Diedré, who let me in the Museum of Modern Art free every day, and I got together. She wanted to quit her job, rent a car, and go to Arkansas with me, but I was unwilling to get that involved. Sure, I could have got a ride, then dumped her, but she was nice. She hated England + N.Y. Also, the dancer's wife, who is a dancer herself, wanted to leave her family and run off to the South, but *no* again. Both of them were beautiful. I drank Cold Duck every night. I listened, saw, did so much. This is what I did. Without telling Cheryl, I packed up and left with Diedré, or however you spell her name.[413] In Washington D.C., while she was visiting her friends, I split from her Mercedes Benz—rented, etc. and caught a bus south. I got drunk with a 89 year old Negro, who was going back to Cleveland,

Miss. to die.[414] He knew my uncle, had actually bought whiskey from him. 100 stories to tell you about N.Y. Lots of beautiful women. I'm in the highest spirits I've been in for a long, long time—almost like after Hollins. A brother is coming by to get me to do a little labor + then go fishing so I don't have time to thank you for all you've done, given me the opportunity to do. Tell me what's happening with the footage. How broke are you? I'll be driving a truck in a few days. I have a couple of your books, you must have some of mine, as I didn't make it to N.Y. with them. Maybe they were left on Cape Cod. I don't care. What has been processed? I guess I told you that guy said the Bell + Howell was fucked up, unless he was fucked up.[415] Keep in touch.[416] {What has happened to Jim. Wrote him. Is he in UCLA?}[417]

yours,
Frank

Before I forget: unless you are planning to go to press soon with that long MS., send it back to me right now, as I have someone to type it over. Try not to mess up page numbers, as it has none. {Mail it 1st Class}[418]

Notes

411. *Eclair*: former film camera company; *Nagra*: producer of portable audio recorders.
412. Stanford was likely seeing the films at the Elgin Cinema. Elgin screened Bergman's *Wild Strawberries* and *The Magician* from August 24 to 26, 1972; Bergman's *The Seventh Seal* and *Through a Glass Darkly* from August 27 to 28; and Bergman's *The Virgin Spring* and *Smiles of a Summer Night* from August 29 to 30.
413. This name is variously spelled "Diedre," "Diedré," "Deidre," and "Deidré" across Stanford's letters. The discrepancies are his own.
414. Cf. lines 74–81 of "Blue Yodel of the Desperado" (and see note 364 above):

> I met up with this English woman with plenty
> That very night
> While she was in the powder room
> I went back to the hotel
> Stole her rubies
> And stowed away on the first rig I saw
> A ship full of wild horses
> Bound for America
> (Stanford, *Light the Dead See*, 65)

415. Bell & Howell, former manufacturer of movie and still cameras.

416. In an October 8, 1972, letter to Cowley, Broughton notes that he is back in Seattle after the cross-country trip on whose projects he had gone "knowingly in the hole" and writes, "Frank who was to spend a yr immersed in the declarations of the city, stuck it out a month. . . . Frank wrote the other day and is cheerful, and it is as if he validated home, or something."

417. *Marginalia: left side, right facing.*

418. *Marginalia: left side, right facing.*

To Irv Broughton: Late September 1972

September, 72
Subiaco

Dear Irv,

I need that MS. pretty bad, because I have to have this girl type some of it to send in with the Guggenheim application, which Dugan has provided me.[419] If I don't have it soon, won't be able to have parts of it typed; besides, the deadline will be up. Go ahead and keep it if you're setting it up for your magazine; I'll feed them a line. Still have doppelgänger thoughts about that parabolic dream, that paramnesiac reverie: either it is worthless, or parts of it are innocently inimitable; it is, if Jim has read it and will understand,[420] a "parallax" of pain, a clairvoyant "dissolve". Are you O.K.?

yours,
Frank

Please keep the page
order the same, as I
have nothing to check
it against.

Notes

419. Broughton returned the manuscript of *The Battlefield* to Stanford in early October; Stanford replied on October 13, noting that Broughton had neglected to include the "partially typed, partially handwritten" synopsis "via bits of paper," adding, "I *need* it for myself." Stanford had sent "an absurd&inadequate synopsis" with the manuscript

to Broughton in July 1972, noting in the accompanying letter, "This manuscript is what drove me mad. I don't want to talk about it. It caused the demise of all that was past and present."

In fall 1972, Stanford applied (unsuccessfully) for a Guggenheim Fellowship, with Dugan and Cowley as recommenders.

420. I.e., Babij.

To George Hitchcock: October 1972

October, 72

Dear Mr. Hitchcock,

Could you look at these? There are several other titles for the first poem; I could just say "For L." I would know, but would anyone else? Or is that a problem at all? Sometimes, I don't know if I'm guilty of meliorism or solipsism, or both in my poems.

yours,
Frank Stanford

Would you consider a long poem?

To William L. Fox: October 1972

October, 1972

Dear Bill,

Yours of the 25th last month at hand.[421] "the mind reader" has never been published, anywhere, so you can use it in your *W.C.P.R.*[422] Maybe I can clean up some confusion by a few details. If you have the MS. *"St. Francis . . . ."*, you should have over 50 poems, of all lengths, written anywhere from 57–64. You can distinguish these poems by the lack of caps. in title and first line and first letter of every line. There is, extant, a long section from a very long poem ⅔'s destroyed. It is called "the battlefield where the moon says I love you,"—about 300 pages long. It is also from St. Francis. It is unnumbered + unstapled, so the only way it can be put together is if I can get hold of the numbered copy—which I'm trying to do. Some of the other poems go up to 15 pages, but you shouldn't have any trouble with them as they are stapled. Could you take 5 minutes and do this, which will make it all much easier: send me a list of all *titles* you have. Also, tell me if you have that long one.

Any poems that have titles in caps. aren't from *St. Francis*. They are newer, probably from a MS. I call *Naegling*, which isn't that good—too literary.

As far as I know, only 4 poems from *St. Francis* have been published: "the buried sword", "keeping the lord's night watch", "the paramour", and "the actresses of night" in *Iowa Review*.[423] However, six editors want to take a look at whatever you don't want—some for books, some for poems in magazines.

There are two poems I don't have copies of that I sort of liked. You took, that is Dave Walker, took one, Esquire the other. They were called: "Nocturnal Ships of the Past" and "The Blood Boot."[424] Maybe you have them around. (I have no idea what L. sent you.)[425]

I'm sorry you have to do all this petty work on account of my laziness and unprofessionalism. Anyway, take whatever you want. Send me that list if you can, please. There is a lot of time for both of us, yet, to talk about poems + backgrounds, etc. Someday I'll tell you, if you don't tell anybody, and don't print it. Until then.

yours,
Frank

(Send mail here) (I saw 100 films in N.Y.)
Coury House
Subiaco, Arkansas
72865

P.S. Another trait of *St. Francis* is:
No spaces, stanzas, white space, indentions.

Notes

421. Fox begins his September 25, 1972, letter to Stanford by sharing that he is thenceforth editing *West Coast Poetry Review* in addition to *Edge* and asks if Stanford's poem "the mind reader" has been published elsewhere in the US, noting that he'd like to use it for *WCPR*. He adds, " 'St. Francis and the Wolf' looks amazing" and mentions that he is hoping to receive, by mail, the version of it with pages that were not "unnumbered."
422. "[T]he mind reader" appeared in the Fall 1972 issue of *West Coast Poetry Review*.
423. See note 186 above.
424. See note 203 above re: "Nocturnal Ships of the Past." "The Blood Boot" is an unpublished poem that appears across Stanford's archives, including in the manuscript *Let Him Lay There: Some Early Poems*. Stanford's work never appeared in *Esquire*.
425. *L.*: Linda Stanford.

P. 32.

The Reunion of the Soul & the Body

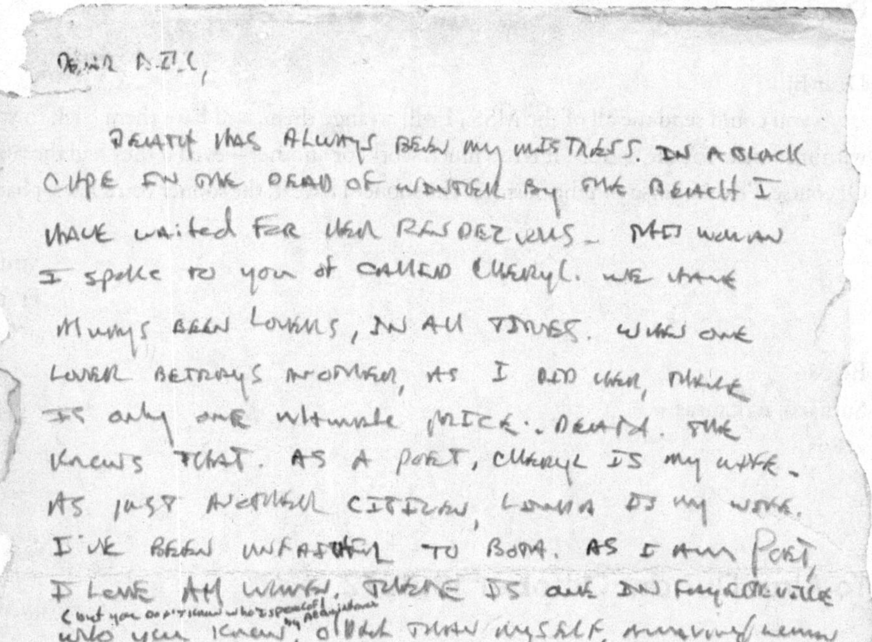

Dear B.I.C.,

Death has always been my mistress. In a black cape in the dead of winter by the beach I have waited for her rendezvous. That woman I spoke to you of called Cheryl. We have always been lovers, in all times. When one lover betrays another, as I did her, there is only one ultimate price. Death. She knows that. As a poet, Cheryl is my wife. As just another citizen, Linda is my wife. I've been unfaithful to both. As I am Poet, I love all women. There is one in Fayetteville (but you don't know who I speak of by acquaintance) who you know, other than myself, a marrying woman with a family. No one knew about us. I will not tell you her name, as I promised never to do so: there is too much to lose, if others should find out. Anyway, it was brief and sweet. If that woman should one day come up to you and ask about me, tell her I loved her (I told her I didn't.) She was another who had to have an abortion. At night I dream of a fleet of coffins which sail, bearing the bodies of dead infants. To all the others I say goodnight. Death lover solitary beach of sorrow I walk, like a ship I sail alone, like a knife I ride in the night: "That I might all forget the human race, and hating no one, love but only her."

Give my love to Cheryl and Linda.

Yours,
Frank

Here and previous: Stanford's ca. late September 1972 letter to Willett and the page torn from *William Blake's Illustrations to "The Grave"* on which it was written—i.e., Stanford wrote the letter on the verso of Blake's final drawing for *The Grave, The Reunion of the Soul & the Body.*

To William L. Fox: October 1972

October, 1972

Dear Bill,

If you could send me all of the MSS., I will arrange them, and have them back to you within a week. You are correct, it is too much work for another—even if they had the time. Of course, I'll reimburse you the postage. The sooner I have it, the sooner you'll have it back.

yours,
Frank

Box 86
Subiaco, Arkansas
72865

To Alan Dugan: October 16, 1972

October, 1972

Dear Alan,

The last few days have proved that the gift of dreaming things before they happened, something I thought I had lost with childhood, is still with me.[426] As you know, I knew we would meet that day in the bookstore. I took my editor's car, over his objection, so that rendezvous would take place. A few days before, why did I pull into the "Cove" gallery asking for directions?[427] Why, when I caught the bus south, eventually running through Memphis + Mississippi, did I sit next to an ancient Negro man, who had heard of my father, who had shot dice with some of the names and men I remember, who was a friend of my uncle's foreman and, who had bought bootlegged whiskey from my uncle himself? How is it that I partially "lived out" the screenplay I had written about the young poet in the monastery? I have had no control over the events that have repeated themselves once again, as if on cue of the dead young man who wrote St. Francis many years ago. What made me select, at random, the poems I sent you? Was it because I knew they were near the truths that were about to happen? I haven't told you about all the premonitions I had in the desolate parts of the forests, when I was working this spring. Alan, you must believe me when I say everything I "saw" in the woods came true. Please don't think I'm deluded when I say these things. How familiar are you with Leibnitz?[428] Have you paid any mind to Alfred Jarry?[429] Paschal?[430]

So I can finish this letter and type my poems, I only want to say these few things: it is midnight, or thereabouts. I am sitting outside on a lighted porch; a quarter mile away on a hill, I can see the top of the monastery bell tower, lit up, which strikes every quarter hour.[431] There is heat lightning all around the dome of the hemisphere. There are 300 boys and 100 monks asleep, and dreaming of the same things. My mother's ducks are standing on one leg; her nine black cats are eating crawdads; the same old brother, who walked in his sleep 8 years ago, is walking tonight. There is something of a meteor shower. The air smells like butchered hogs and soybeans at the feed mill. The homosexual barber who raises bloodhounds is out running his dogs, but the sound you hear is a pack of wolves. Yes, a pack of wolves are howling their crazy love. I have recorded it on tape, but unerased is a hint of Vivaldi.[432] This is not surreal, this is strange, like "that wind blowing in for several thousand miles all night long." If Carl Dreyer were alive to listen to my ramblings![433] If Jean Cocteau could hear me now! The dilemma of Dali + Bunuel![434] Your poem which is so much like "Premonition of the Spanish Civil War."[435] A port for your love. I dream of your father-in-law.[436] And there is that man that draws the shadows of the abbeys at noon, Georgio D'Chirharico;[437] I cannot spell his name. A boat, an egg, a triangle, and one uncovered breast. This is no poem. A long dark arm. A schoolgirl's eyes that can X-ray a watch. The basses of the men singing in the churches bombed six times, as deep as the rocks in the bottom of the St. Francis River.[438] A knife with no gravity. Flower-bed of soft testicles and mystery. Death with its sexual melancholy. NAILS. A woman grading papers with water in her shoes near the Wolfe River.[439] [Specter of my potential in the film genre.][440] I am not a self-promoter, so any screenplay I wrote would go unresolved, any film, however technically incompetent, would go unseen. My agent is the butterfly. I feel like I'm bleeding ALAN when I don't have a chance at films. I am an early riser. I read your poems, some better than Villon, or Lawrence. Listen to this: ASK your wife. I have said all this in rhythms in my poems, BUT: sometimes I think all my songs are sketches that are to be resolved in cinematic drawings. Shelley! Didn't Blake, in his Poetical Sketches, and later on, think in terms of his illustration, printing, with his Songs of I. + E.?[441] But a poem is a poem; it must make its own way. Rossetti said his best poems were paintings, his best paintings, poems.[442] What about us. I've already got a scenario in mind for my friend's proposed work on you. If I had a hand in it, I'd want to shy away from the usual documentary + interviews approach. I would film you strange as you are in your poems, as you were when you wrote me those crazy letters last year, when I dreamed in my cabin, looking at the fire. But this is something we can think on, something different. Child with an amulet and a tattoo, eating shrimp. A mirror that comes up to your waist. A country girl I fucked in the back of her daddy's truck. My saddle-sore ass. Phoenix with lips. The bottom of the class. The hypnotist who can transmute words into acts.

Is there such a thing as a syntax of images (not poetry, Eisenstein collisions[443]) instead of a story accompanied by words? Each day that goes by my senses is an intrigue. "As a medium speaks out of his trance, the poet is unskillful when he speaks."[444] Destiny. NOBLE MUSIC. The same age as I, the labyrinth I saunter through in half-sleep.[445] Some other kingdom. (If I am keeping you from something, go do it.) I feel like I am in space—full of wolves. I can write any kind of dialogue. I would never write these things to anyone but you. Should I be sleeping. Flutes. Unicorns that gallop under water. Both of us are pioneers, not inventors—our thought patterns, nummulites. Women, gimbals for our compasses. Oysters, who would like to weep with Dylan T.[446] We are going to winnow the dark from the hair, weeping around our feet. We are going to *become* the darkening snow. Your dark ship, your wife's dark body. Esmeralda, poolhalls, furrows, men with grey hair and syphilis, weeping at the juke box.[447] The moon that thieves—the colt of darkness. Thorns. Yawns. [I repeat, this is nothing but a letter to lift your exhausted heart.][448] Snow that Judith saw about the time she met you. Terrible + strange enough to blow a cross over. Silence that goes where ever you go. Ubiquitous collisions. Passed over, passed out. Chaste without a woman with a vision without a God. A big house I could live in again. A traveling show, gigolo a way with so many ways. "My locality gave me myself, I have not stopped being local."[449] Seven years without you. A song, an escort to the gallows. A death, mimesis in exile, one more mistress; NONPAROUS. So I can't name two girls Magda and Norn.[450] Parataxis because I see myself in so many weeds. I was baby oblivion. Too many roots, despondent (scrub worms I thought were shrimp). Paregoric. All those old paratactic poems. Telekinesis. Pain. Paramnesia. [All these words from around the same place in the dictionary, describing my manuscripts—I marked them ten years ago!][451] Parallax of agony all poets know. Apophasis. All distance and time. "My eyelids are heavy, my horse is silent."[452]

Parabolic Funambulle[453]

quoting I[454]

yours,

Frank

Notes

426. Cf. the clairvoyant abilities of *The Battlefield*'s hero Francis Gildart; from Stanford's words in a May 10, 1972, letter to Dugan ("A.B. Fact: I was examined for E.S.P. and shit like that a long time ago") and this letter, it appears that Francis's clairvoyance was based on Stanford's firsthand experience. Re: Stanford's "A.B. Fact" (i.e., autobiographical fact), also cf. *The Battlefield*, lines 1328–29: "and I won't have to take no more of them tests to see if / I was a mind reader."

427. The Cove Gallery, an art gallery in Wellfleet, Massachusetts—just south of Truro, where Dugan and Shahn lived—known for showing Shahn's work.
428. Gottfried Wilhelm Leibniz (1646–1716), German philosopher and mathematician who asserted that all possibilities would be actualized—that "the actual universe is the collection of all existent possibles." Quoted in Nicholas Jolley, ed., *The Cambridge Companion to Leibniz* (Cambridge University Press, 2004), 213.
429. Alfred Jarry (1873–1907), French writer who invented the concept of pataphysics, which examines "the laws governing exceptions" and "describe[s] a universe which can be—and perhaps should be—envisaged in the place of the traditional one." *Exploits & Opinions of Doctor Faustroll, Pataphysician: A Neo-Scientific Novel*, trans. Simon Watson Taylor (Exact Change, 1996), 21–22.
430. Blaise Pascal (1623–62), French philosopher, mathematician, and Catholic theologian whose theories (e.g., Pascal's wager—that it is pragmatically more optimal to believe in the existence of God than not to) seminally influenced decision theory and probability theory, as well as Leibniz.
431. Stanford is apparently writing from Dorothy's home in the housing addition west of Subiaco Abbey.
432. Antonio Vivaldi (1678–1741), Italian composer.
433. Carl Theodor Dreyer, Danish filmmaker.
434. Luis Buñuel, Spanish Mexican filmmaker. Dalí and Buñuel cowrote Buñuel's 1929 film *Un chien andalou* and his 1930 film *L'Age d'Or* but fell out while making the latter, largely over political differences (Buñuel holding to leftist beliefs, Dalí sympathizing with fascist ones); Buñuel later cut ties with Dalí, and the Surrealist group expelled him.
435. *Soft Construction with Boiled Beans (Premonition of Civil War)*, a 1936 painting by Dalí. Dalí painted the work six months before the start of the Spanish Civil War and claimed that he had done so to depict the atrocity of the war, which he claimed he had previsioned. Stanford appears to be likening Dugan's poem "On the Civil War on the East Coast of the United States of North America 1860–64" to Dalí's painting; in Dugan's poem, the speaker claims to possess a kind of omniscience and to have fought in multiple wars across centuries.
436. Ben Shahn; see note 370 above.
437. Giorgio de Chirico's paintings, often featuring long shadows adjacent to buildings and Roman arcades, influenced the Surrealists.
438. A tributary of the Mississippi River that flows from southeastern Missouri through northeastern Arkansas, joining the Mississippi River north of Helena, Arkansas. In *The Battlefield*, Francis states, "I know there is such a thing as the St. Francis River" (line 266); C. D. Wright notes in the preface to *The Battlefield*'s second edition that A. F. Stanford built levees along this river. Wright, preface to *The Battlefield Where the Moon Says I Love You*, 2nd ed., by Frank Stanford (Lost Roads Publishers, 2000), n.p.

439. Stanford possibly means the Wolf River—running from northern Mississippi for roughly one hundred miles to Memphis, where it flows into the Mississippi River.

440. Brackets Stanford's.

441. *Songs of Innocence and of Experience* (1794), an illuminated book of poems by Blake.

442. As Rossetti scholar Robert M. Cooper notes, for Rossetti (who was influenced by Blake), "writing and painting were coequal and often interdependent"; Rossetti—who composed ekphrastic poems for his paintings and also wrote of "poetic painting"—stated that "the noblest picture is a painted poem" and wrote, "My poetic tendencies . . . chiefly give value to my pictures: only painting being . . . a livelihood—I have put my poetry chiefly in that form. On the other hand . . . my verse, being unprofitable, has remained . . . unprostituted." Robert M. Cooper, *Lost on Both Sides: Dante Gabriel Rossetti: Critic and Poet* (Ohio University Press, 1970), 22, 112, 188, and 240.

443. Per Soviet montage theory and its leading theorist, filmmaker Sergei Eisenstein, effective, powerful montage arises from the "collision" of dialectical images or shots. Eisenstein, *Film Form: Essays in Film Theory*, ed. and trans. Jay Leyda (Harvest / Harcourt Brace Jovanovich, 1977), 37, 49.

444. A rough quote from Cocteau's 1932 introduction of *Le Sang d'un poète*; see Stanford's February 14, 1972, letter to Dugan above and Stanford's February 18, 1972, letter to Broughton above, both of which also quote from Cocteau's introduction, and see also Cocteau's words in note 218 above.

445. See note 233 above.

446. Dylan Thomas.

447. *Esmeralda*: a character in Victor Hugo's novel *The Hunchback of Notre-Dame* (1831).

448. Opening bracket Stanford's; closing bracket added.

449. From the "Recomendaciones finales" ("Final Recommendations") section of Neruda's "Testamento de otoño" ("Autumn Testament"), the final poem in *Estravagario* (1958): "El pueblo me identificó / y nunca dejé de ser pueblo." As published in Pablo Neruda, *A New Decade: Poems 1958–1967*, trans. Alastair Reid (Grove, 1969), the lines read: "My locality gave me my self / and I have not stopped being local."

450. *Nonparous*: nulliparous—relating to / involving a female who has borne no children. Magda is a common given name, and Norn is a Nordic given name based on the Norns—deities in Norse mythology signifying fate. Stanford could be alluding vaguely to fetuses he begot that were aborted.

451. Brackets Stanford's.

452. Stanford may be quoting himself here; an "(I)" after a quote in a dedication of *The Singing Knives* by Stanford to Dugan (following a quotation blending two excerpts from Byron), inscribed on Eberhart's yacht at Cape Rosier, Maine, in August 1972, appears to mean that Stanford was quoting himself. See, e.g., the phrase "All quotes are mine." Stanford, *What About This*, 544.

453. Stanford is, in all probability, alluding to the Théâtre des Funambules (specifically as depicted in *Les Enfants du paradis*). Stanford's use (in both letters and poetry) of "funambulle" (or *funambule*) has a kind of double meaning, as a funambulist is both a tightrope walker (i.e., an acrobat) and an individual who displays great mental agility (e.g., perhaps, clairvoyance). Cf. *The Battlefield*, lines 5506–7, 9010–11, and 12205–6.

454. See note 452 above.

To Irv Broughton: Late October 1972

Monday, Oct., 72
Subiaco

My Good Friend,

When I was in despair, you helped me, more than you know, get away from it. I know the feeling you must be having now: you *doubt* everything + everyone, including yourself. Each day is an anonymous crook, each person a strand of bobwire for your brow. Don't despair, old friend. I'm writing a poem *for* you, something I don't do. This life is so hard when you do things for others, but, as you know, others are our brothers. We will make these films for these poets, so they may be remembered. No one cares now, but now is not what we intend. To be living is beautiful. We have consecrated our hands to others' hands, beautiful ones, no matter how ugly. If we go under, we'll go down with a little left in the bottle so others can drink.

always
Frank

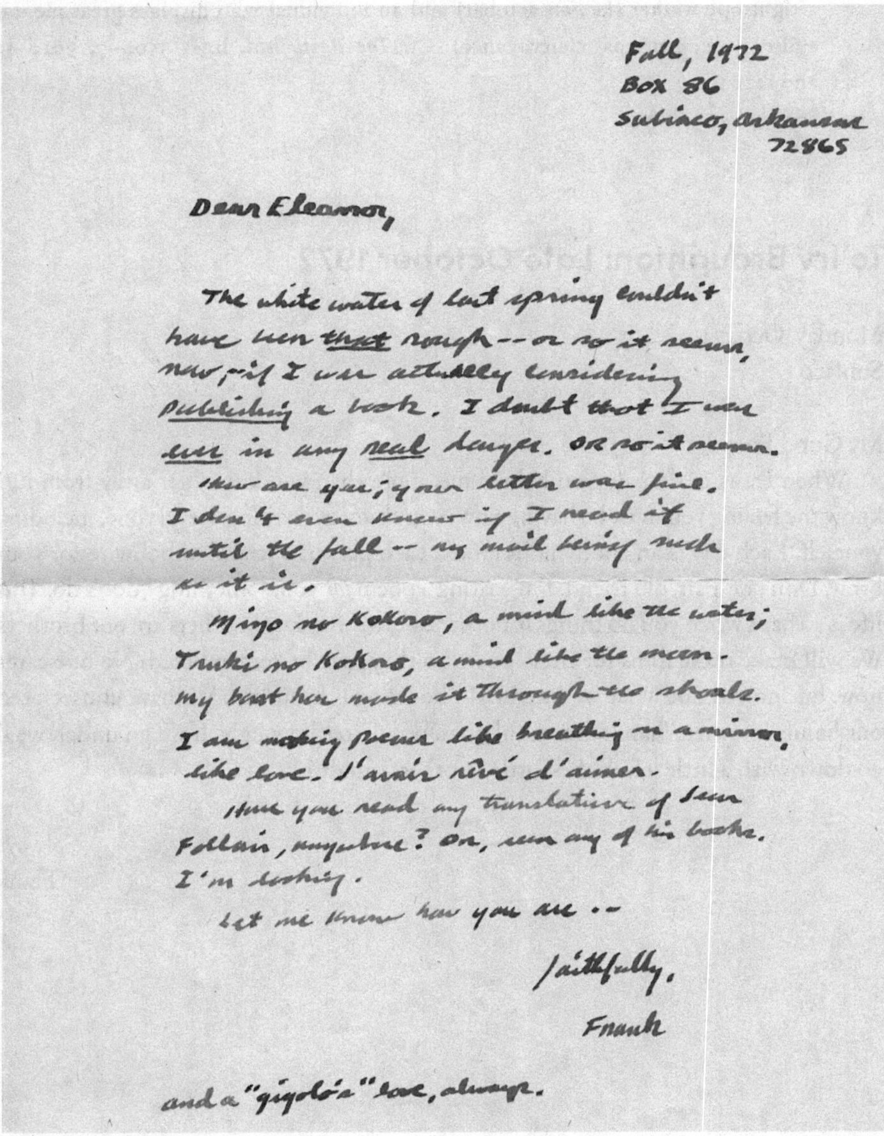

Fall, 1972
Box 86
Subiaco, Arkansas
72865

Dear Eleanor,

The white water of last spring couldn't have been *that* rough -- or so it seems, now, if I was actually considering publishing a book. I doubt that I was ever in any real danger. Or so it seems.

How are you; your letter was fine. I don't even know if I read it until the fall -- my mail being such as it is.

Mizu no Kokoro, a mind like the water; Tsuki no Kokoro, a mind like the moon. My boat has made it through the shoals. I am making poems like breathing on a mirror, like love. J'avais rêvé d'aimer.

Have you read any translations of Jean Follain, anywhere? Or, seen any of his books. I'm looking.

Let me know how you are ..

faithfully,

Frank

and a "gigolo's" love, always.

Starting in late September 1972, Stanford also sometimes wrote in an elegant forward-slanted cursive, especially through his mid-twenties and when writing with a fountain pen. Stanford's fall 1972 letter to Eleanor Bender, which accompanied an inscribed copy of *The Singing Knives*, is an early example.

To Eleanor Bender: Fall 1972

Fall, 1972[455]
Box 86
Subiaco, Arkansas 72865

Dear Eleanor,

The white water of last spring couldn't have been *that* rough—or so it seems, now,—if I was actually considering *publishing* a book. I doubt that I was *ever* in any *real* danger. Or so it seems.

How are you; your letter was fine. I don't even know if I read it until the fall—my mind being such as it is.

Mizo no Kokoro, a mind like the water;[456] Tsuki no Kokoro, a mind like the moon.[457] My boat has made it through the shoals. I am making poems like breathing in a mirror, like love. J'avais rêvé d'aimer.[458]

Have you read any translations of Jean Follain, anywhere? Or, seen any of his books. I'm looking.

Let me know how you are—

faithfully,
Frank

and a "gigolo's" love, always.

[Enclosed is a copy of *The Singing Knives*, inscribed with:]

Today a few weeds
From my garden
One night a rose

For
Eleanor

You know how the evening
Is
All of them strange
Enough to be alike
None of them are
The same
For me you are a part

Of the night
And you know how that is
I don't know you
~~Can you~~
May you always go
With that dark saunter
Even though your hair
Is slowly fair
I don't know I've never seen
You

Frank

Subiaco Abbey
Fall 1972

Notes

455. The placement of this letter and inscription within Stanford's fall 1972 letters herein is based on analysis of his penmanship and the ink and paper used; the correspondence appears to have likely been penned between mid-October and mid-November.
456. A Japanese phrase commonly transliterated *mizu no kokoro* (a mind like the water).
457. A martial arts training phrase.
458. The opening of Robert Desnos's sonnet "Le Paysage" ("The Landscape"), one of his last poems, published posthumously in *Calixto, suivi de Contrée* (1962): "I had dreamed of loving." Trans. Stephen Romer, in *Essential Poems and Writings of Robert Desnos*, ed. Mary Ann Caws (Black Widow Press, 2007), 320–21.

To Alan Dugan: Late October 1972

sometimes in the ridges
the wild dogs sing
tame as monks, and
can be called like the months
of the year to come

October

Dear Alan,

If you were me, here alone, walking through the meadows and mountains, having a vision not too unlike the ones Whitman, Blake, and the singers in the Bible had, not thinking at all in terms of the literary world—but rather cells of inner worlds, almost audible in their movement—or of ever publishing all that you were sensing, would you undertake such a lengthy vision at this time in your life—if you were me?

It was begun years ago, but never had the accompaniment of a mature pen.

It will, if I busy it, be a sung tournament of poems, a sequence.

I'll call it—as it moves now in my womb—*Blue Yodels*. Blue yodel of this, blue yodel of that, etc. Blue yodel of a man crossing the road with an old rope and new strings, Blue yodel of the Recluse Spider, etc. + other, etc.

Are you familiar with how the A. Saxon Ballad + Negro Blues spilled into the same body of water!?[459]

yours,
Frank

I DREAMED ANOTHER POET SWINGING a few days later: last night I could not sleep. I walked until it got dark. Even the day was crazy. I don't know if I had a vision, or what, but I saw a girl ride by. For some reason beyond my control, I got in a fit of depression—the kind where you *write poetry*. {words, once again, a little sweeter to taste.}[460] I typed up some old things, but lost interest; went to something new: "*Blue Yodel of Stinkweed*," and "*Blue Yodel of Three Indian Sisters*." I DID NOT SLEEP. The next day, news came that an old companion of mine, a poet manqué, *hung* himself in his *bed*. Immediately I began a very long poem, it turns out, *Blue Yodel of Poets of Time[s] Past*. Almost a gentle war song of the poet warrior battling to stay alive. It is over 1000 lines already. Too long. A very bad storm knocked the lights out, so I had to write it in the dark. I'll be sending you new poems as soon as I can have them typed. Cheryl wants to come here, and I might let her. The poet's name is Neil Spearman

(Frank means spear!); you met him, I believe. I've read your "Fall" poems for solace.[461] Another poet, unknown, bites the dust. Writing his name in the little chug hole of backwater of ARKANSAS—WE ARE ALONE![462]

Blue Yodel of the Wayfaring Stranger[463]

after Pier Paolo Pasolini

I lean my head up against the juke box in the mountains
And think about the three Indian sisters tending bar
The nighthawks come down to sleep
On the knives in my shoulders
As if I was Saint Francis barefooted and all
They come down to cut their own
Throats in the snow
Which falls like the dandruff
Of Jean Cocteau
And I go on thinking of my white horse
Waiting in the roses
I can tell by the look
In its eyes my baby is dead
All my liquor is gone so is my land
I got kicked out of school for sleeping
And I spent what I had
Going to the picture show
Where I was arrested for putting my fist through a mirror
When this song is finished
I'm leaving this place but first I'm going
Down to the Army Surplus Store
And lay away all I got
On nine guitars

Notes

459. Stanford is alluding to the influence on his *Blue Yodels* of country musician Jimmie Rodgers, whose bluesy music and thirteen "Blue Yodel" songs (1927–33) were influenced by African American blues. Cf. *The Battlefield*, lines 13077–79.

460. *Marginalia: left side, right facing.*

461. Possibly Dugan's "Autumn at Baiae: For Cavafy" (from *Poems 2*, 1963) and presumably "One Waking in a Northern Fall" (from *Poems 3*, 1967).

462. A forty-line excerpt of Stanford's poem "Blue Yodel of Poets of Times Past" was published in *The Boston Phoenix* on December 18, 1973. Neal Spearmon (1946–72) was the fourth roommate of three Fayetteville poet-peers of Stanford's—John Stoss, Ralph Adamo, and Leon Stokesbury—at 815 N. Lindell Avenue from 1971 to 1972. Spearmon had been a physics major, and neither Adamo, nor the late Stokesbury, nor Spearmon's close friend and former housemate Keith Mills (b. 1948) have recalled Spearmon being a poet, but Spearmon's friend Jane Garner is confident that he was—or at least that he wanted, or was trying, to be one. In a November 9, 1972, letter to Cheryl Campbell, Stanford describes Spearmon as "a strange friend of sorts," adding, "We usually spoke poetry and phil. with one another, rather than *of* it."

In late summer or early fall 1972, Adamo, Stokesbury, and Spearmon each moved out of the house, and late into the night on October 13, 1972, Spearmon hanged himself in his bed at his new residence. He tied a rope around his neck and the other end to a cinder block, then threw the block over the bed's footboard; he was found by Mills (Stanford and Willett's backyard cottage neighbor at 221 Buchanan Avenue ca. 1968—see note 98 above—who had been Linda Mencin's boyfriend in 1969 before Mills introduced her to Stanford) and a mutual friend.

Adamo and Stokesbury weren't aware of a friendship having existed between Stanford and Spearmon, but Mills and Garner, who likely served as the basis for Stanford's character Lady Jane, do recall an acquaintanceship or friendship. In any event, Spearmon and Lady Jane are mentioned in a typewritten manuscript page of Stanford's. *What About This*, 544.

Spearmon is also referenced in Adamo's Stoss-centered poem, "A Letter to John, Leaving Marengo," in which the speaker-narrator reflects on "what Neal did": "Three poets and a physicist in one house: / naturally it is the physicist who bows out." *Waterblind: Selected Poems* (Portals, 2002), 58. The full version (in its alleged one thousand plus lines) of "Blue Yodel of Poets of Times Past" is likely nonextant. In a ca. December 31, 1972, letter to Campbell, Stanford writes, "While I was in L.R., I visited Neil's [*sic*] grave, where I scattered the ashes of his long poem. I was drunk, and so I do not know if it was the right grave. The poem was not worthy of him."

463. The version included here is the collected version (*Ladies From Hell*). The version Stanford enclosed presents the title as "BLUE YODEL Of The Wayfaring Stranger," includes no mention of Pasolini, spells "jukebox" as one word, and breaks line 18 into two lines as ". . . fist / Through . . ." Re: "wayfaring stranger": cf. *The Battlefield*, lines 2197, 3122, and 4607—and see mentions of "blue yodel" beginning at line 11949.

To Cheryl Campbell: November 13, 1972

Dear Cheryl,

We, a sphere of dark and light roses, were delivered to the world in the form of a rebus, brought up dripping from the river, in the mouth of the dragon-horse. I paraphrase Eisenstein, who attempted to bring the essences of Yang and Yin to the cinema. I speak after no one, when I say: I love you. 信[464]

More than six weeks since I've seen your bodily form; about six months since I've left Fayetteville and the cabin; about sixteen months that passed between our August twenty-first rendezvous and our earlier one of Spring 71.[465]

I love you so much. This is what it is like without you: I die every minute. I don't believe in you, I cannot believe in myself. If I have faith in myself, then it is impossible to deny you. Your clitoris is a minnow I want to dip out and return to the water, forever. For so long now, TIME has only been a perception rather than a concept. It should, I know, be both, but all I'm able to do in this miserable state is: perceive it past, present, and future, not in any particular order.

Where are you? Where are you my love? I know that we must be together before our minds drift in to despair. O let us go down the roads, love, smoking Coleridge's fantastic pipe, together.

Wish me luck in the morning. If they let me drive their truck, then I'll have found a place by the end of the month. I hope they'll hire me. I must wade in that necessary branch of reality, so I can swim in your waters, so we can dream in peace, so we can live, and create.

I'll let you know: only you, Belle, Cheryl, know that there is music, and if I listened to some of it now, alone, I would merely be dead the next day.

All my love,
Frank

I'm going mad without you.

P.S. Enclosed is a letter, concerning the death of a friend, I would hope you'd post for me. He thinks I'm there, where you are, and so I don't want *anyone* to know any different. I may be getting mail from people wishing to come to N.Y. to see me. GOD FORBID. Tell them I'm in Seattle, or something. You've had one close to you in prison, so I know you'll understand why I was blunt and curt about my whereabouts. I CAN GET INTO *TROUBLE*. Please put up with these seeming trivialities until we are together. I think you don't want me in trouble, just as much as I don't want my friends, or whatever, descending upon you, etc. Keep the faith of our thighs in the darkness.

Love,
F.

(You may open this and read it; but *please mail it.*)

Q: Are you *sure* you're getting all of my letters to you?

Notes

464. Japanese for "believe" or "trust."

465. I.e., between Frank's arrival to Cheryl's residence on Staten Island on August 21, 1972 (see Stanford's first Late August 1972 postcard to Willett above, opening sentence), and, very possibly, the night they shared beneath the stars on Markham Hill in spring 1971; see note 351 above.

To Cheryl Campbell: December 2, 1972

Dear Cheryl,

How did you know to call? I throw down the yarrow sticks, not even knowing what question to ask, and you interpret the configurations—the *answer*.[466]

I "happened" to be there. It is good you stopped over for a night; Dina must have wanted to see her old husband—I figured as much.

The long letter I've been writing you since you left is unreadable, so I won't send it. Perhaps I'll have a poem from it, instead. Somehow, your call erases the letter.

You sounded so *old.* Our conversations by contraption have always been tense, almost as if we were expecting an ambush, or worried the "authorities" were about to separate us, forever.

You must always forgive my manner on the phone; it is so useless, so feeble in conveying what we are about, and becoming. The range of feelings I've had since you drove off, watching me

walk down that dusty road, are as infinite as the music you love. I trust you; you with my life. There have been so many other women, none of them like you, so many around me like flies around shit, and you are the only one I've trusted. Cheryl, you are so unselfish, you want to give so much—so much energy in you.

You are like a source: your movement, your reasons, my strides of thinking, you, who make me sane and want to live, are *so* different from the other diversions

I've sought out, to *keep from* going crazy, dying. Do you know how *sick* I am? Do you know what amnesia is? I would never condemn you, if you were to say

"I cannot endure this." Maybe you will, because you know what lies ahead, and beyond of madness: my genius. It isn't pretentious to say that, either; it's true.

Neither of us, yet, are what we want to become—to ourselves, and to one another, and yet we are enough, as we are. If this journey I ask you to set out on, with me,

at my side, is too frightening, then you must speak up. I am in the hands of time, fate, the gods. This world is all we have to wander, and yet it is so little, when

compared to the worlds I know in my visions. If you flinch at my words, you should leave the ship now. Only if you recognize the magnificent, treacherous

innocence of my soul, will you have any chance at understanding it. I live with the bees, the fish, the hoes, the apples, the fortune tellers, the

Negroes, the gods. I dispense with all beliefs. I am the milt of the poets of times past. I sustain my reverie by loving you, by knowing these who believe

in me. I am not worth spitting between your teeth. If you come on this voyage, you will, as Christ-Gautama said, put the world and its concerns

behind you. I intend to live in the future, by way of the past, *now*. What I'm asking is not easy. It will mean a different way of life—as we spoke of it.

I was so proud of you when you [told] Dina, unselfishly, that in the future your energy, for a while, would flow between us, rather than the void of pettiness and

ego. We have much preparation before our next meeting. I will work, listen to music, and—as I just began last night, translate the poetry of the original

Hebraic Biblical texts. I'm working with Brother Jerome, a young monk, a brilliant scholar and linguist, who has studied all over Europe and Rome.[467] If these things

do not interest you, tell me. There *is* so much strength flowing through me. I want to raise the hard hell of this absurd world, but I want to dream through every

book. I want to dance. What will become of us? You give me the same Book of Changes change I give you.[468] Never again, will two souls like ourselves, with such powers to change + teach + love one another, meet—again? I must give up part of my world, for some of yours, so I can see them both. You must forget some of yours for the one I will let appear for you. There will be some laughter, some companions, some of that which we now know, but it will be so different. If you do not begin with the sun when you think of me, if I am not the breathing form of dark fire of your words, then we should say goodbye.

The world, in all its glory and stench, shall not extinguish me—yet. Are we together? Begin with me, begin reading *Beowulf* again, so you can sing and play and think. Begin with silence, and knowledge of fish, which carry their own changing lights in the deep. Forget your past, your friends, your way of life, and follow me, so I can follow you, so we can lead the spirits who tell us which way to travel in our dreams. You must work up your psyche like a Icelandic warrior, like Choctaw Braves, antediluvian women who worshiped blood and cum. If you are not born with blonde hair and a penchant for fine dresses in my left eye, and if you have not perished naked in the east, smelling of hay, then where is my right eye? Avaunt!

As you can tell, I am taking the bull to the moon for libations. What will become of us. If you do not quake at the thought of me, as you lie awake in the city, remembering everything weak + petty about me, if you cannot penetrate through to the harp that gallops under the oaks and camellias of my soul, then where are we. I, who speak to you, as Solomon sung his song of all songs, I am your destiny—for the living. Answer me. I, who can lose an eye to what you can become, who can lose a life to what you will want me to become: you. I am the thunder with its sexual lightning of silence.

I love you,
Frank

Tell Clive, Liz, Dina, kids, Louise, Leo, the band hello.[469]
{What is the name of Jung's friend, as mentioned by Cerreno about Hesse. The man who wrote about the I Ching? Amnesia you know!}[470]

Dear Cheryl,

I should be able to put this better; all I can say is: I'm lonely for you. I miss you,

I love you,
Frank

Can you run me an errand? I need to know the address + poetry editor of a N.Y. magazine, *The Nation*.

Dear Cheryl,

I hope you don't mind my writing Elizabeth, but I thought it best, since you will be living with her until then, and I would like to be absolved, admitting my evil ways of *being* whatever I was. I am forgiving everyone for everything + all personal relations, not that they have to forgive me, but this is the path I must clear for this journey I speak of. My heart must be free of all injustices, empty of all thoughts, whether realized, inspired, or whatever—when it comes to the well becoming of others, especially the other, your, sex.

The name of the man I can't *think* of is not Wilhelm Reich, but another orientalist, mentioned, I think, in the introduction of your Hesse-Serrano book. Please send it.

(Was his last name something like Reich: say Charles Reich?) Maybe I could borrow your book.

Have you ever read P. D. Ouspensky, who was a student of Gurdjieff?[471]

Don't worry about looking for those books! There are three errands, though: the address + P. editor of The Nation, the address and P. editor of The Quarterly Review of Literature, and 1 small p.b. poetry book, I didn't put down on the list. There is a publishing house in N.Y. called ATHENEUM. They have a book by a French poet, Jean Follain, translated by W. S. Merwin.[472] I need it *soon*. There is so much love and work to look forward to. I'm so glad you called, even if I was strange. Don't worry, we will endure.

Go and make your music, heard, lady that you are——I do miss you, but as you say, it is time for that, and whatever. I'm looking forward for all of your selves sprawled out, nude, on a letter. Please feel free to tell me what is *wrong* with me—as I appeared last weekend. Ever

I love you
Frank

Notes

466. The first twenty-one paragraphs of this letter are written in prose poetry form—with each paragraph containing five manuscript lines.

Per Chinese philosophy, yarrow stalks are a divination tool that can be organized into piles whose meaning can then be referenced in the *I Ching* as a way of consulting the oracle.

467. Fr. Jerome Kodell, OSB (b. 1940), monk and Subiaco Abbey's sixth abbot, from 1989 to 2015. Kodell was ordained a priest, becoming "Father Jerome," in 1965.

468. I.e., the *I Ching*; Cheryl noted, to this editor, that she introduced Frank to the *I Ching* (or *Book of Changes*) in 1971. Text to editor, December 27, 2023.

469. Clive and Liz Thompson and their sons, Christopher and Jason; Dina Cagle, a friend of Campbell's from El Dorado, Arkansas; Louise and Leo, Jamaican wife and husband housemates of the Thompsons and Campbell; and Campbell's band, Catseye Ramble.

470. *Marginalia: left side, right facing.* In Miguel Serrano's *C. G. Jung and Hermann Hesse: A Record of Two Friendships*, sinologist Richard Wilhelm (1873–1930), friend of Carl Jung and translator of the *I Ching*, is discussed.

471. Russian philosopher P.D. Ouspensky (1878–1947) studied with Russian Armenian mystic George Gurdjieff (ca. 1877–1949), later helping, in his own teaching, to advance Gurdjieff's spiritual ideas.

472. Jean Follain's *Transparence of the World: Poems* (1969).

To Eleanor Bender: December 4, 1972

December 4, 1972
Box 86
Subiaco, Arkansas 72865

Dear Eleanor,

A note of inquiry, an excuse for writing you: quite out of the blue, I am becoming "discovered" by various editors and poets. Three small-press books accepted, etc. After the first of the year, *I* don't *intend* to send any more poems out—I'll just work in peace. Since I trust your judgment and remember your kind letter,[473] I'd like you—your time and soul permitting—to look at a few poems only Alan Dugan has seen—no editor. They exist, from the past, quite by chance. Of course, if any of them are worthy to be in print, you can have them. Until I hear from you.

yours,
Frank

As most of the work is
Lawrentian in nature, I'd
rather a woman see them.

Tell about any films
you've seen.

Notes

473. Stanford is presumably referring to Bender's August 5, 1971, letter to him, in which she provided constructive criticism and stated, "I feel that you must be a very extraordinary young man. Your feelings of caution about not wanting to be swept away with the tide of things is very admirable"; asserted that with a poet with some influence backing him for the Yale Younger Poets Prize, Stanford's "poems can stand on their own" and he should win; and noted that she had written to Random House (likely to Nan A. Talese) regarding Stanford and that she could be open to submitting one of his manuscripts to them. On November 10, 1971, Stanford replied, "Your letter was very fine, kind, and informative. It was probably the best letter I've ever received from an editor. . . . I'll always remember your words."

To Malcolm Cowley: December 24, 1972

December 24, 1972

Dear Mr. and Mrs. Cowley,

I am sitting in an illegal drinking establishment in Swiftwater, Mississippi, using a hot T.W. to answer your letter—in my pocket—, sipping buttermilk and cornbread, and waiting on a bus.[474] Since I lost your address, I'll not mail this until I'm sure it'll get to you. (It isn't the liquor which is outlawed, but the *other*: gambling, etc.)

Merry Christmas, and by the time you get this it should be a good New Year. Soon after I left N.Y.—where I ran into an English woman who was kind enough to show me around—I wrote each of you long notes. I don't know if they reached you, since I put down Kent, Ct. In them I said something like this:

Although I've been a stranger to many people and places, under various circumstances, I never had as gracious treatment as you two were kind enough to extend. The afternoon I spent with you is. . . . I know I'm not much of a doc. cameraman, and probably not very much account as a poet, but you made me welcome in your beautiful home. Never will I forget your kindness, as genuine as your garden. At one point, I actually had to hide in the bushes to be alone, I was so moved by your frankness and charm. I've never met anyone in the delta as gracious as Mrs. Cowley. {(There's more, but I don't want you thinking I'm court minstrel.)}

When I was a schoolboy, reading your books and the books by men you shed light on—you are expecting me to come out with something like: "Why, I never dreamed I would one day. . . ." but I will not, because—I DID believe our paths might cross, however much of a foot-trail mine might be. Your voice was just as deep and shaped as I imagined it; a stone on the bottom of the River.

By the way, have you ever heard a black man—say about your age—read any of your poetry? There is such going on right across the boat bottom bar from me. I didn't stage it for your benefit either. It happened right out of the blue; he's reading the first poem in the book you gave me, and has already given a rendition of your famous one on the backcover.[475] The man's voice is high, like you hear in an evening falsetto blues. For some reason, he has improvised "give-it heah" for the second "Mine". Since you are a little hard of hearing now, I'll give you hand signals as to what is going on sonorous-wise: An old man tapping the side of a Jax beercan; snooker balls making fools out of cocky boys—more like pilot fish than sharks; pick-up trucks turning over—no mufflers; hard-boiled eggs and pig feet making speech a little more hushed, just like those cones that some musicians hold over the end of their trumpets; and over by the juke box, in long coat and derby, sits a sly looking wide-eyed man with some kind of affliction of the nerves, which makes him look like a black Harpo Marx strumming his harp.

The paper, like my socks, don't match.[476] The sun going down, now. The delta can be so dreary at times. And there is something about stalks. In the dead of winter, they look like mussed gardens after a party given by Bacchus. There is a stuffed bat on the wall of this tonk and next to it is a picture of a submarine. A hefty woman is cooking a catfish sandwich in a radar range. We were speaking of the inner ear. There is Flying Tiger hanging down from the ceiling, covered with dust, grease, and webs, which reminds of the bombs falling over you know where.[477] The ship in the wine bottle next to the picture of Martin Luther King makes me think of the boat you are taking to England, and the light green bottle brings back the kind of wine you served to the film crew.[478] Now, the bat is like the story you told of the bats getting in. There is an unreadable, dirty poem by Robert Burns next to the mirror. . . .[479] I don't know if you'll be in Scotland by New Year's, but I've often gone out at night in the fog, make believing this country was like the moors, and dipped my bible to the minnows and multitude of marys. And so on.

Missing the land was one of the reasons I left N.Y. so soon. Another reason: Had been promised a job in a bookstore, was to start that afternoon. To pass the time, I went to an old movie theatre. It was full of bums, drunks, and God only knows what else. A lunatic sitting beside me had a cassette recorder, portable, and asked if I wanted to hear some "Whale Songs". I thought the man meant whaler songs, but no, he played actual whale music, with some symphony orchestra to back them up.[480] From whales, I went to the credits of a Greta Garbo film, and from there to Wales and its blue yodeler, and from there to a memory of a poem with no title other than "note" on page 32 of your book.[481] In N.Y. there were alot of folks and artists with five gallon buckets of day-glow black paint. That was about all she wrote for me. In Washington D.C., a man gets on the bus, and he is to be my drinking and tale-spinning companion until Memphis. He was a eighty-four year old black man, who had actually heard of my uncle. In fact, he'd bought whiskey from him several times. (My uncle being a legal bootlegger in Three Way for many years;[482] he took the business over from his father, etc.) In Nashville they kicked us off the bus, along with four other negroes and one white soldier boy. We had a very grand time. I went up to the Vanderbilt campus and examined my conscience. You know, I just never could go along with that fugitive group, however much I tried.[483] Just too much a loner; and I guess I picked that up from Greta Garbo, my father, and a blind man who worked for him.

Whatever, it'll take a fair amount of years of hard work, mostly done alone and apart from any movement and school, if I'm to ever create anything worthwhile. No matter if anyone reads my books or not, I'll always remember my afternoon with the two of you. If you ever come south, and need a chauffeur, fishing guide, a place to stay, please let me know.

Thank you for putting in a word for me. I only applied to the Guggenheim on the advice of a friend-poet. I know my chances will be slim for many years to come, but I know what I want to do, and so I can live in obscurity and poverty.[484] To speak from the heart without a butcher knife or pacemaker in it.

You could probably tell by my actions I've never met many literary people. If only all of them could be as fine, and true as you all. All the wagons of my future will not pass by with any riders as grand and proud as the Cowleys. You use a gentle whip. Please don't take this note, written in haste in a Negro Dive, as a sycophantic ramble, but rather a young man's *honest* respect where it is due.

Shoot, I'd probably feel the same about that afternoon if I had of showed up, hired for the day, to put a little mulch on your roses.

When you get to England, I hope you say a prayer for Coleridge if you visit the place where they put him under.[485] Caedmon is still in unmarked ground I guess.[486]

As soon as I have a few debts out of the way, I'll write to that man in N.Y. about the Yaddo. Thank You Very Much.[487]

After the first of the year, I'll be staying in Hotel New Orleans, Eureka Springs, Arkansas, under the name of Ms. Francis Gildart.[488] Poetry is a good work.

Have the time of your lives and then some.

Faithfully,
Frank Stanford

P.S. Is Sherman named for the bastard who burned Atlanta down? Maybe his grandpappy, as the town seems much older.[489]

Notes

474. Stanford appears to be writing this letter from a rough honky-tonk ("a 'dive' most poets would be afraid to enter," as he notes in a letter to Fox likely written the same day) called the Highway Inn (which may have also been referred to colloquially as Wolfe Brothers)—formerly located on Highway 1 in Swiftwater, Mississippi.

On December 21, 1972, Cowley wrote to Stanford, noting that he had recommended him for a Guggenheim and offering to sponsor him for a Yaddo residency; see note 487 below.

475. "Boy in Sunlight" and "Blue Juniata," the opening and title poems, respectively, of Cowley's *Blue Juniata: Collected Poems* (1968).

476. This paragraph begins p. 2 of the letter—typed on different paper stock.

477. During Operation Linebacker II, the US dropped bombs on targets in North Vietnam for twelve days in December 1972, from December 18 to 29.

478. Cowley had closed his December 21 letter: "The day after Christmas we're setting out for England, to be gone six months." Stanford's concluding paragraph also refers to this sentence.

479. Robert Burns (1759–96), Scottish poet.

480. Stanford was probably listening to Alan Hovhaness's *And God Created Great Whales*, op. 229, no. 1, a 1970 symphonic poem for orchestra incorporating whale sounds that were originally released on *Songs of the Humpback Whale* (1970). *And God Created Great Whales* was first released as an LP in 1971.

481. Cowley's *Blue Juniata: Collected Poems*. The two-paragraph "NOTE" on p. 32, which arguably reads as a prose poem, describes the down-and-out Greenwich Village / East Village living of young people postwar: "In that setting of grime and poverty . . . we had made a kind of religion out of the sordid." Malcolm Cowley, *Blue Juniata: Collected Poems* (Viking, 1968).

482. *Three Way*: possibly the name of the liquor store in Mississippi.

483. See note 136 above.

484. *friend-poet*: Dugan, one of Stanford's recommenders. In his December 21 letter, Cowley wrote: "I wrote a strong recommend, but I'm sure you realize that the chances are against you in asking for help from an organization that doesn't take many chances."

485. Coleridge was originally buried at Old Highgate Chapel in Highgate, Greater London (then Middlesex), England. His remains were reinterred in St. Michael's Church in Highgate in 1961.

486. Cædmon (?–ca. 684), the earliest known English poet to have written in a Germanic language, is buried in the churchyard of St. Mary's Church in Whitby, North Yorkshire, England, though the church was built in the twelfth and thirteenth centuries. A monument, Cædmon's Cross, was erected on-site in 1898.

487. In an October 18, 1972, letter to Broughton, Cowley, who was then at Yaddo (an artists' retreat in Saratoga Springs, New York), explained that he thought he could get Stanford "a period of residence" there and wrote, "Anyhow, will you ask Frank to write me?"

In Cowley's December 21 letter to Stanford, he returned to the notion, mentioning that Stanford could give his (Cowley's) name as a sponsor; Cowley included a contact name ("Mr. Curtis Harnack, Director") and address.

488. *Francis Gildart*: Stanford's given names. He was, on the day of his birth, named Francis Gildart Smith and, upon adoption, became Francis Gildart Alter; upon later adoption by A. F. Stanford, Stanford's name became Francis Gildart Stanford, or

Frank Stanford. Cf. Francis Gildart in *The Battlefield*, who says, "I didn't know what to say when they / asked me my name cause by now I had changed my name so many times I couldn't / recollect which one I was using," claiming that he had "done forgot" his original name (lines 10285–87, 10290).

489. Stanford and Broughton had visited Cowley in mid-August 1972; Cowley lived in Sherman, Connecticut, incorporated in 1802. The town is named for Roger Sherman (1721–93), one of the US's Founding Fathers. General William Tecumseh Sherman (1820–91), whose troops played a part in burning Atlanta in the Civil War's Battle of Atlanta of July 22, 1864, was a distant relative of Roger Sherman's.

To Richard Eberhart: Circa December 29–30, 1972

On The Road
December, 72

Dear Mr. and Mrs. Eberhart,

This letter should have come to you long ago, but there have been good times and alot of bad times, so forgive my inflorescent negligence. I'm writing this somewhere between the monastery and the Hotel New Orleans in Eureka Springs, Arkansas, where I'll be staying. The other day, evening rather, I answered a letter of Malcolm Cowley's in a tavern in Swiftwater, Mississippi. I've always had gypsy blood and, although my thumb is better in pies and gardens, it still works on the road, the backroads at least. In the middle of a story, I just had the urge to return to where I remembered having lived the play: so, I winded up in Mississippi, only to return when hearing of the hospitalization of my mother in Arkansas, and when I got back there, I found out my grandmother was in the hospital in Mississippi. Ever since I was six, I've always carried a copy of one of the Romantic poets whenever I made a journey. In fact, long ago, on one of these inland voyages, on a Trailways bus, as I'm on now, keeping the other passengers awake with my bird of prey pecking, is where I first read a poem by you. This was way before I was taught some of your more famous work by the monks in High School English. For this first reading, we should thank some northern student who had come down to do Summer Project Work when the civil rights movement was in full motion.[490] I use to ride the freedom rider buses often; usually, I came across alot of good reading the students brought with them.[491]

Soon after I left NYC, in the early fall, I wrote ya'll [*sic*] a note in care of Cape Rosier. It was returned. I read the note and decided it wasn't nearly commensurate with the kindness you extended me during my strange working-visit. I've a feeling your graces would have been just as genuine had I not been trying to crank a camera for Irv. As you could probably tell by my backwardness in contemporary literary affairs, I haven't kept that much eastern literary company. Looking to the future, it would be wonderful to think that everyone would be like you two and the rest of your friends and family. To tell the truth, I felt a little out of my element, what with being with Irv and all, but how else would a pipedream come true. You must put yourself in my place, and you can because you are a poet; if someone had told me just a few days before I left the South that I would be at the homes of the Eberharts. . . . . . . I will always keep this memory close to my heart. I've not had sleep in a few days, so please bear with me if I still get carried away with the summer. It was a maze of coinsidences, enchantments, and I was dazed and touched by your "ways". I doubt that I could ever become a doc. cameraman, because I could not remove myself to that objective stance. (One day, I hope to make films side by side with my poems, as Blake drew and engraved.[492] However, at the moment, paper is cheaper.) Really, it all seems like a dream. Byron said, "I had a dream that was not at all a dream."[493] So far, that's how my life has been, so why shouldn't our meeting be that way also?

Believe me when I say I can remember each moment.

There is some line by Pasternak, and Yessenin before him, that not even your first student, Lowell, can imitate;[494] it means, simply, as was the case with both of these men: I shall never forget your goodness. The camera I carried around was a millstone and a chalice, so if I can play the part of the stranger, you have been host to many—I expect. The wedding was so beautiful. How did I get there. I felt like Coleridge's guest, in white suit and panama hat.[495]

New England was a gift, dear folks. You may not even know you gave it. Perhaps I took it with me without you knowing, but now you do. What greater gift, unawares or not, can an older, famous poet and his wife, genuine and charming, make to an unknown poet like me: THE OCEAN. The first time, yes I was still a virgin as far as the sea was concerned, at Undercliff I saw the great motherwater.[496] Dinner at the farm, the swim, the theatre, your home, your gazebo (where I wrote a poem that's been accepted), Dartmouth, the long drive with you two as guides, picking blueberries with Razzi's daughter, the meeting with the Nearings and Hoffmans,[497] Blake's Camp,[498] Mrs. Butcher's party, the caravan of small boats, the cruises, the food, the chance. . . .

If I go on, I won't be able to get off the bus, and I must, so this will have to be cut short, like my visit with you, but I will remember ya'll forever and a day, and this bus is stopping now, have to get off. My companion is an elderly Negro man who can't remember where he is supposed to be, so I'm taking him to the address on his beat-up leather luggage. I'll mail this whenever possible. I remember your sister well, and would write her if I hadn't lost her address.

In a cast-off coat, one can keep warm for miles and miles. My poems may be coming out, soon, like the stinkweeds of Spring, so please don't try to compare them with the lovely flowers cultivated in the yards.

I have known you both. . . . .

Snowdrifting,

Incredible,

The blackberry wine brewed by the monks,

An old man asleep on my shoulder,

The rabbit foot on his belt,

My copy of Keats and Shelly,[499]

A crumpled painting by Chagall in my billfold like a blank check from joy,

Frank

How was I to know the cloud just passing over the moon
was a dark man poling his boat. A chinaman?

Frank Stanford
Hotel New Orleans
Eureka Springs, Arkansas

Notes

490. Stanford is likely referring to the Freedom Summer Project of June–August 1964 (within the US's larger Civil Rights Movement of 1954–68)—launched to register African American Mississippians to vote.

491. Most of the freedom riders (1961) were college students.

492. Blake published most of his books using relief etching to produce illuminated manuscripts, but he used intaglio engraving for most of his commercial work.

493. "I had a dream, which was not all a dream," the opening line of Byron's poem "Darkness" (1816). Sans the comma, the line also appears in *The Battlefield* (line 5493).

494. Robert Lowell's book *Imitations* (1961) includes loose translations of various poets (Villon, Baudelaire, Rimbaud, et al.), including Boris Pasternak (1890–1960). In translation, Sergei Yesenin's surname is typically spelled as such.

495. In a 1981 remembrance essay, Eberhart notes that, on the August 1972 trip to New England, Stanford (and companions) attended the wedding of Eberhart's daughter, Gretchen, in New Hampshire. Richard Eberhart, "Frank Stanford," *Ironwood* 17 (Spring 1981): 137.

496. See the Mid-August 1972 book inscription to Eberhart above.

497. Scott Nearing and Helen Nearing (1904–95), writers, and Daniel Hoffman (see notes 376 and 377 above).

498. Hiram Blake's Camp, a resort on the coast of Cape Rosier, Maine.

499. Feasibly, *John Keats and Percy Bysshe Shelley: Complete Poetical Works* (1932).

Postcard of the New Orleans Hotel in Eureka Springs, Arkansas, where Stanford lived from the close of 1972 into spring 1973. At the hotel, he spent significant time working on various poems, including *The Battlefield Where the Moon Says I Love You*, and fiction. This postcard states that the hotel was built ca. 1890 after an 1888 fire had destroyed the previous frame structure. To Dugan in this January 12, 1973, postcard, Stanford writes, "My luck: this place will probably catch fire."

IV.

THE NEW ORLEANS HOTEL

Eureka Springs, 1972–73

At the close of December 1972, on or just before New Year's Eve and in large part connected to his relationship with Cheryl (who wanted to live in the town after leaving New York), Stanford moved to Eureka Springs—an arts-centered small town located forty-five miles northeast of Fayetteville in the Arkansas Ozarks—and rented a room at the New Orleans Hotel under the name Francis Gildart, his given name. He paid for two months, January and February 1973, in advance. The winter was a productive one for Stanford, who wrote poetry and fiction in his hotel room—room 308—and worked to finish composing and typing (with the help of Cheryl in New York) THE BATTLEFIELD WHERE THE MOON SAYS I LOVE YOU. *On March 3, 1973, on a weekend away from Eureka Springs in Neosho, Missouri, he met Ginny Crouch, a painter with whom he began a lasting relationship. Starting in late winter, he began screening films for audiences at a theater on Center Street in Eureka Springs.*

To Irv Broughton: December 31, 1972

c/o New Orleans Hotel

December 31, 1972[500]
In the last hours
of this year, I'm
thinking of you.

Dear Friend,

Unlike your teaching associates, I haven't lost faith in you. Here you are expending your life's time and energy, not to mention your earnings, and they aren't even willing to help you. You are giving of yourself in your own way, which most people can never do. If I come across any money, I'll try to help. I hope you don't let your present miseries affect your creativity. Remember the good summer; all we spoke of doing! Missus Welty, Walker Percy, and on and on—something of Jim's, etc.[501] I am still with you in spirit, and will be with you in the small quaking bodies of singed poetry. Soon. Look out for yourself.

yours,
Frank

Read Whitman and forgive
your enemies, friends, and self.

Notes

500. Per a letter to Campbell, Stanford was not yet living at the New Orleans Hotel as of December 30, but it appears from this note that he might have moved into his room—room 308, then a center-west room along the hotel's northern wall, two floors above the lobby—by New Year's Eve.

501. Eudora Welty (1909–2001), Mississippi author; and Walker Percy (1916–90), Louisiana author who lived in Greenville, Mississippi, from 1930 to 1945—and whose adoptive father, writer William Alexander Percy (1885–1942), Dorothy Stanford had known. Dorothy Stanford and Ruth Rogers interview by Murray B. Shugars, June 13, 1997. *Jim's*: James Babij's.

To Alan Dugan: January 4, 1973

[Postcard of Eureka Springs, Arkansas, "Little Switzerland of America."]

Alan Dugan
Box 97
Truro, Mass.

Dear Alan,

Your letters forwarded to me here; living in Hotel New Orleans, Eureka Springs, Arkansas, under the name Francis Gildart. Will write you. Send the letter with the poem back.[502] I'm living, loving; glad you two are so well.

yours,
Frank

Notes

502. In Dugan's December 18, 1972, letter to Stanford, he wrote seven lines of poetry (including "The fifty-five knot wind was blowing through our house."). Stanford returned the letter to Dugan with the added annotation: "Good poem. Keep going. Send me more, handwritten, as they come to you, and I'll read + return them. The wind blows the poem out of your house, then back, again."

To Carolyn Gilbert: Circa January 7–12, 1973

[Written in a french-fold greeting card that reads "To Cheer You" and "The Prayer of St. Francis of Assisi" on the front and includes the prayer inside.][503]

I love you and be well

Love
Frank

↙ Open

[Typed in all caps on the inside of the card when fully opened out:]

Dear Gran-Gran,

Will type large so you can pass over this with your eyes easily. Mother just called and said you were ill. Tried to call you a dozen times, Linda Lee too, but the lines are down somewhere in between here and the delta, due to ice and snow storm.[504] Please get well in a hurry, as Mother misses you very much—as do I—and needs you with her. Hope Linda and the baby are O.K. I sent her, am in the process of, a card in care of Indianola Hospital; hope she is there?[505] (There to receive it, but out of care.)

Many trucks, cars, buses have run off the roads in the mtns. And this hotel—which is called The New Orleans because it looks like something in the French Q[506]—is much like a movie, due to all the stranded people who are staying here. Everyone has forgotten their woes, and they're all taking a mid-winter vacation—of course, not intentionally.

This town is one of the strangest places I've ever visited, and that is a litotes. Men and women your age are thriving artists. {There is a fishing guide who thinks he knows the theory of light. I drink with him.}[507] Last week, I had a "date" with a seventy year old woman. She fed me supper, which was honeybread and shrimp and some dish I cannot spell, but which Teressa should be able to since the lady is Lebanese, and then we listened to Bruebeck and Mahler.[508] Everyone is kind to the old people here, especially when there is all this ice on the hilly streets. Uncle Jimmy would be interested to know that most of the young people are farmers who grow and raise just about everything they eat, even down to the yogurt, which they make, that comes from their goats.[509] {There are no negroes, only hill people.}[510] The place is almost Europeon [*sic*]. I'm looking for land, because I intend to have my own farm, rather than hire on to these around here. As Robert Frost said, the only other thing a poet can do is farm.[511] A family lets me ride their horses for helping out with the feeding. They can't get into the mtns always to do it, so I take a very long walk, mulling things over on the way, and do it for them. If I had a chainsaw, I could make an honorable living for the winter. The only trouble is: all the wood to be cut up is in places even the most auspicious of loggers would not try to get to.

The kind of people, the mixture, is so strange. On the one hand you have an elderly glassblower who was formerly a nuclear physicist, then a divorced lady with alot of children who paints and runs her own farm—I've already been invited to supper—, and on the other hand you have someone murdered in a local saloon; hillbillys, Easterners, Europeons, ex-bankers from New Orleans, and my girl friend's best friend who visits Dick Cavett's wife in NYC because they are both from Greenwood.[512] This girl has 1200 acres to herself on the Little Piney River.[513] {That girl from Scotland, the one I met in N.Y., wants to come over here and tour "the south."}[514] All in all, good experience.

Finally, and it is about time, a few checks are starting to roll in from publications. Have four, maybe five, books coming out. One won't be under my name.[515] By the time you are a hundred I hope to have sown all my wild oats and settled down to some genre and form of writing and subject matter, understandable to everyone and something that would make you proud of me. I know most of the things I've done are what you call *épater les bourgeois*,[516] and I wrote most of it when I was a kid, no one knowing about it. Anyway, editors and other poets, etc., are having fun by "discovering" me, and as soon as they get tired of it, I'll have done some readable books in manuscript—I hope, God willing. Other than doing my duty to the people of the universe by way of poetry, the only other thing I wanted to do was work for Uncle Jimmy, and I muffed that. I still love all of you very much, and always have, no matter how crazy and wild I've been, or what you may have read in to what you have seen of my work and life. It is my wish to—one day—carry over all of ya'lls [*sic*] goodness into a book worthy to even be set down on your table. Let everyone thrive and prosper, in their own way, without causing harm to anyone. Get well and visit Mother. Tell everyone I miss them, hope they had a grand holiday season. I may ride up on the white horse of chance in your front yard one spring day. Hope this gets to you and the card gets to Linda Lee and the baby.

Love,
Frank

It was mentioned that Kenneth H. asked about me. You might tell him, to whet his habadasher's [*sic*] curiosity,—meaning no injustice, but rather a gentlemanly jest,—that MALCOLM COWLEY, Faulkner's editor, wants to {sponsor me to "Yaddo" in N.Y. I met he and his lovely wife last summer.}[517]

Notes

503. Re: the prayer, see note 307 above, par. 4.
504. The circa dating of this letter is based on the fact that northwest Arkansas experienced significant cold, ice, and snow between January 5 and January 12, 1973, which began with ice on January 5 and accumulation of snow beginning around January 7.
505. Linda Lee (b. 1940; not to be confused with Linda Lee Mencin, Stanford's first wife), Stanford's first cousin and sister of Jimmy Lee Jr. (b. 1942), on whom Stanford's character Jimmy is based.
506. *French Q*: New Orleans's French Quarter.
507. *Marginalia: left side, right facing.*
508. Dave Brubeck (1920–2012), jazz composer and pianist; Gustav Mahler (1860–1911), composer.

509. *Uncle Jimmy*: James Buford Lee (1915–2010), Stanford's uncle (through marriage to Dorothy's sister Louise) and Jimmy's and Linda's father.

510. *Marginalia: left side, right facing.*

511. In a January 9, 1924, letter, Robert Frost wrote: "Farming seemed the ideal occupation to combine with poetry, if you couldn't have poetry alone, as of course you couldn't." Frost to George H. Sargent, Amherst, MA, *The Letters of Robert Frost*, vol. 2, *1920–1928*, ed. Donald Sheehy et al. (Belknap Press of Harvard University Press, 2016), 392.

512. Dick Cavett (b. 1936), talk show host whose wife, actor Carrie Nye (1936–2006), was from Greenwood in northwest Mississippi.

513. Little Piney Creek, a tributary near the Arkansas River in Arkansas.

514. *Marginalia: left side, right facing.*

515. Stanford may be referring to the publication of his poem "He Was Talking to Himself About Butterflies" in *Seventeen* magazine under the name Francis Gildart, whom Stanford claimed was fifteen years old; a letter to "Francis" from Judy Culbreth of *Seventeen*, dated January 11, 1973, accepted that poem and another, "The Saturday Mail Runs Early," buying the pair for forty dollars.

516. *épater les bourgeois*: a phrase championed by late nineteenth-century French poets such as Rimbaud and Baudelaire, meaning "to shock the middle classes."

517. *Marginalia: right side, left facing.*

To George Garrett: Circa January 7–12, 1973

[On the New Orleans Hotel letterhead.]

SNOWED-IN.[518]

Dear George,

Keep the bottle; don't know if the message is readable, or not—that is, a publishable poem. Someone will find it. I just wanted to say, "Heh."[519]

Some of these come from a new ms. of old poems, *Blue Yodels*. (Not to be confused with "Dream Yodel" and "Frankie's Last Blue Yodel".)

Are we still going to get to see every film ever made, by compiling that book of tragic gags—you said "sure" when I suggested it.[520] John Barrymore in "The Beloved Infidel."[521] Some one ought to film one of Lorca's.

I'm traveling around with a woman from Scotland.[522] Last time I was here, I was with A. Ginsberg, who was eating Huckleberry Pie, and writing post cards to Bob Dylan, Mick Jagger, and Voznesensky.[523]

We swam in one of the springs (grotto of the low born[524]), and I feel like Wycliff, who has just screwed the Loch Ness Monster.[525]

A note on Dickey, Bly, and Ginsberg. None of the 3 intimidate me, not by their work or their way of living. They're all good poets, like the other visionary, Wright.

Since I don't belong to any of these schools, I am, so far, accepted by all of them.[526]

If you have faith with me, not just in me, I will not let you down in the years to come. WATCH.

OUT.

Did you know you're the spitting image of Blake—goggled eyed and all.[527]

On the East Coast the younger editor-teacher-poets are teaching me. The older ones don't like it; I'm corrupting youth with my impurities. They call me "Huckleberry Lautremont" and "Sleepwalking Caedemon."[528] The West Coast calls me "Muhammid Fischer,"[529] while the people I use to run with have it right: "gigolo bastard."

Anyway, *I know* what's left of my old work is a failure. They're just poetical sketches, which need to be resolved in film.[530]

If these are no good, it's because the places I drafted them were fine: Eberhart's yacht and Cowley's shade tree.

Boxed a golden gloves guy the other day;[531] he broke all my ribs.

Let him lay there,[532]

Frank

I try to be ribald,
when, actually, I'm becoming sad.

What do you know about Yaddo? M. Cowley says he will sponsor me to go there. Don't know if I can, because three women (my grand mother, mother, baby girl) in my life are all sick in the hospital in Miss. So, when I wrote this letter I was just happy-go-lucky, now I am two steps from the blues. Anyway, I'm glad I know G.G.[533]

How's Irv and Jack Fischer?[534] Haven't heard from them.

You know your book was good.[535]

Malcolm's address:
80 High St.,
Kenilworth,
Warks,
England

(in case you want him to visit a grave)

{3 or 4 books coming out: poetry, 1957–72.}[536]

Dear George,

If the poems aren't neat enough, send them back to the enclosed address.[537] I live, when I'm there—was living—with a bunch of Jamaican dancers. I say bunch, but they're the best in the world, what with being in Alvin Ailey's American Dance troupe. Just about all of them are Black. They do blues-ballad things, but they also did Bernstein's {(can't spell Jewish)} "Mass". Most of them were the youngest dancers with Martha Graham's company, before she quit. If they get to go to China, I might marry a 6½ foot Black woman, or man, whatever, just so I can go. If Sweet William Faulkner could see me now. Have you read any of Joan William's [*sic*] books? Her old man use to shoot dynamite for my old man.

A Farewell Used by Young Lord Byron

Farewell
Is a word
That must be
Like a sword
That has worn out
The scabbard

Notes

518. This writing appears above the letterhead.
519. Stanford may have meant to write "hey."
520. A "tragic gag" is Cocteau's notion of a gag to which the audience responds somberly as opposed to with laughter; per Cocteau, the concept was actually invented by Buñuel (in *Un chien andalou*).
521. As Gregory Peck (not John Barrymore) starred as F. Scott Fitzgerald in Henry King's film *Beloved Infidel* (1959), Stanford presumably meant to write "The Beloved Rogue" here—i.e., *The Beloved Rogue* (1927), dir. Alan Crosland with Barrymore starring as François Villon; the film was considered lost before being rediscovered in Barrymore's mansion in the 1960s and shown on television in August 1971. Also cf. *The Battlefield*, lines 15332–33.
522. Presumably Deidre (or Diedre), the Scottish or English woman who evidently worked at the Museum of Modern Art in summer 1972.
523. Andrei Voznesensky (1933–2010), Soviet Russian poet.
524. Cf. *The Battlefield*: "I vanished to sing a blue yodel of that low born bastard / brought up by the finest of families" (lines 11949–50).

525. John Wycliffe (ca. 1330–84), priest and philosopher known for promoting translation of the entire Bible into English, and the Loch Ness Monster, a water creature of Scottish folklore.

526. Stanford appears to be referencing correspondence received from Dickey, Bly, Ginsberg, and Wright. No Dickey, Bly, or Wright correspondence, incoming or outgoing, has yet been found. Dugan's March 11, 1973, letter to Stanford noted that a recent letter from Stanford to Dugan included or enclosed a "snotty" letter from Bly to Stanford; Dugan stated, "I think he is out of line in criticizing you."

527. Cf. *It Wasn't a Dream: It Was a Flood*, in which Broughton says to Garrett, "You've been accused of having a William Blake forehead"; when Garrett replies, "Well, you're the first person who's ever accused me of that . . . but that's interesting," Broughton replies, "Frank Stanford says that of you, though. He's the first to notice it." Irv Broughton, *It Wasn't a Dream: It Was a Flood* (Mill Mountain Films, 1975), 16 mm film.

528. Huckleberry Finn, the twelve- to fourteen-year-old character in Mark Twain's *The Adventures of Tom Sawyer* (1876) and *Adventures of Huckleberry Finn* (1884); Comte de Lautréamont (1846–70), Uruguayan French poet; and Cædmon.

529. A fusion of Muhammad Ali (1942–2016), boxer, and Bobby Fischer (1943–2008), chess prodigy and, in early 1973, world chess champion following his win in Reykjavík in August 1972.

530. Cf. Blake's first book, *Poetical Sketches* (1783), and also cf. the opening sentence of Stanford's Mid-August 1972 book inscription to Babij above and Stanford's October 16, 1972, letter to Dugan above, par. 2: "Sometimes I think all my songs are sketches that are to be resolved in cinematic drawings."

531. Per Stanford's correspondence with Campbell, this injury actually occurred ca. early November 1972.

532. An allusion to the final, waterside scene in Elia Kazan's 1954 film *On the Waterfront*, when—after Terry Malloy (played by Marlon Brando) has been beaten up by Johnny Friendly and his thugs and lies barely conscious on the dock—Friendly says, "That's enough. Just let him lay there." Stanford repeats the line in his poetry and in the title of an unpublished manuscript, *Let Him Lay There: Some Early Poems*. Brando was a hero of Stanford's; see, e.g., Broughton's interview with Stanford in *What About This*, 727; Stanford's poem "The Truth" (*Smoking Grapevine*), lines 8–10; and *The Battlefield*, line 12226.

533. George Garrett.

534. John G. "Jack" Fisher, former director of theater at Norfolk State College who led a cinema session at the Hollins Conference; cf. note 59 above.

535. Possibly Garrett's novel *Death of the Fox* (1971).

536. *Marginalia: left side, right facing.*

537. Along with "A Farewell Used by Young Lord Byron" (published as "Farewell" in *Ladies From Hell*), poems included with this mailing were "Dante Gabriel Rossetti with His Head on the Virginal" (*Ladies From Hell*), with the notations "from *Lord Gigolo and the Dancers with Chinese Eyes*" and "Poems beginning D.G.R. are not to be confused with those poems in an old MS. called *The Pre-Raphaelites' Little Brother*—some of which will be appearing in NYQ and other small magazines"; "Youth" (published in *What About This*), with the notations "1963" and "from *Lad Overboard*" (cf. *The Battlefield*, lines 2989 and 4064); and an early draft of "Night Time" (*Shade*).

To Irv Broughton: January 12, 1973

[Postcard of Natural Bridge, Eureka Springs, Arkansas, "Little Switzerland of America."]

Irv Broughton
School of Commune
U. of W.
Seattle, Washington.

Dear Boss,

Got letters from Ferlinghetti and Cowley.[538] I pissed off this bridge, reciting a poem by Hart Crane.[539]

I love you, everyone,
Frank

Notes

538. Lawrence Ferlinghetti, poet and cofounder of City Lights Booksellers & Publishers. Ferlinghetti's "letter"—a postcard dated January 3, 1973, and forwarded to the New Orleans Hotel by Subiaco's postal service on January 8—begins, "Dear Stanford— I do dig many of your poems and would like to hold on to the manuscript so that we might choose a poem or two to publish in a City Lights Journal next Fall, if we do one then. OK with you, I hope. And thanks— Lawrence Ferlinghetti." However, Stanford's work didn't end up appearing in the *City Lights Anthology* (1974), as it was titled.

539. Hart Crane (1899–1932), poet.

To Alan Dugan: January 12, 1973

Nine postcards

[Postcard of Ozark cabin.]

Alan Dugan
Box 97
Truro, Mass.

People live here, and charge money to fools who think they don't.

[Postcard of Roman soldiers entering Jerusalem. Scene from *The Great Passion Play*, Eureka Springs.]

Alan Dugan
Box 97
Truro, Mass.

This is true: the fat Roman, leading the pack, is really a fishing guide, who also owns a grocery and laboratory. He has his own "Theory of Light", but N.A.S.A. "refuses" to listen to him.

[Postcard of street in Jerusalem about 33 A.D. Scene from *The Great Passion Play*, Eureka Springs.]

Alan Dugan
Box 97
Truro, Mass.

This place is crazy. I am Sir Richard Burton, and the 7 Pillars of Wisdom are the kinds of wine they make at the monastery, puked all over my bed.

[Postcard of Christ of the Ozarks statue, Eureka Springs.]

Alan Dugan
Box 97
Truro, Mass.

I guess you know the first time I came here was with A. Ginsberg. We had our picture taken here.[540] He held my hand.

[Postcard of Jesus being accused of treason. Scene from *The Great Passion Play*, Eureka Springs.]

Alan Dugan
Box 97
Truro, Mass.

Am I dreaming?

[Postcard of *The Great Passion Play*'s amphitheater/staging area, Eureka Springs.]

{I go to this place, and shout my grievances, and read my poems to the empty, Elizabethan seats.}

The Greeks?

Goddamnit, Alan, now I don't have any more change for beer.

What will I do for stamps?

[Postcard of the New Orleans Hotel, Eureka Springs, explaining that the hotel was built ca. 1890 following an 1888 fire that destroyed the previous structure.]

Alan Dugan
Box 97
Truro, Mass.

My luck: this place will probably catch fire.

[Postcard of Eureka Springs, Arkansas, aerial view.]

Alan Dugan
Box 97
Truro, Mass.

This is where I am going to write a novel.

[Postcard of swinging bridge, Dinosaur Park, near Eureka Springs.]

Alan Dugan
Box 97
Truro, Mass.

Grendel is here.[541]

Dear Alan,

I pissed, off this bridge, reciting a poem by Hart Crane. Does he live in the belly of a shark like a horse shoe?[542]

Destiny: Malcolm Cowley, the man who slid an ace under the table to [Faulkner—who titled and personally submitted my father's best friend's daughter's first story—],[543] has written me, saying: "I'll personally sponsor you to Yaddo."[544] I doubt if I'll go, but it's fate, and knew it when I was seven. What is Yaddo?

Notes

540. See photo at start of chapter I, "Student Life: Fayetteville, 1969–70," above.
541. *Grendel*: one of *Beowulf*'s three antagonists, "a demon grim" and "wretched wight" whom God had "banished . . . far from the fields of men" and who "made his lair with the monster kin," as translated in *Beowulf: The Oldest English Epic*, trans. Charles W. Kennedy (Oxford University Press, 1940), lines 102, 105–6, 110, a version of *Beowulf* that Stanford used.
542. While traveling by ship in April 1932 with Peggy Cowley (recently divorced—in 1931—from Malcolm Cowley) and wearing pajamas and slippers, Crane jumped overboard into the Gulf of Mexico; his body was never located, but his slippered foot was found in the belly of a shark. Note that this postcard's bridge differs from the natural bridge pictured in the January 12, 1973, postcard sent to Broughton.
543. I.e., Joan Williams's story "The Morning and the Evening"—see note 129 above; Williams's actual first published story, "Rain Later," appeared in *Mademoiselle* in August 1949. Brackets Stanford's.

544. See note 487 above, par. 2; Cowley's words were "If you want to go to Yaddo . . . you could give my name as one of your sponsors." Cowley to Frank Stanford, December 21, 1972.

To George Garrett: Winter 1973

[On the New Orleans Hotel letterhead, on which Stanford has written "Love" and "ulcers" respectively above and below the word "Hotel."]

{Love
ulcers}

Dear George,

Sorry for the lousy poems; it was just an excuse to say, "what's happening."

I've got a chance to earn some quick, needed cash if I can obtain a list of film distributors, and select some films for this particular group of people. They'll pay me as soon as I do it, and the distributors as they show the films, etc.

I've got a BRANDON catalog, but that leaves much to be desired: Bergman, to name one; alot of older, American films aren't there.[545] Anyway, when you, if you, have two minutes spare time, could you have one of your secretaries or beautiful students send me a list. I know you're bound to know some—Janus, etc.—from your past experiences. . . . .[546]

I'd certainly be obliged if you would; it'd keep all the Porlocks out of my keyhole for awhile,[547] and I'd be having fun besides.

Yours,
Frank

Frank Stanford
c/o Mrs. Cheryl Campbell
56 Harvard Avenue
Staten Island, N.Y. 10301 and I'll get it

Notes

545. Brandon Films, a company specializing in 16 mm films.

546. Janus Films, a film distribution company.

547. *Porlocks*: untimely pesterers—from Coleridge having been interrupted by an unwelcome visitor from the village of Porlock, in South West England, while composing "Kubla Khan" (1797). *The Complete Poetical Works of Samuel Taylor Coleridge*, ed. Ernest Hartley Coleridge, vol. 1, *Poems* (Clarendon, 1912), 296; cf. *The Battlefield*, line 14650.

The

LOVE

NEW ORLEANS HOTEL

ULCERS

AND ANNA'S ICE CREAM PARLOR

Phone 501-253-8630

63 Spring Street
Eureka Springs, Arkansas 72632

Dear George,

Sorry for the lousy poems; it was just an excuse to say, "what's happening."

I've got a chance to earn some quick, needed cash if I can obtain of list of film distributors, and select some films for this particular group of people. They'll pay me as soon as I do it, and the distributors as they show the films, etc.

I've got a BRANDON catalog, but that leaves much to be desired: Bergman, to name one; alot of older, American films aren't there. Anyway, when you, if you, have two minutes spare time, could you have one of your secretaries or beautiful students send me a list. I know you're bound to know some--Janus, etc.--from your past experiences.............

I'd certainly be obliged if you would; it'd keep all the Porlocks out of my keyhole for awhile, and I'd be having fun besides.

Yours,

Frank

Frank

Frank Stanford
c/o Mrs. Cheryl Campbell
56 Harvard Avenue
Staten Island, N.Y. 10301 and I'll get it

Stanford arrived in Eureka Springs near the close of 1972; for most of his time there, through the winter and into the spring of 1973, he stayed at the New Orleans Hotel—often using the hotel's letterhead for his correspondence, as in this winter 1973 letter to George Garrett.

To Cheryl Campbell: January 31, 1973

A sunny day;
would that we were together.

Dear Cheryl,

What else can I say, other than, "I love you, and miss you." Please don't ever doubt that; it is the one thing that is eternal. I am sane, and very lonely. Bill helped me remember, but I don't think it is worth our valuable time to try to reconstruct it; let the future, ours, together or apart, take root. Sink down deep into us, my love and yours.

Love,
Frank

P.S. Your letters make me live.

—You may be getting some of my editorial correspondence addressed to you; send it and poems on here. Thank you.

To John McKernan: February 1, 1973

[On the New Orleans Hotel letterhead.]

Feb. 1, 1973

Dear Old Friend,

So now I know where you are. I'm living here, in a houseboat, and with Blake's Our Gang comedy of I. and E.[548] Still think you are one of the best. Read some of your poems to some Greek ladies on Richard Eberhart's yacht last summer. Keep in touch.

yours,
"Huckleberry Rimbaud"
("Muhammad Burns")[549]
↖
Reviews

Notes

548. Stanford is blending *Our Gang* (a.k.a. *The Little Rascals*), the series of theatrical short films produced from 1922 to 1944, with Blake's *Songs of Innocence and of Experience*.
549. Stanford's reviewer (or Stanford, if the reviews are nonexistent) is blending Mark Twain's character Huckleberry Finn and Arthur Rimbaud as well as Muhammad Ali and Robert Burns.

To Irv Broughton: Early February 1973

Item: Letter to one of my best friends.[550]

Item: Eureka Springs has been in Ripley's Believe It Or Not more than any other town in the world.[551] They have a Greek amphitheatre that will seat several thousand; a cast of thousands take part in The Great Passion Play:[552] fishing guides who submit their own theories of light to NASA—and have replies from Verner Von Braun tacked up in their general stores beside prize crappie—play the Romans.[553] Jesus got too fat, turned to liquor, so another was hired. Everyone—all the local billies—are awaiting his arrival. Camels and murder trials; this place is a testament to my clairvoyance. Will send you literature on the place. Looks like Switzerland; all the hicks live in Victorian houses—designed at the turn of the century and before by mad architects and built by dreamers who thought they were going to sea—with stained glass, Much, Beardsly, and so on.[554] Completely insane. Borges, Bunuel, and James Dickey could not contrive such a place and people as this, even if they were on DeQuincy's and Coleridge's Pipe.[555] Mark Twain was supposed to have slept in the old hotel I live in, but not even he and his literary journalism—for all its great southwestern humor—could have dreamed this. There is only one black man in seven surrounding counties of Ark. and Mo.; his name is very simple: "Nigger Richard".[556] I will only tell one episode: passed out in the saloon here about noon one day—normally, the police would have been called, or a hillbilly would have taken advantage of me by knocking the shit out of me; but I'm *reverently*—and rather affectionately—regarded as, "The Poot". (O as in oh said by a woman when you put it in, not the O of the moon.)—and woke up around eight in evening: the place was cleared of its usual noise and drinkers; the bartender was standing back from the counter "protecting his mirror", and a hippy was playing an ozark tune on a mandolin—I say hippy, but all of the young folks who live around here are from cities, are really farming this land that is murder, craftsmen and women, silversmiths, leather workers, and apprentices to what I call the carpentry of dope. That is, these young men rise from their communes, get stoned, and go out atop the sides of these cliffs, where the ancient houses look like they were designed by Ivan's men (minarets, dungeons, etc.) and do some of the best renovative woodwork I've ever seen.[557] (This is the land of 500 underground streams, witches who run dairys, and indianmaids who had their sight restored.)—there was not even the equestrian noise of a que ball, for: the bad Ielees boys and their four hundred pound father had come into town for the first time in three months, down from the mountains, all of whom, excepting for the exception of Big Ize, the father, and a couple sons born him by his wife, but not by him, were stone deaf. I'm bound to the natural strangeness of reality, like a country priest to the mystery of his faith.[558] This is all the god's truth, pardon the irrevocable equation, I add none of the fire of the poet to this place and people. I just woke up and saw, in media res, one faction of the family feuding with the other, standing up on juke box on pool table, table, on one another's shoulders, motioning in sweet legerdemain of the deaf and dumb. So often, you have heard me say, "It was like a dream." Byron said, "I had a dream, which was not all a dream." He said this in the poem, "Darkness".[559] Well, it was dark, and there was the stoned young mandolinist, but these brothers had broken out into a ruckus, which only you and the very few others who have read certain MSS., can appreciate. The father, Big Ize, and those of his sons who were not really his sons, but who were normal in speech and hearing, if you could call the sounds of hill men normal, and ears able to hear the footfall of a fox in a coop of guineas, normal, then I bid you, do it.[560] I meant to say the father had his finger broken by one of the sons, and, in turn, he bit the ear of the boy who did it. I say boy, when some of them had boys of their own, twelve or thirteen. The habanera of these hillfolks' hands turned into a flamenco of rage.[561] I've never seen such rage conveyed in eyes and in stress joints of fingers. After awhile, they began making deep guttural sounds, like you do when you fuck. I looked over in the corner, and there on a pony you put a dime in to ride, was the six year old son, his eyes shut, oblivious to his brothers. I felt like weeping, and would of, if it had not been for "Nigger Richard" to appear outside the picture window on his mule.[562] Before he could stumble in, the owners of the bar had arrived. You are not going to believe this: the owner is a man called Frankie Green, and his wife is Johnny Green.[563] Their son is called little Frankie Green, and the six foot one sixteen year old girl that I've been screwing, regularly, since I got here, beats the fellow up, every other day, in some dark corner of the gymnasium. She is a track star, with some state records, and she hails from Roanoke, of all places.[564] Anyway, Johnny Green took hold of one of the more sawdust deaf and dumb runts and began to shake the daylights out of him. In a matter of a few minutes, the local police came to run them out of town for a few more months. All left but the father and the tot on the dime pony, and I went to the bar for beer. I felt like a somnambulist. Somewhere, I could remember the mandolinist saying, "No", when he broke a string, and the scent of poutoli musk.[565] (Irv, you aren't believing me. All this is so true it hurts. Where else can you see a half-blooded cherokee riding a camel, and a former nuclear physicist, blowing glass ships. Where else can one come and see Judas hung nightly. I look out one window and there is the Crescent moon over the Crescent Hotel,[566] and in the distance I can see the hut of Crescent Dragon, soi-disant appellative of a swan maiden from The Big Apple who writes famous herbal cookbooks,[567] who is rich, and who has parents connected in someway with publishing the best line of children's books in NYC,[568] and you don't believe me still. You wait, mother fucker. I'm going to send you something, a few things that will be like incantations, stilllife. The gift you'll be getting, and the documentation of something I may have to appear in a murder trial over. More about the latter in another letter, and of the former, just you wait.) The boy was mad because he'd bought the incense, a fairly good quarter of his money, thinking they were sparklers. I asked his father what he was saying, and that's how I know. I forgot to tell you, the name of the six foot one blond, who wants to be a masseur, and there are plenty around here, for the body and mind, is Strawberry. Her best friend is Heather, who is pregnant. The other woman I'm seeing is an artist, about thirty, seven years older than eye, fourteen years Strawberry's senior,[569] who is unmarried, but with a six month old child. We were snowed in long ago,[570] and I had a vision seeing them walk by a gazebo, her in her black Napoleonic coat, and the papoose in an Aztec blanket. Two stories drafted about her. Her name is Anna. Almost a Karanina or Magnani, but only because I've always kept aloof from both characters and roles.[571] I made love to her while her child was nursing. Jesus Christ. It reminds me of an old poem where I took milk with a black calf from its mother.[572] I think I know the girl I gave the poem to, but I'm writing it in to a script I'm gonna send Jimbo Babij. Is this why Dugan said I was the greatest living poet, whether or not I wrote another line. Is this why Ginsberg told me, in this very place, in the Spring of 69 (sounds funny doesn't it) that I was the reincarnation of Robert Burns and Robert Johnson, and that I reminded him of Neil Cassidy, which is a fine thing to say, and that I also reminded him of some of Blake, Chatterton, and a toilet paper roll of others who make it sound like a coil of rice paper for the feet of Sumiye painters, etc.[573] Is this why a guy is writing a review of the book you published and a few other little things he's seen, and in it, he says he's going to call me The Marlon Brando of Poetry; an actor and a dancer—and 119 other nouns he's compiled, in parody of my use of a good noun instead of weak links in the fence of adjnoun—who writes about James Dean, Rossetti, and women at the age of eight. (I think you ought to copyright, yourself, calling me the Marlon Brando of poetry, because I think it is something that will stick: the comparisons with Ali and Fischer are ok, but too current.[574] Did I tell you Malcolm Cowley's written me twice, once from England, saying he'll personally sponsor me to someplace Yaddo? Manage me,

Dundee. Didn't I name a character Dundee.[575] It must have been after the Liston Clay fight when I was in tenth grade, fingerfucking Davilee Nevius.[576] To go on about the saloon, which is much more interesting than my career, Big Ize pinched me on the side, where I broke my ribs boxing a few months past,[577] and said to Nigger Richard and the seventy four year old whore who lives here too, and who breaks me fresh bread twice a week, so I don't starve, and who I won't [*sic*] to steal the diamond from her finger, I admit it, I admit the criminal element, and so one, Big Ize, he says, "Just like" . . . . . . (couldn't make out the noun or gerund) "I'd like to bust that horse, wouldn't you Rich." Which all goes to show you no matter how much a buffoon James Dickey is, no matter his diminishing role in poetry—most of which is the finest written—due to the fact professors and knownothing whimperers are taking over the scene—James Dickey has some Vision into the culture of the cancerous buttmilk South, no matter how closed a vision it is. James Dickey is going to turn into something yet. He is the kind of man and poet you hate and love, like the enemy pilot. I say this from the Japanese side. He puts his left toe out, turns it all about, draws a line in the dust at his feet, dares you to cross it, calling it His, mine always, and puts up a good fight. While I, I draw a circle in somewhat the same dust around myself, tell you to move over, into the shade of it, give it to you, there, there you go, now I'm gone before you know it. Ha Ha is a favorite line, no matter who rights [*sic*] it. If James Dickey says he hates me, I know I'm stuck in his craw. If he likes me, I'm "suspect".

Well, I've done it, boss. Rented a building, projector, etc. I'm now the most in debt Shower of Films in the country. Two weeks from today, this morning, a dream come to, if I can't go to it, I'll bring it to me, the Films Of Jean Vigo in Eureka Springs Cinema.[578] The next night, the films of Rossen {Body and Soul, Hustler, Lilith, All King's Men, The Sea Wolf, which he wrote},[579] the next night, the films The Informer and Odd Man Out, the next night, and for the rest of week, a sort of James Ageeish Chess of directors, actors, actresses, writers, cameramen, etc.[580] The Big Sleep, Caine Mutiny, Key Largo, Petriefied Forest (of which I have autographed picture of Louise Fazenda, my mother's friend, and Humphrey Bogart, in a scene from it), Little Caesar and Casablanca, HalWall's best stuff, to Member of The Wedding, Intruder in The Dust, (childhood favorite), other things Faulkner, to Lost Horizon to Renoir, and so on.[581] After the first week, it'll be an every other week double feature. Blake said, "He who respects the Infant's faith, Triumphs over Hell and Death."[582] Remember that line, friend. Remember, the perceptual conception of a boy on a beach, wind, gunpowder, ships, all wrecked in the strands of his hair, his feet smelling of olives, who made what is left of that Ms., then, a progeny from one to all and all for one; it is so, that it is written, it is destiny, via Cowley and Joan Williams, the levees, that The Southerner, the film, was conceived by Faulkner and

Renoir, so I could perceive it, so I could conceive.[583] Parthagenisis [*sic*] of my own poetry.[584] The child knew.

That is why Cinema is my form, it is my drawing, like a flute holding the water of my poetry, just some gentle pressure over the orifices.[585] This art with lips like the mouth of a river. Vision or mission, I don't know which. We must go on. I can write anything, anytime, anywhere, as long as I feel some warmth from humankind. There was a while there, I had my third rate Gethsemene, but I'm full of Action and Mystery, like Marc Chagall, from now on.[586] *Say there, how you felling* [*sic*]. Remember that song. How in the world on the chicktracked barnfloor of a sheet of paper do you convey anything at all about Say there, which is a Song Without Words (Mendohlsohn, and so on, you know what I mean? Maybe not.)[587] and then how you feeeeeeeeeeeeeeeeeelin. Fe Ling was the second daughter to Say No, who was a man of the intellectual fist school of fighting; it was his brother, Bo Die, whom I want to tell about. He had a limp, no scars, and a horse so black it looked blue. He was of the soft fist style.

Everyone I know, I'm threatening with the usury of art. I can get American Films, old ones, for 35.00 a piece, and I'm hitting up every close friend I have to patron one film. I sunk everything I have into this, and if you can't spare 35 Mo for a friend,[588] can you buy, call it that, anything I could write for you. As soon as the wind. I learned how to beg from Saint Francis, Francois Villon, and you.[589] So, we're all keeping good company. After I get a little capital, I can rent foreign films. If there is anyway you can send me films you rent for your courses, etc., I foot postage CoD, etc.[590] Also, get your Sec. to send me a list of all 16 MM distributors. I've got a Brando Catalogue but it lacks all to hell. Notice I left out the n since the guy said I was either great or terrible.[591]

My gift to you, two, one too heavy to mail, is my only cherished object. It is an old butcher knife, over seventy years, which came from the shed of a place on William Faulkner's place. The other is a shoe that came [from] one of his horses; it was shoed by the man, now dead, who was a character in many of his stories. I'm sending the knife. I had another knife that came from the body of a prisoner; I showed you it in Fayetteville. "Remember Me forever" inscribed on the bone handled, falcon shaft. It is gone, like the past.

So I could get this film thing going, I had to sell something I loved: my old spinning wheel. It stood very high and is as long as a casket. The bastard only gave me a hundred for it, and now he's asking threefifty, the bastard is too good a word for him. At least, I can get it back for 125. If you know of anyone who wants such a beautiful spider of wood, let me know. Maybe I can make five bucks on the deal. For bottles of wine, or a week's supply of fresh honey goat yogurt and bananas for my gut. I'm going to commit a sin. I have a whole tow sack of odds and ends I picked up on Faulkner's place, a long time ago: stirrups, cantaloupe seeds with his handwriting on the envelope when he got them, Summer, etc; tw spool, piece of mirror, busted plow, bottle, leather bridle, brush, stuff that a madman would steal. Sometimes, I feel like one of those thieves who entered the tombs of the dead pharaoh. But that is a bad analogy, seeing as to how Go Down Moses was and all, and it was those archaeologists that got cursed and had heart attacks, not the sad thieve.[592] Anyway, I can get 120.00 from someone for it, who will probably sell it to a museum for a ransom of blood money. Just about thirty or forty pounds of stuff. Write me a long letter, dream like Leadbelly.[593]

Frank $$$$$$

Notes

550. The circa dating of this letter is based on context, overlapping content with a February 4, 1973, letter to Campbell, and a letter from Broughton apparently mailed on February 8, 1973, beginning, "Dear Frank, Just got the jelly roll of a letter," which "fell in like nothing in the world."

551. *Ripley's Believe It or Not!*, a series of books, TV shows, etc., covering bizarrely true items and events.

552. *The Great Passion Play*—staged at an amphitheater east of Eureka Springs.

553. Wernher von Braun (1912–77), German American space engineer.

554. *Much*: presumably Alphonse Mucha (1860–1939), Czech artist largely known for his Art Nouveau style, including stained-glass work. *Beardsly*: Charles T. Beardsley (1861–1937), architect known for his Queen Anne, Richardsonian Romanesque, and other period designs.

555. De Quincey's autobiography, *Confessions of an English Opium-Eater* (1821), largely concerns his laudanum addiction; Coleridge was also addicted to laudanum for much of his life.

556. I.e., Richard Banks (1913–75). Banks, the only African American residing near Eureka Springs, Arkansas, at the time of his death in January 1975, was regularly referred to as "Nigger Rich" among townspeople who knew him. Banks may have told friends and others to refer to him as such, though accounts are inconsistent as to whether he welcomed the name or not. Banks, who became a close friend of Stanford's, appears at the beginning of *It Wasn't a Dream: It Was a Flood*.

557. *Ivan*: presumably Ivan the Terrible (1530–84), first crowned tsar of all Russia.

558. An allusion to Robert Bresson's 1951 film, *Diary of a Country Priest*.

559. See note 493 above.

560. Guinea fowl—African barnyard birds related to pheasants.

561. *Habanera*: a Spanish/Cuban dance also called *contradanza*; *flamenco*: an energetic Andalusian dance style.

562. Both Clarke Freeman and Frank Green Jr., longtime Eureka Springs residents, have noted to this editor that Banks did not have a mule and that he actually drove a vintage Plymouth. Freeman and Green texts to editor, September 18, 2023. It appears that when Stanford met Banks, probably in January 1973, he regarded him as bearing similarity to his character Sylvester (in *The Battlefield*, Sylvester Martingale, later Sylvester the Black Angel); see *The Battlefield*, line 2779.

563. Though Stanford mainly frequented the Hi Hat Lounge, on Spring Street near the New Orleans Hotel, in early 1973, this letter's action takes place at another popular Eureka Springs bar, Main Street Bar, formerly located at 63 S. Main Street, at the corner of Benton Street. Both bars were owned in 1973 by Frank Green Sr. (whose wife's name was Kay, not Johnny), both had pool tables and jukeboxes, and neither had a mechanical pony, actually, but Frank Green Jr. noted to this editor that the Main Street Bar—the establishment more resembling a saloon and the one Banks frequented—had mirrors behind its bar and two picture windows that Banks routinely looked into before entering; never fully comfortable inside the bar in the otherwise white town, Banks typically sat at the end of the bar near the front door in case he ever needed easy egress. Frank Green Jr., emails to editor, February 3 and 4, 2026.

564. Roanoke, Virginia—location of Hollins College (now Hollins University), where Stanford and Broughton first met.

565. *poutoli*: patchouli oil, an essential oil popular with hippies and other members of the counterculture.

566. *Crescent Hotel*: a historic nineteenth-century hotel in Eureka Springs.

567. *soi-disant*: self-proclaimed or so-called. Stanford is referring to Crescent Dragonwagon, nom de plume of Ellen Zolotow (b. 1952), author of *The Commune Cookbook* (1972) and *The Bean Book* (1972); Dragonwagon later cofounded the Writers' Colony at Dairy Hollow in Eureka Springs.

568. Dragonwagon was born in New York City to author parents; her mother was an editor and children's author.

569. *eye*: i.e., I; however, Stanford was twenty-four years old (not twenty-three) in February 1973.

570. I.e., in the ice and snowstorm of, roughly, January 6–12, 1973.

571. Anna Karenina from Leo Tolstoy's eponymous 1878 novel and Italian actor Anna Magnani (1908–73) of Italian Neorealism fame, known for starring in Daniel Mann's *The Rose Tattoo* (1955), Pasolini's *Mamma Roma* (1962), and other films.

572. See the closing lines of Stanford's poem "a koto I found in the Rosedale whorehouse":

> if I got hungry enough
> and no one
> was looking
> I might share the teats with a black calf
> (*What About This*, 541)

573. Robert Johnson (1911–38), blues musician; Neal Cassady (1926–68), an influential figure in the Beat Generation on whom Dean Moriarty in Jack Kerouac's novel *On the Road* (1957) is based; Thomas Chatterton (1752–70), English poet who died by suicide at age seventeen; and sumi-e painters.
574. Muhammad Ali and Bobby Fischer; see Stanford's mention of "Muhammid Fischer" in his Circa January 7–12, 1973, letter to Garrett above, par. 10, and note 529 above.
575. No characters in Stanford's published poetry are named Dundee.
576. The Cassius Clay–Sonny Liston fight of February 25, 1964, when Stanford was a sophomore in high school. Clay defeated Liston, becoming heavyweight world champion, and soon changed his name to Muhammad Ali. *Davilee Nevius*: correctly, Davalee Nevius; see *The Battlefield*, line 12509.
577. Cf. Stanford's Circa January 7–12, 1973, letter to Garrett above, par. 13, and see note 531 above.
578. Jean Vigo, French filmmaker best known for *Zero for Conduct* (1933) and *L'Atalante* (1934).
579. *Marginalia: right side, upright*. Robert Rossen, American filmmaker; *Body and Soul*, *The Hustler*, *Lilith*, and *All the King's Men*—1947, 1961, 1964, and 1949 films dir. Rossen; and *The Sea Wolf* (1941), dir. Michael Curtiz and written by Rossen.
580. *The Informer* (1935), dir. John Ford; *Odd Man Out* (1947), dir. Carol Reed (see Stanford's March 1, 1972, letter to Dugan above, par. 2); and James Agee (1909–55), novelist and screenwriter of *The African Queen* (1951) and *The Night of the Hunter* (1955).
581. *The Big Sleep* (1946), dir. Howard Hawks; *The Caine Mutiny* (1954), dir. Edward Dmytryk; *Key Largo* (1948), dir. John Huston; *The Petrified Forest* (1936), dir. Archie Mayo; *Little Caesar* (1931), dir. Mervyn LeRoy; *Casablanca* (1942), dir. Michael Curtiz; Hal B. Wallis, film producer who was married to Louise Fazenda (1895–1962) (Wallis and Fazenda were godparents to Stanford's sister, Ruth); *The Member of the Wedding* (1952), dir. Fred Zinnemann; *Intruder in the Dust* (1949), dir. Clarence Brown and based on the novel by Faulkner (see *The Battlefield*, line 7463, in which Francis notes that the film is his "all time favorite"); *Lost Horizon* (1937), dir. Frank Capra; and Jean Renoir, French filmmaker.
582. "He who respects the Infant's faith / Triumphs over Hell & Death."—lines 89–90 of "Auguries of Innocence," a ca. 1803 poem, from the Pickering Manuscript,

by William Blake. *Complete Writings with Variant Readings*, ed. Geoffrey Keynes (Oxford University Press, 1972), 433.

583. *The Southerner* (1945), dir. Renoir, written by Renoir—with uncredited writing assistance by Faulkner.

584. Stanford means parthenogenesis, a natural form of asexual reproduction.

585. Cf. Stanford's Circa December 29–30, 1972, letter to Eberhart above, par. 2: "One day, I hope to make films side by side with my poems, as Blake drew and engraved."

586. *Gethsemane*: as described in Mark 14, the garden outside Jerusalem where Jesus suffered in agony—or perhaps a reference to the Abbey of Our Lady of Gethsemani in Kentucky, where Trappist monk Thomas Merton (1915–68) had been a member.

587. *Songs Without Words* (*Lieder ohne Worte*, 1829–45), a series of piano compositions by Felix Mendelssohn (1809–47).

588. *Mo*: presumably, money order.

589. Francis of Assisi (ca. 1181–1226), Italian mystic/saint who begged with the poor and after whom Stanford's collection of early writings *St. Francis and the Wolf: Some Poems 1957–1964* is titled. Villon lived in poverty and thieved.

590. *COD*: cash (or collect) on delivery.

591. I.e., Stanford has a *Brandon* catalog. Stanford is alluding to Italian poet-filmmaker Bernardo Bertolucci's words about Brando as published in a cover story / review of Bertolucci's film *Last Tango in Paris* (1972) in the January 22, 1973, issue of *Time* magazine, in which Bertolucci's "verdict" on Brando (as *Time* put it) was (in Bertolucci's words): "An angel as a man and a monster as an actor. He is all instinct, but at the same time he is a complex man." "Self-Portrait of an Angel and Monster," 53.

592. *Go Down, Moses* (1942), a collection of short stories by Faulkner. In the collection, the character Samuel Beauchamp steals from the farm, and cousins Isaac McCaslin and McCaslin Edmonds argue over whether man's attempt to own the land is a curse.

593. *Dream Like Leadbelly* is the title of a currently unpublished screenplay on Stanford's life and death by Broughton. Lead Belly's song "Whoa, Back, Buck!" (1946) plays in *It Wasn't a Dream: It Was a Flood*.

To Father Herbert Vogelpohl: February 21, 1973

Dear Father Herbert,

Thanks for the note. I was getting a remarkable amount of work done, until I got this letter from mother, where she achieved her objective of making me hate myself, once again.[594] The film thing, and good news, has helped me get my mind back, plus make some weekly money. Those kind of letters were the reason I left in the first place. Hope everything is fine with you.

Twice a week I walk eight miles to the top of this mountain and take holy communion at the Episcopal Church.[595]

Say hello to Br. Mike and everyone else.[596]

Notes

594. Fr. Herbert Vogelpohl, OSB (1911–2005), of Subiaco directed Coury House, working closely for many years with Dorothy Stanford, with whom he was close friends.
595. Stanford is hyperbolizing; St. James' Episcopal Church, the only Episcopal church in Eureka Springs—at 28 Prospect Avenue, where it has been located since 1889—is less than a half mile from the New Orleans Hotel at 63 Spring Street, though the church is indeed atop a very steep hill.
596. Fr. Jerome Kodell of Subiaco noted, to this editor, that the "Br. Mike" here would be Br. Michael Fuhrmann, OSB (1920–2005), Fr. Nicholas's first cousin. Email to editor, August 1, 2023.

To Irv Broughton: Circa March 11, 1973

[On the New Orleans Hotel letterhead.]

Dear Irv,

Sorry didn't get your message, March 4th, Sunday Five P.M. Drove two hundred miles to see "Blood of a Poet" again.[597] Got drunk on Yage Chablis and San Gria,[598] then saw "Nothing But A Man".[599] Kicked out of hotel for week due to finances. Hired out on cattle ranch, where breeding calves were dropping from heifers like flies. Made enough for rent. Got my four films in Joplin, Mo.[600] Got drunk, driving through the Bonnie and Clyde & James Bros. badlands, forgot the films were in this girl's trunk.[601] They ended up in Tulsa. Crazy. Talked at two Missouri colleges (small) about films. Got one to build a rear projection unit, buy a new projector. So, when it comes time for our film, we are in the best of hands. If I were to tell you *just* about me and my life at this moment, I would not be able to write. "Nigger Richard" wants me to move in with him, take care of him.[602] Why is it that my past is rejuvenating itself? I'm not consciously trying to relive what I've done and written about!!! Sorry story is so late. But it was locked up with my things in hotel room, couldn't get them until I footed rent. O.K. now, at least until April. Don't know date, only it is raining, warm, and a beautiful woman is sleeping in my bed, her eyes half open. I have a fifth of vodka and enough money for stamps to get all this to you. Have you gotten knife and seeds?[603] Can you sell the other junk? Is there any way you can check out a film and send? Nanook, Louisana Story?[604] You can mail Special Delivery Library Rate for under three dollars, including insurance. This week the doc. filmer Les Blank will be here to show his work on Lightning Hopkins and Mance Lipscomb. He's doing doc. on Leon Russell now.[605] Please read letters enclosed, clear out a space of all clutter to set down my ship of work coming in to you.[606] Interview coming along.[607]

Yours, Spellbound,
Frank

Notes

597. *Le Sang d'un poète*, Cocteau's 1932 film.
598. *Yage*: a principal ingredient in ayahuasca that can be used to produce a hallucinogenic drink. *Chablis*: a French white wine. Sangria is a wine punch.
599. *Nothing but a Man* (1964), dir. Michael Roemer.
600. Presumably, the four films Stanford screened, or intended to screen, for the opening weekend of his theater at 8 Center Street in Eureka Springs—per a February 27 letter to Broughton: *Diary of a Country Priest* (1951), dir. Bresson; *Zero for Conduct* (1933) and *L'Atalante* (1934), dir. Vigo; and *St. Louis Blues* (1929), dir. Dudley Murphy.
601. Bonnie and Clyde passed time in Joplin and Platte City, Missouri, in 1933; late nineteenth-century outlaws Jesse James and Frank James were based in western Missouri.
602. I.e., Richard Banks; see note 556 above.
603. See Stanford's Early February 1973 letter to Broughton above, pars. 5–6, re: Faulkner's knife and cantaloupe seeds that Stanford lifted from Faulkner's property.
604. *Nanook of the North* (1922) and *Louisiana Story* (1948), dir. Robert J. Flaherty.
605. *A Poem Is a Naked Person* (1974), dir. Les Blank, a documentary about musician Leon Russell (1942–2016).

The circa dating of this letter is based on context; the fact that Ginny Stanford (likely the "beautiful woman" mentioned here) has noted to this editor that she met Stanford on March 3, 1973, in Neosho, Missouri, and visited him at the New Orleans Hotel the following weekend (March 10–11); Broughton's apparent reply letter of March 14, 1973 (noting, "Enjoyed your story + letters"); and cross analysis with a letter from Stanford to Broughton likely penned March 19, 1973. Ginny Stanford, email to editor, March 4, 2008.

Assuming that this dating is correct, it appears to conflict with Stanford's mention of Blank visiting Eureka Springs "this week." On March 15, 1973, the *Eureka Springs Times-Echo* noted that Les Blank would be present at Eureka Springs' Gaslight Theatre on Tuesday, March 20, for screenings of his documentaries *The Blues Accordin' to Lightnin' Hopkins* (1968) and *A Well Spent Life* (1971), about blues musician Mance

Lipscomb (1895–1976). The article does not mention Leon Russell, so Stanford's mention here of Blank's visit doesn't appear to be in response to having read the article; Stanford may be using "this week" imprecisely or perhaps was unclear or misinformed on when, exactly, Blank would be visiting town. "Les Blank Film Show Planned Here Tuesday," *Eureka Springs Times-Echo*, March 15, 1973, 1.

606. Stapled together with this undated letter are two other letters from Stanford to Broughton, both also on hotel letterhead, dated February 1 and February 27, 1973.

607. Stanford is likely referring to Broughton's list of interview questions for him; see Stanford's June 11, 1973, letter to Broughton below, opening sentence.

To Irv Broughton: March 14, 1973

[On the New Orleans Hotel letterhead.]

March 14, 1973

Dear Irv,

Should have at least up to page 375 (fragment) of "the battle . . ." to you by the end of month.[608] Beginning to begin again on some stories and novels I've had in mind forever and ever; still have some in MS. I might ought to type up parts of and send to you, request your opinion as to which one is more worthwhile. Just know you won't be able to make out all that green handwriting, etc.

Here is my spiel: I've found a cabin way away on white river I can lease for as long as I want. The area is called SPIDER CREEK.[609] Some rich yankee fishermen have been renting it, perhaps a couple or three months out of the year. I can move in the end of this month if I have the dough for first and last month's rent. I'm doing an incredible amount of work, hoping some of it is good, awaiting your opinion. I read the Lawrence book in two sittings; it put me into a respectable daze, and I intend to work on my work, forfeiting Byronic influences, and ploughing on into "blood-knowledge".[610] Still haven't heard about any of those grants, not expecting anything, but it would help. Being on the river, I can catch and grow my food; I'll also be miles away from a bar. A friend will lend me a canoe, another says I can have a goat—for milk and yogurt—and a saddle horse. If I learn this part of the river, I might be able to make a few books as a guide.[611] It has been a long time since I've done that.[612] What I need to get this place is $150.00. This wouldn't be money down the drain, as I would pay it back, ten dollars a month, promised, or a chapter or a story each month. I know you are broke, and might not be able to make an investment in my writing at this time, but I garuntee [*sic*] good work. In other words, I'd be working for you for ten dollars a month. Waiting to hear from you about this and especially what you think of poems, story, and novel, scenario, story drafts.

Let me know as soon as you can, since I have these people on the hook about getting the place.

Yours,
David Copperfield[613]

Notes

608. The typescript of *The Battlefield Where the Moon Says I Love You*, beginning "tonight the gars" and ending "you're crazy as hell," is 375 pages; beginning at fragment 292, each page's number is labeled as "fragment." In a February 27, 1973, letter to Broughton, Stanford states that Cheryl Campbell is typing up pages/fragments 292–375, though it appears (from typescript analysis and files in her collection) that Cheryl ended up typing, specifically, fragments 292–314 and 326–50.

609. Spider Creek Resort, located about ten miles northwest of downtown Eureka Springs in Busch, Arkansas. Stanford rented cabin no. 7, a one-bedroom cabin with a view of the White River.

610. *the Lawrence book*: possibly *D. H. Lawrence's Letters to Bertrand Russell*; *"blood-knowledge"*: Lawrence's blood-consciousness theories—that visceral intuition and sentiment are more meaningful or wiser than the intellect and shouldn't be regarded as inferior to science—were a central tenet of his philosophy. Per Lawrence's explanation in his December 8, 1915, letter to philosopher Bertrand Russell (1872–1970): "There is another seat of consciousness than the brain & the nerve system: there is a blood-consciousness which exists in us independently of the ordinary mental consciousness. . . . When I take a woman, then the blood-percept is supreme, my blood-knowing is overwhelming. There is a transmission, I don't know of what, between her blood & mine, in the act of connection. . . . This is very important to our living, that we should realise that we have a blood-being, a blood-consciousness, a blood-soul, complete and apart from the mental & nerve consciousness." In *D. H. Lawrence's Letters to Bertrand Russell*, ed. Harry T. Moore (Gotham Book Mart, 1948), 63–65.

    Re: "Byronic influences," cf. *The Battlefield*, lines 13157–58: "but what I really wanted to be was Lord Byron / I was just itching to be him."

611. Stanford presumably meant to type "a few bucks."

612. See the *Chronology* in this book's back matter; Stanford worked as a fishman and guide on Norfork Lake in Mountain Home from 1963 to 1964.

613. Stanford shares some likeness to the titular protagonist of Charles Dickens's novel *David Copperfield* (1850), as neither knew his biological father and both were raised by their mothers until the women remarried, were typically called by names other than their given names (Frankie or Frank in Stanford's case, as opposed to Francis), were sent to boarding schools, and later became writers.

Stanford on the porch of the house on the White River Lodge resort property in which he lived with Ginny Crouch in late summer and fall 1973. On his lap is a copy of *Three Tragedies of Federico García Lorca: "Blood Wedding," "Yerma," and "Bernarda Alba"* (1955). *Photographer: Ginny Stanford.*

V.

SPIDER CREEK AND THE WHITE RIVER

Busch, 1973

In late March or early April 1973, Stanford rented a small cabin for writing at Spider Creek in Busch, Arkansas, northwest of Eureka Springs, and in late spring, he and Ginny Crouch moved in together in a small wood frame cabin near the White River that was part of an old resort in Busch known in that era as White River Lodge. Stanford continued to screen films in Eureka Springs through the spring, and he wrote, returned to land surveying, and worked as a fishing guide and lodge caretaker through the warmer months. In late summer, the couple moved into a larger structure, a house, on the property, across the road from the main lodge. In August, Stanford sent a thick envelope of poems to editor Michael Cuddihy, thus beginning a sustained friendship and correspondence.

To Irv Broughton: April 12, 1973

April 12

Dear Irv,

Thank you for everything and more. Love it here, and plan to stay awhile. (1 year)[614]

Let me hear *how* you are doing, *books*, *living*, etc.

Rain, rain, rain.[615]

Do you want me to film with you, again, this summer or early fall? Who will you work on?

Are my poems any good. I would like to write another Ancient Mariner.[616]

Please let me know what all you are doing,

yours,
Frank

Notes

614. Presumably, Spider Creek Resort's cabin no. 7.
615. March and April 1973 were unusually and nearly consistently rainy in northwest Arkansas.
616. I.e., *The Rime of the Ancient Mariner* (1798)—Coleridge's major long poem (typically 625 lines, 658 lines in the first edition).

To Irv Broughton: June 11, 1973

June 11

Dear Irv,

Promise to have new interview to you sometime in July.

Working outside 10–12 hrs. a day. Sorry haven't written, but you have been on my mind, as I climb the mtns, search the fields for cornerstones. Earning all this living—I am very happy doing it—bites into my time, but I've managed to *finish* several stories, poems, short screenplays.

The girl I am living with is a good photographer and a great artist. Her drawings are wonderful, and her paintings are coming along. You *must* see how she sees all my characters, images, and so on. Do enquire about her work, possibility of using some of it.

I'll be ready to do the films at the end of summer. I can work on your films any time. Where is Babij?

yours,
Frank

To Alan Dugan: June 23, 1973

June 23
Spider Creek
Gen. Del.
Busch, Ark 72620

Dear Alan + Judith,

Four months, or better, have passed since I've heard from you, and it's been longer than that since I last wrote, but I think both of you will be glad to know I've found, and am *soul* [*sic*] caretaker of, what is as close as I'll come to a good and tenable situation: a lodge at the fork of Spider Creek and White River.[617] I'm a fishing guide (more Keatsian than commercial), and groundskeeper part time; and full time land surveyor. I've never made 3.50 an hour before, or $45 a day guiding, so this is the life. I know what it must feel like to be paid for writing poems, now. *No one* visits the lodge, so I love my work. The field book is full of angles and lyrics. I rent canoes, I pay the rent.

The best of all this is the artist I met in a field one day.[618] She is very good, and one day I hope both of you can see her work—especially the drawings + paintings she got from me. She reads one of my poems, drinks a bottle of wine, sits by the river, listens to Mahler, and fills up several sketch books before I return, at sundown, from work.

Somehow, through the French Embassy, I have some very fine films on loan. We watch, on the wall, Cocteau, Carné, and Renoir—also documentaries on Rousseau, de Maupassant, Hugo, Proust, and so on.[619]

This is the life.

Now, tell me, if you wish, about Mexico. When is your book due to be out.[620] I'll never hear, around these parts, unless you tell me. (For the hell of it, I wrote half a dozen short stories and a novella.) When is the *Iowa Review* going to publish that interview? Please let me know.[621]

There are plenty of cabins and rooms and boats, so come visit me. I won't tell anyone you're coming, excepting local folks you'll love drinking + cursing with.

yours,
Frank

Notes

617. The lodge, with current address of 522 County Road 109—on a property that was in that era the old White River Lodge resort in Busch—is a house near the end and on the south side of C.R. 109 that backs up to the White River; it is less than a mile northeast of the point where Spider Creek and the White River intersect.
618. See note 605 above, par. 2.
619. Henri Rousseau (1844–1910), French painter, and Guy de Maupassant (1850–93), Victor Hugo (1802–85), and Marcel Proust (1871–1922), French authors.
620. Dugan's book *Poems 4* (1974).
621. Alan Dugan, "An Interview with Alan Dugan," interview by Michael Ryan, *Iowa Review* 4, no. 3 (Summer 1973): 90–97.

To Eleanor Bender: July 13, 1973

Friday, July 13
Spider Creek
Gen. Del.
Busch, Ark. 72620

Dear Eleanor,

Thank you for your letter of last winter. Are you near the ocean, or in the woods?

I have a job as a caretaker of an old lodge on the river—and as a fishing guide. Rent canoes, etc.

Hope—still—that we may meet one day, so I can make up for my insane, bothersome letters. If you knew me, you would know I'm use to sweat and no hand to be held. Sorry that was your impression.

Sometimes I go see a woman who lives on a 700 acre farm around Neck City or Lamar;[622] that's about as far as I get your way.

They released some of Berryman's correspondence. He had this poem, and liked it; so I send it on to you, hoping you will think it is finished.

What did you think about *Tango* and *Cries and Whispers*?[623]

yours,
Frank

Notes

622. Towns in southwest Missouri; the farm of Ginny Crouch's parents, south of Liberal, Missouri, was located roughly between Neck City and Lamar.
623. *Last Tango in Paris* (1972), dir. Bernardo Bertolucci, and *Cries and Whispers* (1972), dir. Ingmar Bergman.

To Irv Broughton: August 28, 1973

August 28, 1973
Last Night On The River Lodge
Gen. Del.
Busch, Arkansas 72620

Dear Irv,

Ginny just got back from getting the mail and I see there is a thick one from you. I'm typing this, over an unreadable handwritten one, in answer and gratitude for having those poems copied. I'll answer the letter I received today by Sept. 1st I promise.

I have three stories and three screenplays (short) typed-up. When you need (if) any of them, just drop a card and I'll mail them, if you can send me back a duplicate copy.

Although my wages boss is the same, I'm doing four different jobs for him. Surveying land; Caretaking of the Lodge, Grounds, and Cabins; Renovating all the buildings (carpentry, painting, elec., plumbing, etc.); and a Guide. I've had to turn down alot of the latter work because I made a promise to get this place in shape. It is really run down. Strange.

There are seven wood and rock cabins, some with fireplaces, and six rooms in the Lodge.[624] A big kitchen and pinewood&beams fireplace den there, too; plus four rooms I want to make into an apartment. In other words, what a place for a poets get-together. Some kind of small conference maybe. I could rent the whole thing at a pretty low rate for any such meeting. If I had any contact at all with the writers at UofA, they would probably do something here.

I've now seen Beauty and the Beast twenty times.[625]

Another thing you might be interested in. A bunch of hill people in Butler Hollow run a printing press. Only one woman can read. Their commercial work is fine. I know the daddy and son and they want to print books.[626] The daddy wants me to write a manual on turkey hunting with him. Maybe I could use my tape recorder. Ha. Anyway, a person in the East will go Two Hundred and Fifty dollars on a pamphlet of mine if it can come out by Fall. Naturally, I gave them your name, but I wasn't sure if you are including me in an issue of MMR or another book. Whatever, if I can, and they said they would, get a pamphlet done with them, including alot of Ginny's drawings, and a glued or string binding, instead of staple, for two hundred or so, would you accept it as Mill Mtn. Press. I know you've got all your time and money in the fire, so mighten this be of some help. You can select all the poems and drawings. Please, if you agree, let this be something different from whatever you are planning or doing of mine right now. Except for a few dozen, not over fifty, you have copies of all my typed-up poems. The poems are titled, or numbered, and a MSS. name and date should appear on the bottom. Would you, in the next few days or weeks, select the best Fifty, or any number, if there are not fifty worth the trouble, put them in the order of preference, and send a List of the Titles of Poems on to me.

You might just want to sit down at your tape player and go through them, saying which you Don't or Do like. In the next two weeks, I'm going to send you, Cert. Reg. Sp Del. a hundred of Ginny's drawings—based on my poems—the battlefield especially.[627] I think this patron is worth about a thousand dollars if I can get four or five pamphlets done in between now and next year at this time, with their money. What do you say. The drawings are great. Sometimes better than the poem. I think I've outlined the above. Let me hear from you soon, as the daddy and son are going to Oklahoma to hunt treasure, then to and with a bunch of Indians to shoot Elk somewhere out there in your part of the country.

As soon as I stamp this, I'll open your letter just come. You might recall a long one I wrote you from the Hotel.[628] There is a history with this place where I work and live now. The Lodge was a whorehouse, and dance-hall. My place, overlooking the river, was a tavern and gambling joint, with a live spring running through to cool the beer. The stream is still good. Some old bridge pilings, like towers of a Scottish castle, stand up near here.[629] Across the way, there is a beautiful farm, with so many white horses. At night, you can hear coyotes. Red and gray foxes live up in the cedars above us. In the cliff caves and on the bluffs are eagles, hawks, and other non-birds of prey. Water birds too. This is a place where it isn't unusual to see a black panther. Beavers all over. This fall, I'll get some chickenwire and laying hens. Maybe a goat for yogurt. Sorry the Interview was no good. They'll get better. It would have been better if you'd been around.

What is going on in the world of literature.

I'm sure you'll have plenty to say, I hope, about what you are doing. I keep wondering. I'm hoping to find a good poem in your letter. Take care,

Yours,
Frank

Notes

624. See note 617 above.
625. *La Belle et la Bête*, Cocteau's 1946 film.
626. Norman Burton "Burt" Camp (1939–2022) and his son, Warren (b. 1964). Butler Hollow was one of Camp's favorite haunts, but he actually lived in Elk Ranch, southeast of Beaver, Arkansas, a few miles east of Busch; the printing company, Elk Ranch Printing—founded by Camp's mother, Elnora Camp, in 1970—was located at 1436 State Highway 187 in Elk Ranch. Camp and some of his friends and family hunted turkeys, so Stanford and Broughton tended to refer to them as the turkey hunters. With Stanford's close oversight, Camp and Elk Ranch Printing printed Stanford's books *Ladies From Hell* (1974), *Field Talk* (1975), *Shade* (1975), and *Arkansas Bench Stone* (1975).
627. *Cert. Reg. Sp Del.*: presumably, certified, registered, special delivery.
628. See Stanford's Early February 1973 letter to Broughton above, par. 1, in which Stanford details Eureka Springs' colorful past and then-present.
629. The bridge foundations were all that remained (and still remain) of a bridge over the White River that, until its collapse in 1951, had connected what are in present mapping Busch's County Road 107 and County Road 109—along which the cabin and house that Stanford lived in with Ginny and the White River Lodge's riverfront lodge, where Stanford worked in mid-1973, were located; the bridge was a few hundred feet behind, or just south of, the lodge.

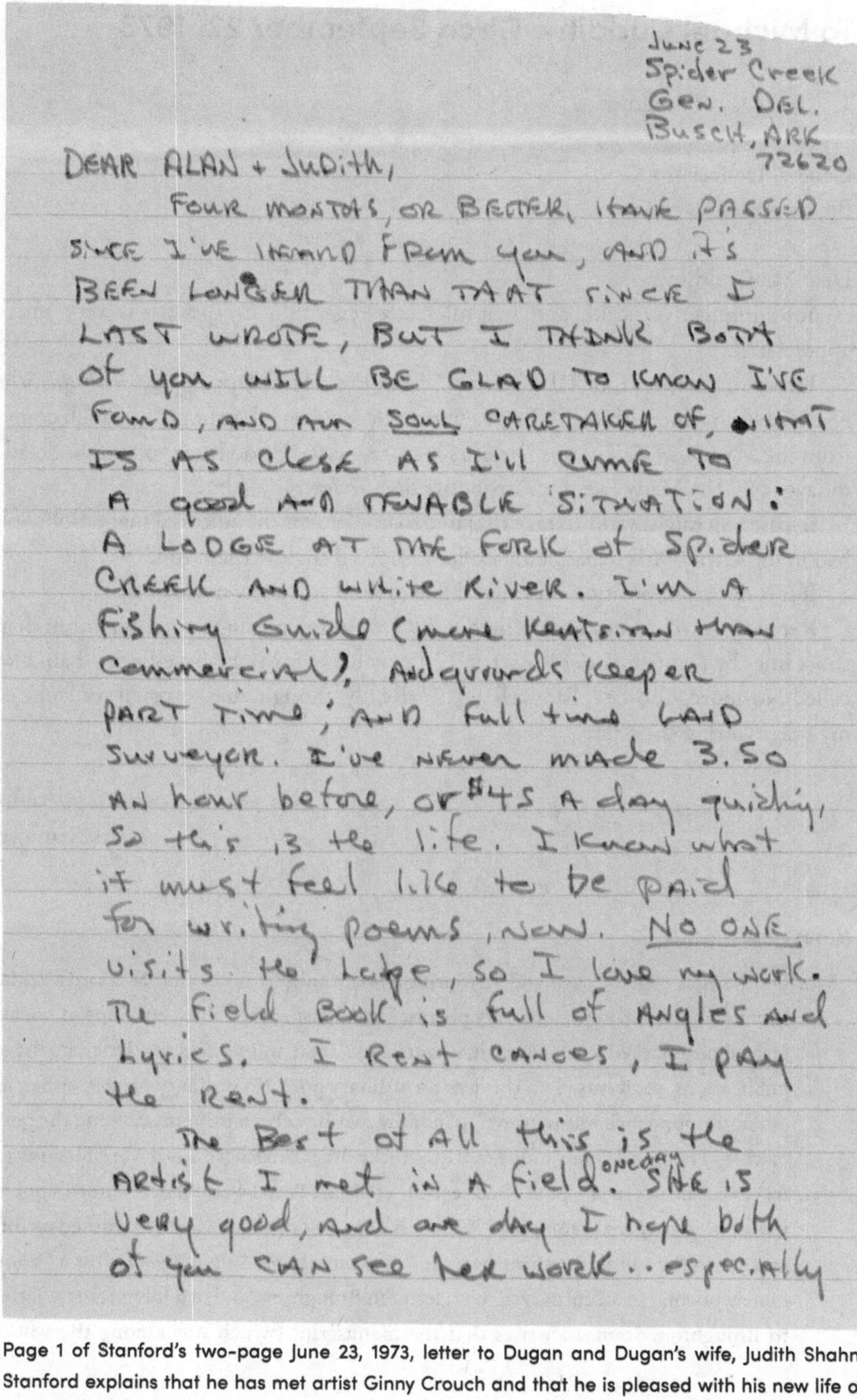

June 23
Spider Creek
Gen. Del.
Busch, Ark
72620

Dear Alan + Judith,

Four months, or better, have passed since I've heard from you, and it's been longer than that since I last wrote, but I think both of you will be glad to know I've found, and am <u>soul</u> caretaker of, what is as close as I'll come to a good and tenable situation: A lodge at the fork of Spider Creek and White River. I'm a fishing guide (more Keatsian than commercial), and grounds keeper part time; and full time land surveyor. I've never made 3.50 an hour before, or $45 a day quickly, so this is the life. I know what it must feel like to be paid for writing poems, now. <u>No one</u> visits the lodge, so I love my work. The field book is full of angles and lyrics. I rent canoes, I pay the rent.

The best of all this is the artist I met in a field one day. She is very good, and one day I hope both of you can see her work.. especially

Page 1 of Stanford's two-page June 23, 1973, letter to Dugan and Dugan's wife, Judith Shahn. Stanford explains that he has met artist Ginny Crouch and that he is pleased with his new life of poetry, films, and work.

To Michael Cuddihy: Circa September 22, 1973

The Last Day of Summer

General Delivery
Busch, Arkansas 72620

Dear Mr. Cuddihy,

Your inquisitive, kind, and helpful letter regarding my poetry is very much appreciated.[630]

Either of parts I, II, or III of "Crest", from the manuscript *Approacheth the Ship and Wonder*, is fine with me.[631] I agree with your revision of "nautalis"—which comes from the MS., *Field Talk: Some Poems 1957–1972*—also.[632] I do hope you might decide in favor of "The Many Evenings" from my *Blue Yodels 1963–1973*.[633]

In case you might want to take the time to implement the editorial suggestions you had in mind for "Milksnake" and "Lullaby . . . .", I'll enclose them too.[634]

If it is not an imposition on you, I'd like to send you a few more poems.

Replying to your question on biography, I wouldn't presume anything more than those lines by Dante Gabriel Rossetti, ". . . . . my name is Might-have-been / I am also called No-more, Too-late, Farewell . . . ."[635] Really, though, maybe you'll see some of my other work somewhere.

yours,
Frank Stanford

Notes

630. On the first page of *Ironwood* 17 (Spring 1981), Cuddihy notes that Stanford's initial submission to him contained only poems: "In August 1973, a thick envelope of poems arrived postmarked Rocky Branch, Rogers, Ark. There was no covering letter, no list of publications, yet it was plain this was no ordinary poet. No ordinary person, either, as our correspondence was to prove." (Cuddihy may have been misremembering the postmark, as Frank and Ginny didn't move to Rocky Branch in Rogers until November 1973.)
631. *Ironwood*, no. 4 (1974), published section 3 ("Some Past Twelve") of Stanford's poem "Crest." *Approacheth the Ship and Wonder* is a manuscript that Stanford worked on, off and on, in the 1970s. Stanford refers to "*Approacheth the Ship in Wonder*" as a "book of new poems" in a February 8, 1972, letter to Broughton, and in a July 22, 1972, letter to Broughton, Stanford writes that the manuscript (which was among the works

burned in late May 1972, he notes), was his "most recent shipwreck of poems—ashes to ashes dust to dust"; however, Stanford evidently returned to *Approacheth* (with "*and*" replacing "*in*")—he mentions in a late 1973 letter to Broughton that "Crest" is "from this Spring," and the manuscript was apparently completed by mid-1976 (see Stanford's June 20, 1976, letter to Broughton below, par. 6).

632. "Nautilus" (*Field Talk*).

633. Published posthumously as "Blue Yodel the Many Evenings" in *You* (1979).

634. Stanford's poems "Milksnake" (*Field Talk*) and "Lullaby to a Child Who They Say Will Not Live Through the Night" (*Field Talk*), neither of which appeared in *Ironwood.*

635. From Rossetti's *The House of Life*, sonnet 97, "A Superscription" (1870), which begins:

> Look in my face; my name is Might-have-been;
> I am also called No-more, Too-late, Farewell;
> Unto thine ear I hold the dead-sea shell
> (Dante Gabriel Rossetti, *Collected Poetry and Prose*, ed. Jerome McGann [Yale University Press, 2003], 170)

See *The Battlefield*, lines 11053–54.

To Alan Dugan: October 13, 1973

Dear Alan,

There is no need to repent for not reading the I.V. in *Iowa Review* with you[636]—which I just now received a copy of, including a cut-out poem from *Atlantic*, and a picture with two poems from some magazine like a newspaper, *American Poetry*[637]—but I am sorry there is *no place* to get one of your books in this fucking state. I *did* like the I.V., but see how he chopped it up. (When you die, I'm not going to make up any lies about you: I'm just going to miss you, and say I loved you, and I'd know you anywhere, you or your poetry, in a honky-tonk, a sea that is rough, a picture show, a factory, a place where the Indians are buried, ...)

I am drunk, but I still dream. I miss you. For me, you're like your old man who read Tennyson. I'll probably never see you again, but I like to think I will.

I'm drinking Medoc wine and German May wine.[638] *St. Matthew Passion*, Mahler, full moon, my wife, Ginny, painting one of the holy terrors of my past.[639]

Oh yes, forgot to say who sent me your poems + picture + interview. A hillbilly friend, whose whole family is in prison.[640]

About the poet + his individual voice. It's true, as you say, we can pick out most folks, but it's almost a fashion with many, not a flesh as it is with your voice.[641]

The other night I had to jump in the river and get my boats. Rain, etc. Cold as monk shit.

My boss, who I just told I'd kill, screwed my wife and I out of $1500 carpentry work, left town. (We've got a warrant out on him.)[642] I'm still land surveying, like Thoreau, so I can pull through it. I see bald eagles, bears, and a wolf sometimes. The guiding is slow, since the fishermen are not spending Nixon's money.

I go out in a canoe, in the fast water at night, and read your poems, or shout them under the moon.

One day, I'd like to think someone unlike myself would do the same for me. What else or who else did you write them for? Would you rather read at some cunt college, land grant, etc., or have me laughing and singing? You are great and therefore worthy of deference, so good luck, and you're with me always, even unto the ends of the earth. (You know how it goes.)[643]

It is OK if you never mention my name in public, but it is essential that you never forget me.[644] In this lonely spot, amongst the fair and gallant poets of the East, I solace in you + your work. I don't send you any poems any more, not because I don't have them to send, but because I feel I *overstepped* my boundry [*sic*] before.[645] You don't have *time*!

Speaking of boundries, I have to plot out a 240 acre woods survey before 6:00 A.M., so I'm killing the bottle, saying goodbye to Neruda, Anna Magnani, W. H. Auden (who I drank coffee with in Conway, Arkansas by chance in the snow in a Holiday Inn), and finishing a poem, and going to bed, and waking up my *new* wife, and screwing.[646] Over-out,

yours,
Frank

The next morning.

Tell Judith hello. I wish she could see some of Ginny's work.

Your last letter was much like a poem: the wind.

Maybe you'll see some of my poems printed somewhere, since about 20 have been accepted in small-time magazines.

Mosquito full of my blood, drowned in wine. Thank you for the fly.[647]

It is raining. (The Eberhart film I worked on is ready. We might shoot Eudora this winter.[648] Also, I'm making a film about the only Black man in seven counties of this state.[649]) Write when you have time.

yours,
Frank[650]

Notes

636. Ryan's interview with Dugan; see note 621 above.
637. Dugan published poems in the January, May, and November 1973 issues of *The Atlantic Monthly. The American Poetry Review*'s May/June 1973 issue published two of Dugan's poems with an accompanying photo of him.
638. Médoc, a Bordeaux region wine.
639. Stanford and Ginny Crouch didn't officially marry until October 17, 1974.
640. Bill Willett (the middle child of eleven in his family), whose younger brother Benny was, as of this letter, facing drug-related charges—following an August 1973 break-in at a veterinary clinic and subsequent fight in the Baxter County Jail—and awaiting trial. "Whole family" is Stanfordian hyperbole.
641. In Ryan's interview, Dugan states, "Because we live in a mass culture, each professional artist is bound to be as individuated as possible, to find his own precise voice. . . . Now any interesting poet can be recognized after reading a few lines. In the old days, in a feudal or aristocratic society . . . the individual voices were indistinguishable."
642. E.W. Brockman, a man from whom Frank and Ginny rented their Busch cabin in spring and summer 1973 and house in summer and fall 1973 and for whom Stanford worked as the resort lodge's caretaker.
643. Matthew 28:20 (AV): "Lo, I am with you always, even unto the end of the world. Amen."
644. Dugan didn't mention Stanford in the interview by Ryan but, when asked of current literary shifts, noted that he perceived "two interrelated directions": "neo-surrealism, and an impetus toward great length in poems and absolute looseness in structure," stating, "We're all coming after the great giants—Eliot, Pound, Williams, Marianne Moore, and the rest of them. So that in the United States of America there's a group of forty or fifty extremely interesting poets right now, but I think that none of us are really large-scale artists in the way they were."
645. Stanford typically misspells "boundary" in letters.
646. W. H. Auden (1907–73), Anglo-American poet. R. S. Gwynn noted to this editor that he, Stanford, Stokesbury, and Kathy Walton traveled in Walton's car to Conway,

Arkansas, on February 22, 1971—an icy, snowy day—to hear Auden read at the State College of Arkansas (now the University of Central Arkansas); following the reading, the four friends had dinner at the Holiday Inn while Auden dined at a nearby table, though none of the four met or talked to Auden. Manuscript and direct messages to editor, November 29 and December 3, 2023; see also Bob Lancaster, "With the Dignity of his Doggerel: Auden Slouches Onstage, Unkempt," *Arkansas Democrat*, February 28, 1971, 2.

647. Dugan's June 27, 1973, letter to Stanford included a fly, taped to the page, that Dugan had killed while penning the letter. Dugan wrote, "It annoyed me, so I killed it and sen[t] it to you." Stanford's response here, on the right side of the page, is written on a large stain.

648. Eudora Welty.

649. Richard Banks. In an August 1, 1974, letter to Dugan, Stanford refers to Banks as "the only black man in seven counties, a sort of hermit." In a ca. January 1974 letter to Cowley, Broughton notes, "I visited Frank last summer, and we filmed the only black man in Carroll County, Arkansas, among other things."

650. Two poems appear to have been enclosed with his letter: "Suspect" (*Ladies From Hell*) and "Fair Trial" (*Shade*)—both with the notation, "from *Yonder* 1965."

To John McKernan: Circa Mid-November 1973

November 73
Gen Del
Busch, Ark. 72620

Dear John,

Your note of the last of last month and *Father Poems* MS. here safe.

You are one of the two or three people I know and remember whose work I will always look forward to reading. Without question, I believe in the magic reality and natural mystery you're feeding your poems with. You're not a vampire, as you say, but a foreboding and desolate cello of a poet. I'm amazed, always, with what you do. You remind one of the music of Delius more than I do.[651] I accept night and your voice.

There is no time now for me to say what I am doing, or about to do, just time enough to get back to your MS., a gradual, green bush of a book. One day I hope all the frenzied, unlucky poets in the country will slow down and give you your due. I consider myself lucky that I can read your poems, and I'm still fascinated by them.

You'll be hearing from me.

yours,
Frank

Notes

651. Frederick Delius (1862–1934), composer.

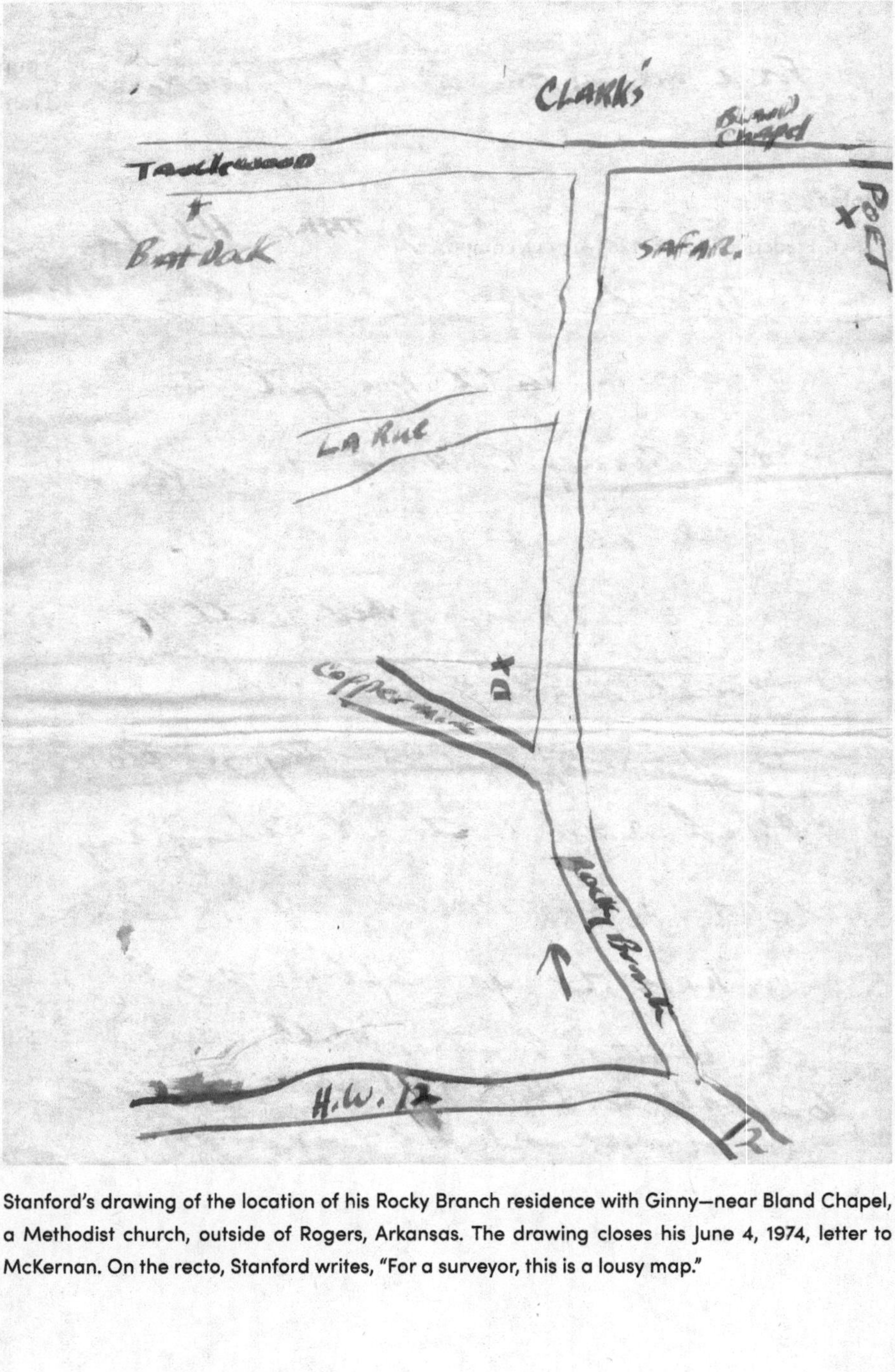

Stanford's drawing of the location of his Rocky Branch residence with Ginny—near Bland Chapel, a Methodist church, outside of Rogers, Arkansas. The drawing closes his June 4, 1974, letter to McKernan. On the recto, Stanford writes, "For a surveyor, this is a lousy map."

VI.

ROCKY BRANCH AND BEAVER LAKE

Rogers, 1973–75

In November 1973, Stanford and Ginny Crouch moved into a rural farmhouse located in northwest Arkansas in an area known as Rocky Branch, about a dozen miles east of downtown Rogers and less than a mile from Beaver Lake. There, the couple worked on their crafts—writing and painting, respectively—and Stanford earned a living as a land surveyor; for a time, his office was in his home. In 1974 and 1975, Mill Mountain Press published Stanford's next four books—each with drawings by Ginny and printed by Elk Ranch Printing, a small printing company a few miles north of Eureka Springs. On October 17, 1974, Stanford and Crouch married. Stanford published poetry and fiction and also laid the groundwork for the press he would later found, Lost Roads Publishers.

To Irv Broughton: November 20, 1973

November 20, 1973
Route 6 Box 342
Rogers, Arkansas 72756

Dear Irv,

Please notice new address. Lodge sold. Had to move. Still screwed out of a thousand and wages and five hundred in expenses—which is against our Mont. Ward account.[652] Goddamn I'm pissed. Just when I had a deal worked out with the Camera Dept. there on a 16 sound. My account is over the limit in shit I bought for the Lodge, so screw that. Working ten hours a day surveying at four bucks an hour. Weather is holding out good. Car went down, still lame. Up and down mountains in little green bug should have rated a commercial. So, put down five hundred on new 412 V.W. Station wagon.[653] We can go anywhere now and shoot, baby. Paying for that and move, plus doctors, etc.

All your film arrived. Going to monastery this T.G. weekend.[654] Will shoot. Got stuff in creek, and more. Soon as I get a load shot up I'll send to you. Also sound. Something drastic, something terrible, something unheard of has happened in WLAC in Nash., Tenn.[655] Alot of white rockshit music. What has happened to my old friends? Surely the gospel still comes through. Will hook up my radio and see.

About books. I have a MS. typed up and blocked, including some great drawings you haven't seen, about 150 pages. I think Dugan wants me to print it as is. Then, take best from that, best from Singing Knives, and best from other and hire a good typewriter and send it to Yale. Whatever, here is the scoop on printing and paper costs here.

I can get good paper and fine covers, any size. Good weight. One hundred copies of a hundred-fifty page book, a limited edition needless to say, will cost in text 75.00. The covers will run a mere five dollars. That's pretty fucking good. The binding will cost 22.50. My contact is still good for the cost of printing on THREE BOOKS OF MINE, but maybe they'd pay for somebody else's, but before I can give you a quote on printing PLEASE LET ME KNOW IF YOU ARE GOOD FOR SETTING THE TYPE. That's what the hillbillies charge for.[656] Goddamn you should see these drawings. The whole gang's there.[657] Ginny wants to do some cover designs for your magazine too. We'll be taking alot of pictures this week. Finally, time.

I know everything you need, and I'm getting it all. Could use that book on mechanics of screenwriting.[658] Tapes and manuscript you wrote I'm editing. You did a good job. I'll send them back to you soon.

Yours,
Frank

P.S. Tear this off. Above reference is for proof on what I'm sending YOU.

Notes

652. *Mont. Ward*: Montgomery Ward, a former department store chain.
653. Volkswagen Type 4's 412 series, an early 1970s station wagon.
654. Thanksgiving weekend—Thursday through Sunday, November 22–25, 1973.
655. WLAC (1510 AM), a radio station in Nashville.
656. In Broughton's November 23, 1973, letter to Stanford, he replies, "Yes, I can set type, and the deal sounds terrific."
657. I.e., the cast of characters in Stanford's poetry.
658. In his November 23 reply, Broughton writes: "Am sending books of screenwriting, and would like them back when you're done with them." To this editor, Broughton noted that (whether in this mailing or otherwise) he sent, among other film books, Lee R. Bobker's *Elements of Film* (1969) and Eugene Vale's *The Technique of Screenplay Writing* (1972) to Stanford. Emails to editor, October 30, 2023.

To Michael Cuddihy: December 15, 1973

Dear Michael,

Thank you for your kind words. I was born about the time you went to Gethsemane, '49.[659] I've been writing since 1957. *Esquire + Iowa Review* and others have published poems I wrote when I was 12.[660] I'm not a monk (although I went to a monastery for schooling after my father died), other than the kind Keats speaks of "my imagination is a monastery and I am its monk."[661]

The lines from "Some After Twelve" are *correct* as you have them and typed them back to me.[662] You may revise "nautalis."[663] Will write as soon as weather gets bad, get off work.

yours,
Frank

Notes

659. Stanford was born in 1948 (not 1949). In an undated fall 1973 letter to Stanford, Cuddihy had written, "You're so good, it's maddening" and noted that "back in '49," he had been to "Gethsemane"—the Abbey of Our Lady of Gethsemani in Kentucky, Merton's home.

660. See notes 186 and 424 above.

661. "My Imagination is a Monastry and I am its Monk—you must explain my metap[rs] [metaphysics] to yourself." John Keats to Percy Bysshe Shelley, August 16, 1820, in *Complete Poetry and Selected Prose*, 469.

662. In his fall 1973 letter, Cuddihy asked about lines 4 and 26 of "Some Past Twelve," which would appear in *Ironwood*, no. 4 (1974).

663. In his letter, Cuddihy suggested a revision to "Nautilus" (*Field Talk*); the poem didn't appear in *Ironwood*, but the book's version includes Cuddihy's suggested edit (viz., that the poem close with "is an appaloosa").

To William L. Fox: January 1, 1974

January 1, 1974
Rt 6 Box 342
Rogers, Ark 72756

Dear Bill,

Sorry I didn't send a note; assumed that you'd probably extended the normal amount of allotted time when it comes to what I've sent you. I knew you were fairly busy, didn't want to bother.[664]

Hope your work, magazine, and job are running smooth. I know alot of poets and editors are having troubles these days.

I've moved three or four times in the last ten months, but only to different houses on the same river.[665] After living with some of the Alvin Ailey dancers in N.Y., I went on a patronized wanderlust.[666] Hotels, monasteries, whorehouses, boxcars, taverns, mansions, cabins, boathouses, and Mercedes.[667] I had a little money left, intended on getting a job on some ship, but met a painter. Got a job on some water I knew as a guide, did part time carpentry, and now I'm a land surveyor. From dawn to dark I'm in the woods, moreorless alone. We live in a farmhouse on the lake.[668]

The man I work for in films, the one who's doing work on Ransom, Eberhart, Cowley, Wilbur, and others—younger, older, famous, and passed out of fame, or never had it, hasn't been able to get enough money together to spread out, which leaves the other kind of films I'm working on in the hopper. However, some graduate people at the UCLA film school accepted some of my poems and screenplays, so I'll let them worry about the finances.[669]

Whatever happened to the man in Maine who used to be your partner? Was his name David Walker? I'd like to have his address if you have it.

Have a story coming out in the Iowa Review.[670] Would like you to read it. Probably long way off yet. G. Hitchcock told me to send you a MS. I'll send it to you, minus the poems Ironwood, Boston Phoenix, Ark Rever R, Dragonfly, Field, and others are taking. I haven't sent them out yet. Sorry, but they are run-on sentences, something you don't like.[671] Take care.

Yours,
Frank

If the MS. interests you, and you'd like to see more, let me know. It's a pamphlet I've got in mind.[672] If you aren't interested, I'd [like] to recommend {the work of} two other poets to you.

Notes

664. In his December 19, 1973, letter to Stanford, Fox noted, "Strange to find poems from you and no note."
665. Spider Creek intersects with the White River, which the former lodge in Busch backs up to; the White River connects with Beaver Lake, near which the Rocky Branch home is located.
666. See note 391 above.
667. Per Stanford, in September 1972, Deidre (sp?) drove a rented Mercedes-Benz; see Stanford's first Late September 1972 letter to Broughton above, par. 2.
668. The Rocky Branch house, with current address of 8475 Twin Coves Road, isn't on Beaver Lake but is near it—just south of Bland Chapel in Rogers.
669. Babij, then a UCLA graduate film student, filmed Stanford's poem "The Singing Knives." In correspondence, Babij also encouraged Stanford to send him "story outlines and/or scripts" and replied that one experimental script Stanford sent was "cohesive" and "cinematic" but that he felt its "marketability" would be "questionable" given Hollywood's "commercial" nature. James Babij to Frank Stanford, n.d., ca. 1973, and July 31 [1973?].
670. Frank Stanford, "A Past: Wintered like a Circus," *Iowa Review* 5, no. 3 (Summer 1974): 39–54.
671. In Fox's December 19 letter, he notes re: *The Battlefield* that he went through "all the pages" of Stanford's "giant" but that he liked some of Stanford's briefer poems, including "Rooms" (*Ladies From Hell*), "better than the run-on sentence ones."

672. In Fox's February 4, 1974, letter to Stanford, he wrote, "I'd kinda like to do a book with you (new poems?) sometime in '75," and in a June 1974 note added, "maybe keep in mind a chapbook for 75," though no book came to fruition.

To Eleanor Bender: January 25, 1974

January 25, 1974
Route 6 Box 342
Rogers, Arkansas 72756

Dear Eleanor,

How are you? After a month of snow and ice and general bad weather, I can work in the woods without a shirt: 60°. As if life were nothing, as if death were nothing, I'm in the forest from dawn until dark, surveying, dreaming about the lives and the poems I will participate in when I return home. I see deer very often, and the sure and graceful and frightened movements of these animals as they leave my sight remind me, very much, of the freedom and youthfulness of our first letters. Hope the calendar will see each day out, well.

yours,
Frank

Please read my long story coming out in Iowa Review?[673]

P.S. I still drink a bottle of Cold Duck and listen to Mahler, or Delius, or Orff, or Bach, or the blues every evening.[674] I don't box anymore; my ribs are shot.[675] My wife paints, and is very good.[676] There are deer in my field most mornings. From time to time, I visit the monks, Negro taverns, and some town where I can sneak a pint into a library or a theatre. I've re-read your last letter, and you seemed, then, somewhat depressed. Don't be: I am writing poetry and dreaming and stalking down a past you probably think about when you are up late and at your desk, alone. Listen.

Notes

673. See note 670 above.
674. Carl Orff (1895–1982), composer.
675. See Stanford's Circa January 7–12, 1973, letter to Garrett above, par. 13.
676. See note 639 above.

To David Walker: February 12, 1974

February 12, 1974
Route 6 Box 342
Rogers, Arkansas 72756

Dear David,

Glad as hell to hear from you, know you and yours are, if not prospering, thriving well. If all your poems are as good as the two you enclosed, then the other David Walkers will have to play second and however many others there are fiddle. The two poems go together like earth and water. Although only twenty lines, the Mandelstam poem has the reader accompany, musically as well, the poet down that long row, which is called Death. I really like it, especially after reading Olga Carlisle's books.[677] Read the poetry of Osip's wife, too.[678] And "In August" is fine.[679]

Your life sounds well, like a deep channel. I can't really remember the last time we were in touch, as you say. I know I spent alot of time, drunk, with nice people on Eberhart's yacht and other folk's boats, looking up and down the coast for Alna, but hell, that was one, no two summers ago—I think.[680]

As you know, I was living on top of a hill in a log cabin in Fayetteville, Arkansas, keeping strange company—some of whom are now dead, trying to plow through the bad soil of every genre known to man—and woman, while at the same time trying to make fourteen years of early, Huckleberry Rimbaud mss. readable.[681] You know, you go down to these strange and ungentle dives and gamble with the creatures and rebuses of your imagination and, by the time you wake up for air, you've lost everything and don't know it, and sometimes no longer know what hand or die or bone you're playing. Whiskey, women, and the bad nights of poetry will always fill your mouth with cold ground: I bit the dust.

For some reason, danger calmed my nerves and made me sleep. As Jean Cocteau said, I think, the old myths are constantly being reborn without their heroes, their victims, knowing it;[682] like lies who always tell the truth, the poet lives beyond his era, thus tragedy, therefore black comedy, ad infi. . . .

Anyway, I left town with nothing, only the clothes on my back. I could have been in bad trouble with the law, an irate husband was going to do me in, besides. I was living nine lives of mystery and real-life madness, still believing my tongue and my dreams and sweet poetry could raise the dead, like an anonymous cathedral of fire, floating through my youth like a barn when the river floods.

The only safe place to go—after I set fire to my cabin, where nothing burned but all my manuscripts—boyuscripts, that's true, was this monastery, where the brothers were the finest consolation, their vision, wine, and song. However, no poontang. So, after letting me share and work and dream with them, one monk showed a rich old fool a bone, promised indulgences, etc, gave me the bread to hit the road.

Fate often delivers an undoomed earl. The bard who wrote Beowulf wrote that, as you know, so we wouldn't be prepared for the good and brave Lord's death at the end.[683]

Anyway, stripped down to the long ago time of having not written a word, which never freed one blue capillary from the dark and sometimes good prison of my heart, every thing burned—I thought, searchless as I had already found what I was looking for, I hit the bottle and virgin page again. In a few months, I'd filled up a few tow sacks full of poems, etc.

(I forgot the part where they put me in the horse pit et al, to dry me out, only Alan Dugan and Cowley and some others found out and called the nuts at the nuts house and tole them let me go. Poetry will put you out of your misery for no charge, and then will do the undertaking cheap and sometimes it rides up out of nowhere like the opposite sister of La Belle Dame Sans Merci and gives you a lap or at least a deathbed to dream in.[684] Here endeth the days of youth. . . .)

Get it?

Got a job with an editor doing films on older poets.[685] Met, filmed, drank, etc, lived, with Eberhart, Ransom, Cowley, Wilbur, and so on. He did Wilbur because McLiesh almost kicked off that summer.[686] Gained experience with camera and personages. An odd way to meet literary people, isn't it.

Lived in NYC with some black dancers and some jamaicans. (No bulletholes, stabs, robbings, etc.) I'd start to work on the cultural side of the city at daybreak and go until about that time the next day. Met alot of people by chance. Really. Everybody I met there, met by chance. Drank and sung in alot of ethnic bars, hate that word. Saw everything in NYC. Helluvalot of experiences but can't go into them here.

Met rich woman from Scotland associated with museums etc. We rode all over in her M. B.,[687] leaving the city, until somewhere, I forget, I got on a bus with nobody but blacks, met an old man who had worked for my uncle in Miss., got drunk, rode buses, trains.

Met up with girl again. SHOWED her the so-called south.

Almost took off on ship on blue swan-path to anywhere, but got drunk, didn't make sailing time. Lived on houseboat. Lived in joints and whorehouses, hotels, just enough money to live and write on, trying not to take advantage of anyone, trying not to rape experience, trying to think more than I feel, passing through fields of men and women, some of whom shall go unrecorded, some of whom are with you and I always.

If I was a pilgrim, I only had a raft and the river was low. If I was a poet, then who was Shelly and that one F. Villon.[688] If I was trying to be somebody else, then why was I becoming myself. If a beautiful woman is death, my own, then how come I'm still alive. (Okra, wine, Keats, etc.) You fill in the blanks.

I winded up in the Hotel New Orleans in Eureka Springs, Ark. Then from there, to a cabin on spider creek on the river as a fishing guide. From there, a farm with no animals on a big lake, working as a field guide for land surveying, the mountains and hills and topography of my soul.

The poets finds another woman.

She is an artist.

Time Passes.

There is rest for the wicked.[689]

I won't bullshit you anymore.

My wife loves living here, alone, old house in timber in fields, with garden, Warm Morning wood stove, two cats, making bread for life and living, and the untold days of the poet.[690]

I bootleg screenpoems to filmmakers working on Masters, etc. in film schools on West Coast. (For awhile, I assumed another name, started a foreign film theatre in a land of hillbillies, and although I'm not a surrealist, no theory accommodates me, I'd like to know of a shenanigan better than that, going over a thousand in debt on film rentals, for the sake of the poor, who didn't understand a word of it, not even the english subtitles, but they did like Klondike Annie,[691] though they did like a good place to drink in the dark.)

David, my life is no longer that of a traveling recluse, since what the doctors told me about being term. ill just didn't happen. I went back, and nothing is wrong. No miracle intended, just thankfulness. (I often think of some monk, down on his knees in the hogpen, a bucket of slop beside him like a censor for the hungry, praying for me—which they do, because they love me. And I love them. I'm still without virtue or faith, but I'm now proud in spirit. Like a tree, a horse, a ship, or a fool.

The only problems I've had, whatsoever, was that of recovering from amnesia, which I didn't include in the previous epic one damn fool. There are still strange streaks that I couldn't tell you about, like heat lightning during a crime or thunder when people make love, but, what with this job of earning a fairly good living, and this lover of love, art, I don't mind. I quit whiskey, but I made friends with wine.

I want you to know this: whatever your intellectual and emotional investment in my ever becoming a worthwhile poet, I hope to pay dividends. I can't tell you when.

I sort of did something dumb in NYC—everything else was stupid, I had a scene with an editor in a bar who had secured a large publishing house for a book of mine. I might still be on the big boy's black list, but hope not.[692] Everyone I hope will forgive and forget when it comes to wild oats sowed, especially when someone else is an aesthetic sow.

Which brings me to that great lot of bacon, those people you met at Meatloaf.[693] (No, I'm just kidding.) That's where this amnesia is a tight rope. I know who a couple of those guys were, as I know the smell of bacon; it is the hickory of the past—or at least part of it, that is hard to come by. There were or are, probably no longer in Fayette Nam, four or five fine writers: John Stoss, John McKernan, John S. Morris, and Jack Butler.[694] I don't know what has become of them. I might have met Miller Williams at a party. The big guy is a fine teacher. They are all good and honorable writers, only better poets advised me not to tow their line of neo-fugative, neo-redneck verse. It is difficult to break with ties, but none I had there were over two years old. I think you will find alot of good work from them and their students though, although I haven't had a chance to read any. They do alot for young writers, I know that.

About "getting on" in poetry. I'll send you a list of the places I've published, accepted under this name.[695] I might throw in *Antioch* and another because they've held alot of my poems for over a year and a half.[696] I'm embarrassed about screwing up an acceptance with a large publishing house, childish, but also about not accepting some smaller press offers, but only for this reason: I hate to say it, but I've never heard of so many poets and presses and, without some sampling of their other work, I didn't feel I should tread. So, those guys might be mad at me, but I feel well knowing some other poet got a book.

I have a heap of Ms. which escaped the tongue of fire and critics. 1957–1974. One book accepted by Lux and M. Ryan of Barn Dream, the former the former editor of I.R., the latter the now editor and Yale winner.[697] Another accepted if I accept. Also, five or six chapbooks at Mill Mountain, formerly of Roanoke, Virginia, now Seattle, Washington, and the editor will move next year again. He is also producer of Mill Mountain Films and editor of MM Review. He is also going to produce some of my shorter films and documentaries. I was advised to become less-"wild" before I send a ms. to Kunitz, which I never did do after a note from him.[698]

I might have sent you a xerox copy of it, but Berryman sure did write me a nice letter. Bless his soul.

This job of land surveying takes from dawn until dark, but it gives us a fair livelihood. And, I still manage to write alot. I'm working on too much fiction for my own good. First story was accepted by Iowa, about fifty pages. "A PAST WINTERED LIKE A CIRCUS".[699]

(first submitted)

My main problem is not enough time. Instead of typing things up for potential publication or sale, I let my imagination go, always on new work, now that's not to say I don't revise or finish.

After I send you some poems, I'd really like your advice about some things. I ask others, but they say, yea, great keep ahead on man, just keep writing. But, believe it or not, I approach poetry like a musician.

I hope you don't flinch from so many words in one dose, but a shy dreamer like me can see a friend.

I'm writing alot, maybe too much, and my wife is painting alot, but my friends are dying off. And one, one of the best from days gone by, is on trial for two counts of first degree murder.[700]

I accept all information and advice. New, good books, poets, films, magazines. And so on.

Sorry to hear about your falling out with Fox and Long,[701] freedom from love and hate, and one's own will should always be tested, have its way.

I'll send you a chapbook if you still want to review it, and the ms. of others coming out, which will give you more to WALK over. Of course, I consider your regard for me very much, and if you wanted to call me sonofabitch I'd still buy you a beer, any brand. You send me some poems long about this spring, too.

Yours,
Frank

Notes

677. *Poets on Street Corners: Portraits of Fifteen Russian Poets* (1968) and *Modern Russian Poetry* (1972)—which both included Osip Mandelstam (1891–1938) and other poets Stanford appreciated, such as Yesenin and Pasternak.
678. Mandelstam's wife, Nadezhda Mandelstam (1899–1980), also a writer.
679. Enclosed with Walker's February 7, 1974, letter to Stanford were two poems: "In August" and "For Osip Mandelstam."
680. Alna, Maine, Walker's hometown.
681. See the signature of Stanford's February 1, 1973, letter to McKernan above and note 549 above.
682. From *L'Éternel Retour* (*The Eternal Return*) (1943), dir. Jean Delannoy and written by Cocteau, a retelling of the Tristan and Iseult romance. Cocteau's opening text overlay notes, "*L'Éternel Retour.* . . . Ce titre, emprunté à Nietzsche, veut dire, ici, que les mêmes légendes peuvent renaître, sans que leurs héros s'en doutent" (*The Eternal Return.* . . . This title, borrowed from Nietzsche, means, here, that the same legends can be reborn, without their heroes knowing it) (ellipsis in original). The Nietzschean notion of the eternal return is that all aspects of existence have been recurring across time and will continue to do so ad infinitum. Cf. the Cocteau epigraph to Stanford's poem "The Sound of Trees," in *What About This*, 664.
683. From *Beowulf*: "Fate often delivers an undoomed earl / If his spirit be gallant!" *Beowulf*, lines 572–73. Cf. *The Battlefield*, lines 4683–84, 10773.
684. "La Belle Dame sans Merci," an 1819 ballad by Keats.
685. I.e., with Broughton.
686. Archibald MacLeish (1892–1982), poet and ninth librarian of Congress.

687. *M. B.*: Mercedes-Benz.

688. Percy Bysshe Shelley and François Villon.

689. A play on a phrase from Isaiah 48:22 and 57:21. From the former (AV): "There is no peace, saith the Lord, unto the wicked."

690. See note 639 above.

691. *Klondike Annie* (1936), dir. Raoul Walsh.

692. Stanford describes this scene with this "well-known but specious editor" for a "slick american magazine" that "isn't worth the trees they cut," which took place "in a cafe full of literary flies," in a ca. December 24, 1972, letter to Fox. Stanford writes that, having supposedly misheard a compliment from the editor, he "threw some vodka in his face and left." Stanford adds, "I do like stories by Borges, though." Stanford appears to be alluding to *Esquire*, which published Borges's story "The Widow Ching, Lady Pirate" in August 1972. *Esquire* may have accepted Stanford's poem "The Blood Boot." See Stanford's first October 1972 letter to Fox above, par. 4; note 424 above; and Stanford's December 15, 1973, letter to Cuddihy above, par. 1. James Dickey was *Esquire*'s poetry editor from 1970 to 1977.

693. Stanford is parodying the name of the Bread Loaf Writers' Conference in Vermont.

694. John S. Morris (b. 1942), poet.

695. See note 726 below.

696. In 1972, Stanford sent much or all of *St. Francis and the Wolf: Some Poems 1957–1964* to *The Antioch Review*'s poetry editor, Eric Horsting; in March 1973, Horsting returned the majority of the poems but held on to eight for further consideration, including "the books," "the mind reader," "the wolves," and "the burial ship." On October 10, 1974, Horsting wrote to Stanford, "I kept your poems for as long as I did while I was editor because they puzzled me. I found them very demanding and sensed they were excellent." He continued, "There's now no doubt in my mind that your poems are first-rate." Horsting had wanted to run a feature on Stanford in an issue but, to this editor, noted that *Antioch*'s editor, Lawrence Grauman Jr., felt that Stanford's poems were "too far out" (Grauman's verbiage, per Horsting). Email to editor, March 22, 2022.

697. Thomas Lux (1946–2017), poet, cofounder of Barn Dream Press, and a managing editor of *The Iowa Review* 1971–72 who corresponded with Stanford for much of the 1970s, and Michael Ryan (b. 1946), poet and associate editor of *The Iowa Review* 1972–74, poetry editor 1973–74. Ryan was never involved with Barn Dream.

698. Kunitz judged the Yale Younger Poets Prize from 1969 to 1976; see note 242 above.

699. See note 670 above; the published version is sixteen pages.

700. On January 24, 1974, Bill Willett's older brother Edward Leon shot and killed two men in his home whom he had believed to be threatening; Leon was indicted on February 1, 1974, and ultimately served his sentence at the Missouri State Penitentiary.

701. William L. Fox and D. S. Long, editors of *Edge*.

To Alan Dugan: March 14, 1974

March 14, 1974
Rt6 Box 342
Rogers, Ark. 72756

Dear Alan,

Down in the bed with the Hong Kong Flu for a couple of days, so have a little time to answer your letters.

Spring is here, and all that shit. Of course, all the dogwoods, redbuds, plums, peaches, and sprouts in our *big* garden are fine to see and smell—their blossoms blowing sometimes like snow, but, the better the weather, the less time I have to write. Now, I'm working in the field 12 hours a day, then some in the garden. I miss those cold days in the dead of winter.

Those poems included in the longer letter are really fine, especially the shorter one in the more recent note. I hope everybody will get to see them. And you are right about "spoor", spelling and meaning. (Down here, I pronounce "spoor", as in footprints or tracks, the same as *spore*, as in free, resistant bodies, capable of developing at once or after a time into an independent organism or individual, which all goes to make the poem better—and I imagine they'll probably pronounce them nearly the same around Boston.)

In fact, I think "On Finding the Tree of Life . . . ." is damn good, a best one.[702]

That survey for the Holy City just happened to be another mountain near land owned by Gerald K. Smith and his fanatics.[703] (I jimmied the S E bearing and chipped off a few acres from the Holy City (which turns in several million a year), thus, giving the land, by rights, to a hillbilly with adjoining property.)

We're working in some rough timber now—a lot of it dead, and when the wind blows, watch out. (Soon, the snakes who have slept all winter will rise.) The other day we got caught in a forest fire. There are many woods stories I can tell you, but I better save them, not that I wouldn't like to begin a de Maupassant TALE, but I just don't have time.

Hope to hell our garden comes up. Had a big rain, chill. North and south of us there was considerable flooding. We're up on a mtn, overlooking a lake. Ginny's planted 12 different kinds of herbs to keep the bugs away, instead of using poison. Don't know how I'll keep the coons and deer away.

Bought me a little boat for 25$ and another wood stove for next year. Also, got a new chainsaw—a John Deere, naturally. Have you ever looked through a Shumway Seed catalog? I keep one in the john, along with Bible, and British literature textbooks.

The other day I was driving down a dirt road in Missouri and came on to G.W. Carver's house. In between Neosho and Joplin.[704] (I guess you know that's where Thomas Hart Benton is from. I think T. H. Benton looks too much like El Greco and Tintoretto.[705] Ask Judith? I'm probably an idiot. And I think Grant Wood looks like early Flemish?[706] Probably, I don't know shit.) But Hurd, Hopper, Sheeler, N. C. Wyeth, W. Homer, Marsh, and before, all are considered realists, but there has to be something deeper and darker, or higher and lighter in their work.[707] What did Shahn think of these artists.[708] What did he think of Andrew Wyeth? WHAT DO YOU THINK OF ANDREW W.?[709] (I won't tell!)

I've heard, from a N.Y.C. artist, Wyeth compared to a poet writing sonnets: Wilbur. Then, I've heard him compared to W. C. Williams, Sherwood Anderson, and, oh my god, Faulkner.[710] (Please enlighten?)

Lawrence said "American artists revel in subterfuge, refusing to say or paint anything explicit—always a double meaning; while realistic on the surface, we have to *look through* the surface into the diabolism of symbolic meaning (what a phrase), otherwise it is all mere childishness."[711]

To get back to my story, in front of this house which was G. W. Carver's, a family was standing; and one of the children (they were a black family) was eating a peanut butter and jelly sandwich.

The kid asked his father: "Daddy, how come that man want to fool round with them peanuts?"

"I don't know son. He was a scientist."

I saw the kid, as they were leaving, throw part of his sandwich in the ditch, and say, "Let's go see *hit*!"

Last summer, I spent a few weekend afternoons in Joplin, looking for Langston Hughes's house, but nobody knew where it was, or if it still existed.[712]

I better get back in bed.

yours,
Frank

Notes

702. Dugan's poem "On Finding the Tree of Life" (published in *Sequence*, 1976, and collected in *New and Collected Poems: 1961–1983*). Lines 8–9 contain: "The spoor around the tree / is old." Dugan, *Poems Seven*, 256. In Dugan's January 25, 1974, letter to Stanford, he transcribed the poem and asked, "Do I use the word 'spoor' accurately?"

703. Gerald L. K. Smith (1898–1976), whose planned religious theme park, Sacred Projects, was a failed project; only Christ of the Ozarks was built.
704. The boyhood home of agricultural scientist and former slave George Washington Carver (ca. 1864–1943) is located near Diamond, Missouri.
705. Thomas Hart Benton (1889–1975), American Realist / Social Realist painter; El Greco (1541–1614), Greek painter; and Tintoretto (ca. 1518–94), Italian painter.
706. Grant Wood (1891–1942), Regionalist painter.
707. Peter Hurd (1904–84), Edward Hopper (1882–1967), Charles Sheeler (1883–1965), N. C. Wyeth (1882–1945), Winslow Homer (1836–1910), and Reginald Marsh (1898–1954), American painters.
708. Ben Shahn; see note 370 above.
709. Andrew Wyeth (1917–2009), American Realist and Regionalist painter.
710. William Carlos Williams (1883–1963), poet, and Sherwood Anderson (1876–1941), writer.
711. From the foreword of Lawrence's *Studies in Classic American Literature* (1923): "The Americans refuse everything explicit and always put up a sort of double meaning. They revel in subterfuge." And from chapter 7 ("Nathaniel Hawthorne and *The Scarlet Letter*"): "You *must* look through the surface of American art, and see the inner diabolism of the symbolic meaning. Otherwise it is all mere childishness." D. H Lawrence, *Studies in Classic American Literature*, ed. Ezra Greenspan et al. (Cambridge University Press, 2014), 12, 81.
712. Langston Hughes (1901/1902–67) was born in Joplin, Missouri, but raised mostly in Lawrence, Kansas.

To John McKernan: April 1, 1974

April 1, 1974
RFD 6 Box 342
Rocky Branch
Rogers, Arkansas 72756

Dear John,

Hell yes, glad to have you on a visit. Of course, I work from dawn to dark, but we can still find time to drink and talk; perhaps you can catch me up on literature. Would write you a longer letter, but no time.

Hope one of your books gets accepted, or all. As yet, I've never submitted to a publisher, although I'm letting some good small presses do chapbooks.

I was supposed to send a MS. to S. Kunitz, but didn't. I'm glad Ryan won.[713] Wish to hell I had time to spend on fiction and films, but just none of it to spare, so I make poetry when not working or sleeping.

Our garden, after frost and alot of rain, is trying to come up again. Trying to grow everything—with these prices in the stores!!

Would send you MSS. of poetry, but my wife won't type—too busy painting, and I can't duplicate, so my only copies go to editors, etc, who I owe work.[714] I've got a few around here, left, I think. Thank you for the invite to your magazine. Sure—anything you want, though I prefer unpublished work.

Hell, it's late, and I have to draw a map and two mountains and a winding creek—all to scale, so will get to it. Then, in the 4 hours of dark left before sunrise, maybe a poem.

yours,
Frank

I'll send a map + instructions to get here, soon.

Notes

713. Michael Ryan won the Yale Younger Poets Prize in 1973, with Kunitz as judge.
714. See note 639 above.

To David Walker: April 1, 1974

April 1, 1974
RFD 6 Box 342
Rocky Branch
Rogers, Arkansas 72756

Dear David,

Yes, I've written alot of poetry, mostly in my youth, when I hadn't the idea of publishing it, maybe too much poetry for my own good.[715]

By God, at last someone with guts who can say what he thinks: I'm grateful for your words on my work. So glad you came right to the mark and said what you think. "You didn't pick scabs or pockets, you picked a flower, you picked a guitar."[716]

My reply: All these poems, for one reason or another, were published.[717] I didn't select the poems for the book or the drawing of me or the illustration, just the title and the color.[718] Was it worth a tree?

There are only two other people who like me enough to tell me when and where it hurts. I really haven't met you, read your work too much in print, and undergone the other natural preliminaries for literary friendship—for that matter, I really don't care for the way editors and teachers and writers *build* bleak auditoriums to house their future business of art, but the truth is in you, and thanks for telling it.

I like universality, but in a particular way, not, as you say, internationalism, what I would call Bly translationese.[719] I like Cocteau's Blood of a Poet and Bunuel's Un Chien Andalou, but I also like the remarks they made about symbols and surreality.[720] Intentional surreality is an easy way to become obscure. However, I don't mind being called surreal, occasionally, as a few others have said, meaning no harm, when actually they had no better words or ways of understanding reality. (Carl Dreyer, for instance, says B+W is more realistic, where the abstractions lie in color, or in perspective elimination, something old painters did. EX: Giotto forfeited natural perspective for a form and color whose main intent is allegory.[721])

Further, Dreyer believes B+W serves the naturalistic, whereas only color is abstract enough to approach a psychological realism.[722] I'm off my bearing, maybe, but you understand: you know what real is, so you don't have to describe what you don't understand as surreal {(like others do)}. Cocteau said: when dealing with mystery, it's always best to use real cards.[723] And, for me, reality has always been, and continues to be, the most mysterious of things.

I wrote most of those poems when my head was full of clouds and the toadfrogs of youth, and so, like the lady bugs my great aunt used to order in the mails for her garden, they were self-indulgent, especially to publish them twice.[724]

Looking forward to your book. When will it be out?[725] Sorry that list was confusing. TSK is the only pamphlet I've published.[726] The rest are *scheduled* to be published, were to have already appeared, etc., but money, etc. kept the printers still. Haven't heard from the editors when any of them will come out. Anyway, all of the other MSS. are longer, much longer than T.S.K., unless they get cut down. That is why they can't afford to print them. When you are talking about 500 copies of a 500 page poem, you are talking yourself into the poor house.[727] The others are under 100 pages. I'd like to do a real small one. I used to think, when I was 16, that, since the poem took so much from me, it should seek its revenge on the reader. Now, I know it should give something.

In a different mail, you will find 375 pages of a 500 page MS.[728] The original was over a 1000 pages, but I got rid of half of it. The other 125 pages are lost somewhere in the mail. The poem, at one time 40,000 lines, is called "the battlefield where the moon says I love you" and it comes from a MS. St. Francis and the Wolf: Some Poems

1957–1964, which is also a partial MS. I believe you liked a poem of mine, "the mind reader" from this MS. This long poem will obliterate your eyes, if you let it, so don't read over 10 pages a day.

Here is what five people have said about it, in toto or in part.

Berryman: "Most poets would give their left eye to have written this, and their other eye to have done what you've done. . . ."

Dugan: "This is better than good, it is great. Publish it with a small press, now, as is, no revision. One day it will explode."[729]

Howard: "Have some mercy and respect for your audience. Weed out most of it, type it up MLA style, and send it back to me as a book. . . . ." + good + bad things too long to quote.

Cowley and Hecht only saw parts of it, but liked it. William Fox said he didn't like it as much as my other poems, too many run-on sentences for him.[730]

The remaining 125 pages are alot different than most of this. I know you think the longer poems in TSK should have been prose, that may be your opinion here, but I hope not. I do write fiction, though.

If the plot gets too labyrinth-like, let me know. I thanked all of the above gentlemen, but flat-out rejected Howard's suggestion.

I know what is good and bad about this. I've forgotten it. I just want you to read it. To remember or forget. Sorry for the shoddy condition of MS., but no book out of it, not even galley proofs.

Keep writing, and sending me poems, and telling me what you think.

Drunk again, reading a book about Carl Dreyer, and so on.[731]

yours,
Frank

$$$ $$$

Try Ironwood and Stinktree and Iowa[732]

Notes

715. In Walker's March 24, 1974, letter to Stanford, he writes, "You must write/have written, a lot if the other several books are as long as *S. Knives*."

716. Re: *The Singing Knives*, which Stanford had sent him in mid-March 1974, Walker writes several manuscript pages in his abovementioned letter. He liked many poems but felt that a couple of longer poems, such as "The Snake Doctors" and "The Gospel Bird," could've been better as prose stories. He didn't particularly like Stanford's use of caesura, and he asks, "And does 'T. of Janus' end in mid-air??" Walker adds, "Well

that's my reaction. I really like the stuff . . . Send me some more sometime" (ellipsis in original).

717. I.e., the poems in *The Singing Knives*. All but a few of the first edition's twenty-three poems appeared in various magazines from 1970 to 1972—the exceptions being "The Blood Brothers," "The Singing Knives," "Transcendence of Janus," and "The Snake Doctors" (a portion of which *Partisan Review* accepted but didn't publish).

718. Cf. Stanford's June 28, 1971, letter to Bender above, par. 3 (re: *The Singing Knives* in manuscript): "I selected them." A front matter page in *The Singing Knives* contains a line drawing of Stanford, and the cover and title page contain an abstract red-and-black illustration; the cover is otherwise dark blue.

719. Of *The Singing Knives*' short poems, Walker writes in his March 24 letter that they seem less Stanfordian than others—"less particularized, more synthetic—international—surreal"—while conceding that he himself admittedly has a predilection for "the concrete."

In chapter 17 of *In Translation: Translators on Their Work and What It Means*, "Translation and the Art of Revision," Susan Bernofsky writes, "When people complain about 'translationese,' it's generally because they feel [that a] sound/sense unity has not been achieved."

720. *Le Sang d'un poète* (*The Blood of a Poet*), Cocteau's 1932 film, and *Un chien andalou*, Buñuel's 1929 film. See note 233 above, and further into his 1946 preface to *The Blood of a Poet*, Cocteau adds: "*The Blood of a Poet* draws nothing from either dreams or symbols. As far as the former are concerned, it initiates their mechanism. . . . As for the latter, it rejects them, and substitutes acts, or allegories of these acts, that the spectator can make symbols of if he wishes." Stanford is likely also referring to Cocteau's front matter essay ("No Symbols") in *Le testament d'Orphée* (*The Testament of Orpheus*): "When a Frenchman no longer understands . . . he either gets angry or he takes refuge in symbols. 'I don't understand, therefore it must be a symbol,' is a typically French way of thinking." Jean Cocteau, *Two Screenplays*, 4, 75.

As published in *"L'Age d'Or" and "Un Chien Andalou": Films by Luis Buñuel* (1968), in 1954, Buñuel stated: "It is surrealism which has revealed to me that in life there is a moral code from which man cannot extricate himself. . . . I have seen in surrealism a discipline to be exercised." Trans. Marianne Alexandre (Simon & Schuster, 1968), 10.

721. See, e.g., Giotto's fourteen allegorical Virtues and Vices (ca. 1305), painted as grisailles (monochrome paintings), in the Arena Chapel at Padua.

722. Stanford is paraphrasing Dreyer's words from the "Imagination and Color (1955)" chapter of *Dreyer in Double Reflection*. Dreyer argues, "A much, much more important means for abstraction is, of course, *colors*. With them, everything is possible" after "breaking the chain that still binds the color film to the photographic naturalism of

the black-and-white film. . . . The realities must be forced into a form of simplification and abbreviation and in a purified state reappear in a kind of timeless psychological realism" and "Perhaps there is an idea for an interesting abstraction in the conscious elimination of the atmospheric perspective." Carl Theodor Dreyer, *Dreyer in Double Reflection: Translation of Carl Th. Dreyer's Writings About the Film (Om Filmen)*, ed. and trans. Donald Skoller (E. P. Dutton, 1973), 184–85.

723. Of artist Christian Bérard (1902–49), Cocteau states: "He was the only man to understand that Wonderland has little use for vagueness, and that mystery exists only in precise things." Jean Cocteau, *Cocteau on the Film: A Conversation Recorded by André Fraigneau*, trans. Vera Traill (Dennis Dobson, 1954), 71. Stanford reproduces this quote in his autobiographical/critical essay, "With the Approach of the Oak the Axeman Quakes"; also cf. the epigraph to Stanford's poem "The Sound of Trees." *What About This*, 240, 664.

724. I.e., to publish the poems in magazines and again in *The Singing Knives*. In Walker's March 24 letter, he notes that the poems in *The Singing Knives* he likes least are the shortest and longest ones: "Some of them, as wholes, hit me as too much a self-indulgence, a gesture."

725. Walker's book *Moving Out* (1976).

726. *The Singing Knives*. With the book, Stanford had enclosed a typescript publication history sheet. In his March 24 reply letter, Walker writes, "Are all those other books out yet, except the 1975 one? Couldn't figure the info. sheet too well."

727. The sheet Stanford enclosed lists the following as chapbooks from Mill Mountain Press: *The Singing Knives* (1971), *The Battlefield Where the Moon Says I Love You* ("1972"), *Approacheth the Ship and Wonder* ("1973"), *Gone* ("1974"), and *Ladies From Hell* ("1975")—with Stanford noting that the "unpublished" latter four are "set in type and awaiting printing." A fifth unpublished chapbook, *St. Francis and the Wolf*, is listed as an anticipated publication by Barn Dream Press with no scheduled publication date. *The Battlefield* was ultimately published as a copublication between Mill Mountain Press and Lost Roads Publishers in 1977, the year on *Ladies From Hell*'s title and copyright pages is 1974 (though it was actually published, it appears, in 1975—see note 882 below), and *Approacheth the Ship and Wonder*, *Gone*, and *St. Francis and the Wolf: Some Poems 1957–1964* were not published.

728. See note 608 above.

729. Dugan's descriptor re: *The Battlefield* was that it was "wonderful"; see his actual words in note 267 above.

730. See Fox's words in note 671 above.

731. *Dreyer in Double Reflection*; see note 722 above.

732. *Ironwood*, Cuddihy's journal; *Stinktree*, a literary journal; and *The Iowa Review*.

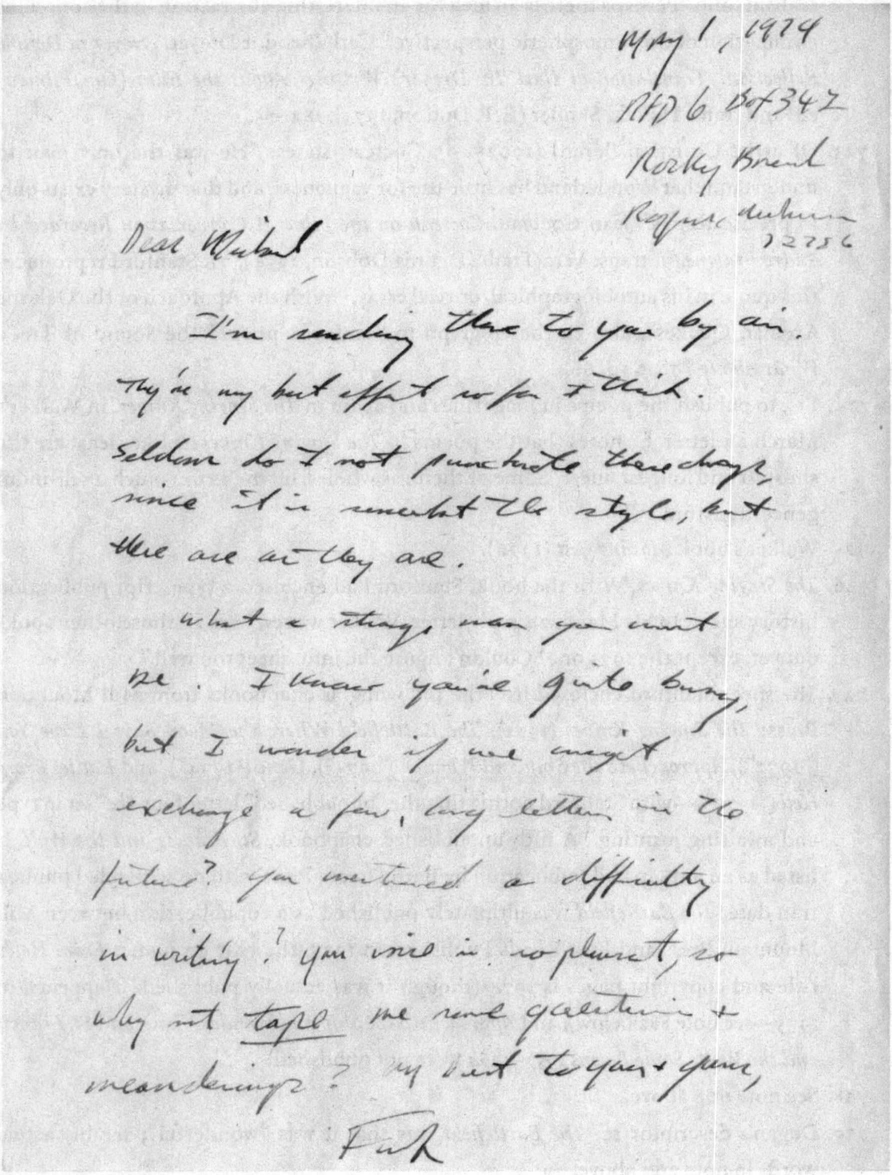

May 1, 1974
RFD 6 Box 342
Rocky Branch
Rogers Arkansas
72756

Dear Michael

I'm sending these to you by air.
They're my best effort so far I think.
Seldom do I not punctuate these days,
since it is somewhat the style, but
these are as they are.

What a strange man you must
be. I know you're quite busy,
but I wonder if we might
exchange a few, long letters in the
future? You mentioned a difficulty
in writing? You write in no plainest, so
why not _tape_ me some questions +
meanderings? My best to you + yours,

Frank

Stanford's May 1, 1974, letter to Michael Cuddihy. Stanford notes that he has by and large shifted from omitting punctuation in his poetry to punctuating and proposes that the two men "exchange a few, long letters in the future."

To Michael Cuddihy: May 1, 1974

May 1, 1974
RFD 6 Box 342
Rocky Branch
Rogers, Arkansas 72756

Dear Michael,

I'm sending these to you by air. They're my best effort so far I think. Seldom do I not punctuate these days, since it is somewhat the style, but these are as they are.[733]

What a strange man you must be. I know you're quite busy, but I wonder if we might exchange a few, long letters in the future? You mentioned a difficulty in writing?[734] Your voice is so pleasant, so why not *tape* me some questions + meanderings?

My best to you + yours,
Frank

Notes

733. Per Cuddihy's May 14 reply, with this letter Stanford sent "The Strange Boy" (*Plain Songs*), which Cuddihy rejected, and "Floating Bridge" (*Plain Songs*) and "Fire Left by Travelers" (*Field Talk*), both of which Cuddihy bought but, by July 1, had changed his mind about—neither poem appeared in *Ironwood*. The latter two poems are unpunctuated, and a version of "The Strange Boy" published in 1975 is as well.
734. In 1951, Cuddihy was stricken with respiratory polio; he was, thereafter, wheelchair bound.

To Lawrence Ferlinghetti: May 20, 1974

May 20, 1974
RFD 6 Box 342
Rocky Branch
Rogers, Arkansas 72756

Dear Mr. Ferlinghetti,

Thank you for the Prévert translations.[735] I'm looking forward to ordering the City Lights Anthology when it is out in Spring.[736] An out of the way bookstore in these parts carries alot of your books, for which I'm glad. I just wish you'd had room for the poems I sent you last year, which you said you liked.

I'm trying to run down Allen's address. When he was in Arkansas a few years ago we travelled around, he wrote some of *These States*.[737] I wanted to take him to a monastery where I used to live, but one of those professors in charge wouldn't let us go. Anyway, at that time, the monks were anxious to have him for a visit, to pray, and read to them from his poetry. By coincidence, some Zen monks from Japan had just visited the abbey. Recently, some religious from India were there. They were animated in the conversation about Allen, pointing out to the monks they'd missed something when he hadn't been able to visit. Every summer, I go back and help with a camp for under-privileged kids. The students have started a small literary magazine with the monks and, since I'm the only one who knows Allen, they've asked me if I might get a poem for their magazine.[738] Of course, no one is interested in a magazine from a monastery published by strange boys and monks, but they'd really be grateful if I could get a poem from Allen. That's why I'd like his address. Charles Plymell is no longer in touch with me, otherwise I could get it from him. By the way, when I said to the monks and students that you'd once turned down some of my work, they were interested in seeing your handwriting, etc. I believe they like your new book better than your play, but I still think they're partial to your *Pictures of the Gone World*.[739] Bukowski is a favorite, as are the drawings by Topor.[740]

I'm enclosing a check for the amount of Allen's book, *The Fall of America*: Poems of These States. If you could get in touch with him in my behalf, or forward this letter to him I would appreciate it.

Yours,
Frank Stanford

Notes

735. Prévert's *Selections from Paroles* (1958)—number nine in City Lights' Pocket Poets Series.
736. *City Lights Anthology* (1974), ed. Ferlinghetti, which included work by City Lights poets (including Ginsberg, Voznesensky, Kerouac, and company) but also various poets outside of the City Lights universe—e.g., Arthur Rimbaud and various Greek poets (appearing in translation), as well as a section on "The Surrealist Movement in the U.S.," which published the work of twenty-three poets, writers, and artists. See also note 538 above.
737. Allen Ginsberg's *The Fall of America: Poems of These States 1965–1971* (1972).
738. *Rock Quarry*, a student literary magazine initiated at Subiaco Academy in 1974.
739. *Pictures of the Gone World* (1955), Ferlinghetti's self-published first book—number one in the Pocket Poets Series. Ferlinghetti's latest book as of 1974 was *Open Eye,*

Open Heart (1973); twenty brief plays were published in his books *Unfair Arguments with Existence* (1963) and *Routines* (1964).

740. Charles Bukowski (1920–94), poet/fiction writer, and Roland Topor (1938–97), illustrator/writer. City Lights published Topor's *Panic* (1965) and, as of 1974, had published two of Bukowski's books (in 1969 and 1972).

To John McKernan: June 4, 1974

June 4, 1974
RFD 6 Box 342
Rocky Branch
Rogers, Arkansas 72756
501-636-7669

Dear John,

Yours of May 26 from El Dorado here. Just got in from a long weekend. Working all over the countryside.

You sound like you might be pulling through here around the weekend of 14, 15, 16 which would be *perfect* for us—and *only* time I'd be here.[741] They've got me working a few hundred miles from here, so I'm just staying in the woods instead of driving back and forth. (Just spent $2,000 on my own equipment, so I can be my own boss.)

Friday, Saturday, Sunday would be *fine*: before that, I'll be off in the sticks, after that I'll be at the monastery taking care of a bunch of young hoodlums at a charity camp. (For 10 days: what a strange vacation! I'll probably have a dream, or someone will get killed!)[742]

If we get too drunk over the weekend, I might not go to work Monday. (I don't give a shit.)

We might have to kill a goat and cook it? I've got plenty of green food from the garden, and Ginny makes pretty good sourdough bread. You can go fishing in my little skiff if you like. My wife drinks cheap, dry wine all day and paints.[743] When she sells something, she drinks expensive, dry wine all day and paints.

Just got a letter from Dugan with a bunch of new, handwritten poems. He's crazy.

Got a copy of your magazine in the mail yesterday.[744] Alright. My wife liked your poems the best. I told her you were crazy, and that I'd seen alot of your shorter things. I've got an idea for a book if you'll write it. When I'm working long hours, I'd rather give the ideas to people. About all I can do with these kind of hours is 6 or 7 poems a week. No fiction or film! Dammit!

I better write Dugan and tell him we're not coming up there to that PROVINCE TOWN WHORE HOUSE, or whatever it is they call it.[745] One of these days, I want to go back to dreaming for a living.

CALL ME, LET ME KNOW WHEN YOU AND YOUR WIFE WILL BE HERE.

yours,
Frank

For a surveyor, this is a lousy map.

GO TO ROGERS, TAKE H.W. 12 towards the LAKE, stay on H.W. 12 until you get to the ROCKY BRANCH turnoff. Once you get on RB ROAD, which is paved, there will be several roads (paved) bearing to your left, but stay on the paved road without taking any left forks. You'll come to where you have to go left or right at Clark's Country Korner. Go right to BLAND CHAPEL, our place is the 1st white house on right.[746]

Notes

741. In McKernan's May 26, 1974, letter to Stanford, he noted that he and his wife would be staying in El Dorado for roughly "2½–3 weeks" and then heading north to Nebraska.
742. Stanford helped out at Camp Subiaco; see note 333 above.
743. See note 639 above.
744. Presumably *The Little Review* 5, no. 1, issue 9 (1974), which published Stanford's poem "Blue Yodel of Those Who Were Always Telling Me" and two single-quatrain poems by McKernan (both titled "Poem").
745. Fine Arts Work Center, a writers residency center in Provincetown, Massachusetts.
746. On the page's verso, Stanford has drawn a map, marking his house with an X and "Poet"; see the map beginning this chapter.

To Alan Dugan: July 1, 1974

July 1, 1974
12:45 AM
Box 342 RFD 6
Rogers, ARK. 72756

Dear Alan:

Just got your March 15 letter mailed + postscripted June 20. We just got back from 10 days at the monastery where I helped with an outdoor camp for orphans, young crooks and idiots.[747] (That's how I took my vacation from work.) Ginny painted monks and drank beer.

Got back here on our place a few hours ago. Went out in the garden to see how the garden is after a week's absence. Good. Growing, eating everything we could get in.

Glad to know you think Andrew W. is a shit. I hate him. Also, I hate T. H. Benton, Hurd-Turd, and especially G. Wood.[748] I really hate T. H. Benton. He is from around where Ginny comes from and his shriveled, pecker, hoe-handled brushes have dribbled over everything in sight. Ginny intends to get a couple of these art magazines, to see what is going on. She knows far less about contemp. art, than I do contemp. poetry. (A new copy of *NY Quarterly* has arrived, along with a *Field*, and my galley proofs for my story in *Iowa R.*—I admire NYQ for trying to do in publishing what our system of justice tried to do for the innocent: better to have guilty men on the loose, rather than one innocent man confined unjustly. Alot of the poetry in the magazines is hard to swallow, but so is this fruit jar of white mule I bought from a blind bootlegger the other day.)

Since neither of us know what we should about contemp. painting, we both feel a little guilty and foolish for trying to discuss it. Although, she is quite familiar with classic and modern work. She's read all she can about their lives, seen what she could when in Europe, painted what she could (including shacking up with a med. student so she could go to anatomy classes, have wine + cheese to eat, and a place to stay in Brussels.) We get drunk and read about "those days of painters, whores, and poets, and politicals in Paris and Zurich," but we don't know what it was like in N.Y.C.[749]

Your letter, describing some of it, is great. I hope you've kept journals about those days. You've probably already written a book {(prose)} about it all, have it hidden somewhere. I like the true tales you remembered and that tall one about the railroad man and the seam in his trousers. It all sounds like a great, tragic, strange, funny hunting story, where the hunters are artistic, all wounded, stalked by their prey, ART.

Got a letter, unexpectedly, from Allen Ginsberg the other week. He said he'd been fasting, etc. for 25 days.[750]

Just finished reading Merton's *Asian Journals* and a book about him *The Man in the Sycamore Tree.*[751] (There was a pilgrim, quite short, who couldn't see Christ over the heads of the crowd, so he climbed a tree.)[752]

You might think me crazy, dipsomaniac, but, for a long time now, Merton appears in my dreams. I am listening to some Greek music, and a fat, Arab woman is about to play on the record player. (By now, the black gospel station is off the air.)

Merton is with me, among others, like many another turning, reposed soul. (In 1964, I wrote an imaginary journey with Thomas. A sort of Twain-Proust-St. John of the Cross memoir.)

A bird is singing outside. It must be an odd bird, because I haven't heard such a voice before? I am letting my black cat out the door to chase fireflies.[753]

I'm about to say fuck the man I'm working for, as my mind is full of slow poems, thick as turtles on the road. This fucking work is getting to me, but I know dough is toilet paper, and when I shit, I like to wipe. (My ass.)

Ginny is having to do hack work for a stupid kind of gallery, plus baby portraits, etc., which have brought her on the verge of having her ovaries removed. She works seriously a good 7 or 8 hours a day, all while I'm gone, taking 2 hour breaks morning and evening to tend to the garden, and some of my shit.

I'm getting too tired to continue this letter. Everything rising and converging, so I'll continue it soon.

***

Pretty goddamn sick; too sick to work, but I wrote a few things. Ginny found out she sold a painting, so we'll get drunk, go fishing, buy a new pair of boots, get the cat spayed, etc.

The goddamn well is just about dry. We['re] watering the garden, instead of bathing. Do that in the lake.

This professor and his wife and kid are supposed to *drop in* on us over the 4th of July weekend. (I must tell you this story. While at Subiaco, a friend of my mother's and dead father's came for a stay. The man is 6'8", has a voice deeper than yours. Missing several fingers on both hands. His father, who was my father's foreman during the early days of levee building, lived in a tent, could neither read or write. When he was seven, his father asked my old man could he have a job picking roots on the levee, running a barr pit pump. The boy was very bright, quit school at the 6th grade. My old man took him under his wing, taught him all he knew about the river, moving dirt, and work. Now in his early 40's, but already the last of the levee legends, he is a millionaire. Drives an initialed Cadillac, smokes with a bone cigarette holder, has a Gainsborough over his bed. —Anyway, he's invited us to come stay with him, and is going to buy a few things from Ginny. He claims to know where all the people I knew in my youth are. Some of them work for him, or he *keeps* them.)[754] Well, on the 4th this editor-teacher-poet is coming, so I caught some catfish, bought some whiskey, made arrangements for some friends to come over, kill + barbecue a goat, etc. One guy is a black Zorba, the other runs a juke joint.[755] (A couple weeks ago the tavern owner's son killed a man. The local paper, formerly owned by Fullbright, read like this: "Roosevelt Murphy was shot in the head three times when Bobby Morgan, now in custody and being questioned, came home and found him taking a watermelon from the latter's refrigerator."[756] The melon was full of dope I figure, but I don't ask about it.

The black preacher I know called up early this morning, inviting me to a memorial service for Mrs. M. L. King, Sr.[757] Some of his remarks, ". . . . what things we dream; men gone crazy as niggers; what it was, I do not know; when I heard it ringing I was looking at the moon coming up, I knew: it's ~~had~~ got to be FRANK."

Do you like jazz by McCoy Tyner or Stanley Turrentine?[758]

Ginny's read your letter several times and would like to hear more from you. Your ideas and opinions on the following: *Gustav Klimt*, Fernand Knöpff, Hippolyte Daye, *W. Kuhn*, Adrian Van Ostad, Vermeer. They fascinate Ginny, and the latter has influenced her the most, along with Matisse + Cézanne.[759]

For my benefit, what do you think of Chagall, Modigliani, Pearlstein, Will Barnett, Leonard Baskin, Perlin, Tooker, Castéllon.[760] I better quit, that's a big job.

yours,
Frank

Notes

747. Camp Subiaco; see note 333 above.
748. Andrew Wyeth, Thomas Hart Benton, Peter Hurd, and Grant Wood—American Realist / Social Realist and Regionalist painters.
749. The quotation here is probably a reference to Dugan's March 15, 1974, letter (missing or lost).
750. Ginsberg's "letter"—a June 9, 1974, postcard—was in response to Stanford's May 20 letter to Ferlinghetti. Ginsberg noted that in fall 1973, he had visited a Buddhist seminary for three months, meditating ten hours a day for twenty-five of the days.
751. *The Asian Journals of Thomas Merton* (1973) and Edward Rice's *The Man in the Sycamore Tree: The Good Times and Hard Life of Thomas Merton* (1970).
752. See the story of Zacchaeus, Luke 19:1–10.
753. Frank and Ginny's cat Debureau; see note 325 above.
754. Per a July 1, 1974, letter to Broughton, Stanford is referring here to a man named James Allen Reece (1932–2002), "last of the old time levee men."

755. Alexis Zorba, the suit-donning, anti-intellectual protagonist of *Zorba the Greek* (1964), which adapted Nikos Kazantzakis's 1946 novel. (Stanford is referring to Jimbo Reynolds, presumably, and to Sherman Morgan.)

756. Roberta Fulbright, widow of Jay Fulbright, owned the *Northwest Arkansas Times* for decades. As reported in the newspaper, Bobby Morgan—Sherman Morgan's son—on May 19, 1974, admittedly had a physical altercation with and was beating Roosevelt Willis at the Fayetteville residence of Willis's son, Billy, either while or immediately before Willis was shot once in the chest and killed; Morgan was acquitted (due to "reasonable doubt") on August 3. Linda Dobkins, "Morgan Found Innocent in Death of Willis," *Northwest Arkansas Times*, August 4, 1974. Stanford is referring to the initial report of May 20, which included the sentence "Police quoted Morgan as saying he had 'whipped' Willis at the Morgan home because he found Willis eating a watermelon which had been in the Morgan refrigerator." "Prosecutor Studies Charge in Murder of Local Man," *Northwest Arkansas Times*, May 20, 1974.

757. The preacher is presumably Claude Ricks. Alberta Williams King, mother of Martin Luther King Jr., was assassinated by Black Hebrew Israelite Marcus Chenault on June 30, 1974.

758. McCoy Tyner (1938–2020), jazz pianist, and Stanley Turrentine (1934–2000), jazz saxophonist.

759. Gustav Klimt (1862–1918), Austrian painter; Fernand Khnopff (1858–1921), Belgian painter; Hippolyte Daeye (1873–1952), Belgian painter; Walt Kuhn (1877–1949), American painter; Adriaen van Ostade (1610–85), Dutch painter; Johannes Vermeer (1632–75), Dutch painter; Henri Matisse (1869–1954), French painter; and Paul Cézanne (1839–1906), French painter.

760. Marc Chagall (1887–1985), Belarusian French artist; Amedeo Modigliani (1884–1920), Italian painter; Philip Pearlstein (1924–2022), American painter; Will Barnet (1911–2012), American painter; Leonard Baskin (1922–2000), American artist; Bernard Perlin (1918–2014), American painter; George Tooker (1920–2011), American painter; and Federico Castellón (1914–71), Spanish American painter. Dugan replied on July 6, 1974: "I refuse to answer your questions, being not stupid enough to be an art critic but stupid enough to be sitting guard on the porch."

To Irv Broughton: July 17 and 18, 1974

NOTE 17
July 17, 1974

Dear Irv,

Just ran out of film in one hundred foot rolls, except a few color rolls. With camera and printing, no way I can buy another roll. Need as much Tri-X, Plus-X, 4-X (or Double X) as you can send me.[761] Done for until then, when I get some.

yours,
Frank

I have complete confidence + faith in your work, be it a film on me, or whatever you choose to use your talents with. Endure.

July 18, 1974
NOTE 18

Dear Irv,

Footage on the way 1st Class. And sound. You'll have to extend deadline till 1st of August on my film because:

1. Camera malfunction
2. Loss of time
3. 1000' approx. bad footage due to interval fuck-up in camera. (Already had it checked here to *save you* processing fees.)
4. I've run-out of 100' rolls of film + magnetic tape.

Footage that has to be done over:

3 rolls → 1. Old men
2. Black patch woman + deaf child
1 roll 3. Fly away in parachute
2 rolls 4. Tall bicycle
5. ! Kid carrying ice, beat-up car with me picking him up!

Keep up the work, keep the faith!
Our garden is burning up.
Trying to do 100 things at once.
Employer fucked-me out of $200, the shit hook.
Deer eating everything.

Drought continues.
! Send Ginny's negatives!
Find pictures of *Roethke* standing in the dark in monk's robe that he liked to effect.[762]
Over and out.
You're great.

Love,
F. + G.

Plan to stay here long as possible.

The easiest thing in the world for me is to come up with a good idea; the next easiest thing is to formulate them, find the interior connections for exterior appearances.

I still have something of the medieval approach, in that a community of anonymous individuals contributes to building the temple they will all pray in.

If my work can teach anyone anything, let me teach others how to care for and cultivate a good crop, even though they didn't plant the seed—even still, *they did the most* work.

I see no reason, whatever, why you can't take full credit for the entire film: I mean, I think it is certainly in your *best interest* to command the respect of the editors and others working on the film, not to mention the sucking blow-flies you have to put up with in your job—I will use the word command and not demand.

That is why *all* my ideas are at your disposal, with no strings attached. That is why you should *show* the editor the suggestions + ideas I have, either in your notes + handwriting, or you should *talk* to her about it, using my notes, which are now yours.

In my opinion, there are only *three* things that can go wrong, and they are these:

1. Lack of money + time

2. A mind set *against* a group of people, rather than *on* a group of ideas—such as the monkey fuckers you work for. Don't let a glaze of contempt or silent rage do anything but *hone* your senses, don't let your situation *dull* your gifts!

3. Due to a sense of pride, on the one hand, or guilt on the other, not using a good idea of mine as your own. Especially, if it comes down to keeping the confidence of your co-workers, editors, *don't hesitate at all* to use what I've sent you. It would be a sin and important loss to the film if you should pass over good material for fear of losing control or respect—this last thing worries me a little. I know you are fair, proud, and generous, and I want you to keep your balance of power—but I'd rather you take credit for something I sent, especially when one of my ideas is better than another.

Most of your ideas and mine are good—it's too bad there won't be enough time for all of them, we will have to cut deep into the film to make it of acceptable length.

I can see now that your approach to the film, an external one, will gradually superimpose *itself* over what I've suggested——and this is as it should be, as there is always a physical layer to things, *even films*.

I can see that you will do an excellent job if you resist the temptation of letting things which mean nothing to me creep into the film. And I don't see much danger here, as you know me pretty damn well.

But since these visuals will *stand* for something, let's don't be tourists taking movies of someone's good life and hard times. I believe the {majority of [the]}[763] audience will be nothing more than tourists in the holy, ordinary city of my soul. If we try to con them, give them the same old show, they'll leave, spiritually broke, and go somewhere else next year.

What we want are pilgrims—so it is essential that we let them experience something as moving as Bach or Mahler, as light as the washboard music "38"—the blues is not really light.

The *tension* of *seriousness* and the *comic is good*. The poking fun, and the somberness of solitude.

Perhaps the worst thing that could happen is our taking the audience for granted, as does most "educational" film. I don't think we should try teaching them "nothing about nobody." Rather, let them learn something by being *entertained*.

There are probably a good 50,000 people in the U.S. trying to be serious poets. There are a good 100,000 or so trying to be serious artists in other fields. I think the potential of this film does lie, however, in writing careers + colleges, etc. If two hundred writing programs or humanities programs or Eng. Dept. or college film programs rented this film at $50.00 bucks a whack, $10,000.00. But forgetting the money, think what would happen if just 100 classes with 20 or 50 in each class saw it?

And so, in conclusion, you will be superimposing your conceptions and perceptions over mine, and I think things will turn out fine, if I don't have to "fill in" or "stand in" to certain spots in the film, otherwise it becomes neither serious or comic, but characture.[764] Ultimately, poets will be looking at it—I don't give a shoot in hell about my image, but I don't want to be anything but honest about it—and they'll be able to smell a phoney and a bad movie a mile off.

The whole point of the music—and only true poets will appreciate it—is that *we live in silence*, and we spend our lives trying to hear, constantly listening to everything. The reasons why *this* music is metaphorically complex—but poets and musicians can understand.

So, you can't use 4 or 3 or 5 min of Rachmaninoff, or Bach, or Orff because it is too heavy—as in Proust, or Vermeer, or Besson or Dreyer,[765] but do use at least a few seconds of it, perhaps a minute—a minute of each piece, a few minutes devoted to mystery.[766]

The poet lives alone in the sanctuary of all those, and all that which he has known, performing the rituals of his imagination, transubstantiating reality into poetry, {and, for a few minutes each week, the congregation of readers—READ, always leaving the papers scattered on the floor as they leave,} which everyone reads for a few minutes each week and leaves behind with the rats.[767]

I like the title:

It Wasn't a Dream, It Was a Flood.[768]

The title implies the transubstantiation of imagination + reality.

I think you are going to have a great film. We don't need fame + fortune, just some recognition and a little money.

Bad news here in that I had a reel of film processed here, suspecting an uneven hum in the camera before it quit running—yes, about 1000 feet of fucked-up footage. (All the stuff you have is good—) Motor in spring caused severe *undercranking*, so as to overexpose film I was shooting at 11, 16, and 22. Footage would appear *too* jerky, then normal, jerky, etc. I'm shooting the shots again.

Notes

761. Kodak Tri-X and Kodak Plus-X, black-and-white film stocks.
762. Theodore Roethke (1908–63), poet. Following this letter, Broughton appears to have mailed a photograph of Roethke, by photographer Mary Randlett (1924–2019), of him dressed in a monk cowl—shot on July 18, 1963, two weeks before his death; later in 1974, Ginny Stanford completed her painting *Roethke* (modeled after the photo), which was used for the cover of *Mill Mountain Review* 2, no. 2 (1975).
763. *Marginalia: left side, left facing.*
764. Stanford either is neologizing—inventing "characture" from *character* and, perhaps, *portraiture*—or means "caricature."
765. *Besson*: correctly, Bresson. An undated note from Broughton to Stanford notes that a piece of music being considered for *It Wasn't a Dream: It Was a Flood* was Sergei Rachmaninoff's symphonic poem *Isle of the Dead*, op. 29 (1909).
766. In addition to clips from blues and folk songs, *It Wasn't a Dream: It Was a Flood* incorporated two clips of classical music: the opening of Johann Sebastian Bach's oratorio *St. Matthew Passion* (BWV 244, 1727), "Kommt, ihr Töchter, helft mir klagen" (Come, daughters, join my lament; approx. 1 minute, 25 seconds), and the opening of act 4 of Umberto Giordano's 1896 opera *Andrea Chénier* (approx. 50 seconds).

767. The grammatical incongruity here is due to Stanford having added "and, for a few minutes . . . as they leave" below, with a line drawn to its insertion point; the modified phrasing doesn't seamlessly integrate.

768. From line 3 of Stanford's poem "The Double Suicide of the Mirror and the Rose" (*What About This*, 660), which was composed pre–summer 1973 (a typescript copy exists in Campbell's papers). The phrase is engraved on Stanford's footstone in St. Benedict Cemetery at Subiaco. The film's title is punctuated with a colon.

To Michael Cuddihy: July 18, 1974

July 18, 1974
RFD 6 Box 342
Rocky Branch
Rogers, Arkansas 72756

Dear Michael,

It was splendid that you called and we were able to talk so long, a luxury you may regret when you get your phone bill.

First of all, glad you want the one poem, and, as I read over the longer one, I'm able to see your suggestions on the last few stanzas, making the line lengths different.

I feel very bad about not being able to *keep up* with contemp. letters . . . . although I've tried to explore the stratas of modern and classical literature. I *think* contemp. poets have an obligation to read their contemporaries. And I try. Merwin and Wright came to my mind—as the best of this generation—as quickly as they came to yours. As for G. Oppen, who I *ought* to know more about, *I do* like his work very much—if he is the same poet who won the Pulitzer Prize in 68 or 69.[769] I remember reading a book of poems of his, then. Yes, his poems in your book, I like *very much*.[770] (I especially am glad to hear he doesn't hustle you.)

Oppen's line reminds me of a poet writing good lines, then letting it, ever so gently, but with a marked force, become a poem. His poetry seems quite the opposite of most [of] the work I see. I like this. I haven't read what *he* writes by *someone else*. In a ritual way, he and Merwin are near. (A long time ago, an editor told me my poetry was too much like Merwin's ((his poetry is, in fact, a bad imitation of Merwin)). The poems he made the remark about were ones I'd written when I was 12. Donald Justice had seen the poems, earlier, and had voiced something to me about my beginning with my voice—although I wrote constantly, early, to find it—and Merwin writing and translating his way into a poem with his voice.)

But now for the shorter poems I'm sending—they're old and 98% unseen. [And as far as those 375 pages of poetry, I never meant, or intended, you publishing a book of it. I just thought you might want a "bit" of wild reading. In fact, I'm still under obligation with another as far as a *book* goes, but magazine-wise, it's free.][771] Dugan is the only poet I know, or have known, or have corresponded with, that I like to mention. (Not because I don't *think the world* of alot of the others, because I do, but because it is hard for me to drop names.) (Especially after they are dead, and especially when alot of them invited me to study with them ($$$$) at various universities, etc., but I declined.)

Anyway, Dugan thought that I should get my early work published "as is".[772]

About those films: neither did I select what poets to film, nor did I have much voice in how they were done. I just ran the camera. If you ever get to see the one on Eberhart, you'll be able to tell my shots and editing suggestions: they contrast greatly from the "T.V." pt. of view!!

In the last two years, those people have shot 10,000 feet at least on me. All these tapes, etc. (I'm against all this mass communication, since, it appears, less and less communication takes place!)

The film, or films, I'm doing will take time—BLOOD OF A POET ~~1957–1967~~. Ha. Ha. The only way I could ever come near a 16mm film is through these folks' generosity. They've given me film galore, a camera, a tape recorder, light meter, and pay the laboratory bill. How's that for kindness? I love to go to films, especially in the fall and winter.

You mentioned seeing *The Children of Paradise*—screenplay by the lovely poet Jacques Prévert.[773] (I've tried to translate alot of his work.) For me, the film is like another childhood, a childhood where you realize you're no longer a child—no more dark glasses.

No one knows it, but a magazine (a poetry magazine) devoted to film—especially poets + cinema is my doing. I didn't send out letters, but I got the guy to do it for one issue.[774] (I've managed to stay out of the issue, as I was leary of squeaking in an essay.)[775]

Our well spring is just about dry, and the garden needs all the water it can get, so we bathe in the lake, let dishes stack-up for days. Drought or flood, no happy medium. About 100° every day.

Every morning I work in the garden, write, and take a swim. In the day I write. And in the evening, more garden and another swim. We're trying to put-up a lot of food for this winter.

I've saved Merton for last, because my connections with him are quite deep, and I don't want to sound like I worship, 10 minutes a day, the itsy-bitsy statues of Zen monks, etc. I don't. No, I want to convey something about Merton: before he even died, I dreamed him, meeting him, not Brigget Bardot.[776] Maybe he wasn't what people said he was, a saint, a prophet, then NONE of us can be. But he comes close, and in so doing, brings us close. What I really have to say about him is quite personal, and I'm afraid it sounds a little "too thick". —The way I found Merton, was not away out, a searching for something or someone. *HE FOUND ME*. In that I dreamed him and knew him before I ever read him or heard of him.

Butterflies at Night

If there was an angel in the garden of love,
if there was ever a garden,
and not a grave with flowers
laid there over a hole,
then I saw his shadow turn to shade,
I soaked my toes, there, in
ten angles of light.
|
not angels
I got soaked to the toes, there, in

From an old dream. (which I no longer recall)

Since several thousand lines of that old manuscript ~~are~~ {were} a mythic encounter with Merton, 500 pages of which I burned, it's really difficult to talk much about it.[777] Late at night, early in the morning. For now,

yours,
Frank

Notes

769. George Oppen (1908–84) received the Pulitzer Prize for Poetry in 1969 for his book *Of Being Numerous* (1968).
770. Stanford is presumably referring to *Ironwood*, no. 1 (Spring 1972), which published Oppen's "A Poem About the Garden" and sections 5 and 7 (unnumbered in the issue) of his "Some San Francisco Poems"; *Ironwood* 3, no. 1, issue 5 (1975) was a special issue featuring Oppen's work.
771. Brackets Stanford's. See note 608 above.
772. Dugan's actual words, re: *The Battlefield* in manuscript, were "as it is"—see note 267 above.

773. In Cuddihy's July 1, 1974, letter to Stanford, he wrote, "Speaking of films, saw 'Les Enfants du Paradis' with Jean-Louis Barrault the other night. Tremendous film."

774. Stanford is referring to Broughton and *Mill Mountain Review*'s (aborted) film issue; see note 892 below.

775. *leary*: a variant of "leery" common especially during the 1960s and 1970s when Timothy Leary was popular.

776. Brigitte Bardot (1934–2025), actor and sex symbol.

777. Re: the burning of early manuscripts—such as works typed up and conglomerated into *St. Francis and the Wolf: Some Poems 1957–1964*, including *The Battlefield*'s 1960s precursor narratives, and other (discarded) work—see several of Stanford's late May–July 1972 letters.

To John McKernan: July 27, 1974

Dear John,

Most likely you're back in W. Virginia working. Sorry we missed each other.

We had some fish (cats), goat, rabbit, and lots of garden vegetables, + all kinds of booze over the 4th of July. My wife and a black cook put it all together.[778]

Too bad about J. C. Ransom kicking the bucket.[779] As you know, I helped compile the footage on a film about him. I loved the old man. Loved his early poetry——when he wasn't a fucked-up preacher, worried over fucking—as M. Cowley puts it. He and I drank some Arkansas wine, he wandered off into the present tense—as if he were still alive—about J. G. Fletcher![780]

Just finished reading *his* draft (t.written)[781] of the titles in the book he was publishing at the time I was filming him.[782] Too bad he spawned off all those lousy, "southern" apologist poets who, he admitted, he did not like.

Well, you keep your eyes out in all those big + little reviews and you're bound to run on to some of my shit. Bout 7 books coming out.

Sorry you didn't get to stay, fish at our place awhile. Would like to have seen you. Wanted you to take a look at my wife's paintings + films.

yours,
Frank

Notes

778. I.e., Jimbo Reynolds; see note 755 above.

779. Ransom died on July 3, 1974.

780. John Gould Fletcher. See note 221 above.

781. *t.written*: typewritten.

782. To this editor, Broughton noted that both he and Stanford somehow left the August 1972 visit to Ransom in Ohio with a single-sheet table of contents for a book of poetry that Ransom planned to publish. Email to editor, March 5, 2025.

To Malcolm Cowley: August 1, 1974

August 1, 1974
RFD 6 Box 342
Rocky Branch
Rogers, Arkansas 72756

Dear Mr. and Mrs. Cowley,

After 58 days without rain, it has finally let-up a little in the Ozarks and our garden is damp. I can't remember the last time I wrote you: whether I was in a houseboat, a boxcar, a monastery, or a hotel. About a year and a half ago I settled down with a painter; she is a fine artist, and we lived on a river where I did fishing guide jobs and rented canoes. After the weather got cold I went back into land surveying and we moved to this small farm near the lake. My job kept me walking the mountains and fields from dawn to dark, but now I'm off for awhile, trying to gather up some stories.

I've also come back from two weeks at the monastery where I help out every year with a camp they give for orphans and the like. My wife painted the monks and I rode herd on the kids. When we returned to our farm, the deer and the drought had done their damage. Last year we lived on homeade [*sic*] bread and wine and goat cheese, and fish, and this year we might just do the same. Our freezer lost its "cool" and we lost hundreds of pounds of produce. We'll put our fall crop in soon, and I believe we'll have enough out of it to give away.

It seems as if all my friends are shooting people. A white friend killed two black men with a double barrel shotgun after they jumped him, and a black friend killed another black friend with a big pan.

I haven't seen Irv since last year when we went to Miss. to film Miss Welty, but she was ill.[783] We filmed another writer, Joan Williams. The young woman Faulkner was interested in. She's the lady that wrote her books at my mother's house when I was a kid.[784] Our fathers knew each other on the levees. Old Irv is still sinking everything but his teeth into his magazine and films. I just recently heard about J. C. Ransom. I never really did go in for that group but I respected them all. Last year sometime I got a letter from him, but when I opened it, he'd forgotten to put the note in.

When school is in session at the monastery, they get me down there somehow to talk about poetry. The boys come from all kinds of backgrounds from all over these states and the world. We usually use Collected Poems by alot of authors which only really excludes a few contemporary poets. Every year they *get* the three poems—from Old English to O'Hara—that they like best, each class does.[785] This year they selected a poem by Dugan, your "Boy In Sunlight",[786] and there is a tie for third between "Fern Hill" by Thomas,[787] a poem by Stafford,[788] and a poem by Roethke. The students and monks have their own little magazine and what they usually do is print the poem and the best commentary on it. Of course, they would need you to permit them to reprint it—and I'm asking. For such a request, my wife wants to give you a painting. If you have a favorite photograph, or idea, or whatever you'd like, let us know.

I am waiting on four black men to come over to go fishing. They probably got drunk and we live so far out of the way they are lost.

Once again, my brief passage with the both of you will never be forgotten.

Yours,
Frank Stanford

Notes

783. Broughton noted to this editor that Welty was not ill but was too exhausted to be filmed because of the attention she was receiving and interviews she was doing after having won the Pulitzer Prize for Fiction that spring. Email to editor, October 30, 2023.
784. See note 133 above; Williams researched *Old Powder Man* at the Stanfords' home in 1964.
785. Frank O'Hara (1926–66), poet.
786. "Boy in Sunlight," the opening poem of Cowley's *Blue Juniata: Collected Poems* (1968).
787. "Fern Hill," a 1945 poem by Dylan Thomas.
788. William Stafford, poet.

To Michael Cuddihy: August 6, 1974

August 6, 1974

Dear Mike,

Your wife called this A.M. and said you were ill and would be tended by doctors for awhile; she also said the both of you had stayed up late and spoken, but what you had said had probably drifted past the lighted harbors of this world—and, as we know—from time to time—, these are the dark waters.[789]

I hope you will soon be yourself and feeling well. I was out by the barn looking at what was left of the moon when she called. Sometimes, early, before light, I do not like to write. I think we poets can easily lose contact with that which we say we understand if we don't keep the connections with "things". From our bedroom window we can see our wilted garden, the moon at some point above it, way in the distance the lake and the hills, and nearby, horseshoes and chains and bits of broken plows picked up out of the old field and secured to a tree, and within a hundred feet or so, our barn with its blown away roof, a wooden ladder leaning against it, my flat-bottom boat on sawhorses, and a rectangular, concrete watering trough—we have no animals now, other than a couple of cats—pets, that is, the others are wild—which looks very much like a tomb. I usually lean my head up against the barn near there, as the sun will be rising to my right—east. I did not like this empty bed, so I shoveled barn floorings, straw, manure, and planted some winter squash there. They have sprouted.

I don't mean to say that I am anti-language or anti-logical, but sort of a-logical sometimes, in respects to the spirit. Perhaps that is why we understand each other. I must say that for all my brooding melancholy, my Harpo Marx antics, my drifting, and drinking, etc., you are not taken in by any of it and quite understand that these are all bright phases the poet must have so he can return to the new and dark part of his soul.[790] There a[re] some people who think I am insane, mean, dangerous, and whatever else. No matter what can of specific fence I put up in my work or in my life, you see that it is all open range, flat and sharp inclines, but always with some music. Whitman said, "I contain Multitudes."[791] I believe we all do. I savor the flesh very much, but I'm always in a sense of awe with anyone who can see through the world, back into the earth. And you might know that one is put at ease in his work and days by knowing there are a few people who can truely [*sic*] understand. I suppose that is why I like to be around monks, the poor—white and black, and alone with myself. The infernal business of this life, especially for one involved in literature and film, seems so far away from the quiet transactions of the poet and his soul—not always quiet. I don't mean we walk around in a field with a group aways behind us looking for something, rather it is like Picasso said, "I'm not searching for anything, it has already found me."[792] I think this is the essence of art and christ and we the people.[793]

At times I do become quite weary of words, and leary of what others make of them.

Contrary to that essay Goethe wrote in 1797, the poet contains tragedy in his epic self—no matter how episodic—as well as when he deals with particulars in a dramatic way.[794] The man acting outwardly is not so different than the man acting inwardly—unless he really is acting. I believe the "plot" of genuine tragedy can require only a little space or it can have a sensuous breadth. Perhaps we have set up all these dichotomies ourselves. Perhaps now what we poets have to do is un-learn. Too many maps and not enough journeys.

I do not think the natural sequence to a problem is a solution.

Although there are paths which we cannot defy, you are one who understands that words may not always hold you in orbit. It does not matter to me when other poets brush me aside, it matters very much when they misunderstand. You see, I think this is the case with some of those that I've known or know. I keep waiting for them to say, "Well, I see now. I see," and I am let down that they don't, because I have and had so much respect for them.

I had hoped this to be a Get Well card, but I guess I'm strange. It is my way of saying Greetings.

Your wife's voice seemed tired, but quite in a daze; she was right that what she wanted to say couldn't occur over a phone, but I think I understood the kind of conversation you had. I heard the ring—two short ones—from the barn, and I was dreaming.

Enclosed is a poem I forgot I ever wrote; it really doesn't sound like me, but I found it a couple of days ago—a day ago—in a box. It is old; there were directions written on the other side and some quotes etc.

My wife is painting an old photograph in three, large panels on a commission which, if accepted, will enable me to write the month of September. She had another, but the idea was so trite she really couldn't go through with it and I couldn't blame her. I'm revising all the stories I wrote last year—I say all, just whatever I can—in hopes of sending them out SOON. *Esquire* has requested to see some of them and, although I have certain reservations about their taste I would like to relieve them of some of their money.

One of these days I'm going to tell you about the genre I'm really interested in, one I'm working in secretly.

I am very glad that your wife called. Rest easy. No doubt you'll be hearing from me soon.

Yours to the both of you,
Frank

more than three quarters of a century has passed
since the death of Guy de Maupassant

an owl hoots
and she shivers

sits up on her bed
puts her hands
to her face
into her hair
and all over her body
and then she walks
down the stairs
as if she were asleep
her long shadow
leaves the house for good
and night on her side
like a beggar on a cross

Notes

789. Mary Cuddihy (b. 1933), Michael Cuddihy's wife.

790. Harpo Marx (1888–1964), comedian/actor who was silent in the Marx Brothers's films. Cf. *The Battlefield*, lines 269–70.

791. From "Song of Myself"—opening poem of Walt Whitman's *Leaves of Grass*. From the first edition: "I am large . . . . I contain multitudes." *Leaves of Grass* (Brooklyn, 1855), 55; ellipsis in original.

792. Pablo Picasso (1881–1973), Spanish artist: "I don't search, I find." The statement opens the front-flap jacket copy for Domenico Porzio and Marco Valsecchi's *Understanding Picasso* (1974).

793. From the US Constitution's preamble, which begins, "We the People of the United States . . ."

794. "On Epic and Dramatic Poetry," a 1797 essay (published in 1827) coauthored by Goethe and Friedrich Schiller (1759–1805), German writer. Goethe and Schiller consider the epic writer a "rhapsodist" writing epic poetry of "individual action" and the dramatic writer an "actor" writing tragedy of "individual suffering"; they assert that the "rhapsodist himself," who "takes his audience back and forth in time, as he sees fit . . . should not appear as a higher being in his poem," while the actor, conversely, "represents a specific individual" and aims "to make us empathize with his mental anguish and his physical suffering, share his difficulties and forget ourselves." Goethe and Schiller argue that plot or action (*die Handlungen*) "of a genuine tragedy can be quite limited in scope," that "the epic poet ranges more freely over a larger area," while "the dramatist normally restricts himself to one locale." Johann Wolfgang von Goethe, *Goethe: The Collected Works*, vol. 3, *Essays on Art and Literature*, ed. John Gearey, trans. Ellen von Nardroff and Ernest H. von Nardroff (Suhrkamp Publishers, 1986), 192–94.

To Donald L. Kemp: October 6, 1974

October 6, 1974

Frank Stanford & Associates
RFD 6 Box 342
Rocky Branch
Rogers, Arkansas 72756
636-7669

Dear Don Kemp,

You may or may not remember that five or six years ago I was in your employ when I was a student at the U of A.[795] For the last few years I've been living in Carroll and Benton counties, employed as a field chief in the land surveying business.

I've become interested enough in it as a means of making a living that last spring I bought a new transit, chainsaw, vehicle, and all other equipment. And by the end of this month I hope to have another K&E, only it will be used.[796] I've worked for three registered surveyors; one has retired, another moved from Arkansas, and the other is still very much in business.

When I worked for you, I didn't much know or care about surveying, and I really wasn't much count as a hand. Since then, though, I've started my own business, been remarried, and published a few books. I've also established good contacts with land owners and real estate agents. Of course, I'm not registered, and that is why I'm writing you.

Anymore, I'm really not interested in working for wages and equipment expenses——that is why I started my own company. When I'm fully responsible for paying the men and dealing with the clients and supervising the work, I can do a much better job, and cheaper. I've found that I'm pretty careful in wrapping angles and "finding" corners when I know I have to pay for everything. And, I'm lucky to have two good hands. One, in his late 30's and another in his late 20's. Both men have brother-in-laws who own their own real estate firms——I get a lot of business from one. I pay these guys three bucks an hour, but I'm always in the field and do all the instrument work myself. However, we have an agreement that time spent finding and correcting busts is not charged to the client or the time sheet. This improves efficiency. So far, I try to keep in close contact with the land owner and try to keep him informed about hours in the field. (I only know of two surveys I've done that are in question. Each time, I was an employee and not the boss. I had no control over the bill, which I thought was too high under the circumstances of rain, one hand, someone else's equipment breakdown.) The closer the tabs I can keep with the client, the better.

My time as a writer is valuable, and so is all the equipment I bought from Triangle, so I'm not interested in wasting time, since I'm paying for it. I like to do the survey as soon as possible, but I do enough research in the beginning so that I don't have to fool around. If things work out, I'd like to become a member of the association Bennie Edwards told me about that's started up in NW Arkansas. Eventually, I might like to work to get a license.

Of course, I can make more money with my equipment than without it, but I'm not interested in making a killing in surveying. My wife is a fairly well-known artist, and I sell my work regularly. However, that isn't enough to make a living. Being outdoors all day is the best kind of work for me I've found out the last few years. A couple months a year I wouldn't be in the field at all, as my wife and I would probably want to spend the time renovating a farmhouse on 400 acres of land near Joplin; we're part owners in the place with parents.[797]

I am currently associated with a reg. surveyor, but it is just too much driving to his place. And I don't like Newton county to work in or working around Jasper.[798] The last time I checked, in June, I was averaging over a 1000 miles per four or five days. I could probably get associated with an older surveyor, near by, but I'm not interested in that, or a real large operation.

I hope you might have the time to discuss the possibility of my company working with your company. If not, at least I hope you'll let me hear from you, and maybe I could buy you a beer and we could talk about surveying in general.

Moneywise, I'm talking about something like this: I get the job, do the job paying all labor in the field and vehicle and expenses, and what office work I can, and you approve it. I collect the bill, and we split, after wages & wage taxes, 50-50.

If you want to have one of your men do all the calculations, computer, and drafting, then you get 100% of the office work you do. I can draft, but I'm not fast. And my experience on a Monroe computer is limited, but I can punch it.

If you wanted to do the calculations, and you got 100% of that, and all I could do is the field work and research and some office, you would pull down, depending on the hours in the field, somewhere in between 150–300 dollars per week. Your only cost would be a draftsman. If you wanted me to do the drafting, you'd make less.[799]

I am hoping you might be interested in this, I know I liked working for you in the past. My phone and address are enclosed.

Yours,
Frank Stanford

P.S. I'll be listed in most of the area phone book yellow pages.

Notes

795. Donald L. Kemp (1936–85), land surveyor in Fayetteville; Stanford had worked for Kemp's prior company—Kemp, Christner and Associates—four years earlier, in summer/fall 1970, with Gwynn.
796. *K&E*: Keuffel and Esser, former manufacturer of land surveying equipment.
797. Ginny Stanford clarified to this editor that her family's farm—in southern Missouri, north of Joplin—was 260 acres (not 400 acres). Email to editor, September 7, 2024.
798. Jasper, Arkansas, a town in Newton County roughly seventy-five miles southeast of Stanford's Rocky Branch home.
799. Enclosed is a one-sheet costs/wages breakdown of the business collaboration Stanford had in mind, showing how much Kemp could expect Don Kemp & Associates to be paid per week, depending on whether Stanford's surveying crew would be a two- or three-man crew.

To Alan Dugan: November 18, 1974

November 18, 1974 Monday
FRANK STANFORD
LAND SURVEYOR
RFD 6–Box 342 Rocky Branch
Rogers, AR. 72756
501-636-7669[800]

Dear Alan,

Just a note because I'm busy as hell this time of year——I hope the work keeps up!

This weekend we went to the Nelson in Kansas City to see the W. Kandinsky exhibit.[801] Ginny bought a paperback on your Father-In-Law.[802] I got a teach yourself Trig. as I need it for my job.[803]

Poems coming out here and there. Got a letter from G. Lish and he wants me to revise "fix" a story I sent them.[804] Man am I going to get drunk if they take it.

What are you doing? In this country still? Ginny has painted her best since I last wrote you. Will send you a few slides as soon as I have time, unless they get bought before I can shoot them. The U. of W. gave this friend of mine 3 Grand to do an issue of his magazine on Roethke.[805] He is the one who did that little pamphlet of mine. Ginny did a painting of Roethke and I think they are going to use it on the cover. Also, she did a drawing of Cocteau and I hope that one is used in another issue.[806] I'd still like to see your bi-ling. poem. Wish you'd drop me a copy. Are you still interested in publishing it?[807]

Enclosed is something you can send the slides back in—when you're done with them. Ginny would like to read that letter you wanted me to send back.[808] Hope we can keep in touch.[809]

Yours,
Frank

P.S. The Am. Academy of Poets wouldn't accept for consideration my MS. for the W. Whitman award; said it was too long to read. Horseshit.[810]

Notes

800. This is the first letter herein employing a rubber stamp that Stanford used from ca. early November 1974 into fall 1975. In a March 23, 1975, letter to Cuddihy, Stanford writes, "It was just for work, but now on other correspondence. It saves so much time that the coldness is worth it."
801. The William Rockhill Nelson Gallery of Art (now part of the Nelson-Atkins Museum of Art) and Wassily Kandinsky (1866–1944), Russian painter.
802. Ben Shahn; see note 370 above.
803. *Teach Yourself Trigonometry* (1940), a book by P. Abbott reprinted for many decades.
804. Gordon Lish, *Esquire*'s fiction editor from 1969 to 1977. Lish wrote to Stanford on October 30, 1974, noting that of his submitted stories, "only TANCREDI'S LIGHT comes close to really getting me.... It may be that you will want to give the piece another once-over and show it to me again." Stanford sent two more stories (one of which appears to have been "The Dream of the Rood") on November 15. On November 25, Lish replied, "You have massively interesting ideas and a remarkable hand at housing them."
805. *U. of W.*: University of Washington. Broughton's *Mill Mountain Review* 2, no. 2 (1975), a special issue "In Memory of Theodore Roethke," featured Ginny Stanford's painting of Roethke as cover art (see note 762 above) and published Stanford's poems "Sketches Instead of Drawings," "Dream Horse of Marlow Hollow," and "Two Blue Yodels Driving to the State Line" and his short story "The Farmhouse Where the Old Man Went to Die in the Arms of the Young Woman."
806. I.e., *Mill Mountain Review*'s (aborted) film issue; see note 892 below.
807. In Dugan's May 23, 1974, letter, he asked Stanford if he knew of any Spanish-English journals that might consider a long bilingual poem he sought to publish, adding that he was "tempted to publish it as a pamphlet as a vanity publication." After checking with Broughton, Stanford wrote to Dugan on July 24: "I talked to one guy I trust. He would like to do it as soon as you would."
808. I.e., Dugan's March 15, 1974, letter to Stanford (mailed June 20), which Stanford returned to Dugan with his (Stanford's) July 24 letter, per Dugan's request. (According

to Dugan's July 6 letter to Stanford, Judy Shahn was upset with Dugan for not having saved a copy of the letter, so Dugan asked Stanford to return it.) The letter is missing or lost. With his December 21, 1974, reply, Dugan enclosed a letter from Judy to Stanford about Ginny's work (see note 821 below).

809. On December 21, Dugan replied, "I, too, 'Hope we can keep in touch.', but living can get so complicated even for people like Judy and me, whose desire is for what?, working solitude?"

810. The Academy of American Poets' guidelines for the first annual Walt Whitman Award in 1974 noted, "Suggested length is between fifty and one hundred pages." On November 16, the Academy of American Poets wrote to Stanford: "Dear Mr. Stanford: We just cannot accept a manuscript for the W. Whitman Award competition that is significantly longer than 100 pages. If you are not able to cut down your entry to that length, then you should not send it in to this particular competition. Academy of American Poets, Inc." On December 21, Dugan wrote to Jeffrey Mitchell at the Academy, quoting Stanford's postscript to this letter and adding, "I think you have made a mistake. Stanford is a brilliant poet and just because he is ample in his work, like Whitman, is no reason not to consider his manuscript. . . . He should be encouraged in his amplitude rather than rejected for it. I've been reading his work for the last four years or so and I'm convinced of his genius as a writer."

To John McKernan: December 1, 1974

FRANK STANFORD
LAND SURVEYOR
RFD 6–Box 342 Rocky Branch
Rogers, AR. 72756
501-636-7669

December 1, 1974

Dear John,

Hope the poems reached you in time. Maybe some of them are good enough for *The Little Review*. If not, please send them back. If so, could you send me xerox copies of what you take——I've promised my wife to keep a practical file.[811]

I wish more of the smaller magazines would stick with your type format, forgetting all the Japanese paper and do-do bird eggshell binding and ink pigment ground from genuine Cherokee shit, and pay attention to what is read and seen, as well as paying the poet and not union shop printers.

My wife just got a painting accepted for a cover of a magazine dedicated to Roethke.[812] Also, another drawing of Jean Cocteau for a cover. Right now I'm more interested in her work than my own.

I wish John Morris wouldn't give up the ghost. I really like his work. Last year I had a chance to pick a MS. for publication by a small press: wrote him but never got an answer——although I still hold a vote. It may be a little premature to say so but a snake in the grass whispered to me that a magazine was considering me to be its editor for a year, something of which I know nothing, not even jack shit. So, I may be calling on you.

Haul off and write me a long letter sometime. The galley proofs of four of my pamphlets are sitting on the desk but I'm not interested in looking at them.[813] I'm reading maps and listening to music and cutting wood.

Tell me what is going on soon as you can.

Yours,
Frank

Notes

811. McKernan published twelve of Stanford's poems in *The Little Review* 5, no. 2, issue 10 (1975); see note 882 below.
812. See notes 762 and 805 above.
813. Presumably *Ladies From Hell* (1974), *Field Talk* (1975), *Shade* (1975), and *Arkansas Bench Stone* (1975). *Ladies From Hell* was, it appears, not finalized until 1975 (see note 882 below). Though *Field Talk* is typically referenced as being Stanford's third book (per the "Books by Frank Stanford" front-matter pages in his five 1974–76 books), it may not have been finished until 1976, after publication of *Arkansas Bench Stone* (see Stanford's June 20, 1976, letter to Broughton below, par. 6). As well, *Shade*'s front matter feigns that the volume was first published in "1973" and that the 1975 edition is the "SECOND EDITION," but it is, in fact, the first edition.

To Alan Dugan: December 26, 1974

Dec 26, 1974

Dear Alan,

Visiting my mother and grandmother at the monastery over the holidays. Ginny is trading recipes. We've just come down from her folks' place in Missouri and I have all the planting tipis I'll need this planting time. Hoping for another good garden.

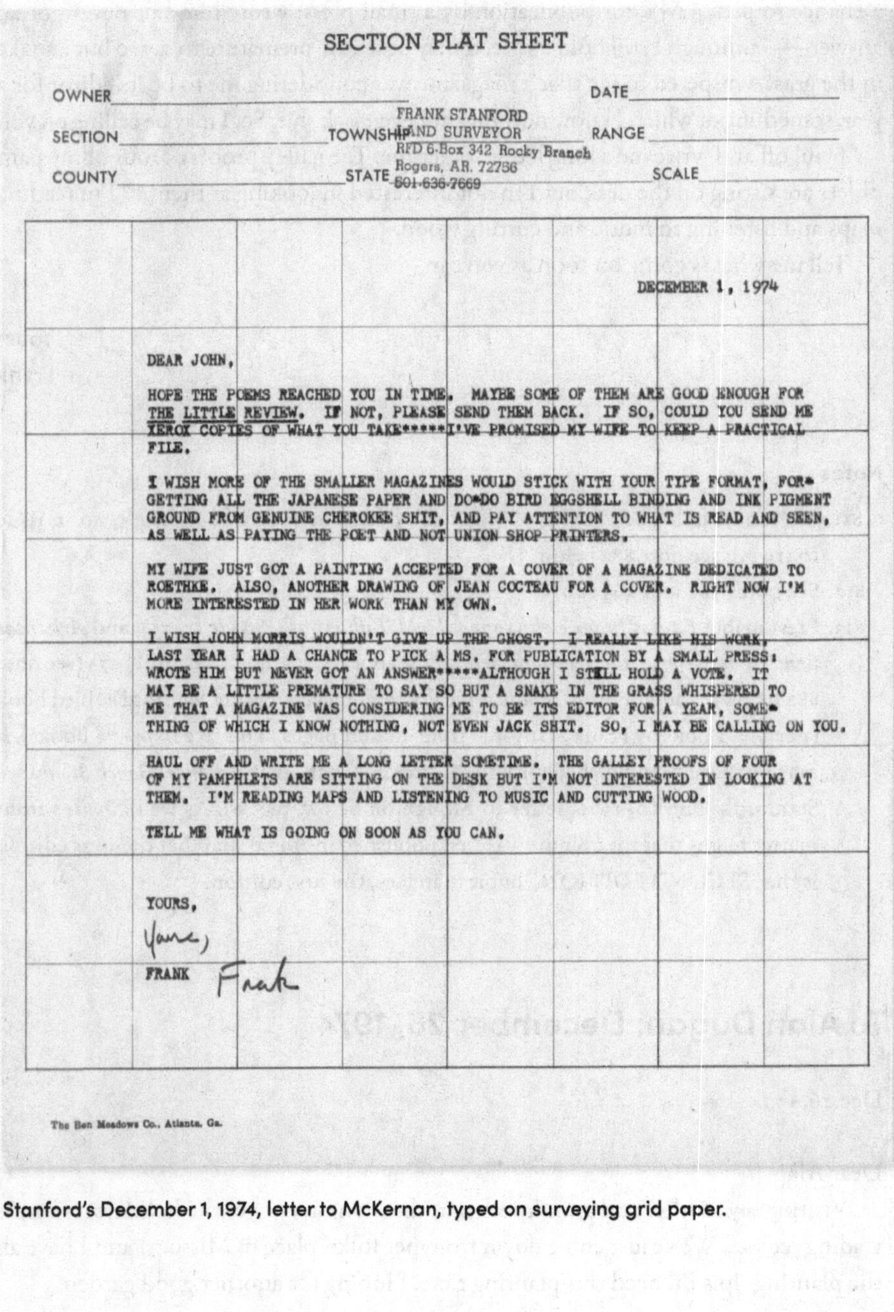

SECTION PLAT SHEET

OWNER ______ DATE ______

FRANK STANFORD
LAND SURVEYOR
RFD 6-Box 342 Rocky Branch
Rogers, AR. 72756
501-636-7669

SECTION ______ TOWNSHIP ______ RANGE ______

COUNTY ______ STATE ______ SCALE ______

DECEMBER 1, 1974

DEAR JOHN,

HOPE THE POEMS REACHED YOU IN TIME. MAYBE SOME OF THEM ARE GOOD ENOUGH FOR THE LITTLE REVIEW. IF NOT, PLEASE SEND THEM BACK. IF SO, COULD YOU SEND ME XEROX COPIES OF WHAT YOU TAKE*****I'VE PROMISED MY WIFE TO KEEP A PRACTICAL FILE.

I WISH MORE OF THE SMALLER MAGAZINES WOULD STICK WITH YOUR TYPE FORMAT, FOR-GETTING ALL THE JAPANESE PAPER AND DO-DO BIRD EGGSHELL BINDING AND INK PIGMENT GROUND FROM GENUINE CHEROKEE SHIT, AND PAY ATTENTION TO WHAT IS READ AND SEEN, AS WELL AS PAYING THE POET AND NOT UNION SHOP PRINTERS.

MY WIFE JUST GOT A PAINTING ACCEPTED FOR A COVER OF A MAGAZINE DEDICATED TO ROETHKE. ALSO, ANOTHER DRAWING OF JEAN COCTEAU FOR A COVER. RIGHT NOW I'M MORE INTERESTED IN HER WORK THAN MY OWN.

I WISH JOHN MORRIS WOULDN'T GIVE UP THE GHOST. I REALLY LIKE HIS WORK. LAST YEAR I HAD A CHANCE TO PICK A MS. FOR PUBLICATION BY A SMALL PRESS; WROTE HIM BUT NEVER GOT AN ANSWER*****ALTHOUGH I STILL HOLD A VOTE. IT MAY BE A LITTLE PREMATURE TO SAY SO BUT A SNAKE IN THE GRASS WHISPERED TO ME THAT A MAGAZINE WAS CONSIDERING ME TO BE ITS EDITOR FOR A YEAR, SOME-THING OF WHICH I KNOW NOTHING, NOT EVEN JACK SHIT. SO, I MAY BE CALLING ON YOU.

HAUL OFF AND WRITE ME A LONG LETTER SOMETIME. THE GALLEY PROOFS OF FOUR OF MY PAMPHLETS ARE SITTING ON THE DESK BUT I'M NOT INTERESTED IN LOOKING AT THEM. I'M READING MAPS AND LISTENING TO MUSIC AND CUTTING WOOD.

TELL ME WHAT IS GOING ON SOON AS YOU CAN.

YOURS,

Yours,

FRANK

Frank

The Ben Meadows Co., Atlanta, Ga.

Stanford's December 1, 1974, letter to McKernan, typed on surveying grid paper.

Ginny received from her folks a large book on Hopper and I got a two volume collection of "poetry in manuscript," only 1,500 copies printed.[814] My 89 year old grandmother and I are going over the handwriting of the poets all dead and gone with her reading magnifying glass.[815] My uncle and his family were here; we played poker and drank until time for Midnight Mass which my mother *made* us all attend. The Gregorian chants were worth the late hour, as was the special and rare invitation to dine with the monks after the service—monk bread, monk wine, and monk sausage and honey, etc.

Hope you got my telephone-o-gram about *Poems 4* which I like the best of your books.[816] I'll say more about that in another letter. I showed them to my uncle (from Mississippi now living in Texas; he fought in the Battle of the Bulge and has had a hard life since his boyhood.[817]) He says, "I didn't know anybody wrote poetry (("POETREE")) about work and women and drinking and living. If I'd known anybody wrote like this . . . . well, this is right down my alley!" His name is Robert Gilbert and he likes your work.[818]

I'm still hungover from the texture and diction. It seems like these poems were written before *Poems 1*.[819] Then again, these poems could have only been written after *1, 2, 3*, and nights like only you have spent . . . . but we have all spent these nights but only you have had the guts to withstand.[820]

Ginny appreciates the note from Judith. Yes, all her work does have a *brownish* glow to it, coming from that part of the Ozarks where the fields of Missouri meet the plains of Kansas as she does. One of these days she is going to amount to something. I wish you could see her work up close, scale and color.[821]

It will take awhile.

Goddamn, I wish I'd written *Poems 4*.

We went into a bookstore. Saw the new book on Picasso.[822] Liked it. Saw a book called *Jericho*. What a pile of shit by Dickey and {(not-worth-a)} Shitworth, "Southern Living Pseudo-South."[823] Willie Morris, who raved about it, is a complete fool.[824]

Saw a book ~~by~~ of Casper David Freirich; really liked it.[825]

I'd like a copy of that magazine which will be featuring you.[826]

Where is E. Honig editor?[827] *Partisan*? They took a poem of mine.[828] I can get the whole poem published for you, would be an *HONOR*.[829]

I've got a lot of work sprouting up.

Thanks for writing the jerks at the Am. Acad. of Poets.[830] I figured they'd at least look at the thing, considering the name "Whitman" on their award. It cost me $200 to have the thing typed. When they wrote back, saying they couldn't consider it, I got pissed but didn't write them back.

Maybe I'll be able to subsidize my poetry with fiction? My job is keeping me busy and food on the table, etc. So we don't have any worries, only petty bourgeois things, like getting a pick-up, etc.

If *Poems 4* are the kind of poems you're writing, you shouldn't have any worries other than living through them. Keep at it. All best.

yours,
Frank

Notes

814. *Autograph Poetry in the English Language: Facsimiles of Original Manuscripts from the Fourteenth to the Twentieth Century*, a lavish collection that reproduces "poetical manuscripts" ("poets' own manuscripts") of 146 poets, many of whom were influential for Stanford—including Blake, Burns, Coleridge, Byron, Shelley, Keats, Poe, Whitman, Rossetti, Dickinson, Stevenson, Lawrence, et al. P. J. Croft, ed., *Autograph Poetry in the English Language*, 2 vols. (McGraw-Hill Book Company, 1973), xii.
815. In December 1974, Stanford's maternal grandmother, Carolyn Gilbert, was eighty-six (not eighty-nine) years old.
816. Dugan's book *Poems 4* (1974).
817. The Battle of the Bulge, a 1944–45 World War II battle fought in the Ardennes.
818. Stanford's adoptive uncle Robert Lloyd Gilbert (1921–2004).
819. Dugan's book *Poems* (1961).
820. Dugan's books *Poems*, *Poems 2* (1963), and *Poems 3* (1967).
821. Stanford is referring to Judith Shahn's December 21, 1974, letter to him in which she responded to slides of Ginny's work that Stanford had sent to Dugan, writing, "I got no sense of the scale of the work from the slides—obviously—and I'm not sure about the color: whether most of her work actually does have a brownish cast." Shahn went on to critique the strengths and weaknesses she perceived in Ginny's work.
822. Possibly Domenico Porzio and Marco Valsecchi's *Understanding Picasso* (1974) (or its republished version, *Pablo Picasso: Man and His Work* [1974])—see note 792 above—though numerous books on Picasso were published in 1974.
823. *Marginalia: left side, upright.* Stanford is referring to *Jericho: The South Beheld* (1974), a book of text by Dickey and drawings/paintings by Hubert Shuptrine.
824. *Jericho*'s jacket included a blurb by Mississippi writer Willie Morris (1934–99), heralding the book as "extraordinarily haunting," adding, "It moves through the South as a vision revealed." Hubert Shuptrine and James Dickey, *Jericho: The South Beheld* (Oxmore House, 1974).
825. Caspar David Friedrich (1774–1840), German Romantic landscape painter. The book was presumably Helmut Börsch-Supan's *Caspar David Friedrich* (1974).
826. In his December 21, 1974, letter to Stanford, Dugan noted that the magazine *Arion's Dolphin*, which was folding, would be giving him "a full issue . . . with a series of letter-poems to the ghost of C. P. Cavafy." No work by Dugan appeared in any further

issue of *Arion's Dolphin*, but his book *Sequence*, beginning with six epistolary poems addressed to Greek poet Constanine P. Cavafy (1863–1933), was published by Dolphin Editions—*Arion's Dolphin* was edited by Greek writer/editor Stratis Haviaras (1935–2020), a founding editor of Dolphin Editions—in 1976.

827. Edwin Honig (1919–2011), founding editor of Copper Beech Press.

828. *Partisan Review* accepted part of "The Snake Doctors" for publication on December 10, 1971, but didn't publish the poem.

829. See Stanford's November 18, 1974, letter to Dugan above, par. 4, and note 807 above.

830. See note 810 above.

To Michael Cuddihy: December 30, 1974

Dear Mike,

As I was digging potatoes this evening such a great thought came: try applying the theory of time to poetry, poetry thought, dreamt, and in motion.

If we could think or dream, sending out a fleet of poems at the speed of light, or approaching the speed of light, what would we actually be doing. If a poem could travel the same distance light could in a year, then a poem I would launch now would be 15 years old and passing thru this galaxy's edge and I would have been dead 45,000 years.[831] There is something to all this and death.

For about four years I haven't been able to finish what I was saying. It is dark and raining and fog. Soon it will be light.

I got waylayed by a thought.

The destination of any poem departing for an eternity is another infinity, but I feel as if we are points of interception for our own poems. Depending on the arc or degree of curve a poem or dream would pass back through us, but at what time I don't know. The faster the poem the sooner our death. As the time increases from the point of our deaths, the further are our poems.

It is very difficult to write about this, so I will turn to other things. The money you sent we bought our garden seeds with.

Can't get off the subject. What's so strange is the poem "the burial ship," I wrote when thinking the same thing I'm thinking now.[832]

Wish I could write a decent letter but this thought won't let me. I'll be keeping in touch as soon as I can concentrate.

Yours,
Frank

Notes

831. It has long been known that our Solar System is located approximately halfway between the Milky Way galaxy's center and its outer rim (and about 500 light-years from the vertical edge), based on an understanding of the galaxy's diameter being roughly 100,000–180,000 light-years; so Stanford's calculation is based on the greater estimate—of the galaxy's horizontal edge being roughly 45,000 light-years from us. (New research, published in 2020, indicates that when including a vast halo of dark matter, the Milky Way may actually be 1.9 million light-years in diameter. Alis J. Deason et al., "The Edge of the Galaxy," *Monthly Notices of the Royal Astronomical Society* 496, no. 3 [August 2020]: 3929–42.) Per Einstein's special theory of relativity, traveling at the speed of light would actually not age the poem (treated as a physical object in Stanford's thought experiment) at all; for the poem to have aged fifteen years, it would need to have traveled at 99.99999444% of—or "approaching"—the speed of light. Stanford may be thinking specifically of "the burial ship"—an "early" poem (per an April 1974 letter to Cuddihy; see also note 696 above) from *St. Francis and the Wolf: Some Poems 1957–1964*, which (per Stanford's manuscript dating), could have been, give or take, fifteen years old in 1974. Also cf. *The Battlefield*, lines 14573–74.

832. Near the end of "the burial ship" (which Cuddihy published in *Ironwood* 3, no. 2, issue 6, in 1975), when the boys set the coffin ship ablaze, a spark cracks. The poem's last lines read: "it kept on going towards the heavens / it was a shooting star." Frank Stanford, *Light the Dead See*, 99.

To Alan Dugan: March 1, 1975

FRANK STANFORD
LAND SURVEYOR
RFD 6–Box 342 Rocky Branch
Rogers, AR. 72756
501-636-7669

March 1, 1975

Dear Alan,

Coming is a ms. which I intend to send Mr. S. Kunitz at Yale. I remember him saying I was "wild" but "for real" in a note to you four years or so ago, so I have left out most of the nut&gut work, and even some head gut things which are a tad longish.[833] You might remember a half dozen or so poems from before, and maybe you've seen some of the others in magazines? I figure it is about time for me to start looking for a publisher.

I wish you'd send me the address of that Greek magazine you'll be in, and the addresses of any others.[834] What ever happened to the bi-lingual poem?[835] What does Honig edit?[836] Partisan? The latter took one of my poems four years ago but I've never checked to see if it was published.[837]

I hope things in these times aren't making ya'll reach too deep in the pocket. If you're back teaching, I hope you have some good students with tough-ass minds.[838]

I want to thank ~~Ginny~~ Judy again for the words she had to write on Ginny's work. She did take them to heart. It always works when a well-known artist tells another not-so known to use their "own" voice.[839] She's been doing that recently and what do you know? She won first place in a fairly old&well-known Art show in these parts & another painting placed too. "Now And At The Hour Of Our Death" was the title.[840] Seven young women surrounding an older woman.[841] It had something to do with a friend of ours, a hermit like fellow who lived in the mountains, the only member of his race—the hillbillies called him "The Nigger Richard".[842] For the last few years he'd been telling me he had sawdust in his eye, and he always wanted Ginny to get it out. We found out it was cancer. They took his eye out. Cancer had set in on him and took hold like kudzu. Sometimes in my work I'd pass by his house.[843] He said if he ever had a white handkerchief tied to the tree outside his window, then I better stop and see in on him. He got so that he couldn't lift his own firewood the pain was so bad. When people told me they could hear him yelling at night, stirring up the dogs, then I got him in the hospital. (The fucking county govt. wouldn't give him his pension, etc., because they said he couldn't prove his age. There was a flood here in the mountain valley land when he was born, and the old timers all marked their X's at the courthouse saying so[844]—he did have close friends among them, especially a woman named Crow, who was the mother of the 12 deaf&dumb children I was telling you about.[845])

I suppose he'd a rather died in his house with his dogs and cats, but he couldn't take the pain anymore—even whisky wasn't doing any good. I knew he was done for when he said he didn't want a drink. He's gone, now.

The juror was Alexander Hogue, a fairly old man who's known here and around and especially in England—for some reason.[846] I couldn't understand him, his speech was muttering. He's a Woody Gutherie man, and I think he said he knew Judy's dad, but he didn't want to talk much, as if the past was a missed train.[847]

The winter didn't really come here until the turn of the year. Cold rain and snow all the time, but we've got 16 rows of peas in, waiting to get the rest of the early garden in. Last year we raised enough to eat all year, we want to double our garden because there are a few people, older, in town who are a little down in the dumps; good food would help their health. Our place used to belong to a blacksmith who tended a graveyard. When they flooded the land to the 1136 feet elevation, the people around here didn't want the Corps of Engineers digging up the graveyard. There's a retired preacher in the next hollow who likes to tell how he run all the G-men off. As my father was always yelling—above the sound of machinery—at "G-men", I can conjure the scene.[848] Where they kept the hogs and mules we've got our garden planted. We've done lots of composting so the soil is pretty good by Ozark standards. I quit making liquor when the price of sugar went up, but my friend a few counties to the east called the other night to say his stuff just topped off. As soon as the roads are good I'm going to drive over there and get drunk&survey his farm. Some hippie from NY just bought some land next to his and is running a wild fence on the wrong assumption that he can claim what he puts under fence.[849] Since the developers and out-of-state rich have descended, land has gone sky-high, and the only way you can keep track of your ~~corner~~ stones is if you bury relatives at your corners. Greed and hard times are coming.

All this shit about the spys and infiltration and CIA is making me wonder if we won't all be in prison in a decade?[850] Nixon would have had us all there. I'm losing sleep over such things now, hope it doesn't turn into my freedom. I heard something about how many years back a New York farmer was hauled into jail on bad debts by the sheriff. The local farmers rose up and took the courthouse, then the sheriff and his boys took it back. It seems 500 farmers rode in from Massachusetts and took it back. I don't think these boys up in D.C. realize what some of the populas populis (can't spell on this elec. TW[851]) ((my fingers are too cold, 4:30 A.M., just stoked the stove)) will do? When the banks start coming for peoples' land, then they better hold their hats—if they'd want to die with something on their head. I'm not preaching violence here, but the Govt. is inspiring it. I really do believe that the whole fucking Gov't is a lot of wheeling dealing bastards, making it while they can. The top 1/5 keeps getting more, while the lower 2 gets the peelings. populace I believe is the way you spell it.

One day maybe you could take a swing through here for a visit—if not a visit, we could always arrange to be away for a few weeks—at the orphan camp this summer at the monastery[852]—so you could have the place to write&draw to yourselves—if you didn't mind watering and cutting a few weeds in the garden. I'd like to see you again, but I doubt there is much chance I'll get up there unless I become famous or publish. So, if you ever get it in your blood to travel, you might do well to travel this way—in between poems or teaching posts, a change might be conv. & diff.[853]

I hope both of you keep well, keeping good at your work. Sorry it's been awhile since I've really written, but please don't feel obligated to answer if you're in the middle of things more vital.

Yours,
Frank

If I may suggest a magazine that pays which is good: *Ironwood*, po box 49023, Tucson, Arizona 85717, Mike Cuddihy. Issue 5 is devoted to G Oppen.

Notes

833. Kunitz did write that Stanford was "for real" but not that he was "wild." See note 242 above.
834. *Arion's Dolphin.* See note 826 above.
835. See note 807 above.
836. See note 827 above.
837. See note 828 above.
838. In his July 6, 1974, letter to Stanford, Dugan had mentioned that, for financial reasons, he might have to return to working or teaching, and in his December 21 letter, he noted that he was returning to teaching.
839. In her December 21 letter to Stanford, Shahn wrote of Ginny's work, "I think my strongest reaction is that she has not yet found her own voice. . . . I kept having the feeling that she was looking at things with various other people's eyes, as well as her own. . . . This is often the case with young painters." Re: "voice," see also Stanford's July 18, 1974, letter to Cuddihy above, par. 4.
840. Ginny Stanford's painting *Now and at the Hour of Our Death*—titled by Frank (Ginny noted to this editor) with a line from the Hail Mary, a traditional Catholic prayer. Email to editor, September 13, 2023. The painting won the twenty-fifth annual Art Center Competition at the Fort Smith Art Center (now the Fort Smith Regional Art Museum) in March 1975.
841. *Now and at the Hour of Our Death* ("one of my favorite paintings," Ginny notes) was purchased by Fayetteville banker Obert Undem and stolen several years later; the painting remains unrecovered. Email to editor, September 13, 2023.
842. Richard Banks; see note 556 above.
843. Clarke Freeman, at whose family's motel, the Joy Motel, Banks worked from ca. the early 1950s until shortly before his death in 1975 (and for whose grandfather Banks had also worked beginning ca. 1930), notes to this editor that Banks's home was northwest of Eureka Springs' downtown, near where Thorncrown Chapel is currently located. Email to editor, January 14, 2026.
844. The Great Flood of 1913—in March; Banks was born later in the year, in December.
845. Freeman notes that Banks's friend was Maxine Crow, who was legally deaf and had several deaf children (perhaps four to six in total)—who all studied at the Arkansas School for the Deaf—but that "12" is certainly Stanfordian hyperbole. Email to editor, August 14, 2023.
846. *juror*: the art competition's judge. Alexandre Hogue (1898–1994), American Realist painter.
847. Woody Guthrie (1912–67), American folk singer-songwriter afflicted with Huntington's disease for many years; *Judy's dad*: Ben Shahn, artist (see note 370 above).
848. *G-men*: government men.
849. Willett affirms that Stanford is referring to him here—noting that Stanford surveyed some of his land in Rush, Arkansas (in Marion County, three counties east of

Benton County, where Stanford lived), on which Willett had an encroachment by someone from New York that was resolved in court in the late 1970s—but clarifies that he was not making any moonshine. Texts to editor, August 12, 2023.

850. Numerous news articles published across several months of 1975 outlined how the Central Intelligence Agency kept files on thousands of individuals and opened people's mail, wiretapped people, etc.

851. *elec. TW*: electric typewriter.

852. Camp Subiaco; see note 333 above.

853. *conv. & diff.*: presumably, convenient and different.

To Father Jerome Kodell: Circa Late Winter 1975

Dear Father Jerome,[854]

Long time no see. You're probably the most snowed under monk in America, but I need some help. How is your Italian? I'll tell you what I need later.

You will probably remember that essay you gave me some time ago concerning poetry. Well, I showed it to a few people, one guy is interested in it if you can "translate" a few more of the psalms. I think he's mainly interested in the passages about the psalms.[855] A letter can't explain what I'm getting at. I'll be down soon, and we can go over it.

Congratulations on your new job. I hope you aren't overworked.[856] I don't have time to do half of what I want to do, now that I'm running a crew of surveyors. Like a few other poet-surveyors before me, Whitman-Thoreau, etc., the combinations of the naturals and the arts work together well, only infernal business gets in the way.[857]

As I said, we'll get together on the psalms soon, but here is something else.

These are some poems by Bertolucci.[858] What I'm doing—when possible—is taking the originals, finding a literal-non-poetic translation of them into English, then adapting them to poems. Half-translation and half-versions. Not like Lowell's "Imitations".[859] I don't even need the translations to be in poetry margins, just a prose version will do. I'm not sure you'll like this guy, I'm not sure you'll even want or have time to do it. If so, let me know. Really, they don't have to be that accurate.

If you don't like this guy, you might enjoy a poet I will be doing the same thing with next ~~year~~, the filmmaker-poet, Pier Palo Pasolini. A great filmmaker and good poet. I'm trying to get hold of his publisher in Italy, a certain book you may have heard of: L'usignolo della Chiesa cattolica.[860] ???????

I hope you have time, or are interested. You'll get credit, and if any money comes out of this—which seldom happens in poetry—I promise half to the abbey. I know you and I have the same problems, no time and other responsibilities. If you'd like to give it a crack, let me know. All I need are approx. prose translations of titles and poems. It is important that you know that you don't have to take the time to do all of these at once. I'm sending some envelopes so you can mail each poem back as you finish. As I get them, I will work on my end. It should only take up about 15 minutes of your time per poem—unless you have forgotten your Italian. I'm not really in a bind for them, except I would like to have one or two as soon as you get time.

Hope to be hearing from you.

Yours,
Frank

You might be interested in knowing that Domenico Grasso of the Pontifical Gregorian University likes Bertolucci.[861]

Notes

854. Fr. Jerome Kodell noted to this editor that he never received this letter and that he didn't collaborate with Stanford on translating any poems by Bernardo Bertolucci or Pier Paolo Pasolini. The letter is housed at Yale University, whose Stanford collections include primarily incoming correspondence; Stanford apparently never mailed the letter. Kodell, emails to editor, February 8, 2022.
855. Kodell's essay on poetics and the biblical Psalms, "The Poetry of the Psalms," *Bible Today*, March 1973. Kodell argues that the Psalms bear the hallmark traits of real poetry by drawing analytical comparisons to Dickinson, Whitman, *Beowulf*, and other poets and works. Kodell noted that he had shown the essay, in manuscript, to Stanford for him to critique and that Stanford had been complimentary of it. Kodell clarified that he didn't translate any psalms for the essay, though cf. Stanford's December 2, 1972, letter to Campbell above, pars. 19–20. (Stanford's writing of "one guy" being "interested in it" suggests that Stanford may not have known of the essay's 1973 publication.) Email to editor, February 8, 2022.
856. From 1975 to 1987, Kodell was Subiaco Abbey's director of formation.
857. Thoreau worked as a land surveyor, though Whitman didn't; Stanford could perhaps be using the term metaphorically (e.g., of Whitman surveying the American landscape).
858. Stanford was working from *In cerca del mistero* (In search of the mystery) (1962), a book of poems by Bertolucci published by Longanesi in Milan.
859. See note 494 above.

860. *L'usignolo della Chiesa Cattolica* (*The Nightingale of the Catholic Church*) (1958), a book of poems by Pasolini published by Longanesi.

861. Fr. Domenico Grasso (1917–88), Roman theology professor at the Pontifical Gregorian University in Rome. The January 22, 1973, cover story / review of *Last Tango in Paris* in *Time* magazine (see note 591 above) notes that Milan's newspaper *Corriere della Sera* had just run a dialogue on the film between Grasso and novelist Alberto Moravia (1907–90) and that "both men gave the film high marks aesthetically"; despite reservations regarding some scenes, Grasso had concluded that the film was "an appreciable work." "Self-Portrait of an Angel and Monster," 52.

To Michael Cuddihy: March 15, 1975

March 15, 1975

Dear Mike,

Just a note to say thanks for the OPPEN issue, congratulations;[862] it looked good, read good, and there was just enough of it to thrill and not "go-on". Now IRONWOOD will last as long as the libraries. I wonder why other editors haven't taken the time and expense to do what you've done? I can think of only a few, though my expertise is limited. I bet OPPEN was pleased as much as the reading public.

Also, Ginny won first place in a fairly old&established Art show, and the other painting placed. The juror was an old, well-known artist, here in this country and abroad.[863] The winning painting was called NOW AND AT THE HOUR OF OUR DEATHS.[864] Wish you two could see it. Anyway, that is the reason we haven't sent the painting we wanted to give you yet. It placed in the show and will have to hang for a month or so, and if you don't mind, she would like to enter it in one more show before it retires to your living room since people remark on it as much if not more than the larger painting. Some are so taken with her work that word has got around to some place that wants to see slides of her past work. As you have the only ones, perhaps you could get them back to her. I'm sorry if I've rushed you with them, but this all just came up, and it could prove to be something for her.

She is now painting some 12 hours a day, huddled next to the wood stove. Old man winter is just now coming. Cold rain, ice, snow for the last six weeks has not done our garden good, but we do have 16 rows of peas ~~in~~ which the snow can only sweeten.

Since things are finally looking up in our pocketbooks enclosed is some money for two issues of the OPPEN issue. They will be collectors items I'm sure. I think the other buck ought to get the slides back pretty fast, too.[865]

How is your health? And is Mary well? I hope you'll always let me know when things are good and bad.

What do you think about this typewriter? It will type like this, too. As my other two old ones bit the dust, I am having to rent this for 20.00 per month.[866]

I am going to tell you something I hope you will not repeat until I have it all worked out. As you know, I've long had an interest in those poets who are also filmmakers, as was Blake an artist, Rossetti, etc.[867] Well, it is easy to gain access to Cocteau and Prevert, and sometimes Pasolini, but I have secured a copy of the very rare, first book of young B. Bertolucci.[868] You don't have any idea how hard it was for me to get the book! It has taken about two years. Now, a brother Jerome and myself will translate it, if that is the word.[869] He lived in Rome and the hinterlands of Italy for awhile. By the time I get through with the translations, they will be versions. But still good poems, I hope. I don't plan to stick with the end rhymes. You know, of course, that Bert. started off working for Pasolini, and Pasolini for Fellini. I am afraid to let a big publisher know about this because they would only get a well-known poet to do the book, making a lot of money for all concerned. (After this one, I want to do another small book of Bertolucci&Pasolini together.)

If I were to make any money, I would like to start a chapbook series in the form of a magazine. That is, each issue is a different book, the only imprint being on the title page and spine, not saying # this or that, but just the name of the publisher. If I could print 8 or 10 books by people I think deserve books, then I would feel more like I was doing my part—as I am not a teacher, or editor. I sometimes feel like an oddball, in that I am not a publisher or teacher. It would still be a magazine in that subscribers would get all books published during the year. I would impose something a little different; no manuscripts other than subscribers would even be considered, unless vouched for by a subscriber. Does that seem unfair? You must find it hard sometimes to consider work by someone who hasn't bought your magazine or seen it? This may all be an early morning pipedream, but the small book of BERTOLUCCI is not.

I don't have a publisher and I've not inquired, but as soon as the ms is finished I will. Fortune is on my side in that I did a survey on a printer's farm. The printer was happy with my work but not with what the court decreed, so he couldn't pay for it. Rather than having an uncollectable bill, I now have about a 1,000 credit, which would publish a 1000 copies of the book I have in mind.[870] If I have to publish myself, I will, but I think that is a little odd. If it were advertised in the right places, I believe it would sell to more than just poets. {Any body interested in cinema.}

I have the address of the publisher in Italy,[871] but I need some one to tell me my rights as well as the publisher's rights. I would have to use Bertolucci's name of course in the title somewhere, and I would say that my poems were versions or something to that effect, not translations literal {no originals en face,}, etc.[872] What do I say to his publisher? What language should I use and what do you suggest. Say when W. Matthews did some Follain translations, did he really have permission from the publisher to translate? I noticed that nothing was said in the title page of the magazine?[873] What all do I have to do if I publish 20 pages or so bound like your OPPEN issue. I would have to call it off if the publisher in Italy wanted a lot of money, etc. Please suggest the best way to handle it, the easiest, as soon as you have time to let me know. Please keep all this under your hat.[874]

Yours,
Frank

I'm not making a pitch to you to publish this; I *really* do need *advice*, though.

I wrote this note to you last summer!

Dear Mike,

Just remembered one more time where I have heard of Oppen.[875] In the Spring of 1969 a poet named A. Ginsberg came through these parts. He was with a poet named P. Orlovskey (sp.).[876] I told him that when I was a kid I was fairly impressed with Pound, but not much anymore, because it was hard for me to keep my eye on the intent of the grandstand and on the ball at the same time.[877] He told me about two poets, one called Charles Plymell (who was married to the daughter of the woman who first published Joyce[878]) and Charles Reznikoff (sp.).[879] He said he liked Reznikoff. And then he said something about Oppen, the exact words I can't remember. I am looking forward to reading about him.

His poems remind me of a beer can vibrating on some machine. Something man-made moving something else man-made.

Frank

Notes

862. *Ironwood* 5 (1975).

863. Alexandre Hogue; see note 846 above.

864. Correctly: *Now and at the Hour of Our Death*; see note 840 above.

865. *Ironwood* 5's price was two dollars. Cuddihy's March 18, 1975, letter to Stanford notes that he mailed Ginny's slides back the previous afternoon after receiving this

letter—which he calls "beautiful," writing, "My amazement grows with each letter. I sometimes feel as if there are several dozen Frank Stanfords, all of them intelligent and considerate, but each one incorporating a different facet of the All."

866. In a March 23, 1975, letter to Cuddihy, Stanford notes that this rented typewriter is an IBM Executive model—with proportional letter spacing and the ability to effect expanded spacing.

867. See note 442 above.

868. See note 858 above.

869. See notes 467 and 854 above.

870. The printer Stanford is referring to is Burt Camp of Elk Ranch Printing; see note 626 above. In a July 12, 1974, letter to Broughton, Stanford explains:

> I did two free surveys, personally, for two tracts of land the turkey hunters own as a family. I've got about 800 bucks of time and labor in it, but I didn't charge them a penny. There is a several hundred thousand dollar lawsuit involved as there was a fist fight among the turkey hunters women and a no count preacher and real estate agent. . . . As soon as time permits, I have to spend three or four days surveying another tract of land around a H.W. [highway, presumably] and mountain for them. It is a great coinsidence that they are printers and we need each others' services. . . . They are going to teach us how to print, and they'll do small books of mine for cost. That's how come I didn't charge them.

871. Longanesi in Milan.

872. *Marginalia: left side, upright. no originals en face*: no poems in Italian included (i.e., the edition would not be bilingual).

873. *Ironwood*, no. 1 (Spring 1972), published six prose poems by Follain translated by William Matthews and Mary Feeney.

874. In his March 18 letter, Cuddihy replies that he won't "breathe a word" about Stanford's translation project and notes that Stanford wouldn't need permissions if he printed "individual poems or groups of poems in a magazine," explaining, "It's only if you want to do a whole book."

875. Cf. Stanford's July 18, 1974, letter to Cuddihy above, pars. 3–4.

876. Peter Orlovsky; see note 1 above.

877. Re: "grandstand," see Stanford's February 14, 1972, letter to Dugan above, pars. 1, 4.

878. Plymell's wife, Pamela Beach Plymell, is the daughter of translator Mary Beach (1919–2006), a distant cousin (multiple times removed) of Sylvia Beach (1887–1962), who published Joyce's novel *Ulysses* (1922).

879. Charles Reznikoff (1894–1976), poet.

[Stanford, Frank
Mar 4, 1975]

March 15, 1975

Dear Mike,

Just a note to say thinks for the OPPEN issue, congratulations; it looked good, read good, and there was just enough of it to thrill and not "go-on". Now IRONWOOD will last as long as the libraries. I wonder why other editors haven't taken the time and expense to do what you've done? I can think of only a few, though my expertise is limited. I bet OPPEN was pleased as much as the reading public.

Also, Ginny won first place in a fairly old&established Art show, and the other painting placed. The juror was an old, well-known artist, here in this country and abroad. The winning painting was called NOW AND AT THE HOUR OF OUR DEATHS. Wish you two could see it. Anyway, that is the reason we haven't sent the painting we wanted to give you yet. It placed in the show and will have to hang for a month or so, and if you don't mind, she would like to enter it in one more show before it retires to your living room since people remark on it as much if not more than the larger painting. Some are so taken with her work that word has got around to some place that wants to see slides of her past work. As you have the only ones, perhaps you could get them back to her. I'm sorry if I've rushed you with them, but this all just came up, and it could prove to be something for her.

She is now painting some 12 hours a day, huddled next to the wood stove. Old man winter is just now coming. Cold rain, ice, snow for the last six weeks has not done our garden good, but we do have 16 rows of peas in which the snow can only sweeten.

Since things are finally looking up in our pocketbooks enclosed is some money for two issues of the OPPEN issue. They will be collectors items I'm sure. I think the other buck ought to get the slides back pretty fast, too.

How is your health? And is Mary well? I hope you'll always let me know when things are good and bad.

What do you think about this typewriter? It will type like this, too. As my other two old ones bit the dust, I am having to rent this for 20.00 per month.

I am going to tell you something I hope you will not repeat until I have it all worked out. As you know, I've long had an interest in those poets who were also filmmakers, as was Blake an artist, Rossetti, etc. Well, it is easy to gain access to Cocteau and Prevert, and sometimes Pasolini, but I have secured a copy of the very rare , first book of young B. Bertolucci. You don't have any idea how hard it was for me to get the book! It has taken about two years. Now, a brother Jerome and myself will translate it, if that is the word. He lived in Rome and the hinterlands of Italy for awhile. By the time I get through with the translations, they will be versions. but still good poems, I hope. I don't plan to stick with the end rhymes. You know, of course, that Bert. started off working for Pasolini, and Pasolini for Fellini. I am afraid to let a big publisher know about this because they would only get a well-known poet to do the book, making a lot of money for all concerned. (After this one, I want to do another small book of Bertolucci&Pasolini together.)

If I were to make any money, I would like to start a chpbook series in the form of a magazine. That is, eash issue is a different book, the only imprint being on the title page and spine, not saying # this or that, but just the name of the publisher. If I could print 8 or 10 books by people I think deserve books, then I would feel more like I was doing my part--as I am not a teacher, or editor. I sometimes feel like an oddball, in that I am not a publisher or teacher. It would still be a magazine in that subscribers would get all books published during the year. I would impose something a little different; no manuscripts other than subscribers would even be considered, unless vj uvouched for by a subscriber. Does that seem unfair? You must find it hard sometimes to consider work by someone who hasn't bought your magazine or seen it? This may all be an early moring pipedream, but the small book of B ERTOLUCCI is not.

I don't have a publisher and I've not inquired, but as soon as the ms is finished I will. Fortune is on my side in that a survey I did on a printer's farm. The printer was happy with my work but not with what the court decreed, so he couldn;'t pay for it. Rather than having an uncollectable bill, I now have about a 1,000 credit, which would publish a 1000 copies of the book I have in mind. If I have to publish myself, I will, but I think that is a little odd. If it were advertised in the right places, I believe it would sell to more than just poets. Any body interested in cinema.

No originals en face,

I have the address of the publisher in Italy, but I need some one to tell me my rights as well as the publisher's rights. I would have to use Bertolucci's name of course in the title somewhere, and I would say that my poems were versions or something to that effect, not translations literal, etc. What do I say to his publisher? What language should I use and what do you suggest. Say when W. Matthews did some Follain translations, did he really have permission from the publisher to translate? I noticed that nothing was said in the title page of the magazine? What all do I have to do if I publish20 pages or so bound like your OPPEN issue. I would have to call it off if the publsiher in Italy wanted a lot of money, etc. Please suggest the best way to haddle it, the easiest, as soon as you have time to let me know. Please keep all this under your hat.

Yours,

Frank

I'm not making a pitch to you to publish this; I really do need advice, though.

Here and previous: Stanford's March 15, 1975, letter to Cuddihy—poet and founding editor of *Ironwood*—using an IBM Executive model typewriter that Stanford rented briefly in 1975 for (he notes) twenty dollars per month.

To John McKernan: March 17, 1975

March 17, 1975

Dear John,

Got your letter dated February 21st. Sorry took so long to answer, but we are snowed under with work, and just plain snowed under with snow. Essential now that we get the garden in while there is a break in the weather.

Ginny, my wife, just won 1st place in 25th annual Arts Center competition in Fort Smith—about the oldest art show in Arkansas.[880] Hope her "*Roethke*" cover comes out soon at the U of W in Seattle.[881] And her photographs are really taking hold. She really has a vision.

I'm O.K.ing on all the poems you accepted, including changes, except "*Soaking Wet*" which seems to me now needing much more than a little trimming.[882] In fact, the poem went by me like a bullet—I must take some time to find out from where the shot came from, or where it hit. If I find out soon, I'll give it back—if there's time, or publish it elsewhere if there is no time. Whatever, I'll make up for the loss of one poem with another I was just about to send to *Field*. Your editing did improve the other poems, no shit. Thanks.

Yea, the printer owes me, and I'll have him print them on the kind of paper you suggested according to the signature size you specified.[883] Is your circulation really 1,000? I don't think he'll do but about 500 for the money he owes me. Just drop me a line and say how many copies you need for *The Little Review*. When they're done, I'll have him ship them to you, but tell me where: Boston or Huntington?[884] The whole process will take about 3 weeks I think?

There is a chance a magazine might offer me a guest editorship for an issue or two, maybe a chapbook selection, etc. I don't know a goddamn thing about editing, etc., but I know, think so, a good poem and a for real voice when I hear one. There are two or three unpublished (book-wise) poets around who I'd really like to see get in circulation. You are one of them. A couple years ago I offered John Morris a chance to do a chapbook, but full size, but he never wrote me back, so my chance to get someone published passed. You're next if they tap me. It would be fine looking, and of course your poems would be good, but you would still be in contention for YALE, etc., as it would be a chapbook.[885] I can't confirm anything yet, but if and when I do, you won't have to wait around forever and a day. So, if they give it to me, I'll hit you; let's leave it there until Fall, when I'll know. I hope you publish a book in the mean time, though.

Send back those poems you rejected, if you don't mind.
Let me hear from you about the above.

Yours,
Frank

Notes

880. See note 840 above.
881. See notes 762 and 805 above.
882. In his February 21, 1975, letter, in response to Stanford's poems sent in fall 1974, McKernan writes, "I love them & want to print up eight of them": "Lap," "Mouths Full of Spit," "Their Names Are Spoken," "Monk's Dog," "Women Singing When Their Husbands Are Gone," "Soaking Wet," "Lament of the Land Surveyor" (which McKernan assesses as "unbelievably beautiful"), and "Tale." *The Little Review* 10 (1975) published seven of the above eight poems (all but "Soaking Wet") plus "Blue Yodel," "Island," "Will," "Shed," and "Blue Yodel of the Quick and the Dead." All of these poems appeared in *Arkansas Bench Stone* except "Women Singing When Their Husbands Are Gone" (which appeared in *Ladies From Hell*); inclusion of *The Little Review* in *Ladies From Hell*'s acknowledgments section thus suggests that the book was actually published in 1975 (not 1974 as the book's front-matter pages state). "Soaking Wet" appeared in *The Ark River Review* in 1976.
883. In McKernan's February 21 letter, he wrote, "Can you get someone to print them up on 8½×11 rag paper using AW IBM with carbon ribbon or a Verifax machine? If you can't (I think you mentioned you could) then I'll have to find some machine."
884. Huntington, West Virginia—location of Marshall University, where McKernan taught for decades.
885. *YALE*: the Yale Younger Poets Prize.

To William Stafford: April 8, 1975

FRANK STANFORD
LAND SURVEYOR
RFD 6–Box 342 Rocky Branch
Rogers, AR. 72756
501-636-7669

April 8, 1975

Dear Mr. William Stafford,

Since 1964 or so, when I was about 15, I have had the pleasure of reading your poetry. When I left the lake and the monastery school to attend college, I again encountered your work. A poet by the name of Don Justice came to Arkansas once and told me how I could get a Xerox copy of one of your early books from the U of Iowa.[886] For this I was thankful.

From time to time I see new work by you in the poetry magazines—sometimes I'm in them, too. I especially liked a poem "Whenever It Is".[887] And your work in *Field* and *Iowa* came close to me, also.[888]

As I am not what you could call a part of the poetry world, I haven't kept up with your new books—or anyone's. Though I'm not there in body, maybe I am in spirit. My work keeps me in the woods most of the time from dawn until dark, but I still keep a log of poems and I read the magazines various poets and editors send me. This summer I hope to have some time off. So, if you could be kind enough to tell me the name of your latest books, and the publishers from which I can obtain them, I would be obliged. I'd like to fill the gap.

In the past ten years I've had the gumption to write two other perfect strangers. Mr. Berryman answered.[889] If you don't have the time, I certainly understand. If I get into a city, perhaps I'll run onto one of your books.

I like your poems, Mr. Stafford.

Yours,
Frank Stanford

Notes

886. Stafford and Donald Justice had both studied at the University of Iowa, receiving PhDs in 1954.
887. Stafford's poem "Whenever It Is," *Ironwood*, no. 4 (1974).

888. Stanford and Stafford had indeed been brushing up against each other in print; they appeared in *Mill Mountain Review* 1, no. 3 (1971), in the Summer 1972 and Spring 1974 issues of *The Iowa Review*, in *FIELD*, no. 10 (Spring 1974), back-to-back in *Ironwood*, no. 4 (1974), in *Mill Mountain Review* 2, no. 2 (1975), and in *Poetry Now* 2, no. 2, issue 8 (1975).

With this letter, Stanford enclosed a copy of *FIELD*, no. 12 (Spring 1975), which published four of his poems. Stanford also followed up by sending an inscribed copy of *Ladies From Hell*; Stafford replied on June 16, noting that "Death in the Cool Evening" was his favorite poem in the collection. (Incidentally, Ginny Stanford later wrote, in a 1997 essay, that Stanford read the poem to her the day they met. She added, "It remains my favorite simply because it was part of such a remarkable and life changing encounter." "Death in the Cool Evening," *Portable Plateau* 1, no. 1 [1997].) *The New York Quarterly* published the poem in Summer 1973 with the date of 1964; to Cheryl Campbell on December 12, 1972, Stanford had stated of its composition, "I wrote it near the shore by my house on Lake Norfork. I was 15 years old, and in love with my death."

889. The second "perfect stranger" (i.e., in addition to John Berryman) to whom Stanford is referring here is not clear, though he wrote to other established poets. Stanford sent a manuscript version of *The Singing Knives* to Anthony Hecht (via *The Hudson Review*) in late July 1971 (Hecht responded very favorably on December 29, 1971) and appears to have also written in the early 1970s to James Wright (see Stanford's July 20, 1972, letter to Irv Broughton above, postscript) and Robert Bly (see note 526 above)—but none of Stanford's correspondence to these four poets (including Berryman) has yet been found.

To Irv Broughton: June 22 or 29, 1975

Sunday[890]

Irv,

Arkansas Bench Stone looks great, thanks for being so fast.

How is the *Roethke* issue coming?[891]

The MMR V is driving me crazy.[892] How would you like to work with printers who couldn't even read? They're so fucking slow and stupid. They are thinking of selling out of all their equipment in the printing business after our jobs are over. They do have some fairly good equipment. I'd like maybe to get the hand press they have at least. Don't know what they're asking. Their goddamn lawsuits are what is holding things up.

It'll come out.

Ginny, Mother, and I are going down to see James Allen over the fourth of July.[893] We intend to look at old pictures and see who we can dig up. He is willing to cooperate on everything, and also he has asked Ginny to do some more paintings for him.

Shade ought to be out anytime.[894]

And *ABS* will be out as soon as you send me back enclosed corrections.[895]

Hey, are the INTERVIEWS with Eberhart and Stafford upcoming in American Poetry Review yours?[896]

Your book will have a gloss white cover with green ink showing maps and title, etc.[897] Really look professional. Be getting ready for it.

MMR V will have two different kind of covers. Black gloss for those going to those colleges, and regular for those going to subscribers, etc.

I've seen the list of all the magazines and presses that have won substantial grants. Even a shit sheet gets 500 bucks, so you ought to rake up after they see the looks of my books, all 7 of them.[898]

No more ribbon.[899]

Frank

Notes

890. This letter's dating is based on its relation to a June 13, 1975, letter to Broughton in which Stanford states, "Urgent that you send *Arkansas Bench Stone* or else it will cost alot to get done."
891. See note 805 above.
892. *Mill Mountain Review* 2, no. 1 (the magazine's intended fifth issue), or "MMR V." Broughton noted to this editor that the issue—the film issue, slated to include poems and essays—never was published; it doesn't exist (though vol. 2, no. 2, the Roethke issue, does). Broughton sent Stanford the money for the turkey-hunter printers to print the issue, but the project, which had been in development for several years, was never completed. Irv Broughton, email to editor, July 26, 2023.
893. James Allen Reece; see Stanford's July 1, 1974, letter to Dugan above, par. 16, and note 754 above.
894. Stanford's book *Shade* (1975).
895. *ABS*: Stanford's book *Arkansas Bench Stone* (1975).
896. The July/August 1975 issue of *The American Poetry Review* included an interview with Stafford conducted by Sanford Pinsker, as well as two poems by Eberhart. The May/June 1977 issue included an interview with Eberhart conducted by Broughton.
897. Broughton's book of poems *Surveying* (Lost Roads, ca. 1975)—a thirty-two-poem early version of the book that ultimately became *The Blessing of the Fleet* (Lost Roads No. 6, 1977); the book has an off-white gloss cover with green titling.
898. The front matter sections of Stanford's 1974–76 Mill Mountain Press books list phantom publications—viz., *St. Francis and the Wolf: Some Poems 1957–1964* ("1972"), *Let*

Him Lay There: Some Early Poems ("1974"), and *Approacheth the Ship and Wonder* ("1976"). Camera-ready plates were made for these titles, but the books were not published; see Stanford's June 20, 1976, letter to Broughton below, par. 6. Had the first two titles above actually been published in 1972 and 1974, *Arkansas Bench Stone* (1975) would have been Stanford's seventh published book.

899. The ink is fading toward the close of this letter.

To John McKernan: July 28, 1975

JULY 28, 1975

Dear John,

Glad you liked the book, and the poems. The latter are from a book, *Arkansas Bench Stone*, due out soon. My favorites are ones I sent which you hadn't seen.

Round up your best 20 or so poems, more or less, long or short, and send them to me. Be sure to enclose the ones from *Field*, *Prairie Schooner*, *Paris Review*, *Atlantic*, and elsewhere, giving credits where published, or where will appear. I've already got your book accepted, now you send it so it can make their Fall List.

Of course, they'll advertise it in some paper like *Poetry Now* or *American Poetry Review*—did you see my poems there?[900]

This fucking work is lasting longer than I thought. I love what I do and make a fair living, but shit I didn't know I'd be so far in to it deep in the summer like this. I dusted my broom pretty good last year, but don't know what kind of things I'll get written this year. If I don't revise my short story collection, it won't get published until next year.

Today, exactly, it has been 8 months since I've sent anything out, story or poem. For awhile there, every time I sent something out, they'd take it. I need to type a few things up and send them out, especially stories.

Whatever happened to all those poets that were in that workshop that summer. All I did was chew Day's Work and eat watermelon.[901] I was about drunk half the time. The Mill Mountain Editor said a couple of those poets that were big dogs when I was sitting in there sent him some ms., but he rejected them all.

Guess I'll hit the hay now.

Yours,
Frank

Notes

900. Stanford's poems "The Strange Boy" and "The Village with the Dark Sun" (later revised to "Village with Dark Sun") appeared in *Poetry Now* 8 (1975), and his poems "What About This" and "They Really Do" appeared in *The American Poetry Review* 4, no. 2 (March/April 1975).
901. Days Work, a brand of chewing tobacco.

To John McKernan: October 1, 1975

OCTOBER 1, 1975

Dear John,

Your ms. is just what the doctor ordered.[902]

You are the best UNPUBLISHED published poet I've seen.[903]

Can't promise anymore than 500 copies, unless you win an award for the book, then maybe another run of same. Will see to it you get as many copies as possible.[904]

See if you can get Mark Strand to write a few lines about your book, *Walking Along the Missouri River*.[905] Whitehead seemed to think he and another might be the best. Jim and Miller wrote something pretty good for Steve Morris.[906] As soon as you can get a line or two or paragraph from Strand and someone else, your book will go to press, proofs to you then, etc.

Frank

Hurry! Peter Davison?
Mark Strand?
David Ignatow?[907]

Notes

902. Following a September 1, 1975, letter and a follow-up note from Stanford, both requesting McKernan's manuscript, McKernan replied on September 11 with a manuscript for *Walking Along the Missouri River*.
903. I.e., a poet who has not yet published a book but has published poetry in magazines (as McKernan had).
904. In McKernan's September 11 letter, he asked Stanford to have the press's editor write him (McKernan) a letter telling him "exactly how many copies will be printed

(500 is my understanding) and also telling me how many copies of the chapbook I am to receive (hopefully 80 or more)." Whether McKernan understood Lost Roads to have a different editor than Stanford or thought that his book would be published by a different press, such as Mill Mountain, is unclear.

905. Mark Strand (1934–2014), poet. McKernan's book was ultimately published as Lost Roads No. 5 in 1977.

906. I.e., John S. Morris. Whitehead wrote a blurb for *Bean Street* on August 28, 1975, but when C. D. Wright's, John Stoss's, Ralph Adamo's, John S. Morris's, John McKernan's, Irv Broughton's, and Stanford's books (Stanford's being *The Battlefield Where the Moon Says I Love You*) were finally published as Lost Roads Nos. 1–12 (1977), none included blurbs.

907. Peter Davison (1928–2004), poet and poetry editor of *The Atlantic Monthly*, and David Ignatow (1914–97), poet. This postscript, expounding on Stanford's request for a blurb in par. 4, includes an arrow drawn from "Hurry" to "Mark Strand" in the paragraph. McKernan closed his reply letter: "I will start writing those dreadful blurb-seeking letters. OK?" Stanford replied on October 12: "About the blurb bit. You and I both know this is a dumb thing. You have never seen them on the back of my 7 books." (See note 898 above.)

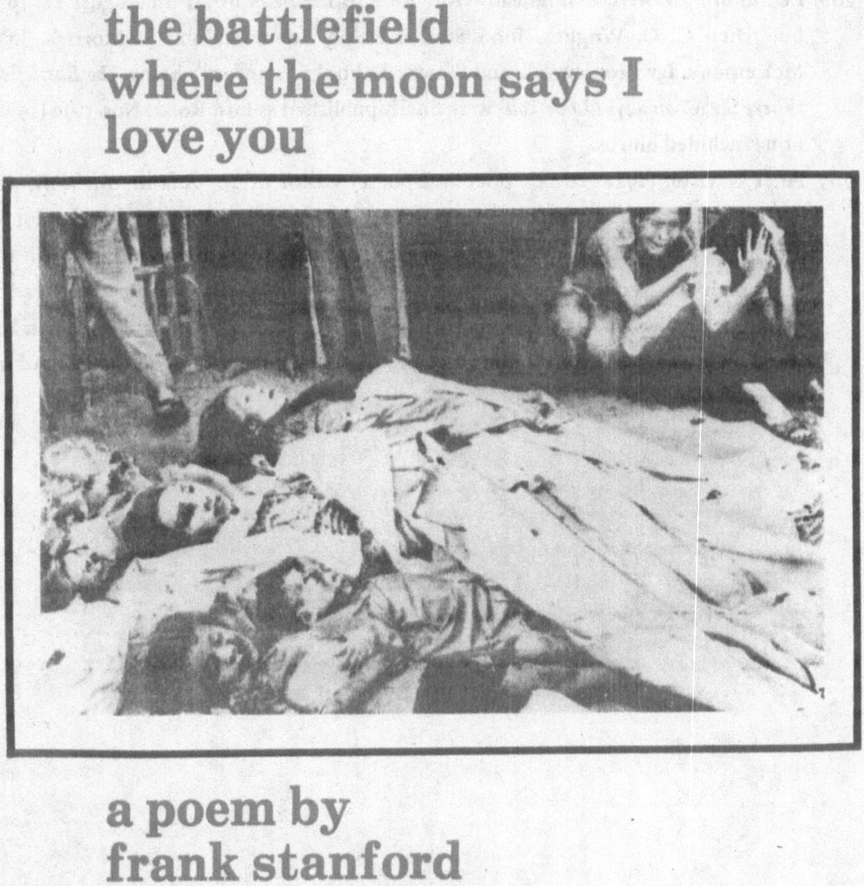

The cover of the first edition of *The Battlefield Where the Moon Says I Love You*. The book's copyright page notes that the photo was taken on April 29, 1975, at the Tân Sơn Nhất Airport in Saigon.

VII.

THE LOST ROADS

Rogers, Liberal, and Fayetteville, 1976–78

In 1976, 1977, and early 1978, Stanford worked on getting his new press, Lost Roads Publishers, off the ground, applying in 1977 and 1978 for funding from the National Endowment for the Arts to publish Lost Roads' first titles. In 1976, Stanford shut down his land surveying office; he was partnering in Fayetteville with Don Kemp, for whom he had worked, with R. S. Gwynn, in 1970. In fall 1976, the Stanfords moved from Rogers into a house south of Liberal, Missouri, north of Joplin, on the farm that Ginny Stanford's parents inherited from her maternal grandparents. However, Frank was living a double life, as he had begun a romantic and professional relationship with poet C. D. Wright, whom he had met in fall 1975 and who lived in Fayetteville; also in fall 1976, on October 1—around the time that he also moved to Missouri with Ginny—Stanford and Wright moved in together in Fayetteville at 705 Jackson Drive, where they based Lost Roads and, starting in spring 1977, their new printing company, White River Printers.

To John McKernan: January 22, 1976

[On Lost Roads Publishers letterhead.][908]

1/22/76

Dear John,

Glad you understand delay.

Why do you want to pull "After Entertaining . . . ."? Copy of "Dawn" enclosed.[909]

Not sure, but it may be too late to pull the former?

John S. Morris's book, *Bean Street*, will be out in March, and your book, *Walking Along the Missouri River*, will be out in APRIL. *Ascend*, by John Stoss, out in May.[910]

I put in for 5 grand to the NEA, but I was too late. I will try CCLM. Am in the process of getting this Company listed with all the places, etc. If you have any addresses of use, send them. I need to know how to get the address of that Books In Print catalog service, etc.

Hope I mail this. Written you ten letters, never mailed them.

Yours,
Frank

Notes

908. The subhead for all Lost Roads Publishers letterhead until fall 1977 reads "A Magazine in Book Issue."
909. McKernan's poems "After Entertaining Some Friends at My Mother's House in Omaha I Go Out in the Back Yard to Get Some Fresh Air" and "The Dawn" appeared in *Walking Along the Missouri River*.
910. Stanford is presumably referring to early or intended versions of Lost Roads books by these poets. A forty-one-poem early version of Morris's *Bean Street* was printed in a very limited, perhaps mock-up, Lost Roads edition in 1975—similar to Broughton's *Surveying* (precursor for *The Blessing of the Fleet*); see note 897 above and Stanford's June 20, 1976, letter to Broughton below, par. 7. Morris's *Bean Street*, McKernan's *Walking Along the Missouri River*, and Stoss's *Finding the Broom* were ultimately (and officially) published as Lost Roads Nos. 4, 5, and 2, respectively, in 1977.

To Ralph Adamo: March 27, 1976

[On Lost Roads Publishers letterhead.]

3/27/76

Dear Ralph,

John is back from NO and says you are doing OK.[911] I have your book.[912]

Because I have a surveying business to run, I only read in March, April, and May for publications in September, October, and November, vice versa.

Promise to let you know by June 1st. Will see you when you are here?

Yours,
Frank

Notes

911. John Stoss; *NO*: New Orleans.
912. I.e., manuscript.

To Alan Dugan: March 29, 1976

[On Lost Roads Publishers letterhead.]

3/29/76

Dear Alan,

Long time, no see, no hear.

Still here, working, and so on. Decided to publish a few books while it is possible . . . . all by other folks, of course.[913] Wish I could print a limited edition of something by you?

Each book is self-contained, titled work by one author, perfectly bound, printed on 75 weight text, about 500 copies.

Hey, I know a guy who is interested in applying for Provincetown.[914] He has a book of poems coming out, and has written two novels and a play—unpublished. He is big, fat, crazy, but a kind and genuine soul—34 years old.[915] His name is John Stoss. I guess any mail should go to him c/o Ben Kimpel, Chairman of the Dept. of English, U of A, Fayetteville, Arkansas 72701.

Where are you working now? One of these days run into each other again. You have any new books?

Yours,
Frank Stanford

Notes

913. Except that Stanford self-published (as a copublication with Mill Mountain Press) *The Battlefield Where the Moon Says I Love You* as Lost Roads Nos. 7–12.

914. See note 745 above.

915. John Stoss was thirty-five years old (not thirty-four) as of the writing of this letter.

To John McKernan: April 5, 1976

[On Lost Roads Publishers letterhead.]

4/5/76

Dear John,

Got your note today—please notice that I am quick to answer. Congratulations on your poem in the New Yorker—I'm just as happy as you are.[916]

Well, you ought to have copies of the uncorrected proofs by now. Of course, I'll make the revision in the acknowledgments, and I'll hold off distribution as long as you want.

Yours,
Frank

P.S. Yea, I like Dugan. I think he's pretty damn great.

Notes

916. McKernan's poem "Winter Letter to Dan Marsteller from South Boston January 1975"—published (under a slightly different title) in *The New Yorker* on June 7, 1976, and collected in *Walking Along the Missouri River.*

To Irv Broughton: June 20, 1976

[On Lost Roads Publishers letterhead.]

June 20, 1976 Sunday

Dear Irv & Connie,

I feel bad about not writing you in so long a time. What can I say?

I blame everything on the tribulations of earning a living. I hired and trained a guy to save me time, and what happens is: it takes three people twice as long to do what one man and I could do. This costs me 160 dollars for three men for two days instead of 24 dollars for one man for one day. Also, they aren't doing the work correctly, while I spend three times the hours in the office that I was. I can't charge for any of this either. Haven't done much of anything. Between now and the 1st I plan to change all of this. You just can't win for losing. Everybody is a crook, more or less. I am just now getting paid for jobs I was doing when you were here!! Enough of business.

Glad to hear the both of you are working—not that there is any merit in working—sometimes there aren't even any rewards——but I know you aren't starving.

This week is the first time at home I've spent since you all left. Strange isn't it? I wrote a new book of twenty poems since then, one of them quite long—ten pages or so. I call the book *Crib Death*. The long poem, a little in the mud of "The Snake Doctors", I call "Nigger Blood."[917]

Carolyn's book is out and I am sending you a good many copies.[918] Frank Jones's book has been done a long time—I just haven't been over to pick it up.[919] I think Roger Brown's is done, too?

The camera ready copies of St. Francis (from 7 poems), Let Him Lay There, Constant Stranger are sitting in the closet. Approacheth The Ship And Wonder and also You are ready ms typed-wise. They are sitting there, too. I think Field Talk is about printed.

I am going to re-print *Surveying* and *Bean Street* this summer. You and John S. Morris will really like how they will both end up looking. The text will be better paper, the cover will have a photo, also I will have you re-set a page or two in your book where there are missed words.[920] Also, send me—when I get ready and ask you—eight more poems. I want a full size 40 poem book—50 pages long. Stoss's book and McKernan's book will come out this fall. I want to apply for about 4 grand at least. I have six or seven quality mss. but I can't afford to accept them now.

Of course, I would like to go in to my life with Carolyn, but I don't even have time to do that now. You would not believe her poetry now. She has moved beyond what she was doing, and is writing some of the best things I've read—outside of John Stoss. Have you time to read it?

My life is all work and no play. Fuck it.

Carolyn has typed up the whole long poem so a typesetter can read it. This is what I promised to you by July 1st. And you will have it by then. As we went along we found many errors and such, so I took it upon myself to make minor revisions. At the moment, she is giving me advice about where and when to white space certain transitions. This is for the reader's benefit. The text is large and double spaced for the benefit of the ~~read~~ person who is doing the typesetting. Before anything else goes too far, I want to see several examples of typestyles in 10 and 11 point, especially Century and Times Roman.[921]

About how much it is going to cost. He said he could do 1200 copies for 3000.00. The film issue he can do for 600.00. I will take up the extra. He can have the film issue done within 30 days of when he is paid and has the stock. He can do it sometime in July. He would rather wait until the end of the summer to do the long thing.

I intend to get behind the book. I will write a few folks I know and get some advance notices. Also, I think I will end up coming out to Seattle for a month or so after it comes out. I have some people who may be able to get us some money—sell it to a trade publisher. Anyway, you and I have a lot of Art to talk over and I could use a vacation. Of course, I would bring Ginny or Carolyn with me. Wish life were so that I could live with both. But not so. We'd be able to help with your rent and food while we were there. My father in law may lend me some money so we can take out some ads in the right places.

Shouldn't I dedicate this book to the moths who shared the light with me while I wrote it, and who died gently.

I feel, for the first time, as if things are going to happen.

Love & everything else that drives along the night roads of the past & future.

Frank

Notes

917. Stanford may have meant to type "mood" instead of "mud" here. Also, many close to Stanford have noted that since he was adopted and never learned his biological parents' identities, he suspected that (or at least wondered if), partially given his skin's particular complexion, he might be at least part Black.
918. *Alla Breve Loving* (Mill Mountain Press, 1976), a book of poetry by C. D. (Carolyn Doris) Wright (1949–2016). Stanford's mentions of "Wright" from here forward refer to C. D. Wright.
919. *The Myth of the Pierced Rock* (1975), a long poem by Yvan Goll (1891–1950)—translated by Frank Jones, illustrated by Ginny Stanford, and published by Mill Mountain Press.
920. In a January 1976 letter to Stanford, poet Phyllis Franklin Morris (1932–2022), Morris's wife, noted that (the early version of) *Bean Street* had arrived but that the book's binding was "poor—the pages literally fall out as you turn them." See note 910 above.

921. Cf. Wright's description: "I had 'set' it, riddled with errors, on a proportionally-spaced typewriter. I stripped in hundreds of corrections and missed hundreds more. Frank took little interest in the process." C. D. Wright, preface to Stanford, *Battlefield*, 2nd ed., n.p. Also consider Forrest Gander's words from a note in the second edition's second printing: "CD Wright had used [Stanford's typescript] to typeset the first edition on a proportional spacing IBM typewriter heavy as a bank safe." "Note," in Stanford, *Battlefield*, 2nd ed., n.p. (The typewriter's make, notably, is uncertain—it might have been an Olympia.)

To Ralph Adamo: July 15, 1976

[On Lost Roads Publishers letterhead.]

July 15, 1976

Ralph,

Sorry I didn't have time to get back in town and talk to you about your book. This is what I wanted to say:

600 Mss.—24,000 poems, more or less, later—I like some of your poems the best.

You are a poet and you write poetry—rare. Sometimes, you write beautiful poems, constant as night.

Let's say I'm interested in 16–20 here, but would really like it if you send me, from time to time, new work, or whatever. Your ms. is very good as is, but knowing you I think you can come up with something incredible. I really like you.

If I'm bad on letter writing, sorry. No time. We've got all year to put this together.

Depending on the God Fucking Buck, let's say anywhere from 500–1500 copies, *at least* 100 hardcover.[922]

Take your time.

Yours,
Frank

Notes

922. All seven of the first Lost Roads titles prepared during Stanford's lifetime—C. D. Wright's *Room Rented by a Single Woman* (Lost Roads No. 1), John Stoss's *Finding the Broom* (Lost Roads No. 2), Ralph Adamo's *Sadness at the Private University* (Lost Roads No. 3), John S. Morris's *Bean Street* (Lost Roads No. 4), John McKernan's *Walking Along the Missouri River* (Lost Roads No. 5), Irv Broughton's *The Blessing of*

the Fleet (Lost Roads No. 6), and Frank Stanford's *The Battlefield Where the Moon Says I Love You* (Lost Roads Nos. 7–12)—have both hardcover and paperback International Standard Book Numbers (ISBNs), but none received a hardcover release.

To Robert T. Motter Jr.: September 20, 1976

[On Lost Roads Publishers letterhead.]

9/20/76

Dear Mr. Motter,

We are interested in using your services for perfect binding, both paperback and hardback.[923]

Our runs are from anywhere between 120 books to 1200 books. In particular, I need estimates on the following work orders:

400 paperback, glued *or* S. sewn, 60 wt stock, approx. 160 pages, 6¼ × 9¼ untrimmed, trimmed to 6 × 9.[924] (12½ × 9¼ sig—2 up)[925]

1200 books (800–1000 paperback & 200–400 hardback), glued or S. sewn, 60 wt stock, approx. 552 pages—not exceeding 1½" in the spine, 8.75 × 7.50 untrimmed, trimmed to 8.5 × 7.25. (8.75 × 15 sig—2 up)[926]

250–500 books (80% paperback & 20% hardback), glued or S. sewn, 70 wt. laid stock, approx. 32–64 pages, 8½ × 5½ untrimmed, trimmed to minimum. (8½ × 11 sig—2 up)[927]

On the spine of the hardback we would require a gold, red, or silver AUTHOR'S NAME, TITLE, PUBLISHER. We would like to use dark green, blue, or black as colors. Of course, we would furnish the paperback covers.

If possible, could you please send me the following estimates, and also samples of your work?

Yours,
Frank Stanford

P.S. I can be reached at 501-636-8405 in the evenings.[928]

Notes

923. Robert T. Motter Jr. (1924–2010), Oklahoma-based bookbinder whose Motter Book Binding Company apparently bound Stanford's *The Battlefield Where the Moon Says I Love You.*

924. *S. sewn*: Smyth sewn—a type of bookbinding in which groups of pages are stitched together with thread; *60 wt stock*: sixty-pound paper stock, a strong, standard weight.

925. Stanford's January 20, 1977, letter to Broughton, noting a balance due on "film issue + big book," suggests that this paragraph likely refers to the aborted *Mill Mountain Review* film issue; see note 892 above.

926. This paragraph refers to *The Battlefield*; the first edition (1977) is 542 numbered pages—552 pages if including unnumbered pages. The book's spine width is approximately 1 9/16"; the book's dimensions are 8 9/16" tall by 7⅛" wide. Re: *The Battlefield*'s print run, see note 980 below.

927. This paragraph refers to Lost Roads Nos. 1–6; the books range from thirty-two numbered pages (Morris's *Bean Street*) to fifty-four numbered pages (Stoss's *Finding the Broom*). All six books' dimensions are 8¾" tall by 6¼" wide.

928. Per Stanford's November 9, 1976, letter to Cuddihy below, par. 11, (501) 636-8405 was the Stanfords' private home phone number in Rogers.

To Ralph Adamo: October 20, 1976

[On Lost Roads Publishers letterhead.]

10/20/76

Ralph,

Yes, let's consider it final. I want to do a beautiful book of at least twenty poems, the same amount Stoss and Wright will have in their books. (The other three books contain forty poems each, but that is just too much poetry.[929] Anyway, one of your kind of poems has the drive of several poems.)

Thanks for the poems you sent, will be pulling some of them I know for the book. Find enclosed xeroxes of poems I wish you would revise so I can include. Please. I will be sending you a xerox of something I've found for the cover, and I think it will blow you down. I hope.

Also, as soon as I make the final choices, will be sending you a standard contract and copyright claim. (Of course, it will be done in your name, all rights reserved for you, not me.)

If you are interested in having a Library of Congress Cataloging in Publication Data info above your copyright and also listing in Bowker Books in Print, talk to some of your friends and get the essential forms, etc. so I can do that for you. I'll be sending you a list of final selection and everything back so you can get the others off to another Press.

Frank

The poems you sent are good, good, good.

I will be letting you know about a place for the *Rose* poems. Kind of busy now, but give me a month or so to get on it. Maybe MM?[930]

Have you seen Leon's book?[931] Nice poems, funny. As you know I had a book of his (20 poems) printed, but had changed his mind when the Texas Press started their Poetry Series. I'll probably send him what I have.

Ellen will be moving back to NO and wants to work with you on your BR and get it going.[932]

Did you know that Carolyn is buying a lot of printing equipment and will soon be in the business of duplicating words? This will be nice for all of us price wise, I'm sure. You ought to keep her in mind.

I like the Tabloid format lots—when it has a circulation of up in the thousands.[933] Otherwise, people throw them away. You may want to check costs with Carolyn when she gets set up for work.

Notes

929. The 1977 published versions of Lost Roads Nos. 1–6 (see note 922 above) each contain twenty poems.
930. *MM*: Mill Mountain Press; Adamo's book *Hanoi Rose* (1989) was ultimately published by New Orleans Poetry Journal Press.
931. Stokesbury's *Often in Different Landscapes* (University of Texas Press, 1976).
932. Ellen Gilchrist (1935–2024), fiction writer/poet. Gilchrist began studies (briefly) in Arkansas's MFA program in 1976. *BR*: *Barataria Review*.
933. *Barataria Review*, no. 2 (for which Adamo was an associate editor), was published in a newsprint format.

To Ralph Adamo: Circa Fall 1976

[On Lost Roads Publishers notepad letterhead.]

Ralph,

Ellen showed me the revisions for

"The Other Man"

"Pinnace"[934]

Yes. Please make them for me.

Would like to put one *of* two poems in for "The Children of the Oven . . . ."[935]

?

Only make *essential* revisions, please?

$$$$
Frank

I need

1. Cover ideas:
   Design, photo, etc.
2. Photo of yourself.
3. Bio & vita.
4. Blurbs—*two*; or send names of two people you want words from.
5. *Complete* list of publications, herein:
   magazine, poem, editor, *address*!!, volume, issue, number, date.
6. Advice.
7. Your corrected typescript proofs.
8. Signed agreement—copyright form.
9. Pres-Aply—labels.[936]
10. ?

Notes

934. Poems in Adamo's books *Hanoi Rose* and *Sadness at the Private University*, respectively.

935. Adamo's recollection is that a tentative working title for *Sadness at the Private University* may have been *The Children of the Oven*, a reference to the book's cover art—*Le Medecin guarissant Phantasie* (*The Physician Curing Fantasy*), an anonymous seventeenth-century illustration depicting various creatures (including children) rising as smoke from an oven (the cover was credited to Ginny Crouch Stanford in the book).

936. Correctly: PRES-a-ply.

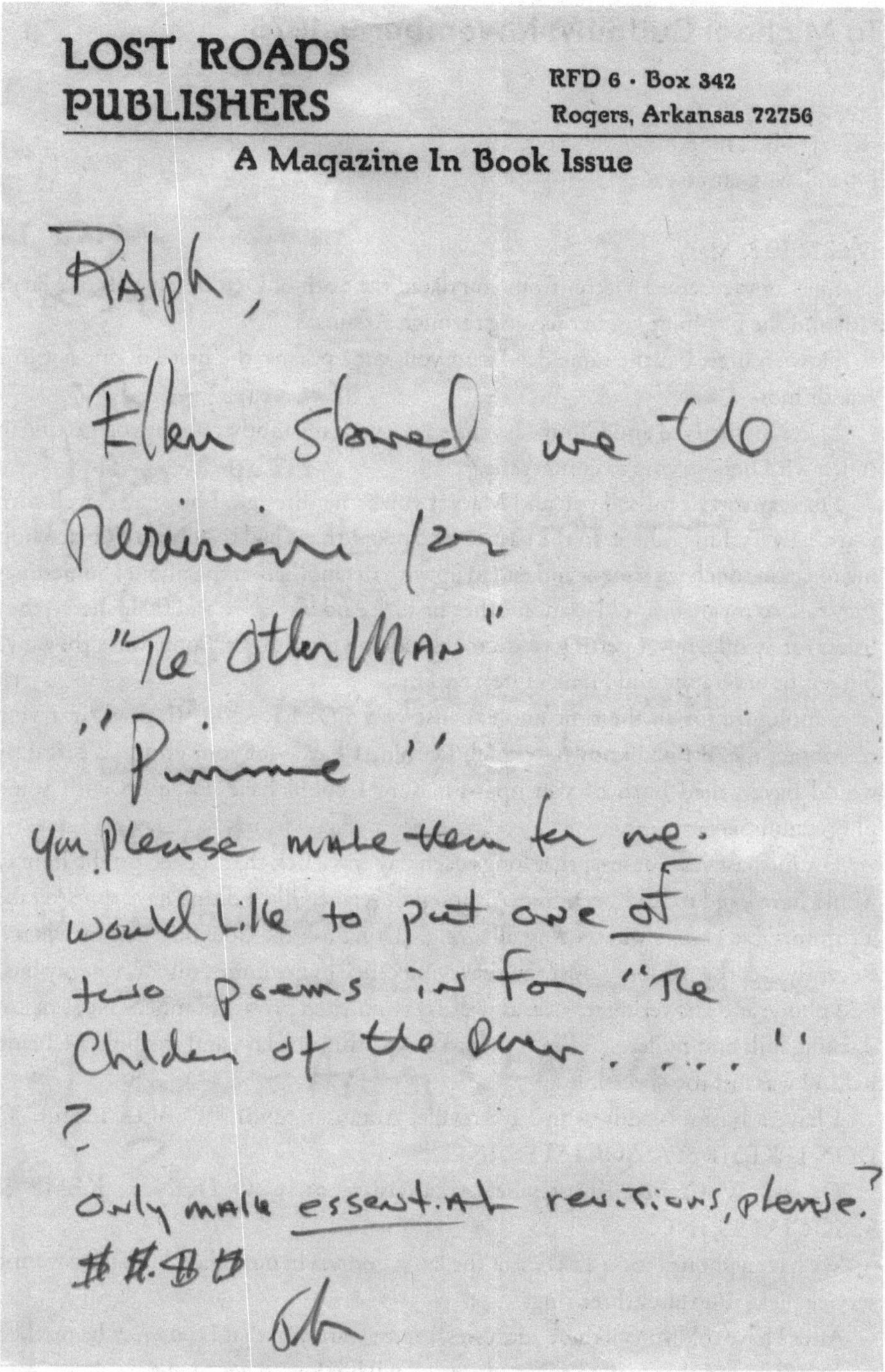

LOST ROADS PUBLISHERS

RFD 6 · Box 342
Rogers, Arkansas 72756

A Magazine In Book Issue

Ralph,

Ellen showed me the revisions for "The Other Man" "[illegible]"

you please make them for me. would like to put one or two poems in for "The Children of the River ....." ?

Only make essential revisions, please?

[illegible]

[illegible]

Page 1 of Stanford's ca. fall 1976 letter to Ralph Adamo on early Lost Roads notepad letterhead, mentioning poem revisions in the planning stages for preparing Adamo's *Sadness at the Private University* (1977) for publication.

To Michael Cuddihy: November 9, 1976

November 9, 1976
{RT 1}[937] Box 108A
Liberal, Missouri 64762

Dear Mike & Mary,

I just now received a letter from you dated the 20th of October. It tells of Mary's visit and the possibility of her passing through Arkansas.[938]

How strange. On the same day I sent you some poems, the first I'd sent out in a year or more.

I have just arrived and Ginny says she spoke with my mother about you getting in touch with her—trying to contact me.[939]

I'm very sorry I missed you and Mary if you came through. I hope all is well with you all. Everything is here. In the past several people have had to contact Subiaco hoping to get in touch with me—and ended up with my mother on the phone! Sometimes they talk to my 90 year old grandmother first.[940] And if they've had their sherry, they listen for awhile, never getting to do much talking themselves. Sometimes they give out a spot biography and Frank's Greatest Hits.

I apologize for all the time and expense you must have gone through in trying to contact me. If I had known—which I couldn't have—of your efforts, I certainly would have called both of you up—I'm sure I could have come up with some phone numbers.

For the past year (at least that long) each day was a tick that sucked on the hours I would have liked to have been free. Although it seemed like I didn't have time to take a comfortable crap, I was writing all along. (Don't ask me how or when or where.) Recently, I chose to close down the surveying office in my home, disconnect my business phone and answering service, as well as my unlisted private number. (No, I'm not ducking bills and police. . . . I'm trying to stay within the law, and the bills are being paid.) I was just too accessible.

I have a business address in Fayetteville, Arkansas 72701, PO BOX 1001, C/O DON L. KEMP & ASSOCIATES, INC.[941]

Or, 118 W Center, Fayetteville, Arkansas 72701, C/O DON L. KEMP & ASSOCIATES, INC.

We have a phone (501-4424152) at the latter address in our office, but an answering service picks it up after three rings.

After I have told you all these addresses, I must warn you that I can *never* be reached in the office, and that mail to these addresses will be slow to get to me.

The old RFD 6 BOX 342 Rogers, Arkansas 72756 address, with the private phone 636-8405 and the business phone & answering service 636-7669 are now all gone.[942]

The above address {RT 1} BOX 108 A, Liberal, Missouri 64762 is now applicable to Ginny all the time and to me some of the time. That is, I am in the field, earning a living Friday through Monday, usually in Arkansas—about four counties, and am here Tuesday through Thursday.[943] The number is listed under Ginny Crouch Stanford, Jasper, Mo. information, 417-394-2859. It would be best to get me in the evenings of those midweek days.

I still pick up mail in Rogers, Arkansas at the Post Office once or twice a week as I pass through on my way to work from the farm. The address there is PO BOX 1303, Rogers, Arkansas 72756.

I have an address in Fayetteville and a phone which no one knows. I will send them to you in case you need to get hold of me over the weekend. (When I say no one knows, I mean *no* one.)

I would like to tell you about this new place in Missouri, but I'm a little tired right now. Very different geography & people. Twelve miles due East of Pittsburgh, Kansas;[944] and twenty-four miles North of Joplin, Missouri. I will tell you about it, most probably in poems.

Business and being a publisher are completely cut out of this place. I only write here, and take care of this old, two-story house on 400 acres.[945] (The tillable land is leased out to a local family of kin-farmers by Ginny's mother and dad).

I have been very lucky in life and poetry. As John Lee Hooker would put it, Born in Mississippi, Raised up in Tennessee—I would add, Come Into My Own in Arkansas.[946] The move from the Delta to the Ozarks—by way of Memphis, was pressurized carbon. Now, this. Just out of the Ozarks and at the edge of the plains, so near Kansas, not too far from Oklahoma.

So, what is going on? What do you have coming up? Are my poems any good?

Recently, I really got into Ai's poetry.[947] Don't know if I'm still into it or not? Someone I've recently discovered is Philip Levine.[948] What an underrated poet. I think he is great.

The three poets I have coming out with Lost Roads, John S. Morris, Irv Broughton, and John McKernan, have been a little difficult to deal with. They have really been pushing me to get their books out, the latter being subject (of course) to my time and money. I think they're all doing something different, doing it THEIR OWN WAY. However, I will confide this to you only, I am not too thrilled anymore with their poetry. HOWEVER——

There are three other poets I've come across who are able to keep me up all the time. They are, in my mind, just wonderful. John Stoss, Ralph Adamo, CDWright. I have just completed working with them on their mss., but I won't be able to publish them until late 1977. I don't want to send you the first three mss. because the books are so near publication, and because of my lack of enthusiasm. (Don't get me wrong—I still like their poetry, it's just that I've moved along so far myself it is too much like looking back.)

I don't want to send you the other three mss. Is it too pretentious for me to say "so you can have first crack at them"? Of the three, Adamo has published before in magazines. I am actually including some of his poetry ~~that~~ which appeared several years ago in small journals now forgotten. John Stoss is a rare poet. Their work is not at all the same, but each poet is beautiful. I can't wait to lay ten of CDWright's poems on you. I think she is the most powerful poet I've read since Ai—but oh so very different.

(I hope you will have the time to read&consider them. Of course, if you don't like the poetry, I want to know why—and they will want to know. I have told them about you, they've read *Ironwood*, and they know they will get an honest opinion.

There are so many things I would like to talk about, but there is plenty of time. Did I mention that Mill Mountain got a grant to publish The Battlefield Where The Moon Says I Love You, all 542 pages, Spring 1977?

Love Supreme per John Coltrane[949]
Frank

Notes

937. *Marginalia: Left side, upright.*
938. Per Cuddihy's memoir, he and Mary traveled in October 1976 to Alabama to visit her brother, and Cuddihy "had hoped to see Frank" as well. Just before the trip, Stanford had sent to him an envelope "thick with poems" carrying "a sense of urgency"; he had thought that Frank or Ginny "had died or been injured" and, so, phoned them, attempting (unsuccessfully) to reach them. Michael Cuddihy, *Try Ironwood: An Editor Remembers* (Rowan Tree, 1990), 72, 75.
939. Cuddihy noted that, after returning to Arizona, he phoned Subiaco Abbey and spoke with Dorothy. When he connected with Stanford, at the farm in Missouri, Cuddihy proposed that the poems Stanford had sent to him in October be the groundwork for a book. *Try Ironwood*, 75, 88.
940. Carolyn Gilbert was eighty-eight years old (not ninety) as of the writing of this letter.
941. Kemp was Stanford's surveying associate in the late 1970s.
942. Stanford continued using Lost Roads Publishers letterhead with the RFD (i.e., Rural Free Delivery) 6, Box 342 address in Rogers well into the middle of 1977.

943. Cf. Stanford's May 21, 1978, letter to Ginny and C. D. below, par. 8.
944. Pittsburg, a small city in southeast Kansas.
945. See note 797 above.
946. *Born in Mississippi, Raised Up in Tennessee* (1973), blues album (and title track) by John Lee Hooker (1912/1917–2001), who was born in the Mississippi Delta and lived, in the 1930s, in Memphis.
947. Ai (i.e., Ai Ogawa, 1947–2010), poet. Seven of Ai's poems appeared in *Ironwood*, no. 1 (Spring 1972) and *Ironwood*, no. 2 (Fall 1972); three more of her poems appeared in *Ironwood* 4, nos. 1/2, issue 7/8, in December 1976.
948. Philip Levine (1928–2015), poet.
949. *A Love Supreme* (1965), jazz album by John Coltrane.

To Irv Broughton: Circa Late 1976

[On Don L. Kemp & Associates, Inc., letterhead.]

Irv,

I *have* to have a check (made out to *Overstreet Printing*) in the amount of $677.50 by Jan 1st! If it will bounce, make out check and let me know when they can spend!

F.S.

You may want to register letter.

Also, make out a check for whatever printing you need done.

Did *House of Books* in Fayetteville send you a check for $40.00? They were supposed to send it to me.[950]

Frank

Notes

950. The content of a January 20, 1977, letter from Stanford to Broughton—in which Stanford inquires whether House of Books (formerly Fayetteville's main bookstore, at 518 W. Dickson Street) sent a check to him and notes a similar balance ($697.83) due to the printer—suggests that this note was penned ca. late 1976.

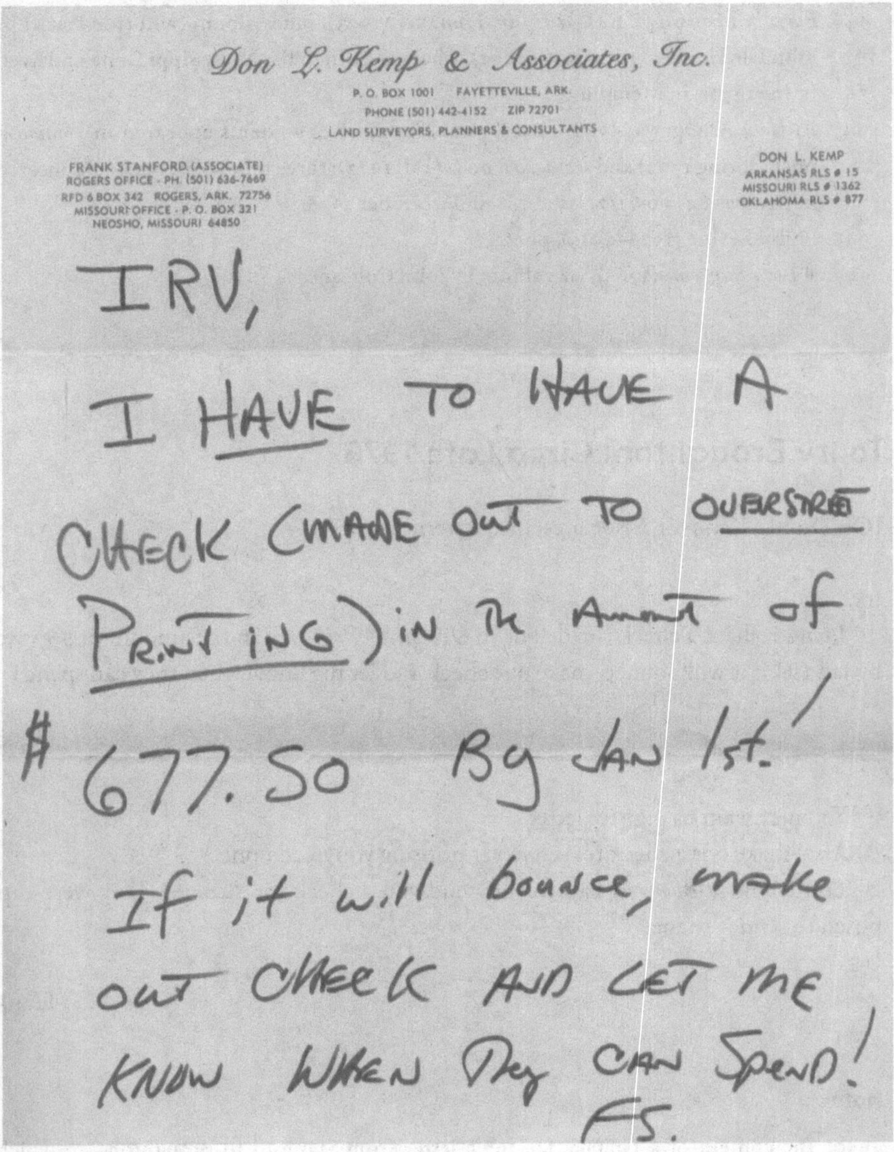

Don L. Kemp & Associates, Inc.

P. O. BOX 1001 FAYETTEVILLE, ARK.
PHONE (501) 442-4152 ZIP 72701
LAND SURVEYORS, PLANNERS & CONSULTANTS

FRANK STANFORD (ASSOCIATE)
ROGERS OFFICE - PH. (501) 636-7669
RFD 6 BOX 342 ROGERS, ARK. 72756
MISSOURI OFFICE - P. O. BOX 321
NEOSHO, MISSOURI 64850

DON L. KEMP
ARKANSAS RLS # 15
MISSOURI RLS # 1362
OKLAHOMA RLS # 877

IRV,

I HAVE TO HAVE A CHECK (MADE OUT TO OVERSTREET PRINTING) in the Amount of $677.50 By JAN 1st.!

If it will bounce, make out CHECK AND LET ME KNOW WHEN they CAN SPEND!

FS.

Page 1 of Stanford's ca. late 1976 letter to Irv Broughton—unusually penned on Stanford's and Don Kemp's business letterhead.

To Ellen Gilchrist: January 15, 1977

[On Lost Roads Publishers letterhead.]

1/15/77

Dear Ellen,

Enclosed are four copies of the contract as drawn up by Judge Wright.[951] Also, a copy of his letter explaining the tax situation for you.

If you could sign and send two copies back to me with the check, I will file them at the courthouse, deposit the check in the account, and begin publication right away.[952]

There is no way I can thank you except with the publication of the great poetry herein mentioned. What you are doing for these authors, including myself, is very fine. I believe we all may be stepping into that big cow chip called literary history?

Love,
Frank

Notes

951. Judge Ernie E. Wright (1915–2009), C. D. Wright's father.

952. The enclosed "Contract for Book Publication" notes that Ellen Gilchrist Kullman contributed $5,000 to Lost Roads Publishing Company toward publication of the early Lost Roads titles by Wright, Stoss, and Adamo and the second edition of *The Singing Knives* (published in 1979) and that Stanford would pay Gilchrist 50 percent of "all the profits realized."

To C.D. Wright, John Stoss, Ralph Adamo, John S. Morris, John McKernan, and Irv Broughton: April 1, 1977

[On Lost Roads Publishers letterhead.]

NEW ADDRESS:
Lost Roads Publishers
PO Box 210
Fayetteville, Arkansas 72701

4/1/77

Dear Six Authors,

This is to notify you of what is happening: After spending two years of getting everything together and about 6,000.00, the first book is on its way out. I have secured Library of Congress CIP Data and ISBN Data for all your books,[953] and so they will be catalogued and listed in all Bowker publications, BOOKS IN PRINT, etc. I have also arranged more financing for national advertising—always open on suggestions. Of course, send me a list of where you think I should advertise. I want to be able to run something around or through your local college or hometown, too. As for distribution, it will be done by someone employed by me the first six months, and after that we will have someone else handle it. The books will also be available in catalogues from Spring Church and Quarto, etc.

You will find enclosed only a typescript of what I will be using to typeset your book. The only changes in this typescript which are allowed at this point are for errors. Please don't attempt to make revision, cosmetic changes, or order changes. The books are being set in 11 pt. Century Light, titles in 12 pt. Century Bold. Book size will be 6¼ × 9¼ more or less, perfect bound.[954] We are printing on 70 wt. Carnival Offset, Ivory Vellum. Covers on 65 wt. Carnival Antique. There will be dust jackets on paperback and hardback.[955] The printing will run somewhere between 1000–1250 copies.[956] I am really not sure how many hardback copies will be done at this moment. By the time all six books are out and advertised, I will have spent 12,000.00, and another year of time.

Once this typescript is corrected I will send you xerox copies of your galley proofs, and also a new contract drawn up entirely from the author's point of view: re-print rights, re-print payments, all reserved under your name, copyright under your name, first rights to remainder stock, and option to purchase plates, the amount of copies you will receive—how and when, review copies, discounts to you, and of course ROYALTY

& ADVANCE. Right now, I plan to pay you either 5.00 per poem or 5.00 per page in advance of publication. I don't know how soon after you sign the contract this will be. I am talking about between 600.00 and 845.00, so it is hard for me to say. You will also receive about 300.00 worth of free books. ~~also~~ In other words, an author will get at least a hundred bucks in cash and about a hundred books.[957] (But please don't give your books away to people who will buy them.) If and when I receive a NEA grant, I will up this to 10.00 per poem. As far as royalties go, I am glad to say that you will receive 30%. That is six times what a University Press gives and three times what a Trade Press gives. The pb will sell somewhere between 3.00 and 4.00 each. The hb will sell somewhere between 6.00 and 8.00 each. Royalties will be paid every six months. Of course, I will be submitting your books for all the awards. I am only aware of about 3 or 4, so please send me whatever you have about this or any goddamn thing you want.

This all started out on a small scale in a small way. The more I read your poetry the more I knew I had to do to make it reach the most people. I selected your six books from over 600 other pickings. I am very sorry it took over two years to get this all off the ground. When you finally get your book, receive a check, have your royalties rolling in, I hope you think it was all worth it. So far, only one author has failed to return the original agreement I sent with the raw typescript. They were corrected per your instructions, and I have put together your books from them. Also, five of you have sent me the lists of names I really needed. Thank you. This really helps me out.

Remember, no poet has over 20 poems in his book.[958] The reason for this is very simple. I have never read a book with over 20 or so good & powerful poems in it.[959] There is no fat or padding in these books. Other poets and editors across the country who have seen some of the typescripts haven't yet recovered from seeing so much good poetry at one time.

Remember, as soon as you've proofed this typescript and I get it back, I will send you a contract. As soon as I get that back, your typescript will go to the typesetter. Between then and publication date, you will receive your advance. Remember, the book will be *printed* months before publication date. I have listed publication dates as I have solely for your benefit: reviews, awards, readings, etc.

Yours,
Frank

P.S. The printing order of the books is based upon the order in which I received your agreements and proofs, etc. Also, don't hold onto this typescript too long. I want to take care of everything as soon as possible.

Notes

953. *CIP Data*: Cataloging-in-Publication data.

954. See note 927 above.

955. None of the Lost Roads Nos. 1–6 titles included dust jackets, and see note 922 above.

956. A seeming discrepancy exists between "1000–1250 copies" here and language in the Lost Roads author agreement—signed and notarized, in at least three poets' contracts, by Stanford on October 20, 1976 (Adamo was officially brought in a month later), copies of which are housed in the Lost Roads Publishers Records at Yale University—to which Stanford refers in the postscript, which states that the poet's book will be printed in "limited editions of 250 copies, not to exceed 2 editions, or 500 copies in total." If by "1000–1250 copies," Stanford means *per title*, then the intended print runs substantially increased between October 1976 and April 1977; however, he probably means 1,000 to 1,250 copies to be the likely run for all six titles—in total. Stanford's accounting sheets sent to the National Endowment for the Arts (NEA) in an August 15, 1977, letter state that one thousand copies of each book were printed, but the claim was likely duplicitous—both Adamo and Broughton firmly disbelieve that the number of copies printed of their books exceeded the low hundreds. Lost Roads Publishers Records, Yale Collection of American Literature, Beinecke Rare Book & Manuscript Library; Ralph Adamo, direct message to editor, January 13, 2026; and Irv Broughton, email to editor, January 13, 2026.

957. The price listed on each of the first six Lost Roads titles is three dollars.

958. See note 929 above.

959. Notably, both *Ladies From Hell* and *Field Talk* contain exactly twenty poems, but several of Stanford's own books—*The Singing Knives* (see note 157 above), *Shade*, *Crib Death* (see note 1053 below), and *You*—contain more (as many as thirty poems).

To Fred Overstreet: Early May 1977

Frank Stanford
PO Box 210
Fayetteville, Arkansas 72701

501-521-5244[960]

Dear Fred,[961]

Made my contacts with the backers of the books, and it looks like things are clear on the big book—providing you can have it printed as of two weeks of the 3rd of this month.[962] We will have to make at least three dummies up as I cannot wait to get copies where they HAVE to go. You would have to make at least one dummy anyway to know where and how to locate spine, cover, back material on cover.

Please have Dave or his wife call me as soon as you have something screened and something to look at as to how the cover will look. You could experiment on some of that back side of the waisted [*sic*] cover stock on Constant Stranger I saw in your dark room, per Larry ?#%&*.

Before you wrap and crate, please make sure you have three sheets of each for dummy. Also, please check quality to make sure there are no bad imprints. After you wrap, mark so

2	3
1	4

or

4	1
3	2

or whatever order they are in.

Then, we will have two books accounted for.[963] An accounting of what you have rec'd and what you are allowed to credit is on the back—less cost of boxes, of course.[964] And, I do have a tax number.

I could not prevail on the other six books though.[965] I paid you, paid 50% down with another printer, and now the backer wants money refunded, which is legally within rights. Since I can't pay for these things three times, I need the amount listed below, less boxes, paid to me as soon as possible. If you can't repay me all at once, as I paid it, please come up with it in weekly or monthly installments, but don't take over two or three months. I can probably borrow some money if you can't come up with the entire sum all at once, but please work with me on this. See you soon.

Frank

Notes

960. Stanford's and Wright's home number at 705 Jackson Drive in Fayetteville.
961. Fred Overstreet (1947–2007), longtime resident of Bentonville, Arkansas, and founder of Overstreet Printing Company.
962. A letter from Overstreet to Lost Roads, dated May 3, 1977, closed by noting that *The Battlefield*, which was "now on the press," was "expected to be finished in the very near future, approx. 2 weeks."
963. Stanford's books *Constant Stranger* (1976) and *The Battlefield Where the Moon Says I Love You* (1977). Overstreet's May 3 letter explains that "only one book has been published and a second book is now on the press" and notes that Stanford had given

"the other six books" to "another printer." The printer for Lost Roads Nos. 1–6 was Stanford's own printing company, White River Printers.

964. The enclosed sheet notes that Overstreet had received $3,287 for purchasing paper, printing *Constant Stranger*'s 43 pages, printing a 547-page book (i.e., *The Battlefield*), and picking up paper—totaling $2,471.16 of work and thus leaving an amount due to Stanford, according to his accounting sheet, of $815.84 (less cost of boxes).

Constant Stranger is a book of 48 numbered pages (plus four flyleaves), but five of those numbered pages are blank.

The Battlefield's first edition is a book of 542 pages, plus five non-blank front matter pages and one non-blank back matter page (plus one flyleaf). Stanford may be forgetting the back matter page here, as the number of non-blank pages in the published book totals 548, not 547.

965. Lost Roads Nos. 1–6; see notes 922 and 963 above.

To Ralph Adamo: May 30, 1977

5/30/77

WHITE RIVER PRINTERS
705 Jackson Drive
Fayetteville, Arkansas 72701

Re: *Barataria* #3

Dear Ralph,

We got the rest of the G.P. today, Monday, instead of this coming Wednesday, so we are still a couple of days ahead of schedule.[966] The rest of the G.P. will be mailed Wednesday, June 1st. We can begin printing as soon as we hear from you with C.G.P.'s.[967]

As soon as Louis has the fiction put together the way he wants it, send it along. We can begin on it Wednesday, June 1st, and have it to you in a week or two.

So far, no cover and no check?

Yours,
Frank

P.S. 6/1/77 We are ready anytime to print #3 and to typeset #4?
1610.00 for 1000 copies, 96 pages.[968]
1450.00 for 1000 copies, 80 pages.[969]

Notes

966. *G.P.*: galley proofs.

967. *C.G.P.'s*: corrected galley proofs.

968. Penciled scribbles in the margin show Stanford's calculations, with $1,610.00 being broken down as $960.00 + $450.00 + $200.00.

969. In published versions, *Barataria*, no. 3, is eighty-five numbered pages; *Barataria*, no. 4, is seventy-six numbered pages.

To C. D. Wright, John Stoss, Ralph Adamo, John S. Morris, John McKernan, and Irv Broughton: June 1, 1977

[On Lost Roads Publishers letterhead.]

6/1/77

Dear Six Authors,

So, you have everything but a contract and some advance. The NEA was supposed to let me know last month about how much money I was getting. If they don't let me know within ten days, I will send along contract, as is, @5.00 per poem, but I want to be able to give 5.00 per page, at least 10.00 per poem. Whatever, check your mail for the contract. You will be getting a check soon after.

If you have not returned EVERYTHING listed in blue on my last note/checklist by the 10th of this month your book will be left off some very important lists.[970] This does not mean I won't publish your book or print it (any minute now), it means it will just sit in a box for 12 months.

I hope the Galleys look O.K. Shit or get off the pot.

Last Call,
Frank

Notes

970. Stanford may be referring to the twenty-item checklist at the close of his May 1, 1977, letter to the six authors, though no items are listed in blue on the copy of that letter housed at Yale University.

To Michael Cuddihy: June 15, 1977

6/15/77

LOST ROADS PUBLISHERS
PO BOX 210
FAYETTEVILLE, ARKANSAS 72701

Dear Mike & Mary,

Hello. The last issue is wonderful.[971] I think I've shown it around enough so that you ought to be getting subscribers from Fayetteville and New Orleans.

It is very dry up at the farm, harvest time for certain crops. This is good. It is not good for those people with new crops in. The peas and lettuce are over, the corn and tomatoes are making. I hope the people down the way will get rid of their hogs, because the SW wind is fairly strong.

Everyone is working in their own way. Recently, I purchased with some others on a long term low interest note a complete print shop: about 16,000 worth of used and new equipment and supplies. Call it WHITE RIVER PRINTERS and we have done the first three LOST ROADS books, Wright, Stoss, Adamo. Next, we do issues of the *Barataria* out of New Orleans.[972] Next, the other three LOST ROADS books, Morris, McKernan, Broughton. Next, issues and books for MILL MOUNTAIN, not if their grant does not come through though. (These won't be any books by me.) So, we have three regular customers as long as they have regular funding. Only poets work for us. I pay 4.00 an hour. The main printer is a man who hasn't been out of prison long—manslaughter or murder?[973] One of his poems appeared in the P.E.N. writers in prisons issues.[974] Of course, we have no editorial say on anything, just layout and design suggestions. There really is an editorial flow in all honesty. I have declined to do printing jobs for crummy books, but I think this was an error. I think it was elitist and un-democratic. From now on the printing company and the publishing company and poet's mind won't get mixed up. In fact, I felt so guilty towards these people, I arranged to have their work printed by another printer at a very low cost through a sort of professional trade-off.

So far, we need the accounts of about nine other fairly regular small press/little magazines. We ~~won't~~ {want} to offer quality service at low costs to other poets and editors. If we can't get enough on a regular basis, we will have to print menus and letterheads and advertisements, etc. You will see an example of our work as soon as the books get back from the bindery. (perfect, sewn)

1000 copies of a 48 page book on warren old style paper, baskerville type, perfect bound-sewn, runs about 1000.00. 500 copies about 742.50. 1000 copies 96 page runs about 1710.00. I am told that this is about ⅔ cost in Northwest and Deep South. I hope some other small press people can shed some light on their real costs, so we can know about our prices?

Well, enough of that.

Everybody was impressed with the new issue of *Ironwood*. Wright sent some more poems out, *Field* took 3 or four. I still haven't sent anything out.

Have you seen that text book by that *Field* editor, Turner.[975] It probably doesn't look like what I told you about last year, I was a bit surprised at the way it looked. Anyway, it took them a pretty long time to get it out and it isn't really what I expected it was going to be. It has my essay and poem "Death and Arkansas River" but they have left out a few passages of the essay as per I explained them to you last year—about filming, etc.[976]

I have some other essays but I don't think they are worthwhile, maybe too personal and not very academic?

About *Crib Death*, here are 20 poems, 2 of which you haven't seen. I have 10 more to send you to select from, also. It would make about 40–48 pages (three 8up-8down signatures in printer talk).

I have several suggestions about a cover, which of course you are under no obligation whatsoever to use or even consider. {Photos already exist.}[977] One is a very fine color photograph taken at night with a full moon and pumpkins in an upstairs window (candles inside). This would require maybe 4 color separation and so too costly and out of question. The other is a very good black and white which is toned in sepia. The other is a drawing by Gauguin done in brownish-red of a devil man and a naked woman in a bed.[978] Most people have never seen it or heard of it. (But this is Arkansas, you know.)

Some make-up dummy copies of *The Battlefield Where the Moon Says I Love You*, all 550 pages, should be done by the 20th of this month, the day Mitchell goes to prison. Finally, John Mitchell is going to the slammer.[979] The book is not being printed by us and is delayed and probably won't have much quality printing to it. The cover is interesting. The release date is Dec 31 77. I doubt if I'll send it out to see if anyone wants to publish any of it. None of it has been so far.[980]

Why don't you send me some poems. Are you in SF? Have a good summer,

your friend
FRANK

{Flash! Ginny will be in San Francisco 1st of July, will you be there? What is your address?}[981]

Notes

971. *Ironwood* 5, no. 1, issue 9 (Spring 1977)—which, Cuddihy wrote in *Try Ironwood*, was published in April—featured seven Stanford poems ("Taking Your Life," "Amaranth,"

"A Woman Driving a Stake into the Ground at Midnight," "Strange Roads Before Light," "Only One Set in the Singer's Eyes," "The Angel of Death," and "Death and the Arkansas River"), as well as work by Wright, Oppen, Stafford, et al.

972. *Barataria Review*'s last two issues (published as *Barataria*): issue 3 (Spring–Summer 1977) and issue 4 (Fall 1977)—both edited by Adamo (poetry editor), Louis Gallo (fiction editor), and Gilchrist and Everette Maddox (associate editors).

973. Jess Henderson, who was charged with a heroin-related crime in 1974.

974. PEN International, a global association of writers, runs the Writers in Prison Committee.

975. *Fifty Contemporary Poets: The Creative Process* (1977), ed. Alberta T. Turner—a founding editor of *FIELD* and, for many years, an associate editor there. The anthology published Stanford's poem "Death and the Arkansas River" and his essay "With the Approach of the Oak the Axeman Quakes."

976. The essay's published version omits no text from the ca. fall 1975 typescript draft in Stanford's papers, which includes his discussion of filming *It Wasn't a Dream: It Was a Flood*'s waterside scene.

977. *Marginalia: left side, upright.*

978. Presumably *Tahitian Woman with Evil Spirit* (ca. 1900), an oil-transfer drawing by Paul Gauguin.

979. John N. Mitchell (1913–88), sixty-seventh US attorney general (1969–72) and Watergate conspirator as chairman of Nixon's 1972 presidential campaign. Mitchell's prison sentence actually began on June 22, 1977.

980. Several poets in Stanford's circle saw copies of *The Battlefield* prior to his death; some limited number of "dummy" copies were finished and bound in 1977, but the book is effectively a posthumous publication. C.D. Wright later wrote that the copies of *The Battlefield*'s first edition, which had been printed by Overstreet Printing in Bentonville (with some, if not all, copies printed as early as May or June 1977), were bound after Stanford's death in Tulsa, Oklahoma ("At the time of Frank Stanford's death, in 1978, the poem was printed but not bound"), and Willett noted to this editor that he drove to Tulsa after Frank's death, in late 1978's warmer months, to pick up a large number of copies (hundreds, at least). Wright, preface to Stanford, *Battlefield*, 2nd ed., n.p.; Bill Willett, texts to editor, September 25, 2023. The binder appears to have been Robert T. Motter Jr.; see Stanford's September 20, 1976, letter to Motter above. The exact print run of *The Battlefield* is slightly unclear; a January 31, 1978, Lost Roads letter (housed in the Ginny Crouch Stanford Collection of Frank Stanford, Yale Collection of American Literature, Beinecke Rare Book & Manuscript Library) signed by Deborah Nolan (now Luster; photographer, b. 1951, who worked for Lost Roads) but likely written by Stanford states that the "proposed" print run for *The Battlefield* was "more or less" one thousand copies, but in a February 18, 2008, email

to this editor, Wright noted that *The Battlefield*'s first-edition print run was fifteen hundred copies, more than five hundred copies of which "were destroyed in a flood in the basement of The Grapevine . . . in Fayetteville, Arkansas, where I had left them in storage when I moved to San Francisco. Even so it took 20 years to sell the first edition out." See note 1056 below as well.

981. *Marginalia: left side, left facing.*

To Louis Gallo: June 20, 1977

6/20/77

WHITE RIVER PRINTERS
705 Jackson Drive
Fayetteville, Arkansas 72701

Re: *Barataria* #4

Dear Louis,

Have rec'd. typescripts, should be out of typesetting in a week. Please send rest of *Barataria* #4 and check in the amount of $796.00 right way. We need the money to get the ball rolling on typesetting and paper, etc. We need the rest of the *stories* (other matter can wait) to get to the typesetters.[982] Keep it all flying.

Yours,
Frank

PS Ralph, can you fly me a color copy of what you want on the cover pronto. Other copy got left in N.O. Also, name of artist.[983] Louis, can you send along cover you want for #4, name of artist?[984] Please comply.

Notes

982. *Barataria*, no. 4 (Fall 1977), was a fiction issue for the magazine (Gallo was fiction editor).

983. *Barataria*, no. 3 (Spring–Summer 1977), was a poetry issue (Adamo was poetry editor); the issue's cover was a painting by John Moisant.

984. The cover of *Barataria*, no. 4, was Bernard Zalon's pen and ink drawing *Subway*.

To John McKernan: Late Summer or Early Fall 1977

Frank Stanford

Arkansas Land Surveyors
PO Box 1303 Rogers, Arkansas 72756

White River Printers
705 Jackson Drive Fayetteville, Arkansas 72701

Lost Roads Publishers
PO Box 210 Fayetteville, Arkansas 72701

Wife & Farm
Route 1 Box 108 A Liberal, Missouri 64762

Dear John,

Some people claim to have troubles getting in touch with me, so here. You tell Tom Lux to write me a goddamn letter. Sounds like there is a pretty good poker game up there, a lot of good hands.

Very pleased you liked books, sorry I didn't send galleys of #4 & #6.[985] Making covers, and then to binders. Your cover by a man here who was with Minor White at *Aperture*;[986] cover for Bean Street (John S. Morris) by student of above;[987] cover for Irv Broughton's The Blessing Of The Fleet by Ginny.[988]

Yes, I am having to stay in the woods most of the time to stay at the layout table and in the darkroom. Don't worry, Mike Cuddihy is publishing a new book of poetry, Crib Death, this fall.[989] Ginny stayed with Mike & Mary in San Francisco this summer. Been off liquor and meat for a good while now so health is good, brain full of little Roland Kirk tadpoles like the cosmos is stars.[990]

Next year am doing a book by a woman from New Orleans will blow everybody off the road.[991] Been working with her for couple of years. Also, may do three books of photography. Quality of work & equipment getting better and better. Yea, I read about 600 mss. Still keep mostly to myself around here, but do use UofA library and film theatre a lot.

Don't send out poems anymore at all; once to *Field* and *Ironwood* in last 2-½ years. Would say "don't know why" but sounds too much like jazz. Have finished two books: Flour The Dead Man Carries To The Wedding & Last Panther In The Ozarks.[992]

Another magazine I like is *Ark River Review*.[993]

Yes, hope the NEA gives L.R. a grant.[994]

Tell everyone hello. Sending out permission requests to reprint to editors this month, taking care of contracts, etc. Will hold publication dates up until poems have appeared in magazines, so no one gets a wild card.

Frank

J.

Enclosed you will find an unbound galley & cover of #7–12 by Frank Stanford.[995] You may be wondering why it is called a Mill Mountain Book, etc. Well, MM published my other ten books in limited editions and also got a grant from NEA to publish this one.[996] As it turns out, they didn't get enough money. It was printed somewhere else and just sitting in boxes getting wet so I tended to it. Tom Lux knows all about this book. It won't be released until 1978 sometime. I know some ~~poem~~ won't like the idea of white paper and reduced typewriter, was my idea. For that matter, there are many who aren't going to like the poem. But so far, everyone is coming out shaking my hand. If you think anyone might be interested, let them have a look-see.

F.

Notes

985. Morris's *Bean Street* (Lost Roads No. 4) and Broughton's *The Blessing of the Fleet* (Lost Roads No. 6).
986. *Aperture*, photography magazine. Richard Albertine (1944–2016) is the photographer of the photograph appearing on the cover of McKernan's *Walking Along the Missouri River*; photographer Minor White (1908–76) is pictured in the photo.
987. Richard Leo Johnson (b. 1955), a student of Albertine's, is the photographer of the photograph appearing on the cover of *Bean Street.*
988. The cover of *The Blessing of the Fleet* (credited to Ginny Crouch Stanford) was the engraving *St. Brendan Holding Mass on the Back of a Whale* from the book *Nova Typis Transacta Navigatio, Novi Orbis Indiæ Occidentalis* (1621) by Honorius Philoponus (pseudonym of Caspar Plautius, Benedictine abbot).
989. Stanford's book *Crib Death* (Ironwood Press, 1978).
990. Rahsaan Roland Kirk (1935–77), jazz instrumentalist.
991. Gilchrist's *The Land Surveyor's Daughter* (1979).
992. *Flour the Dead Man Brings to the Wedding* and *The Last Panther in the Ozarks*, small-scale works (each with fewer than eighteen poems, most of them brief) published posthumously in *What About This* (pp. 509–31 and 489–504, respectively).
993. *The Ark River Review*, a magazine edited by Jonathan Katz, A. G. Sobin, and (through vol. 3, no. 1) Arthur Vogelsang; the magazine published Stanford's poems

"In Plain View" and "Pasture Dream" in vol. 3, no. 1, in 1974 and "Soaking Wet" and "The Unbelievable Nightgown" in vol. 3, nos. 2/3, in 1976.

994. *L.R.*: Lost Roads.

995. *The Battlefield*.

996. Prior to *The Battlefield*, Mill Mountain Press had published six (not "ten") of Stanford's books; if including the phantom titles listed in *Constant Stranger*'s front matter, he would have published nine books through *Constant Stranger* (or ten through *The Battlefield*). See note 898 above.

To Ralph Adamo: October 31, 1977

Oct 31, 1977

Ralph,
Your book came out today![997]

Frank

Notes

997. Lost Roads Nos. 1–6 were prepared in 1977, with 1977 copyrights and some copies released, but like *The Battlefield*, the books were not officially published until 1978; see Stanford's February 15, 1978, letter to Karl Elder below, par. 4.

To Ellen Gilchrist, Ralph Adamo, Louis Gallo, and Everette Maddox: November 1, 1977

11/1/77

WHITE RIVER PRINTERS
705 Jackson Drive
Fayetteville, Arkansas 72701

Re: Barataria #3 & Barataria #4

Dear Editors,[998]

You should have received both issues of your magazine by now. Ralph Adamo asked us to keep some here for us to distribute. He is also mailing some out from here.[999]

I apologize for being behind schedule. We should have had #3 ready by the 1st of September and #4 ready by the 1st of October. Things developed both here and New Orleans which caused this delay.

A bill for services rendered and an accounting of payments received is enclosed.[1000]

Thank You,
WHITE RIVER PRINTERS

Notes

998. Though mailed to Gilchrist in New Orleans, this letter and its enclosed statement are technically to the four editors of *Barataria* issues 3 and 4; see note 972 above.
999. Adamo noted to this editor that he often visited Fayetteville in the late 1970s but that Stanford presumably means here that Adamo had asked him and/or Wright to mail out some copies of *Barataria* from Fayetteville on his behalf. Direct message to editor, October 18, 2023.
1000. The enclosed sheet notes that, for issues 3 and 4, $2,490 had been received against $3,160 billed (including shipping), leaving a remaining balance due to White River Printers of $670.

To Michael Cuddihy: November 21, 1977

11/21/77

Route 1 Box 108-A
Liberal, Missouri 64762

Dear Mike & Mary,

I am sorry I got hold of you at what seems to be the wrong time. You know, I certainly didn't intend for you to feel that I was pulling the rug out. My intentions were good.

Please find enclosed all the poems you originally wanted + all the poems that were going to be in *You*.[1001] When you find variations in titles or lines, you make your choice. I feel as if I have encroached on your territory. In your letter of this time, more or less, last year you say, "If it's not too late, I'd be willing, eager even to do a book of these poems, provided I could have some say about which ones were left out." (You add a compliment which I won't repeat here.) "Possibly forty-eight pages perfect-bound." In going over your offer again, I see where I have gone off course. I apologize.[1002]

Also included is "Death And The Arkansas River" + some others.[1003]

About my idea for "Notes" at the back, please let me know if you want to kill this?[1004]

The above + the fact you didn't like my new poems that much was a let down, but that is the risk we all have to take. I am very glad to hear you don't beat around the bush.

Could you tell me what "8vo" means at it appears on your bookmarks for forthcoming books?[1005]

I understand that it will take you some time to decide which poems will be in the book, and if you want any for the magazine. I await your choice.

I will be thinking about you, and especially Mary when she has to go to the hospital.

Yours,
Frank

Notes

1001. *You*, Lost Roads No. 15 (1979), a posthumously published book of Stanford's.

1002. The letter from Cuddihy to which Stanford is referring here appears to be missing or lost, but in *Try Ironwood*, Cuddihy notes that he proposed to Stanford in late 1976 that the poems Stanford had sent to him that October—which had "moved" and "worried" him (as he told Stanford), making him "instantly apprehensive"—form the basis of the book that became *Crib Death*. *Try Ironwood*, 75, 88. See also notes 938 and 939 above.

1003. Stanford's poem "Death and the Arkansas River," first published in *Constant Stranger*, was republished in *Crib Death*.

1004. No notes appear in *Crib Death*.

1005. *8vo*: octavo, a term used for books smaller than folios or quartos in which each page consists of an eighth of the original printed sheet.

To Alan Dugan: Circa Late 1977

[On Lost Roads Publishers letterhead.][1006]

Dear Alan,

Never hear from you anymore? How is everything going? Here is what I've been doing with most of my money and time the last three years. I still have the surveying company, which made a publishing company, which made a printing company. I am still poet company, but never in company with poets.

I will tell you more about everything if I hear from you.

I tried to get *Sequence* from that Greek, I'll write again.[1007]

All ten books are OUP.[1008] Ironwood is going to publish a book in a year or two called *Crib Death*. Sent a ms. to Simpson at Walt Whitman.[1009] The publication date on these books is Spring, 1978, so no rules broken.[1010]

I would appreciate a line or two, maybe another dead fly; I still have one you sent me.[1011]

Yours,
Frank Stanford

Notes

1006. This is the first letter herein on Lost Roads Publishers' later letterhead (sans "A Magazine in Book Issue"), which Stanford had begun using earlier in fall 1977.

1007. Dugan's *Sequence*; see note 826 above.

1008. Stanford means "OOP" (out of print) here, though he had published only six books as of this letter; see note 996 above. A January 1, 1978, Lost Roads letter (signed by Nolan but likely written by Stanford) claims that Stanford's "ten" Mill Mountain Press chapbooks "are now all out of print."

1009. Louis Simpson judged the Walt Whitman Award in 1978, selecting *Wonders* (1980) by Karen Snow.

1010. Stanford appears to have enclosed Lost Roads Nos. 1–12 with this letter (see note 922 above); see, e.g., Stanford's February 15, 1978, letter to Elder below, par. 4. The Walt Whitman Award is for a poet's first book (excluding previously published chapbooks);

Stanford apparently means here that his 1977 submission to the Walt Whitman Award preceded *The Battlefield*'s official publication (in 1978, though its copyright was 1977; see note 997 above).

1011. See note 647 above.

To Leonard Randolph: December 15, 1977

[On Lost Roads Publishers letterhead.]

December 15, 1977

Director
Literature Program
National Endowment
For The Arts
Washington, D.C. 20506

Dear Director:

Ten months ago I applied for a grant proposal for small presses to publish six books of poetry. I wrote several letters to your organization requesting some information, but had no word. Four months ago I sent a registered letter, but still heard nothing.[1012]

Of course, I know from others who got grants and who didn't, but could you send me the list, and also a formal notice of rejection. My application number was A11961-77.[1013]

On another note, I never received a formal rejection for my individual grant application. Could you send me one of those lists? My application number was A10806-77.

By the way, I'm enclosing the six books I sought assistance for. I have several things planned for next year and I hope you will keep me posted on the next set of deadlines. As with the first six books, I plan to publish poetry, photography, and so on with or without your assistance, but it would be very helpful if someone up there would answer my letters.

Yours very respectively,[1014]
Frank Stanford

FS:dn[1015]
Enc

Notes

1012. Stanford is referring to his August 15, 1977, letter (with accounting sheet) to Randolph.
1013. Following this letter, Philip H. Robins of the NEA spoke by phone with Stanford and, in a December 28 follow-up letter (which Stanford appears not to have received until ca. late January 1978), apologized for delays. Robins enclosed two letters from Randolph: a small-press rejection letter with the date August 16, 1977, stamped above a prior date of May 20 and an undated rejection letter re: Stanford's application for an individual NEA fellowship, for which the NEA had received 1,627 applications in poetry.
1014. As opposed to "respectfully." Wright closed her August 12, 1978, letter to Robins the same way, preceding the closing with "As Frank signed his letters, and couldn't be convinced to do otherwise." The complimentary closes of the January 1, 1978, and January 31, 1978, Lost Roads letters signed by Deborah Nolan (see notes 980 and 1008 above) both use "respectively" as well.
1015. I.e., Frank Stanford:Deborah Nolan.

To Philip H. Robins: February 1, 1978

[On Lost Roads Publishers letterhead.]

February 1, 1978

Philip H. Robins
Literature Program Specialist
National Endowment For The Arts
Washington, D.C. 20506

Dear Philip H. Robins:

Thank you for your call and promise of forthcoming letter concerning grant proposal. As you can see though, it is a full month before I received it?[1016] Anyway, I have everything ready to go. My bookkeeper and lawyer have been going over my budget as they are preparing an IRS proposal for a non-profit status for me.

I suppose it is already too late, but I'm enclosing everything anyway. I did appreciate your kind letter and explanation, and thanks for the help.

You will find in one envelope my 1978 Application, and in two more envelopes six copies each of two of the 12 numbers we published. In another envelope you will find all my 1977 Application correspondence and figures, as futile as it was. Also, you should have all 12 numbers we published on file.

Please contact me at the above address or by phone 501-442-4152; if you get my answering service, I'll call back with the phone trick you mentioned.[1017]

I hope you will stay in touch with me about any developments.[1018]

Yours, very respectively,
Frank Stanford

FS:dn
Enc

Notes

1016. See note 1013 above.

1017. In his December 28, 1977, letter to Stanford, Robins wrote, "If you have questions while filling out the forms, call me, person to person collect. . . . We will refuse the call, take your number, and call back. Okay?"

1018. On June 6, 1978, Robins wrote, "Dear Frank: I have tried and tried to get in touch with you—with no success. Either your answering service has not passed the messages on or you don't want to talk to us . . whatever, now the future of your grant is *entirely in your hands*" (ellipsis in original). Robins went on to state that he couldn't let Stanford know "the *final* results" of the review process for his application but that some technical budget calculation issues with the application needed to be "ironed out" by Stanford "*immediately*," noting that "the timing factor is quite serious now"; Robins closed, "Please call. Please. We think highly enough of you to recommend funding at your requested level. But you must get in touch. Call." Robins's letter was written and arrived too late, though, as Stanford had died on June 3.

After Stanford's death, further discussion occurred between Wright and Robins, including the August 12, 1978, letter to Robins, in which Wright wrote, "I read over Frank's correspondence with the NEA over the past two years. Sad. He earned this grant. He didn't have to die for it. . . . We are doing the work he was committed to. Even in his will he expressed concern for the status of his grant. . . . We are desperate, friend. And determined." On August 21, 1978, Stanford's grant of $7,850 was posthumously awarded toward Lost Roads' 1979 publications of Wright's *Terrorism* (No. 13), Gilchrist's *The Land Surveyor's Daughter* (No. 14), Stanford's *You* (No. 15), Justin Caldwell's *The Sleeping Porch* (No. 16), Adamo's *The End of the World* (No. 17)—which replaced Cuddihy's *Bark*, as he withdrew his manuscript after Stanford died—and the second edition of Stanford's *The Singing Knives* (No. 18).

To Ellen Gilchrist: February 1, 1978

[On Lost Roads Publishers letterhead.]

February 1, 1978

Ellen Gilchrist
1563 Webster
New Orleans, Louisiana 70118

Dear Ellen:

This is to let you know I have been taking care of the hell and highwater ambient to love, love, and work.[1019] Many thoughts as to the title of your book. Still like the moon moving always eastward through the stars or some such but not so much the sea anchor anymore. Have gone over my dictionaries but can't find illustration. Some new ideas though. Now, pursuant to a dream lecture in my sleep by JCL,[1020] after reading of his lecture at the strange movies, I looked up the word anchorite, thence ♀ anchoress, thus to find anchor light, and so on to your available light, then again back to CJL feelings about light, then into metaphorical adventures of tombs as anchors of light then to the light anchors or the light anchor. Tell me what you think.[1021]

You will now notice that I have left out the word life and put love in twice in my flood control.

We are doing some work on the singing knives. If we can get some warm weather to operate press will have something before long.

I will be sending you info on CCLM and ISSN.[1022] You should be aware that the best set-up for funding is a magazine 2 or 3 times a year, which also publishes books or chapbooks or pamphlets 2 or 3 times a year. But to cut down on the cost and time a magazine done twice a year with the third yearly issue being a book, etc. would also qualify. You would still be eligible for NEA and CCLM funds. Your editors should be working on this.[1023]

I have been having CJL appear in my dreams lately, sometimes as a priest, sometimes as a blind man with peacocks, sometimes as a ventriloquist. Now ginny wants to paint him as such......

Can you find out from him what the name of that photograph was about the burned room, charred beam on mantle, spectre, dead room, night of living dead, don't look now, saw it at Freeman A.[1024]

LOVE,
F...

Notes

1019. A variation on (or possibly a mistyping of) the phrase "life, love, and work." If typed intentionally, Stanford appears to be alluding to his double life between Ginny and C. D. (See par. 2.)

1020. Correctly: CJL—Clarence John Laughlin (1905–85), New Orleans–based American surrealist photographer.

1021. Per Stanford's February 1978 NEA grant application and a February 25, 1978, letter from Gilchrist to Laughlin, *The Light Anchor* was an early title, and "definitely" (per Gilchrist) the one she wanted (at least at that time), for the Lost Roads book that became *The Land Surveyor's Daughter* (1979).

1022. Coordinating Council of Literary Magazines (CCLM) and International Standard Serial Number (ISSN).

1023. Stanford is seemingly referring to Gilchrist's coeditors for issues 3 and 4 of *Barataria*; see note 972 above.

1024. *Spectre in a Dead Room* (1953), photograph by Laughlin—exhibited at a 1976 show at the Freeman-Anacker Gallery on Decatur Street in New Orleans.

To Karl Elder: February 15, 1978

[On Lost Roads Publishers letterhead.]

February 15, 1978

Karl Elder
Seems
Department of English
Southwest Missouri State University
Springfield, Missouri 65802

Dear Karl Elder:

You're getting pretty close up there in Springfield; don't know if our paths will ever cross, hope so. I got the copy of *Seems #9.*[1025] So far, just digging on the fiction, as I'm snowed under with all kinds of work right now.[1026]

Maybe we can catch each other this Spring. I'm hoping to get a jazz group out of Memphis and thereabouts down here to help bring out Lost Roads Number 13, *Terrorism* by C. D. Wright.[1027] Maybe you saw some of Carolyn's work in *Field* or *Ironwood*?[1028]

Can you help me out on something? Trying to find out the publisher of V. H. Cruz's *Mainland*?[1029] Would like to get a copy somewhere.

I'm enclosing Lost Roads Numbers 1 through 12. The publication date on Numbers 1 through 6 is April 1, 1978.[1030] The publication date on 7 through 12 has not been set.[1031] A review of the books would help if you can get into it. By the way, John Stoss is from Kansas.[1032]

Carolyn Wright is going to be in Springfield somewhere between the 22nd and the 24th of the month to catch something called "Open Eye Theatre", so maybe she'll try in [*sic*] get in touch with you.

Let's stay in touch.

Yours,
Frank Stanford

Notes

1025. *Seems*, a literary magazine for which Elder (b. 1948) was poetry editor. *Seems*, no. 9 (1978), published Stanford's poem "Living the Good Life" (*Crib Death*). Elder had apparently solicited Stanford for a submission ca. early 1975. Stanford replied, "It is always a fair feeling, indeed, for an unknown poet like me, in these parts, to get such a request." Elder replied, on October 3, 1975, that the poem would appear in issue 9, which was still several issues out.
1026. *Seems*, no. 9, published fiction by Sharyn Jeanne Skeeter and Gordon Mennenga.
1027. Presumably, the George Caldwell Sextet (sometimes Quintet), a jazz group from Memphis that performed at Stanford's wake on June 10, 1978.
1028. Both Stanford and C. D. Wright published work in *Ironwood* 9 (Spring 1977).
1029. *Mainland* (Random House, 1973), a book of poems by Victor Hernández Cruz (b. 1949).
1030. See note 997 above.
1031. *7 through 12*: *The Battlefield*.
1032. Stoss was born in Great Bend, Kansas, and attended Fort Hays State University; Elder received an MFA from Wichita State University in 1977.

LOST ROADS PUBLISHERS

PO BOX 210 • FAYETTEVILLE, ARKANSAS 72701

February 15, 1978

Karl Elder
SEEMS
Department of English
Southwest Missouri State University
Springfield, Missouri 65802

Dear Karl Elder:

You're getting pretty close up there in Springfield; don't know if our paths will ever cross, hope so. I got the copy of SEEMS #9. So far, just digging on the fiction, as I'm snowed under with all kinds of work right now.

Maybe we can catch each other this Spring. I'm hoping to get a jazz group out of Memphis and thereabouts down here to help bring out Lost Roads Number 13, TERRORISM by C.D. Wright. Maybe you saw some of Carolyn's work in FIELD or IRONWOOD?

Can you help me out on something? Trying to find out the publisher of V.H. Cruz's MAINLAND? Would like to get a copy somewhere.

I'm enclosing Lost Roads Numbers 1 through 12. The publication date on Numbers 1 through 6 is April 1, 1978. The publication date on 7 through 12 has not been set. A review of the books would help if you can get into it. By the way, John Stoss is from Kansas.

Carolyn Wright is going to be in Springfield somewhere between the 22nd and the 24th of the month to catch something called "Open Eye Theatre", so maybe she'll try in get in touch with you.

Let's stay in touch.

Yours,

Frank Stanford

Stanford's February 15, 1978, letter—on later Lost Roads letterhead—to Karl Elder, poetry editor of *Seems*. Beginning in 1978, Elder became the journal's editor and publisher.

To Ralph Adamo: February 20, 1978

[On Lost Roads Publishers letterhead.]

Dear Ralph,

Everything going far into the clear and naked and shining and fast breathing snow.

Really, I'm having a good time. Just working and listening to jazz, enjoying the house by myself. Many women and rivers to cross but staying dry. Saw two great movies: *The Mother and the Whore* & *The Harder They Come.*[1033]

Ironwood going to press soon with my book, out early fall. It is my best but I think he has decided to keep it around 48 pages.[1034] He was going to make it about 60 with some very new work. He is doing another book, too, besides Orlen's and mine, Michael Burkhart.[1035] The poet is very good, ask J. Biguneut.[1036]

I have finished another book. It is like a B&W movie made by a new director, except it is printed instead of filmed.

Carolyn's *Terrorism* is very good, the best so far.[1037]

Caldwell's book knocked over Cuddihy.[1038]

Almost finished selecting what I want from Ellen's.[1039] Hope she is writing some good new work, original, not just writing, but good poems.

I lose sleep over Stoss. After the new poetry, plays, stories, novel, autobiography, even if I didn't have to run into him all the time and work with him, have come to the sad but honest conclusion that he can't write, that he is inept. I intend to call my notes on his work *The Man Who Doesn't Bleed.* The legend about Stoss is no longer romantic, it is sad. I've decided to spend some time to edit his work, and to see if he can take it from there. But this will be difficult at his age.[1040] What an incredible and rare creature Stoss is! The work now though is not wild and strange from youth it is awkward and manic from frustration. He is such a child. But his is not Zorba.[1041] Zorba was not pure, or was he high minded.[1042]

When I told John C. D. had *Machines* and was trying to get it into shape so I could at least get some shape out of it he got furious.[1043] Now he has calmed down. Everyone has contributed to Stoss's legend, but no one has taught him how to write. I know I can't teach him. He's catching on though.

Are you getting any response from poets I got to look you and *Barataria* up? Hope so.

How are you for doing some short reviews of a couple of poetry series? Not of LR, two other poetry series?[1044]

I can pay you a little. I don't mean a hit-man cut-down review, just a few words, citing a couple of poems, and some intelligent remarks?

I have 5 books from Cleveland State Poetry Center Poetry Series. And four books from Ironwood Chapbook Series. I am interested in that free space as yet untravelled between prose poem and essay—as far as good comment goes. Let me hear. For a long time only shit hooks and political powers were doing essays and reviews—now young poets are. You could do it Ralph.

When is Ellen going to send me the reviews of the LR books? She promised. From here south 20 people have said they wanted to review them, but Bignet will probably be the only one to come through.[1045] I'm not worried about West, Midwest, or the East. You wouldn't believe how good McKernan is in helping us all out. Sold 100 books in a month, and got 25 bookstore orders because of him since 1st of year. I still plan to hit new york, he plans to take boston. If my friend Thomas Lux would respond, he is a boston dude. I want the books out of print April 1, 1979.[1046] And I want 24 small press reviews. I'm not shitting. I'm hoping I can get somebody from here that's going to that AWP thing in San Francisco to do some distribution there.[1047]

Keep in touch about what is happening—any good music or folks coming up down there. Send me copies of the courir and figerour?[1048]

Well, maybe 1980 and 12 reviews.

frank

2/20/78

Ralph,

My records indicate that you should have received to date a total of 75 copies of *Sadness at the Private University*, 50 copies of *Finding the Broom*, and 50 copies of *Room Rented by a Single Woman*.[1049] A shipment of books got there about a week before I did also—via Ellen. I have to have an accounting right away. If this is or is not correct, please notify me at once, certainly no later than 3/1/78, or it will hold up my non-profit status application.

I have shipped today 25 copies each of Numbers 1 through 6, and also an additional 50 copies of *Sadness at the Private University*.

All copies shipped so far should be regarded as *for sale* copies and accountable. I am sending out 100 copies of each book with press releases. Of course you will eventually receive 100 copies free of your own book, but let's sell a few first and not give them away.

Everyone is getting this kind of letter and should be getting a more detailed letter by the 1st of the month.[1050] Am getting a non-profit status and must supply records.

Watch the mail or bus.

Frank

Been working 3 weeks in a row on L.R. distribution. Check with Ellen about # books rec'd and where they are, where they went, bookstores, friends, review copies, out of hand sales, ###'s.

You have to send me those labels (100) or your book is not going out.

Notes

1033. *La maman et la putain* (*The Mother and the Whore*) (1973), dir. Jean Eustache, and *The Harder They Come* (1972), dir. Perry Henzell.
1034. *Crib Death* is fifty-five pages; the poetry runs from pp. 7–50.
1035. Steven Orlen (1942–2010), whose book of poems *Separate Creatures* (1976) Cuddihy had published, and Michael Burkard (1947–2024), whose book of poems *None, River* Cuddihy published in 1979.
1036. John Biguenet, poet/dramatist.
1037. Wright's *Terrorism* (1979).
1038. Caldwell's *The Sleeping Porch* (1979).
1039. Gilchrist's *The Land Surveyor's Daughter* (1979).
1040. Stoss was thirty-seven years old as of this letter.
1041. Stanford may have meant to type "he is not Zorba" here.
1042. See note 755 above.
1043. *Machines Always Existed* (1984), a novel by Stoss.
1044. *LR*: Lost Roads.
1045. *Bignet*: correctly, Biguenet—i.e., John Biguenet.
1046. Viz., within one year of publication.
1047. The 1978 Associated Writing Programs (AWP) "Annual Meeting" was held in San Francisco from March 9 through 11. University of Arkansas MFA faculty William Harrison and John Clellon Holmes (1926–88) attended as panel members; Whitehead was AWP's president in 1978.
1048. The *Vieux Carré Courier* and *Figaro*, free New Orleans weeklies; Gilchrist was a contributing editor of the *Courier* in the late 1970s.
1049. Adamo's, Stoss's, and Wright's books.
1050. Stanford sent versions of this February 20, 1978, accounting note to the other Lost Roads poets as well; the number of copies of their books that they had respectively received varied, according to the letters.

To Michael Cuddihy: March 20, 1978

[On Lost Roads Publishers notepad letterhead.]

March 20, 1978

Mike

I've read your ms. and I like it.[1051] Right now it would be unfair for me to go into what I do and don't like about it because of unbelievable lack of time I have. Trying to beat the Spring leaves on many jobs so I won't have to work my ass off come full bloom. I intend to go over everything in detail, soon.

I can see my way into 18 poems at the moment, but I am more interested in coming up with either 24 or 30 for a book. So, we are already talking in terms of a book. I am very impressed by the new poem after Gerald Stern, "Loyalties".[1052] You take a different turn with this poem. I like it, and maybe you will write some new poems with this kind of digging in. From time to time I will be writing you notes and I hope you will be sending me new poems. I just need to decide on using two more poems before I can say I accept very much this ms. I was in the opinion to take them from the 36 but getting the new one changed my mind. Also, haven't I seen in print or in the mail from you other poems you did not send?

Now about me. I hope you can decide on 24 or 30 poems. I am on some new things if you can't find 30 you like.[1053] Thanks for taking those two poems and for the check. I am will[ing] to revise *Terrorism* and cut all but the first line in the title to *Memory Is Like A Shotgun. . . .*[1054] Thanks for letting me know what you will be using, and what you are thinking about. You never can tell, I may get hot just before the gun and send you ten new poems!

Frank

Notes

1051. Stanford is presumably referring to Cuddihy's manuscript *Bark*, which, at the time of Stanford's death, was slated to be published by Lost Roads; Cuddihy withdrew the manuscript shortly thereafter.

1052. "Loyalties" was published in Cuddihy's pamphlet *Celebrations* (1980).

1053. *Crib Death* contains thirty poems.

1054. In a ca. early 1978 letter to Stanford, Cuddihy noted that he was accepting Stanford's poems "The Light the Dead See" and "A Milk Truck Running into a Crazy Maid at the Corner of Getwell and Park"—which would be published in *Ironwood* 6, no. 2, issue 12 (Fall 1978)—and asked Stanford to revise "Terrorism" and the title of "Memory Is Like a Shotgun Kicking You near the Heart" (because of its content/meaning) for *Crib Death*; the former two poems indeed appeared (along with "In This House" and "The Boy Who Shot Weathercocks") in *Ironwood* 12, and all four poems appeared in *Crib Death*, with the title of "Memory Is Like a Shotgun Kicking You near the Heart" unedited.

To Dorothy Stanford and Carolyn Gilbert: April 16, 1978

[On Lost Roads Publishers letterhead.]

Sunday 6:00 PM 4/16/78

Dear Mother & Gran-Gran,

I know it made you feel bad when Ginny and I didn't come down St. Patrick's Day for the birthday.[1055] I had to go to Oklahoma on that Sunday.[1056] We were both planning to come. I've just been snowed under. I've had to stay away from the Farm a lot because of everything I do, and that hasn't set too well with Ginny. I certainly don't blame her. We see each other every week there and sometimes she comes here, but ever since Christmas or so I haven't been really living there as I did.[1057]

I just returned from the Farm and I hope Ginny will come here this week to see me. I hope you don't think there is anything very wrong with us, because there isn't. We still love each other, have been together five years, and plan to go on being together forever. We aren't getting a divorce or anything like that. We just both have to get together and figure out how and where we are going to live given our respective jobs and concerns. We can't afford to have a place here and I can't afford not to do my kind of work. And we can't afford not to take advantage of the farm.

The main problem is all the time it takes. Ginny and I have both talked about this a lot. As you know my surveying company is here and so is my publishing and printing companies. We can't do this all at once, but what we plan to do is move at least two of these concerns to the Farm. We would have to re-model an outbuilding. Ginny would also use the building for a natural light studio. The other thing I can do to average out my time better is purchase expensive distance measuring equipment (Electronic Infra-Red), which I have already done last month with my partner. It is very expensive on the lease-purchase plan, but we share the cost.[1058] The best thing about it is that eventually it will enable me to save a great deal of time and also hired labor expense. I also got a mini-computer the same way. So, practically speaking, I will be able to work out of the mire of work, etc. Also, managing Ginny's art career takes a great deal of planning and time. I know I am doing too many things at once now, but I hope to ease up. We are both in good health, mind and body.

The only reason in the world we haven't been down is that I am so busy, and she doesn't want to make the trip alone. But because of work I've been neglecting the ones I love too long, you, Gran-Gran, and Ginny.

We both have bright futures, though the present is a little dark here and there. I hope you both will keep one strong feeling I have in mind: that is this, Ginny and I, unlike a lot of other artists, don't plan to base our personal successes by hurting others. Neither one of us go along with the myth you have to hurt the ones you love.

I really do plan to get there, even for a day, as soon as I can. As I say, Ginny would probably feel a little uneasy being there by herself, and I think she would come with me if she thought you all wouldn't all be upset. Please don't be upset.

If there was something seriously wrong, you would be the first to know.

Please tell Father Herbert and Nick we both said hello and love and to not worry about anything.[1059] If I was worrying, I'd be right down there on your doorstep with my tail tucked under.

Finally some good weather, but hate to see the leaves, ticks, and chiggers back in force, not to mention the snakes.

Much work to do here, soon some of it done, I'll be down. Nobody worry about anything.

I love you, Frank.

Notes

1055. I.e., down to Subiaco. On Saint Patrick's Day (March 17, 1978), Carolyn Gilbert turned ninety years old.

1056. Why Stanford traveled to Oklahoma is not clear, but Don Kemp was licensed to survey in Oklahoma (in addition to Arkansas and Missouri), and Stanford sometimes worked weekends; see Stanford's November 9, 1976, letter to Cuddihy above, par. 12. Otherwise, Stanford's trip could have been bookbinding related, as the vast majority of copies of *The Battlefield*'s first edition were, in the first half of 1978, not yet bound; see note 980 above.

1057. By "here," Stanford means Fayetteville. By "there," he means the farm belonging to Ginny's parents in Missouri, where Frank and Ginny moved in fall 1976; see Stanford's November 9, 1976, letter to Cuddihy above.

1058. In Stanford's will, dated May 22, 1978, he writes, "I give [Don] my share of new equipment, based on the rare breaks he gave me. I was able to write, support other artists, and make a living. Thank you, Don."

1059. Fr. Herbert Vogelpohl and Fr. Nicholas Fuhrmann of Subiaco Abbey.

To Dorothy Stanford: May 12, 1978

[On Lost Roads Publishers letterhead.]

Friday 3:00 PM 5/12/78

Dear Mother,

Here is a note I mailed you a long time ago. Ginny said you never got it; maybe it was because I didn't have a Zip on it? Anyway, I'm glad I made a carbon. I'm just used to making carbons on everything for surveying and writing.

Ginny says Gran-Gran isn't there and that you aren't feeling too well. I was expecting a note or letter from you c/o above or Farm. But since you didn't get my letter I guess you didn't want to write.

This dadgom rain is throwing me off schedule, but I'm still doing OK. We are planning on seeing you Mother's Day the 14th on Sunday, or the day after on Monday? Don't know which yet. I'll call Sunday to let you know when to expect us.

Ginny said you and Ruth and her family are no longer talking.[1060] That just goes on and on. You and I haven't had a real argument in over five years going on six; I think that is pretty good don't you?

Rained me out today, but I was able to get a good half day in the field and when it is like this I can always do office work.

Don't go to any trouble fixing anything big. Just let Ginny make some bread and we'll make something. If you do want to make a dessert, I sure won't stop you.

Speaking of eating, I've been running for several months now. Always run two miles every day, and three and four when I'm feeling good. I like to run early in the morning before work. The other day I got up real early and drank some coffee, then ran. What a mistake! Give everybody my love and we'll see you shortly.

I love you, Frank.

Notes

1060. Stanford's sister, Ruth Rogers. Ruth later noted to this editor that May 12, 1978, was the last day she saw Stanford—at the hospital in Ozark, Arkansas, that evening for the birth of her third daughter, Carrie. Email to editor, December 8, 2008.

Frank Stanford on the evening of June 2, 1978, at the home of Ellen Gilchrist and Fred Kullman in New Orleans. *Photographer: Frederick Kullman.*

VIII.

THE MUSIC OF THE SOUL

New Orleans and Fayetteville, 1978

On May 18, 1978, Stanford traveled to New Orleans, Louisiana, for a little more than two weeks—spending time with poets Ellen Gilchrist, Ralph Adamo, and Kay DuVernet and other friends. The day Stanford left for New Orleans, Ginny Stanford found love letters among his poems. Subsequently, Ginny and C. D. spoke by phone and then in person in Fayetteville, assembling the many fragments of Stanford's accumulated mendacities. They phoned and talked with Stanford in New Orleans, from where he then wrote a lengthy letter to Ginny and C. D., attempting to explain his transgressions.

To Ginny Stanford and C. D. Wright: May 21, 1978

New Orleans
Sunday 5/21/78

Dear Carolyn & Ginny,

Two and a half days here now, and two days since I talked to you both. It is very strange and lonely here. There are no stars in New Orleans. I feel like someone who has finished a nightmare the length of a journey. Rest.

Feeling is coming back to me. I can feel. And I can now say what I feel. I don't have anything to defend or protect anymore. Both of you are gone from my life, I feel. Wherever you are at this minute, whatever you are doing, I am thinking of you, and for the first time in many months I can speak without fear or trembling or hesitation or premeditation.

I remember how I would be lying down after love, with Carolyn asleep, and thinking about you. I remember how Ginny would come and I would want you to be there.

It was so lonely being with one of you and not the other. I wanted to wake up and see both your faces. I wanted to see you close and sleeping and friends. I never thought you would be lovers, I wanted you to be friends.

I would dream about us together, with no children, just poems and paintings and films, changing things for other people in the world. I saw us politically and I saw us personally. I dreamed us in the garden, working, growing things.

One time, after C. and I had come back from a movie, I put the covers in my mouth and said your name.[1061] Once, at the farm, while Ginny was asleep, I was writing; all I could type was your name over and over.

You and you were my desire.

In the beginning things were very simple. I met C. at a gathering of writers. I loved her poetry, not so much for what it was then, but for what it was to become. I fell in love with C. Made love to Ann, her roommate, but thought of C. I began to stay away from home—J. W. Hanes business as a cover, to see C.[1062]

I don't remember when, how many months or years later, that C. asked me if G. knew about her. I can't really remember.

But C. thought G. knew about our love, I told her G. knew. C. was always afraid I would leave her.

G. knew nothing.

Sometimes C. and I would fantasize in our love about G. This went on until one day C. pulled away when we were making love.

As time went on C. would never let me express anything sexual about G. without hurting her feelings or disturbing her. Many times, just before I was to leave Fayetteville, C. would want to make love. I think she was afraid I would make love to G.

I remember how G. cried when she saw the pictures I took of Carolyn.[1063]

I remember how G. would flinch when I spoke of love or loving with another woman.

I contrived that C. was gay and a bitch and that G. was spiritual and celibate. I knew neither of you could accept my love for the other, yet.

I thought, that in your hearts, you knew I was in love with you both and loving you both.

My dream was for all of us. As time went by I saw how impossible it would be for me to live without you both. The more I dreamed my way into your art, the more I needed you both.

I dreamed constantly of the future, always. I had been with G. 2½ years and her work was coming forward. C. needed me the most. G. was stronger than C., more spiritual[ly] akin. I wanted C. to understand this spiritual courage and strength. Through making love and friendship I thought this was going to happen. I thought G. could hold on & accept; I thought C. would ~~come to~~ {change}. I would dream us working in a garden, going somewhere and listening to music, etc. The ideal and our friendship grew further apart.

I can understand how you hate me for my manipulations and not telling you the truth and causing you to be crazy and lonely. I hurt you very much but that was never what I wanted to do. I thought that if I could ever get you to be friends, based on your mutual dislike for me, I could one day tell you everything. For over two years I was obsessed with the idea of your friendship. I would imagine everyday scenes. I even devised a way to have you share our sexual experiences. I could have you think I was fantasizing about you and other men, but I would be thinking about all 3 of us loving.

Sometimes just the everyday things became so difficult that it was very tempting to stop it all—but this meant death for me. I began to think in terms of us as something good and wonderful and able to change the world. It was essential to our existences as artists to survive together.

God, how I wanted us all to be together. I missed you so much, Ginny. Never think I forgot about you or never wanted to make love to you. And Carolyn, it was so lonely to be at the farm or at Subiaco without you. Wherever I was, whoever I was with, you were in my thoughts. After I saw that I no longer had your trust or friendship, I looked for the first friend to come along—Merideth.[1064] She was very nice to me. I hurt her, too. She wanted a friend and a lover. I was her lover, but I was not a good friend. I never was honest with her. As was the case with you two.

I wondered how I could ever bring you two together, but I also worried about keeping you apart until the right moment. I did not know how to live if we were apart. I wanted you both to share a friendship outside of your common enmeshment with me.

We all three lived in our own reality. As time went on I wondered if the only reason either one of you had any thing to do with me was because of my eternal and constant belief in your work. Although I knew your feeling toward my work, I really began to see that the real reason you put up with me was my relationship with your own. And nothing whatsoever is wrong with this. But I never wanted to be a teacher, just a friend in the jungle. Not a mean jungle, a beautiful jungle. Whatever I wanted, whatever we had is as ancient as childhood. Anyone who was nice to me I drew to. Lucinda was wonderful to be with when C. was gone.[1065] I felt free from danger, as I had with M.[1066] I wanted everyone to be friends with her, I didn't want the same thing to happen again as it did with M. There were chances I didn't take, what I really mean there really seemed a chance of all these things working out in my plan of the future for us through another person. I just had no idea of the extent of your bitterness towards me. And I thought I was giving you a lot of leeway in your true feeling about me. But it seems it is more than that. I came to see how much you despised me. I could foretell everything that was going to happen, but I somehow didn't intervene . . . I was weary of controlling everyone's reality.

As I saw how I was losing contact with you I needed contact with someone. I felt this with Marlissa.[1067] We were never lovers. I felt a strong attraction towards her, but all I wanted was friendship. I knew time was running out on us and I thought through her, if I told her everything, she, another woman, could possibly get closer to you than me. I knew I was a ghost. I could see in your eyes when you looked at me you didn't know what you were looking at. I was very weary and very determined about you, but I just wanted to lay my head on Marlissa's shoulder and rest, rest, rest. But Marlissa just didn't mean a comfortable go-between for me. I see in her, as I see in you, many things to come, as an artist & as a woman.

The closest things ever came to fulfillment was when C. drove up to the farm that night and she and I drove to Kansas and talked. Had G. or C., either one, acted alone with my courage wanting you to act, wanting you to understand your freedom, I think things would be different now. If C. had stepped in the door, instead of going through me and saying "tell her it's OK I won't come in" or if G. had gotten out of bed and told C. to come in, instead of going through me and saying "tell her she can come in and I can leave if you want to talk."

I meant everything I said to C. that night—my feelings about us, all 3 of us. If we can't all be friends, then none of us really can. But now you are trying to, and I'm happy. If I thought you would not be friends, I would be very sad. But you will understand there will always be something missing, as I understand. No matter what love, or what pleasure, or what understanding, no matter how many gifts and messages, there is always a loneliness. I don't mean there is any real satisfaction or resolution, because two people can have that when there are 3 involved, you always have whatever you have. I mean the feeling of the desert of identities, waking up with one woman in Fayetteville, or with one woman on the farm, and knowing wherever or whenever you wake up another part of you is missing—a part another part has never even had a chance to love, and chances are if love ever comes, it will mean, chances are, that your love will be lost.

I fear that both of you have forgotten many of the things we said, and now in a frenzy, arising from another part of the brain, you are making a terrible mistake. I don't think you know what you are doing, what you've done, what you will do. You don't know how dangerous to your soul it can be, I do. In these next few weeks I'm sure you will be choosing ways to seek some kind of revenge on me, but I hope you won't hurt yourselves or any innocent people.

I do have some hope that you will try to resolve your amazement and pain by simply not using the bad plumbing of the moment, not trying to explain or figure out or fathom everything about me and us by understanding the plumbing. This shit has nothing to do with you, me, or our souls. It has nothing to do with my world, or what yours should and could be.

I'm sure this is all bullshit to you, so I am trying to write something shorter, more to the point, to mail you both c/o Jackson Drive. This is a letter that will [not] get mailed. I'll just leave this on your doorstep some night?[1068] I know what I have done to you. I am now finding out what I have done to myself.

My love.
Frank

Notes

1061. *C.*: Carolyn—i.e., C. D. Wright. Later in this letter, *G.*: Ginny. In this and subsequent letters to Ginny and C. D., the "you" shifts irregularly between singular and plural use. Cf. Stanford's posthumously published book *You* (1979), which, per Stanford's directive in his will, is "for" Ginny and Carolyn.

1062. See Stanford's November 9, 1976, letter to Cuddihy above, par. 12.

1063. On September 3, 1976, Ginny Stanford completed a painting of Wright titled *Carolyn Wright Readies Herself for Another Evening* in which Wright twice appears clothed before appearing a third time partially undressed; as Ginny frequently painted portraits from photographs, Stanford may be referring here to photographs of which one or more were used as basis for the painting.

1064. Merideth Boswell (b. 1954), Arkansas native and (now) film production designer.

1065. Lucinda Williams (b. 1953), musician and daughter of Miller Williams.

1066. *M.*: Boswell.

1067. Marlissa is an as-yet-unidentified woman in Stanford's biography.

1068. Stanford indeed did not mail this letter. Per the police report on Stanford's death, on the evening of June 3, 1978, Investigator Mary Mueller of the Fayetteville Police Department separately interviewed Ginny and C. D., who both stated that Stanford had, that afternoon, wanted them to read the letter that "he had written" while "in New Orleans," though neither of them wanted to read it.

To Dorothy Stanford: May 31, 1978

[On Lost Roads Publishers letterhead.]

New Orleans
5/31/78

Dear Mother,

I'm fine and having a very good time. This is a wonderful city full of wonderful people.

I was supposed to take the plane today, but have found a ride. May stop off at Greenville on way back to see little Jimmy & family.[1069] As soon as I pass through, etc., will call you.

Been in Pass Christian and other parts of the coast last few days.[1070] Don't worry, I'm well, fine, feeling good.

Could you deposit a check for 175.00 or 200.00 to my acct. in Ark, via the enclosed stamped envelope. I'll send you a check for same soon as I get back to my mail box in Fayetteville. Have several uncashed checks from clients there. (Just endorse my name signature on back.)

See you this weekend or before.

Love,
Frank

Hello, Gran-Gran if you are there.

Notes

1069. Jimmy Lee Jr. and probably his father, James Buford Lee. Stanford didn't end up returning to Fayetteville by automobile via Greenville or Subiaco; he flew from New Orleans to Fayetteville.

1070. Pass Christian, Mississippi, a small coastal town roughly sixty miles east of New Orleans.

To Ralph Adamo: May 31, 1978

5/31/78 Wed. 7:30 PM

Ralph,

Got back from 2 days on coast. Sorry to miss you, brother. Will be going back early in the morning.[1071] Take care of everything, keep your eye on the moon, your poetry.

Love,
Frank

Notes

1071. Stanford returned to Fayetteville on Saturday morning, June 3, 1978—not June 1; Adamo noted to this editor that Stanford modified his travel plans multiple times. Stanford and Kay DuVernet (1947–2009), photographer/poet, spent the night of Friday, June 2, at Adamo's home before Stanford's return to Arkansas.

To Ginny Stanford and C. D. Wright: June 3, 1978

Saturday 3rd June

Dear Ginny & Carolyn,

Since I have been in New Orleans I have been preparing for something which will soon take place. My only doubts about myself and what I am going to do occurred this morning before my take-off and after I talked to you. Except for late night rides on the street cars, during the early part of the 1st week in NO, this morning was the first time I was alone—Kay Duvernet brought me to the airport and left.[1072] Naturally, I was sad. She has been my companion and friend most of my stay in NO. We are not lovers or in love in the ordinary sense, but we are in an extraordinary way. She revived something in me, something which both of you loved. And she completed something in me, something which both of you desired, respected. If it were not for her, all my feelings would be dark and terrible. I feel light and I feel pain going away. Meeting her, I once again met both of you. I remembered myself, and recalling myself, I felt happy. The last two weeks have been very strange, melodic, ecstatic, and preparatory. I have known about this journey for a long time, I even knew how it would come about. I was certain, beyond a doubt, when Carolyn and Debbie and I were in the truck.[1073]

At that moment, or even during the dreams I had the night before, I could have delayed things, could have put them off, but I was weary of controlling my spirit and yours. The person who is writing this is Frank Stanford, poet. The person who has been in New Orleans, listening to the music of his soul, is not the same person who left two weeks ago, or the person you have not trusted for so long, the person you hate now. The man writing this is the creature of the poems, the man you loved and desired, and who loved and desired you.[1074] Forget this other man, but don't allow yourselves to hate him. If you allow this hate to drive you off course, you might find yourselves far from the place you wanted to be, and you will have to travel back through the hate to begin a new journey of your love. The poet never allowed himself to be injected by this hate, and so don't you. I should have more hate for this man than anyone, because he lost for me my life, loves, & work,[1075] but I forgive him.[1076] The poet is writing to you now under the full powers of love, freedom, and joy.[1077] I would not be honest if I said I ~~wasn't~~ was ~~just~~ totally free of fear and sadness. There is sadness and there is fear. But I feel like an explorer, embarking on a journey I have been charting and studying for many years.[1078] I know something of death, so do not be afraid or terrified or lonely. The living spirit, now, is my concern. If anybody can, if anybody ever has, I will still know you and you know me. The days of our friendship, loving, and work are not over. I am not letting you down, I am not committing a violent act against myself or either of you. I believe you understand.

Notes

1072. Kay DuVernet, who could well have been a quondam acquaintance of Stanford's, had managed and lived at the New Orleans Hotel in Eureka Springs in the early 1970s. See McWilliams, *Life and Poetry*, 489, and cf. note 1071 above.

1073. *Debbie*: Deborah Nolan.

1074. Stanford may or may not have intended "creator" in place of "creature."

1075. Cf. note 1019 above.

1076. Cf. Stanford's July 5, 1972, letter to Campbell above, par. 2: "That which made me betray you, wants my life, now."

1077. Stanford's wording here closely aligns with the title of his poem "Freedom, Revolt, and Love" (*You*), a fifty-four-line narrative poem in which two illicit lovers are found out and murdered; in an unpublished ca. 1981 essay titled "One Poem from *You*" in which he analyzes the poem (housed in the Lost Roads Publishers Records at Yale University), Whitehead proffers that the poem's lovers might "have a life together *after* death. Freedom, revolt, and love then become the rewards of an afterlife."

1078. Cf. Stanford's words in a late September 1974 letter to Cuddihy: "I was studying about death."

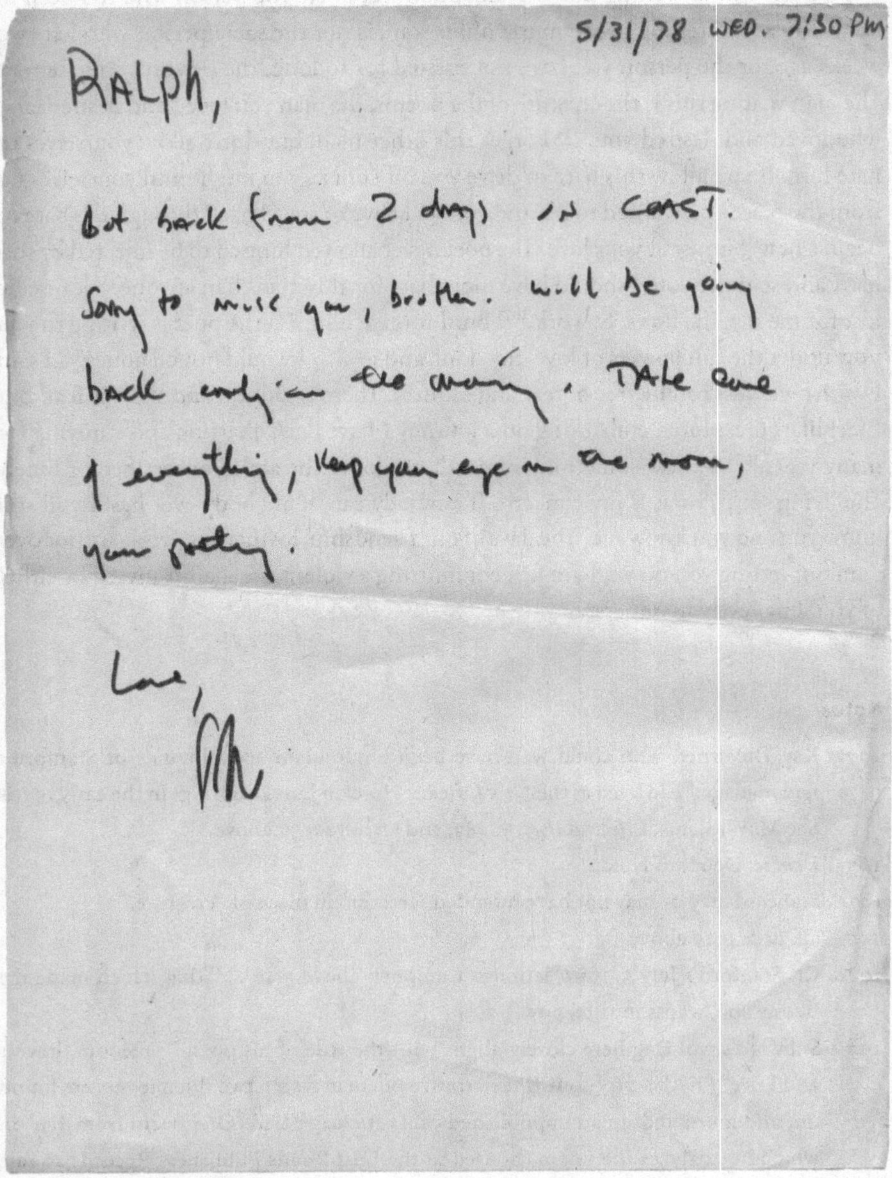

5/31/78 WED. 7:30 PM

Ralph,

Got back from 2 days on coast.

Sorry to miss you, brother. Will be going back early in the morning. Take care of everything, keep your eye on the moon, your poetry.

Love,

Following his return from Pass Christian, Mississippi, on May 31, 1978, Stanford penned this parting note to Adamo (though he didn't end up returning to Fayetteville until June 3)—which closes with "keep your eye on the moon, your poetry."

To Ginny Stanford and C. D. Wright: Circa June 3, 1978

I am disturbed that you are now trying to "grab at straws", as you say, to figure this labyrinth out.[1079] Several things have been mentioned to me by you which you are in someway trying to piece together. One is my feeling of a lack of recognition for my work. Another is my need to "make conquests" of women. And also that I am a "weak person." Lastly, I think, though there are other feelings you have toward me, in your conception of me as a ruthless, manipulative person, engaged in a war with you, that in fact, I am "Rasputin" like, and mad or evil; that I have used you to protect myself, and that I really had no respect for either of you.[1080]

I believe I can give a fair and objective account of everything I have done and been. I fell in love with Carolyn and what her work would become in the same way I fell in love with Ginny. Like a charge of lightning I suddenly saw I was in love, very deeply, with two women, and their work.[1081] Before I knew what was happening I dreamed an ideal life of us together as friends, lovers, workers, and artists, working to change things. Because of the great feeling and understanding you both had and were showing me, I peered into a new world, much more desirable than the old world, where everyone was equal. Shortly after I met Carolyn, and even when she knew Ginny knew nothing of our love, I saw my destiny become wonderfully but dangerously encircled in this idea of 3 people willing to change things. I no longer had the desire to live the other kind of life. My only desire was to achieve a new kind of experience. Each of you became more and more essential to my work and my life. I felt myself undergo great changes. My love for the ideal and my desire were so great I knew my existence was founded on its conception.

These are the splendid ideas poets have, their dreams. But I am a man in this world, and so I became obsessed in any way whatsoever in bringing my ideal to fruition. I took it upon myself as a man, to tamper with the rare and special knowledge of the artist, and to use that magic to control you. I was not only determined as an artist to this ideal, but was carefully practical as a man to make this come true. I would do anything to insure the existence of our love, its future.[1082] You see, all the time you believed your lives and your work were dependent on me, I was totally nurtured by you. This was my secret, my reason for existence.

Notes

1079. A note atop page 1 of this letter reads: "Found on floor of Front Room." The letter's composition time and, arguably, date are uncertain.

1080. Grigori Rasputin (1869–1916), Russian mystic regarded variously as seer and charlatan.

1081. Cf. lines in an undated—possibly ca. 1973 (based on typewriter analysis)—typescript poem of Stanford's seemingly titled "Their Smell," which begins, "I love two women. / And they love me." The poem goes on to contend that if the women are not in love with each other, "Then the man falls in love with his death," and closes, "Then the women meet finally at the grave of the man who loved them, / Finally." Ginny Crouch Stanford Collection of Frank Stanford, Yale Collection of American Literature, Beinecke Rare Book & Manuscript Library.

1082. Stanford may or may not have intended "ensure" in place of "insure."

EPILOGUE
The Living Spirit

On May 22, 1978, in New Orleans, Frank Stanford had also written a will, bequeathing his entire literary estate to Ginny and C. D. and including instructions for the posthumous publication of some of his works. Ginny filed for divorce on June 1. On the morning of Saturday, June 3, Stanford returned to Fayetteville, via Little Rock, by plane. After first being unable to locate him, Ginny and C. D. found him outside, behind his and C. D.'s home at 705 Jackson Drive. Frank, Ginny, and C. D., together, discussed his misrepresentations of his respective relationships with them but didn't quarrel. Stanford visited his surveying office, mentioning to C. D. that he wanted to phone his mother. Back at the house, Frank, Ginny, and C. D. continued their discussion, but no attempts at reconciliation were successful. Shortly after 7:00 p.m. in the evening, Stanford walked into the home's southern bedroom and, with a Hi-Standard Double-Nine, a .22-caliber double-action revolver, belonging to Don Kemp, ended his life with three self-inflicted wounds in his chest near the heart.

ACKNOWLEDGMENTS

I AM INDEBTED TO EACH OF the following individuals, many of whom knew or corresponded with Frank Stanford and have contributed in broad capacities, at various points in my Stanford research, to a greater and fuller understanding of the poet. The conversations and communications occurred variably in person or via email, postal mail, phone, text, or social media:

Steve Allen, Thomas R. Atkins, James Babij, Mari Andrejco Bath, John Biguenet, Ezra D. Bowen, Matthew Bowen, Gen Whitehead Broyles, Jack Butler, George Caldwell, Justin Caldwell, Warren Camp, William Carpenter (of Maine), William Carpenter (of Minnesota), Franklin Stanford Coleman, Floyd Collins, Mary Cuddihy, the late Robert Day, Karl Elder, William L. Fox, Clarke Freeman, the late Father Nicholas Fuhrmann, Louis Gallo, Jane Garner, Frank Green Jr., Carole Hess, Eric Horsting, Larry Johnson, Richard Leo Johnson, Father Jerome Kodell, Jimmy Lee, D. S. Long, the late Thomas Lux, the late John McKernan, Linda Mencin Bond, Keith Mills, Bill Monie, John S. Morris, Brother Ephrem O'Bryan, Charles Plymell, Pamela Beach Plymell, Carrie Rogers Prysock, the late David Ray, Judy Ray, David Reich, Debbie R. Ricks-Douglas, Philip H. Robins, the late Ruth Rogers, Michael Ryan, R. M. Ryan, Brother Jude Schmitt, Murray Shugars, A. G. (Anthony) Sobin, Steve Stern, the late Leon Stokesbury, the late John Stoss, the late Brian Sulkis, Leslie Ullman, Robert Vas Dias, Mark Vinz, Arthur Vogelsang, the late David Walker, Kathy Walton, Michael Waters, the late John Wood, the late C. D. Wright, and the late David Young.

I also thank friends, colleagues, and other individuals who have helped bring this project to fruition, whether inadvertently or through intentional or other specific support, including: Keith Althaus, Yi Bian, Michel Brix, Mary Ellen Budney, Marty Cain, Philip Coleman, Mark Cronin, Meoghan Cronin, David Scott Cunningham, Jeff Danos, John Erwin, Janet Foxman, Jonathan Galassi, Ryan Haas, Ian T. Hall, Andrew Haringer, Andrew Heitert, the late Matthew Henriksen, Katie Herman, Christopher Hurley, Benjamin Lee, Melinda Malik, Tom Mancuso, Calista McRae, Ata Moharreri,

Amanda W. O'Neal, Bryce Patton, David Quinn, Aidan Ryan, Heidi Jon Schmidt, Paul Tenngart, Frances Silenzi Walker, M. Keith Walton, Roger Weingarten, and Joshua Youngblood.

To the following individuals, my gratitude extends far beyond my appreciation expressed here: Ralph Adamo, Irv Broughton, Catherine I. Brown, Forrest Gander, R. S. Gwynn, Eleanor Hamilton, Leo A. Lensing, James McWilliams, Nils Nelson, John Öwre, Cheryl E. Ross, Ginny Stanford, Pamela Jody Stewart, Bill Willett, and Annabelle Williams.

I would also like to extend my gratitude to the Marion and Jasper Whiting Foundation and Saint Anselm College.

BIOGRAPHICAL SKETCHES OF KEY CORRESPONDENTS

Adamo, Ralph: B. 1948. Poet, editor. Born in New Orleans, Adamo graduated from Loyola University New Orleans and received an MFA from the University of Arkansas in 1974. Has edited *Barataria Review*, *New Orleans Review*, and *Xavier Review*. Stanford published Adamo in *Preview: Eight Poets* in 1971, then published Adamo's book *Sadness at the Private University* as Lost Roads No. 3 in 1977; C. D. Wright later published his book *The End of the World* as Lost Roads No. 17. Lives in New Orleans. Other works include *Waterblind: Selected Poems* (2002), *Ever: Poems 2000–2014* (2014), and *All the Good Hiding Places* (2020).

Bender, Eleanor: B. 1942. Editor. Bender founded the poetry magazine *Open Places* in New York in 1966. She moved to Columbia, Missouri, in 1968 and, in 1970, began teaching at Stephens College, where she edited and published *Open Places* until 1987. Following Stanford's initial submission to *Open Places* in March 1971, he and Bender began a correspondence that continued into 1974. Now Eleanor Hamilton, she lives in Seattle.

Broughton, Irv: B. 1941. Publisher, editor, poet, writer. Born in Orlando, Broughton grew up in Florida and Massachusetts. Met Stanford at the Hollins Conference on Creative Writing and Cinema at Hollins College (now Hollins University), where Broughton was a graduate student, in June 1970 and became Stanford's publisher via Mill Mountain Press, which Broughton founded and which published Stanford's poetry across several issues of the *Mill Mountain Review*. Mill Mountain also published Stanford's first six books (in 1971, 1974, 1975, and 1976) and copublished (with Lost Roads Publishers) *The Battlefield Where the Moon Says I Love You* (in 1977); it published C. D. Wright's first book, *Alla Breve Loving* (1976), as well. Broughton also directed the 16 mm short film about Stanford *It Wasn't a Dream: It Was a Flood* (1975). Stanford published Broughton's book *The Blessing of the Fleet* as Lost Roads No. 6 in 1977. Broughton lives in Spokane, Washington. Other works include *The Gracious*

Afterward: Delta Stories (2015) and *The Levees That Break in the Heart* (2016), as well as an unpublished screenplay and unpublished musical, both about Stanford.

Campbell, Cheryl: B. 1946. Multi-instrumentalist. A love of Stanford's from 1971 to 1973, first in Fayetteville (1971), later on Staten Island (1972) and via letters (1972–73). Born Cheryl Crites in Cape Girardeau, Missouri, Cheryl was a French horn major and viola minor from 1964 to 1969 at the University of Arkansas. She met her first husband in summer 1970, and they moved to Greenland, Arkansas, just south of Fayetteville. After their brief marriage failed (though she continued to use her new last name), Cheryl met Stanford circa January 1971 at a birthday party at a cabin on Markham Hill in Fayetteville. In late winter 1971, Cheryl moved into Stanford's small writing studio in Fayetteville on Lindell Avenue (between Cleveland Street and Eagle Street), where she typed many of his poems and letters in late winter / spring 1971—with Stanford sustaining a short-lived double life between Linda, his long-term girlfriend, on Mount Sequoyah and Cheryl, his paramour, at his studio. Circa June 1971, Cheryl discovered that she was pregnant with a (male) child conceived with Stanford, but shortly thereafter, likely in early July, she miscarried. In August, Cheryl moved to New York City and began living on Staten Island with dancer Clive Thompson and his family at 56 Harvard Avenue—where Stanford visited her in August and September 1972 after his marriage to Linda failed. Upon leaving New York, she saw Stanford a final time in 1973 at the New Orleans Hotel. Now Cher Ross, she lives on Whidbey Island in Washington.

Cowley, Malcolm: 1898–1989. Writer, poet, editor, critic. Met Stanford in Connecticut in August 1972 when Stanford and Broughton traveled through there and filmed him, and he and Stanford corresponded irregularly over the subsequent couple of years. Works include *Blue Juniata: Collected Poems* (1968).

Cuddihy, Michael: 1932–2000. Publisher, editor, poet. Born in New York City, Cuddihy studied at the University of Notre Dame and settled in Tucson, Arizona. Founded the literary journal *Ironwood*, which he edited from 1972 to 1988 and which published fourteen of Stanford's poems while Stanford was living—across three issues in 1974, 1975, and 1977. Cuddihy's Ironwood Press published Stanford's book *Crib Death* in 1978—published posthumously, though much of it was prepared while Stanford was living. Corresponded with Stanford from 1973 to 1978. Cuddihy's wife, Mary, is also mentioned herein. Cuddihy's two poetry books are dedicated to her, and his book *Celebrations* (1980) is additionally dedicated to Stanford, "who knows now."

Dugan, Alan: 1923–2003. Poet. Dugan visited the University of Arkansas in early November 1970 and was impressed with Stanford's poetry—declaring, provocatively, that Stanford was the only worthwhile poet of the group surrounding the graduate poetry workshop. Stanford wrote to Dugan following the visit, but that first letter is missing or lost; Stanford wrote again on April 27, 1971, thus beginning a lengthy correspondence and friendship. Dugan resided in Truro, Massachusetts, on Cape Cod for decades with his wife, artist Judith Shahn, and Stanford visited him there in August 1972 on his New England trip. Works include *Poems* (1961) and *Poems Seven: New and Complete Poetry* (2001).

Eberhart, Richard: 1904–2005. Poet. Met Stanford, along with traveling companions Broughton and James Babij, in early August 1972 in New Hampshire; the travelers attended the wedding of Eberhart's daughter before journeying to Eberhart's cottage in Maine, where they spent time on his yacht. In 1981, Eberhart published a remembrance article titled "Frank Stanford" in *Ironwood* issue 17, noting that he was "astonished . . . by the originality and power" of Stanford's poems, observing that Stanford had "produced a remarkable, unforgettable body of work," and asserting that Stanford's "language is taut and fine" with "not a word out of place, remarkable hits, few errors. Truth and honesty throughout" (137–38). US poet laureate from 1959 to 1961. Works include *Collected Poems: 1930–1986* (1988).

Fox, William L.: B. 1949. Poet, writer, editor, artist, critic. Born in San Diego, California, Fox assumed editorship of *West Coast Poetry Review* in 1972, editing the magazine and West Coast Poetry Review Press from 1972 to 1988 and publishing Stanford in 1972 and 1974. Lives in Reno, Nevada.

Garrett, George: 1929–2008. Poet, writer, playwright, critic. Organizer of the Hollins Conference at Hollins College in June 1970. Garrett also cofounded the Associated Writing Programs (now the Association of Writers & Writing Programs), or AWP, in 1967.

Gilbert, Carolyn Gildart: 1888–1980. Stanford's adoptive grandmother and Dorothy Stanford's mother. Carolyn's husband, Stanford's adoptive grandfather, was Judson Malcolm Gilbert (1877–1948), who died less than three weeks before the poet was born. Carolyn lived in Mississippi and, in some of her last years, in Subiaco.

Gilchrist, Ellen: 1935–2024. Fiction writer, poet. Born in Vicksburg, Mississippi, Gilchrist studied briefly in the MFA program at the University of Arkansas. Worked as a contributing editor for New Orleans's *Vieux Carré Courier* from 1976 to 1979. Stanford worked with Gilchrist on her first book of poetry, *The Land Surveyor's Daughter*, which was published as Lost Roads No. 14 in 1979. Gilchrist's husband in 1978, Frederick Sidney Kullman, took the photo of Stanford reproduced herein at the beginning of chapter VIII. A recurring character in Gilchrist's fiction is Francis Alter (named and modeled after Stanford), of whom the narrator of "A Wedding in Jackson" (in *The Age of Miracles*) states, "He was my first true writer friend. The first blessed, gifted, cursed poet that I knew. Also, the most beautiful human being I have ever seen. To be in his presence was to understand why men became the disciples of Christ. Existence changed when he was around, became finer, clearer, more alive. He dedicated his life to beauty, to art, poetry, freedom. Then he killed himself" (39). Gilchrist biographer Mary A. McCay writes (in *Ellen Gilchrist)*, "Frank Stanford was certainly the most influential poet in Gilchrist's life. In fact, he may well have been the most influential person" (xi). Other works include *In the Land of Dreamy Dreams* (1981) and *Victory over Japan* (1984).

Ginsberg, Allen: 1926–97. Poet and leading figure of the Beat Generation. Works include *Howl and Other Poems* (1956) and *The Fall of America: Poems of These States 1965–1971* (1972).

Justice, Donald: 1925–2004. Poet. A well-regarded teacher of poetry whom Stanford respected. Met Stanford in 1969. Justice published four early poems of Stanford's in *The Iowa Review* in 1972.

McKernan, John: 1942–2025. Poet, editor. McKernan received a master's in English from the University of Arkansas (and, later, additional degrees from Columbia University and Boston University). Editor, from 1968 to 1980, of *The Little Review*, which published fifteen of Stanford's poems—across three issues in 1971, 1974, and 1975. Stanford published McKernan's book *Walking Along the Missouri River* as Lost Roads No. 5 in 1977. McKernan taught for decades at Marshall University. Other works include *Resurrection of the Dust: Selected Poems* (2007).

Stanford, Dorothy: 1911–2000. The poet's adoptive mother. Born in Greenville, Mississippi, to Judson Gilbert and Carolyn Gilbert (née Gildart), Dorothy Stanford (née Gilbert) was the oldest of six children. Finished high school at age fifteen, wrote and sold short stories to little magazines as a teen, and worked for Sears for ten years beginning in 1932—in Memphis and then (following her divorce from her first husband, Carl Alter) in California from 1939 to 1942. In the 1940s, she was reportedly the first woman in the US to manage a Firestone tire store. On August 1, 1948, as Dorothy Alter, she adopted the poet on the day of his birth in Mississippi—as purportedly the first single woman in Mississippi to adopt a child. In March 1952, she remarried, to A. F. Stanford, becoming Dorothy Stanford, and following his 1963 death, she became—for many years, starting in fall 1964—caretaker of Subiaco Abbey's retreat center, or guest lodge, Coury House. "Frank was my heart," she wrote of her late son to Michael Cuddihy on March 29, 1979. "It is so difficult to get through the nights.... The days are not quite as horrible."

Stanford, Ginny: B. 1950. Artist. Born Virginia Crouch in Missouri, Ginny met Frank on March 3, 1973, while he was visiting a friend in Neosho, Missouri, on a weekend away from Eureka Springs, Arkansas, where he was living in the New Orleans Hotel. Ginny and Frank lived together in spring and summer 1973 in a small wood cabin on the White River Lodge resort's property in Busch, Arkansas, northwest of Eureka Springs, then, beginning in late summer, in a house on the same property. In November 1973, they moved to Rogers, Arkansas, near Beaver Lake. Ginny married Frank on October 17, 1974. Collaborated with Stanford, contributing artwork to his books *Ladies From Hell* (1974), *Field Talk* (1975), *Shade* (1975), and *Arkansas Bench Stone* (1975). Relocated to California in 1981. Was commissioned by the Smithsonian's National Portrait Gallery to paint *Hillary Rodham Clinton*, the first NPG portrait of a First Lady, in 2006. Author of two essays on Stanford, "*Requiem*: A Fragment" (1994) and "Death in the Cool Evening" (1997).

Walker, David: 1942–2008. Poet. Born in Alna, Maine, Walker corresponded with Stanford in the 1970s, first while coediting *Edge* in 1971 and 1972, then again in 1974 as a poet-contemporary of Stanford's. Of Stanford's suicide, Walker stated (in a March 5, 2008, phone call) to this editor, "I'm not the most sane person in the world, but that strikes me as insane." Works include *Moving Out* (1976) and *Voiceprints* (1989).

Willett, Bill: B. 1947. A close friend of Stanford's—and Stanford's longest-running friendship, from 1961 to 1978. Was born into a large family in Gassville, Arkansas, and grew up in Little Rock, Pine Bluff, Mountain Home, and elsewhere. Met Stanford as they entered eighth grade at Mountain Home Junior High School in late summer 1961 when the two were thirteen years old. The second edition of *The Battlefield Where the Moon Says I Love You* is dedicated to Willett—"closest, longest friend of the late Frank Stanford." Lives in Mountain Home, Arkansas.

Wright, C. D. (Carolyn Doris): 1949–2016. Poet. Born in Mountain Home and attended Mountain Home High School one year behind Stanford, though she and Stanford did not know each other then. Met Stanford in 1975 in Fayetteville while an MFA student at the University of Arkansas, becoming a lover, colleague, and friend of his until his death. Her first book, *Alla Breve Loving*, was published by Broughton's Mill Mountain Press in 1976. She assisted Stanford with establishing Lost Roads

Publishers, which published her early book, *Room Rented by a Single Woman*, as Lost Roads No. 1, in 1977; she continued editing the press after Stanford's death for several decades, for most of that time with her husband, Forrest Gander. Her fourth book, *Translations of the Gospel Back into Tongues* (1982), is dedicated "to Frank" and "for" Kay DuVernet. Taught at Brown University from 1983 to 2016. Other works include *Terrorism* (Lost Roads, 1979), *Steal Away: New and Selected Poems* (2002), and *One With Others* (2010).

CHRONOLOGY

1948 Born Francis Gildart Smith on August 1 in southeast Mississippi. Adopted the same day by a single divorcée, Dorothy Gilbert Alter of Greenville, Mississippi. Stanford's adoption is finalized by the State of Mississippi on August 20; Stanford's name becomes Francis Gildart Alter. Affectionately called "Frankie," he is first raised on a farm outside of Greenville. On September 5, Stanford is baptized at St. James Episcopal Church in Greenville; Albert Franklin (A. F.) Stanford (1884–1963), or Frank Sr., is listed as one of the baptismal sponsors.

1949 Dorothy adopts a second child, Bettina Ruth, "Ruthie"—Stanford's younger, adoptive sister.

1950 Dorothy and the children move into town: Greenville, a western Mississippi Delta town located on an oxbow lake along the Mississippi River.

1951 Edna Alexander Stanford, longtime wife of A. F. Stanford, passes away in August.

1952 Dorothy Alter remarries, on March 7, to A. F. Stanford—a successful levee engineer based in Memphis, Tennessee, twenty-seven years Dorothy's senior. The couple, Frank, and Ruth move to 1157 Knox Road (now Knox Avenue) in the Frayser neighborhood of North Memphis.

1950s Stanford, his parents, and Ruth spend summers in levee camps along the Mississippi River south of Memphis, where A. F. Stanford builds levees and Dorothy cooks.

1954 Stanford begins first grade at the elementary school in Snow Lake, Arkansas, a levee camp village.

1955 Stanford completes first grade in Memphis at Our Lady of Sorrows Elementary School, where he also attends second grade. On November 21, Stanford is formally adopted by A. F. Stanford; Stanford's name changes a final time to Francis Gildart Stanford.

1956 Stanford switches schools to West Frayser Elementary School, where he attends third grade.

1957 In the summer, the Stanfords move to 1116 Oakridge Drive in an affluent neighborhood of East Memphis. Stanford switches schools again, to Sherwood Elementary School, where he attends fourth through sixth grades. Per Stanford's manuscript dating, he composes the earliest poems later compiled into manuscripts titled *St. Francis and the Wolf: Some Poems 1957–1964* and *Field Talk, 1957–1972*.

1958 In April, while in fourth grade, Stanford places fourth, with his poem "the sphinx," in the fourth-through-sixth-grade division of a poetry contest for students in the Memphis and Shelby County Schools.

1959 Per Stanford's dating in later letters, he composes "the mind reader," a lengthy narrative poem ultimately published in 1972.

1960 This summer appears to be the last full one that Stanford spends at the levee camps. His magnum opus, *The Battlefield Where the Moon Says I Love You*, contains flashbacks to the 1950s as well as flash-forwards, but the bulk of the narrative is set in and around the levee camps circa 1960. Stanford begins seventh grade at Sherwood Junior High School.

1961 On May 14, Stanford is confirmed at All Saints' Episcopal Church in Memphis. A. F. Stanford retires with ailing health at age seventy-six, and in summer the Stanfords move to 27 Mallard Point Road on Norfork Lake outside of Mountain Home, Arkansas, in the Ozark Mountains. Stanford lives most of the rest of his life in northern Arkansas. Entering eighth grade at Mountain Home Junior High School, he meets Bill Willett, who becomes a lifelong friend.

1961–62 Circa 1961–62, Stanford gives poems to a friend, who later recalled the poems' "nocturnal" vocabularies ("knives, prows, wolves, and the cold, wet lure of the moon"—per C. D. Wright's 2006 description, in the *Oxford American*, of the friend's response). In 1962, Stanford begins ninth grade at Mountain Home High School.

1963 A. F. Stanford dies of kidney problems on August 29 at age seventy-eight as Stanford, age fifteen, is starting tenth grade. Stanford works at Norfork Lake's Cranfield Boat Dock, as a fishman and guide, until fall 1964.

1964 In summer, author Joan Williams and her sons visit Dorothy, Frank, and Ruth at Mallard Point for a month. Per Stanford's dating in later letters, he composes an early draft of the poem that becomes *The Battlefield* (though the early version was typed up, with revision and expansion, including via compilation with other early poems, in the early 1970s), which later becomes part of *St. Francis and the Wolf: Some Poems 1957–1964*. Around this time (and possibly beginning as early as 1963), the family converts to Catholicism.

1964–66 Starting in eleventh grade, Stanford studies at Subiaco Academy—a Benedictine boarding school in the Ouachita Mountains of western Arkansas—developing friendships with monks including Fr. Nicholas Fuhrmann and Br. (later Fr.) Wolfgang Mimms. Stanford receives a rigorous classical education, reads voraciously, and writes poetry. Also starting in fall 1964, Dorothy begins as caretaker of Subiaco Abbey's guest lodge, Coury House, a position she holds for the rest of Stanford's life.

1966 Stanford graduates from Subiaco in May and matriculates at the University of Arkansas in Fayetteville in fall, first enrolling in the College of Business.

1966–70 Stanford lives in at least ten different residences as a college student—including in apartments on Dickson Street, Buchanan Avenue, Whitham Avenue, and Florene Street—sometimes with Willett as a roommate.

1967 In fall, Stanford switches from the College of Business to the College of Arts & Sciences, where he studies English.

1968 At the close of summer, Stanford tells Willett that he has learned that he was fully adopted—that his mother is not his biological mother. The realization is regarded as having been devastating to his psyche and having instigated a metamorphic change in his disposition, general outlook, and approach to writing. Stanford meets James "Jim" Whitehead, English professor and cofounder (in 1966) of the university's MFA Program in Creative Writing.

1969 At Whitehead's invitation, Stanford joins the graduate poetry workshop, which he takes in both spring and fall. An early version of Stanford's poem "Living" appears in *Preview: 1968–1969*, the university's literary journal. In early May, Allen Ginsberg visits the program and is drawn to Stanford's poetry. Stanford meets his future wife Linda Lee Mencin, with whom he travels to Washington, DC, for the Second Moratorium to End the War in Vietnam on November 15. Stanford's known surviving correspondence begins.

1970 Four of Stanford's poems appear in *Preview: The Literature* (the journal's 1970 issue), for which Stanford is associate editor. Stanford publishes "Early Times in a Mississippi Liquor Store" and "The Hole" in spring in *Tansy* 1—his first professional publication. He attends the Hollins Conference on Creative Writing and Cinema in June, meeting his future publisher, Irv Broughton. In summer and fall, Stanford begins working as a land surveyor alongside R. S. Gwynn, a poet-peer. Stanford moves with Linda into a cabin at 115 Skyline Drive atop Fayetteville's Mount Sequoyah neighborhood. Alan Dugan visits the MFA program November 8–14 and declares that Stanford is the only poet of merit among the students. That month, Linda discovers that she is pregnant; she has an abortion. In late 1970, Stanford also publishes in the *Mill Mountain Review*, edited and published by Broughton.

1971 At least partially resulting from costs relating to Linda's abortion, Stanford does not return to classes in spring; he never completes his degree. Circa January, Stanford meets Cheryl Campbell, with whom he initiates a romance and who soon moves into his writing studio on Lindell Avenue; Stanford thus begins a short-lived double life between Linda on Mount Sequoyah and Cheryl at the studio. He begins publishing widely, including in *Chicago Review*, *kayak*, *The Little Review*, *The Nation*, *New American Review*, and *West Coast Review*. Having received no response to a first letter, Stanford writes a second letter to Dugan in April—establishing a years-long friendship. Stanford also edits the 1971 issue of the university's journal, *Preview: Eight Poets*, despite not being enrolled as a student. In June, as his relationships with Linda and Cheryl become known by both women, Cheryl discovers that she is pregnant, and in early July, she miscarries. Stanford stays with Linda. Cheryl moves to Staten Island in August before Stanford and Linda marry, on August 21—in northwest Arkansas, with Fuhrmann officiating and Willett and longtime friend "Big Time" Sonny Morris serving as Stanford's groomsmen. Stanford begins typing up his juvenilia, with many of the poems compiled into a manuscript he titles *St. Francis and the Wolf: Some Poems 1957–1964*.

1972 Stanford continues typing up much of his juvenilia and other early work, further selecting poems for *St. Francis and the Wolf*, and works on *The Battlefield Where the Moon Says I Love You*. He publishes in *The Hollins Critic*, *The Iowa Review*, *The Massachusetts Review*, *Open Places*, *Poetry Australia*, and *West Coast Poetry Review*. The Stanfords separate at the close of April or in mid-May, and Stanford is anguished; he burns large portions of his early work. He enters the Arkansas State Hospital from June 2 to 12, then spends some weeks at Subiaco. Stanford is suicidal in the weeks leading up to Linda's divorce filing on July 7 but is immediately jubilant upon reconnecting with Cheryl—receiving on July 5 her July 1 reply letter to his June letters, in which she expresses her love for him. His first book, *The Singing Knives*—published by Broughton's Mill Mountain Press—appears (with a copyright date of 1971). In August, Stanford travels to New England with Broughton and James Babij, interviewing and filming first John Crowe Ransom (in Ohio), then Richard Eberhart, Richard Wilbur, and Malcolm Cowley, and visiting Dugan. Stanford then visits Cheryl on Staten Island, living for several weeks with her. Returning to Arkansas, he spends the fall at Subiaco. The Stanfords' divorce is finalized on October 18. At the close of December, Stanford moves to Eureka Springs, Arkansas.

1973 Stanford lives in the New Orleans Hotel in winter and into early spring, working on various poems, including *The Battlefield*, and fiction. On March 3, in Neosho, Missouri, he meets Virginia "Ginny" Susan Crouch. Stanford rents a small cabin for writing at Spider Creek Resort in Busch, Arkansas, and soon after, he and Ginny begin living together in a wood cabin at an old resort nearby known as White River Lodge. He publishes in *The New York Quarterly* in summer and in *The Boston Phoenix* in May,

August, and December. Frank and Ginny move into a house on the same resort property later in summer, and Stanford begins a correspondence with Michael Cuddihy, editor of *Ironwood*. In November, Frank and Ginny move again, to a house east of Rogers, near Beaver Lake.

1974 Stanford and Broughton collaborate on a film about Stanford, *It Wasn't a Dream: It Was a Flood* (which also includes footage shot in 1972 and 1973). Mill Mountain publishes Stanford's second book, *Ladies From Hell* (which doesn't actually appear, seemingly, until 1975). Stanford also publishes in *FIELD* (twice), *The Iowa Review* (including his first published story), *Ironwood*, *The Little Review*, *Poetry Australia*, *Prairie Schooner*, *West Coast Poetry Review*, and elsewhere. Stanford and Ginny marry on October 17 in northwest Arkansas.

1975 Stanford publishes three books with Mill Mountain: *Field Talk* (which may not have been released until 1976), *Shade* (as a "second" edition, though it was the first), and *Arkansas Bench Stone*. These books (and *Ladies From Hell*) contain drawings by Ginny Crouch Stanford. *It Wasn't a Dream: It Was a Flood* is finished and is selected by judges as one of the winning works at the Northwest Film & Video Festival in August. In fall, Stanford returns to Fayetteville and meets C. D. (Carolyn) Wright, with whom he begins a professional and romantic relationship—thus beginning what becomes a double life between Ginny and C. D. He publishes poetry in *The American Poetry Review*, *FIELD*, *Ironwood*, *The Little Review*, *Mill Mountain Review*, and *Poetry Now*.

1976 Stanford's sixth book, *Constant Stranger*, is published. He also founds Lost Roads Publishers, which he had conceived as early as 1974. In October, Stanford and Wright move into 705 Jackson Drive in Fayetteville, and that same fall, the Stanfords move to a house in southwest Missouri, north of Joplin, on a farm originally belonging to Ginny's maternal grandparents.

1977 Securing a loan, Stanford and Wright purchase a printing press, camera, plate burner, and light table and borrow a typesetting machine and launch White River Printers—aptly named since the White River flows along or near most places Stanford lived in his life, including Snow Lake, Mountain Home, Fayetteville, Eureka Springs, Busch, and Rogers. To help fund the press's publications, Stanford applies for funding from the National Endowment for the Arts (NEA) in February. He begins publishing (with copyright dates of 1977 but publication dates of spring 1978) the first six Lost Roads titles out of the Jackson Drive house: books by Wright and poet-peers John Stoss, Ralph Adamo, John S. Morris, John McKernan, and Broughton. *The Battlefield Where the Moon Says I Love You* (Lost Roads Nos. 7–12), Stanford's major epic, is prepared for publication. Stanford also publishes in *Barataria* issues 3 and 4 and *Ironwood*, and his work appears in the anthology *Fifty Contemporary Poets: The Creative Process*. Stanford's small press and individual NEA grant applications are rejected.

1978 Stanford reapplies for an NEA grant in February. His separate relationships with Ginny and C. D. grow increasingly complicated, with Stanford continuing to misrepresent his relationship with each woman to the other. On May 18, he travels to New Orleans for a little more than two weeks to visit friends. Ginny finds love letters among Stanford's poems, Ginny and C. D. communicate with each other and with Stanford, and he attempts to explain his deceits in a letter that he writes but doesn't mail. In New Orleans, he spends time with Adamo, Ellen Gilchrist, Kay DuVernet, and others and writes his will. Ginny files for divorce on June 1. Stanford returns to Fayetteville on June 3 and, after talking at length with Ginny and C. D. about his transgressions and penning his last correspondence, walks into one of the Fayetteville house's bedrooms and fires three shots into his chest near the heart with a Hi-Standard Double-Nine, a .22-caliber revolver. At the time of his death, *The Battlefield* is printed, but the vast majority of copies are not yet bound. Wright successfully receives the NEA grant for which Stanford had applied and also finalizes publication of *The Battlefield*. *The Battlefield* and *Crib Death* are published posthumously.

1979–91 *The Singing Knives* is published in a second edition (1979), and *You* (1979; "for Ginny and Carolyn"), *Conditions Uncertain and Likely to Pass Away* (1990), and *The Light the Dead See: Selected Poems of Frank Stanford* (1991) are published posthumously.

1994–97 Ginny Stanford publishes remembrance essays, "*Requiem*: A Fragment" (1994) and "Death in the Cool Evening" (1997).

2000 Lost Roads, under the editorship of Wright and Forrest Gander, publishes the second edition of *The Battlefield Where the Moon Says I Love You*.

2008 New editions of *The Singing Knives* and *You* are published.

2015 Editions of Stanford's collected and uncollected poetry are published: *What About This: Collected Poems of Frank Stanford* and *Hidden Water: From the Frank Stanford Archives.*

2025–26 *The Life and Poetry of Frank Stanford*, the first full-length biography of Stanford; the third edition of *The Battlefield Where the Moon Says I Love You*; and *Letters of a Poet Dying: The Selected Correspondence of Frank Stanford* are published.

DESIGNATIONS

Letter Formats: Manuscript–M | Typescript–T | Typescript with Manuscript Postscript / Marginalia / Insertions–TM

69.11.10-AG	M
69.11.23-AG	M
70.7.13-CP	M
70.10.6-JM	M
71.2.10-IB	M
71.3.1-*TMR*	M
71.3.15-*k*	M
71.3.26-*OP*	M
71.4.11-JM	TM
71.4.27-AD	M
71.c.l4/5-EB	M
71.5.10-JM	M
71.5.24-JM	M
71.6.21-AD	M
71.6.28-EB	T
71.7.26-AD	M
71.7.27-DJ	M
71.7.27-EB	M
71.7.31-IB	M
71.10.19-DJ	M
71.11.30-GH	M
72.l1/e2-DJ	M
72.2.1-EB	M
72.2.14-AD	M
72.2.18-IB	M
72.2.28-IB	M
72.3.1-AD	M
72.5.9-AD	M
72.5.15-TS	M
72.5.15-16-AD	M
72.c.l5-IB	M
72.5.26-AD	M
72.5.27-AD	M
72.c.l5-EB	M
72.c.6.1-WF	M
72.e6-IB	M
72.6.16-AD	M
72.6.19-WF	T
72.c.7.3/4-AD	TM
72.7.5-CC	M
72.7.10-EB	T
72.e7-AD	T
72.c.m7-IB	M
72.7.12-EB	M
72.7.15-CC	M
72.7.19-CC	T
72.7.20-WF	M
72.7.20-IB	T
72.7.29-CC	M
72.8.6-CC	M
72.8.7-CC	M
72.8.7-AD	M
72.8.11-CC	T
72.8.11-BW	M
72.m8-RE	M
72.m8-JB	M
72.l8-BW	M
72.l8-BW	M
72.9.13-BW	M
72.c.9.15-BW	M
72.c.l9-BW	M
72.l9-IB	M
72.l9-IB	M
72.10-GH	M
72.10-WF	M
72.10-WF	M
72.10.16-AD	M
72.l10-IB	M
72.fall-EB	M
72.l10-AD	M
72.11.13-CC	M
72.12.2-CC	M
72.12.4-EB	M
72.12.24-MCo	TM
72.c.12.29-30-RE	TM

72.12.31-IB	M
73.1.4-AD	M
73.c.1.7-12-CG	TM
73.c.1.7-12-GG	M
73.1.12-IB	M
73.1.12-AD	M
73.wint.-GG	TM
73.1.31-CC	M
73.2.1-JM	M
73.e2-IB	T
73.2.21-HV	TM
73.c.3.11-IB	T
73.3.14-IB	T
73.4.12-IB	M
73.6.11-IB	M
73.6.23-AD	M
73.7.13-EB	M
73.8.28-IB	T
73.c.9.22-MCu	M
73.10.13-AD	M
73.c.m11-JM	M
73.11.20-IB	T
73.12.15-MCu	M
74.1.1-WF	TM
74.1.25-EB	M
74.2.12-DW	M?
74.3.14-AD	M
74.4.1-JM	M
74.4.1-DW	M
74.5.1-MCu	M
74.5.20-LF	T
74.6.4-JM	M
74.7.1-AD	M
74.7.17-18-IB	M
74.7.18-MCu	M
74.7.27-JM	M
74.8.1-MCo	T
74.8.6-MCu	T
74.10.6-DK	TM
74.11.18-AD	TM
74.12.1-JM	T
74.12.26-AD	M
74.12.30-MCu	?
75.3.1-AD	T
75.c.l.wint.-JK	T
75.3.15-MCu	TM
75.3.17-JM	T
75.4.8-WS	T
75.6.22/29-IB	T
75.7.28-JM	T
75.10.1-JM	TM
76.1.22-JM	T
76.3.27-RA	T
76.3.29-AD	T
76.4.5-JM	T
76.6.20-IB	T
76.7.15-RA	T
76.9.20-RM	T
76.10.20-RA	T
76.c.fall-RA	M
76.11.9-MCu	TM
76.c.l-IB	M
77.1.15-EG	T
77.4.1-CW et al.	TM
77.e5-FO	TM
77.5.30-RA	TM
77.6.1-CW et al.	T
77.6.15-MCu	TM
77.6.20-LG	T
77.l.su/e.fa-JM	T
77.10.31-RA	M
77.11.1-EG et al.	T
77.11.21-MCu	T
77.c.l-AD	T
77.12.15-LR	T
78.2.1-PR	T
78.2.1-EG	T
78.2.15-KE	T
78.2.20-RA	TM
78.3.20-MCu	T
78.4.16-DS/CG	T
78.5.12-DS	T
78.5.21-GS/CW	M
78.5.31-DS	M
78.5.31-RA	M
78.6.3-GS/CW	M
78.c.6.3-GS/CW	M

CONCISE BIBLIOGRAPHY

Ackroyd, Peter. *Blake*. Ballantine Books, 1997.

Adamo, Ralph. *Sadness at the Private University*. Lost Roads No. 3. Lost Roads, 1977.

Adamo, Ralph. *Waterblind: Selected Poems*. Portals, 2002.

Allen, Esther, and Susan Bernofsky, eds. *In Translation: Translators on Their Work and What It Means*. Columbia University Press, 2013.

Atkins, Thomas R. "Studied: 250 Films in 14 Days at the Hollins Conference on Creative Writing and Cinema." *Film News: The International Review of AV Materials and Equipment* 27, no. 4 (September 1970): 12–15.

Babij, James. "Footsteps of the Poet." *Ruthenians.net*, May 7, 2020. https://www.ruthenians.net/kArpatia/2020/05/footsteps-of-the-poet/.

Babij, James. "Portland to Portland." *Ruthenians.net*, July 29, 2014. https://www.ruthenians.net/kArpatia/2014/07/portland-to-portland/.

Baudelaire, Charles. *Intimate Journals*. Translated by Christopher Isherwood. Beacon, 1957.

Blake, William. *Complete Writings with Variant Readings*. Edited by Geoffrey Keynes. Oxford University Press, 1972.

Blake, William. *William Blake's Illustrations to "The Grave."* Double Elephant Folio & Quarto, 1969.

Bédouin, Jean-Louis. *André Breton: Une étude par Jean-Louis Bédouin; Œuvres choisies, bibliographie, dessins, portraits, fac-similés*. Editions Pierre Seghers, 1955.

Beowulf: The Oldest English Epic. Translated by Charles W. Kennedy. Oxford University Press, 1940.

Borges, Jorge Luis. *Labyrinths: Selected Stories & Other Writings*. New Directions, 1964.

Breton, André. *Manifestoes of Surrealism*. Translated by Richard Seaver and Helen R. Lane. University of Michigan Press, 2001.

Breton, André. *Nadja*. Translated by Richard Howard. Grove, 1960.

Breton, André. *Selections*. Edited by Mark Polizzotti. University of California Press, 2003.

Broughton, Irv. *The Blessing of the Fleet*. Lost Roads No. 6. Lost Roads, 1977.

Broughton, Irv. Interview by A. P. Walton. June 28, 2023.

Broughton, Irv, dir. *It Wasn't a Dream: It Was a Flood*. Cinematography by Irv Broughton and Frank Stanford. Mill Mountain Films, 1975. 16 mm film.

Bulfinch, Thomas. *Bulfinch's Mythology: "The Age of Fable," "The Age of Chivalry," "Legends of Charlemagne."* Modern Library, n.d.

Buñuel, Luis. *"L'Age d'Or" and "Un Chien Andalou": Films by Luis Buñuel*. Translated by Marianne Alexandre. Simon & Schuster, 1968.

Byron, Lord. *Childe Harold's Pilgrimage*. Edited by A. Hamilton Thompson. Cambridge University Press, 2013.

Byron, Lord. *The Complete Poetical Works*. Edited by Jerome J. McGann. 7 vols. Clarendon, 1980–1993. Vol. 6 coedited by Barry Weller.

Byron, Lord. *The Works of Lord Byron*. Rev. ed. *Letters and Journals*, vol. 5, edited by Rowland E. Prothero. John Murray, 1901.

Camus, Albert. *The Rebel: An Essay on Man in Revolt*. Translated by Anthony Bower. Vintage International, 1991.

Cocteau, Jean. *Cocteau on the Film: A Conversation Recorded by André Fraigneau*. Translated by Vera Traill. Dennis Dobson, 1954.

Cocteau, Jean. "*Le Sang d'un poète*." In *French Film Theory and Criticism: A History/Anthology, 1907–1939*. Vol. 2, *1929–1939*, edited by Richard Abel. Princeton University Press, 1988.

Cocteau, Jean. *The Blood of a Poet: A Film by Jean Cocteau*. Translated by Lily Pons. Bodley, 1949.

Cocteau, Jean. *Two Screenplays: "The Blood of a Poet," "The Testament of Orpheus."* Translated by Carol Martin-Sperry. Penguin, 1969.

Coleridge, Samuel Taylor. *The Complete Poetical Works of Samuel Taylor Coleridge*. Edited by Ernest Hartley Coleridge. 2 vols. Clarendon, 1912.

Cooper, Robert M. *Lost on Both Sides: Dante Gabriel Rossetti: Critic and Poet*. Ohio University Press, 1970.

Cowley, Malcolm. *Blue Juniata: Collected Poems*. Viking, 1968.

Crinnin, Max, and Aidan Ryan, eds. *Constant Stranger: After Frank Stanford*. Foundlings, 2018.

Croft, P. J., ed. *Autograph Poetry in the English Language: Facsimiles of Original Manuscripts from the Fourteenth to the Twentieth Century*. 2 vols. McGraw-Hill Book Company, 1973.

Cuddihy, Michael. *Celebrations*. Copper Canyon, 1980.

Cuddihy, Michael, ed. *Ironwood*, nos. 1–17 (1972–81).

Cuddihy, Michael. *Try Ironwood: An Editor Remembers*. Rowan Tree, 1990.

Cuddihy, Michael. *A Walled Garden*. Carnegie Mellon University Press, 1989.

Deason, Alis J., Azadeh Fattahi, Carlos S. Frenk, et al. "The Edge of the Galaxy." *Monthly Notices of the Royal Astronomical Society* 496, no. 3 (August 2020): 3929–42.

Desnos, Robert. *Essential Poems and Writings of Robert Desnos*. Edited by Mary Ann Caws. Black Widow, 2007.

Dreyer, Carl Theodor. *Dreyer in Double Reflection: Translation of Carl Th. Dreyer's Writings About the Film (Om Filmen)*. Edited by Donald Skoller. E. P. Dutton, 1973.

Dugan, Alan. "An Interview with Alan Dugan." Interview by Michael Ryan. *Iowa Review* 4, no. 3 (Summer 1973): 90–97.

Dugan, Alan. *Poems Seven: New and Complete Poetry*. Seven Stories, 2001.

Dumoulin, Heinrich. *A History of Zen Buddhism*. Translated by Paul Peachey. Pantheon, 1963.

Durrell, Lawrence. *The Alexandria Quartet*. Faber and Faber, 1970.

Eberhart, Richard. "Frank Stanford." In "Chinese Poetry & the American Imagination." Special issue, *Ironwood* 9, no. 1, issue 17 (1981): 137–38.

Ehrenreich, Ben. "The Long Goodbye." *Poetry Foundation*, January 18, 2008. https://www.poetryfoundation.org/articles/69003/the-long-goodbye.

Eisenstein, Sergei. *Film Form: Essays in Film Theory*. Edited and translated by Jay Leyda. Harvest / Harcourt Brace Jovanovich, 1977.

Eliot, T. S. *The Sacred Wood: Essays on Poetry and Criticism.* 7th ed. Methuen, 1950.

Essick, Robert N., and Morton D. Paley. *Robert Blair's "The Grave" Illustrated by William Blake: A Study with Facsimile.* Scolar, 1982.

Fisher, Burton D., ed. *Mozart's "The Magic Flute."* Opera Journeys Publishing, 2005.

Follain, Jean. *Transparence of the World: Poems.* Translated and edited by W. S. Merwin. Atheneum, 1969.

Frank Stanford Papers. Yale Collection of American Literature. Beinecke Rare Book & Manuscript Library.

Frost, Robert. *The Letters of Robert Frost.* Vol. 2, *1920–1928,* edited by Donald Sheehy, Mark Richardson, Robert Bernard Hass, and Henry Atmore. Belknap Press of Harvard University Press, 2016.

Gauguin, Paul. *The Letters of Paul Gauguin to Georges Daniel de Monfreid.* Translated by Ruth Pielkovo. Dodd, Mead, 1922.

Gilchrist, Ellen. *The Age of Miracles: Stories.* Little, Brown, 1995.

Ginny Crouch Stanford Collection of Frank Stanford. Yale Collection of American Literature, Beinecke Rare Book & Manuscript Library.

Ginsberg, Allen. *The Letters of Allen Ginsberg.* Edited by Bill Morgan. Da Capo, 2008.

Goethe, Johann Wolfgang von. *The Autobiography of Goethe: Truth and Poetry, from My Own Life.* Translated by John Oxenford. London, 1897.

Goethe, Johann Wolfgang von. *Goethe: The Collected Works.* Vol. 3, *Essays on Art and Literature.* Edited by John Gearey. Translated by Ellen von Nardroff and Ernest H. von Nardroff. Suhrkamp Publishers New York, 1986.

Haralson, Eric L., ed. *Encyclopedia of American Poetry: The Twentieth Century.* Routledge, 2012.

Hart, Henry. *James Dickey: The World as a Lie.* Picador USA, 2000.

Jameson, W. C. *Lost Treasures of Arkansas's Waterways: Hidden Mines, Buried Fortunes, and Civil War Artifacts.* Plum Street Publishers, 2015.

Jarry, Alfred. *Exploits & Opinions of Doctor Faustroll, Pataphysician: A Neo-Scientific Novel.* Translated by Simon Watson Taylor. Exact Change, 1996.

Jolley, Nicholas, ed. *The Cambridge Companion to Leibniz.* Cambridge University Press, 2004.

Keats, John. *The Complete Poetry and Selected Prose of John Keats.* Edited by Harold Edgar Briggs. Modern Library, 1951.

Keats, John. *The Selected Letters of John Keats.* Edited by Lionel Trilling. Farrar, Straus and Young, 1951.

Kodell, Jerome. "The Poetry of the Psalms." *Bible Today,* March 1973, 1107–13.

Lancaster, Bob. "With the Dignity of his Doggerel: Auden Slouches Onstage, Unkempt." *Arkansas Democrat,* February 28, 1971.

Launius, Carl Judson. "It Was a Flood: The Life and Poetry of Frank Stanford." PhD diss., University of California, Davis, 1988.

Lawrence, D. H. *The Collected Letters of D. H. Lawrence.* Edited by Harry T. Moore. 2 vols. Viking, 1962.

Lawrence, D. H. *The Complete Poems of D. H. Lawrence.* Edited by Vivian de Sola Pinto and Warren Roberts. 2 vols. Viking, 1964.

Lawrence, D. H. *D. H. Lawrence's Letters to Bertrand Russell.* Edited by Harry T. Moore. Gotham Book Mart, 1948.

Lawrence, D. H. *Selected Poems*. With an introduction by Kenneth Rexroth. Viking, 1959.

Lawrence, D. H. *Studies in Classic American Literature*. Edited by Ezra Greenspan, Lindeth Vasey, and John Worthen. Cambridge University Press, 2014.

Lehman, David, ed. *The Oxford Book of American Poetry*. Oxford University Press, 2006.

"Les Blank Film Show Planned Here Tuesday." *Eureka Springs Times-Echo*, March 15, 1973.

Levee Camp Pay Rolls. Peters Job, July 14–20 and July 21–27, 1958. Private collection of Irv Broughton.

Little Review, vol. 2, no. 2 (issue 4), and vol. 5, nos. 1–2 (issues 9–10) (1971, 1974–75).

Lost Roads Publishers Brochure. Lost Roads Publishers, 1980.

Lowell, Robert. *Imitations*. Farrar, Straus and Cudahy, 1961.

McCay, Mary A. *Ellen Gilchrist*. Twayne Publishers, 1997.

McKernan, John. *Resurrection of the Dust: Selected Poems*. Backwaters, 2007.

McKernan, John. *Walking Along the Missouri River*. Lost Roads No. 5. Lost Roads, 1977.

McWilliams, James. *The Life and Poetry of Frank Stanford*. University of Arkansas Press, 2025.

Mencin Bond, Linda. Interview by A. P. Walton. January–July 2014.

Mill Mountain Review, vols. 1 and 2 (1969–75).

Morris, John S. *Bean Street*. Lost Roads No. 4. Lost Roads, 1977.

Myles, Eileen. "A Man's World." Review of *The Light the Dead See: Selected Poems of Frank Stanford*, by Frank Stanford. *Village Voice*, October 6, 1992.

Neruda, Pablo. *A New Decade: Poems 1958–1967*. Grove, 1969.

New American Review, no. 11 (1971).

Parra, Nicanor. *Poems and Antipoems*. Edited by Miller Williams. New Directions, 1967.

Pasolini, Pier Paolo. *The Selected Poetry of Pier Paolo Pasolini*. Edited by Stephen Sartarelli. University of Chicago Press, 2014.

Perkins, David. *A History of Modern Poetry: Modernism and After*. Vol. 2. Belknap Press of Harvard University Press, 1987.

Plato. *Complete Works*. Edited by John M. Cooper. Hackett, 1997.

"Poetry Contest Winners Are Announced." *Memphis Press-Scimitar*, April 14, 1958.

Porzio, Domenico, and Marco Valsecchi. *Understanding Picasso*. Newsweek Books, 1974.

Prawer, S. S., ed. and trans. *The Penguin Book of Lieder*. Penguin Books, 1964.

Ransom, John Crowe. *The New Criticism*. New Directions, 1941.

Richie, Donald. *Japanese Cinema: Film Style and National Character*. Anchor Books, 1971.

Robinson, W. R., ed. *Man and the Movies*. With assistance from George Garrett. Louisiana State University Press, 1967.

Rossetti, Dante Gabriel. *Collected Poetry and Prose*. Edited by Jerome McGann. Yale University Press, 2003.

Schumacher, Michael. *Dharma Lion: A Biography of Allen Ginsberg*. Expanded ed. University of Minnesota Press, 2016.

"Self-Portrait of an Angel and Monster." *Time*, January 22, 1973.

Shackelford, George T. M., and Claire Frèches-Thory. *Gauguin Tahiti*. MFA Publications, 2004.

Shelley, Percy Bysshe. *Shelley's Critical Prose*. Edited by Bruce R. McElderry Jr. University of Nebraska Press, 1967.

Shugars, Murray B. "What the Moon Says: Frank Stanford's Quest for Poetic Identity." PhD diss., Purdue University, May 2000.

Shuptrine, Herbert, and James Dickey. *Jericho: The South Beheld*. Oxmore House, 1974.

Stanford, Dorothy, and Ruth Rogers. Interview by Murray B. Shugars. June 13, 1997.
Stanford, Frank. "A Past: Wintered like a Circus." *Iowa Review* 5, no. 3 (Summer 1974): 39–54.
Stanford, Frank. *Arkansas Bench Stone*. Seattle, WA: Mill Mountain Press, 1975.
Stanford, Frank. *The Battlefield Where the Moon Says I Love You*. Lost Roads Nos. 7–12. Mill Mountain; Lost Roads, 1977.
Stanford, Frank. *The Battlefield Where the Moon Says I Love You*. 2nd ed. With a preface by C. D. Wright and (in the 2nd printing) a "Note" by Forrest Gander. Lost Roads Publishers, 2000.
Stanford, Frank. *The Battlefield Where the Moon Says I Love You*. Edited by James McWilliams and A. P. Walton. 3rd ed. University of Arkansas Press, 2026.
Stanford, Frank. *Conditions Uncertain and Likely to Pass Away*. Lost Roads, 1990.
Stanford, Frank. *Constant Stranger*. Mill Mountain, 1976.
Stanford, Frank. *Crib Death*. Ironwood, 1978.
Stanford, Frank. *Field Talk*. Mill Mountain, 1975.
Stanford, Frank. *Hidden Water: From the Frank Stanford Archives*. Third Man Books, 2015.
Stanford, Frank. "Irv Brought[on] Talks with Frank Stanford." Interview by Irv Broughton. Ca. 1972–74; mislabeled as 1972–73. Transcript (uncut). Frank Stanford Papers. Yale Collection of American Literature. Beinecke Rare Book & Manuscript Library.
Stanford, Frank. *Ladies From Hell*. Mill Mountain, 1974.
Stanford, Frank. *The Light the Dead See: Selected Poems of Frank Stanford*. Edited by Leon Stokesbury. University of Arkansas Press, 1991.
Stanford, Frank. *Shade*. Mill Mountain, 1975.
Stanford, Frank. *The Singing Knives*. Mill Mountain, 1971.
Stanford, Frank. *The Singing Knives*. 2nd ed. Lost Roads No. 18. Lost Roads, 1979.
Stanford, Frank. *What About This: Collected Poems of Frank Stanford*. Edited by Michael Wiegers. Copper Canyon, 2015.
Stanford, Frank. "With the Approach of the Oak the Axeman Quakes." In *Fifty Contemporary Poets: The Creative Process*. Edited by Alberta Turner. Longman, 1977.
Stanford, Frank. *You*. Lost Roads No. 15. Lost Roads, 1979.
Stanford, Frank, ed. *Preview: Eight Poets*. University of Arkansas Press, 1971.
Stanford, Ginny. "Death in the Cool Evening." *Portable Plateau* 1, no. 1 (1997).
Stanford, Ginny. "*Requiem*: A Fragment." *New Orleans Review* 20, nos. 3/4 (Fall–Winter 1994): 150–67.
Stokes, Richard, ed. *The Book of Lieder: The Original Texts of over 1000 Songs*. Faber and Faber, 2005.
Stokesbury, Leon, ed. *Preview: 1968–1969*. University of Arkansas, 1969.
Stokesbury, Leon, ed. *Preview: The Literature*. University of Arkansas, 1970.
Stoss, John. *Finding the Broom*. Lost Roads No. 2. Lost Roads, 1977.
Trussell, Robert. "Frank Stanford: A Poet's Dreams, Death and Legacy." *Stage & Scream in Kansas City*, January 16, 2012. https://kansascitytheater.wordpress.com/2012/01/16/frank-stanford-a-poets-dreams-death-and-legacy/.
Villon, François. *Poems*. Translated by David Georgi. Northwestern University Press, 2013.
Villon, François. *The Poems of François Villon*. Translated by Galway Kinnell. University Press of New England, 1982.
Walton, A. P. "Compendium of Characters in Frank Stanford's Poetry." In Crinnin and Ryan, *Constant Stranger*.
Walton, A. P. " 'Full of Wonder, and Wistfulness, and Strange': Frank Stanford in the Light (and Shadow) of D. H. Lawrence." *D. H. Lawrence Review* 46, nos. 1/2 (2021–24): 75–94.

Walton, A. P. "Lives & Works: From Myth to Mythology." In Crinnin and Ryan, *Constant Stranger*.

Walton, A. P. "Toward Innumerable Futures: Frank Stanford & Origins." Master's thesis, Lund University, Spring 2015.

Whitman, Walt. *Leaves of Grass*. Brooklyn, 1855.

Willett, Bill. "Correspondence from Frank Stanford to Bill Willett, with Commentary by Bill Willett." Edited by Matthew Henriksen. *Fulcrum: An Annual of Poetry and Aesthetics*, no. 7 (2011): 408–14.

Wood, John. "With Allen in Arkansas: An Ozark Diary." *American Poetry Review* 41, no. 5 (September/October 2012): 47–49.

Wright, C. D. "A Note on *The Battlefield Where the Moon Says I Love You*." In "Chinese Poetry & the American Imagination." Special issue, *Ironwood* 9, no. 1, issue 17 (1981): 157–61.

Wright, C. D. Introduction to "Frank Stanford: Blue Yodel of a Wayfaring Stranger, Nine Previously Unpublished Poems by the Virtuoso Dreamer of the Ozarks," by Frank Stanford. *Oxford American*, Winter 2006, 99–100.

Wright, C. D. *Room Rented by a Single Woman*. Lost Roads No. 1. Lost Roads, 1977.

CORRESPONDENCE, POETRY, AND IMAGE SOURCES

Correspondence by Stanford to the following recipients and letter images appear from the collections of the respectively named institutions, to which grateful acknowledgment is here made:

Bender, Eleanor (and *Open Places*): *Open Places (Columbia, Mo.) Records. The State Historical Society of Missouri.*

Cowley, Malcolm: *Malcolm Cowley Papers. Newberry Library.*

Cuddihy, Michael: *Michael Cuddihy Papers and Ironwood Press Records, 1932–2000. The University of Arizona, Special Collections.*

Dugan, Alan: *Alan Dugan Papers, 1861–2003. Stuart A. Rose Manuscript, Archives, and Rare Book Library, Emory University.*

Eberhart, Richard: *Richard Eberhart Papers. Rauner Special Collections Library, Dartmouth College.*

Fox, William L.: *West Coast Poetry Review Records. John Hay Library, Brown University.*

Garrett, George: *George P. Garrett Papers, 1929–2008. David M. Rubenstein Rare Book & Manuscript Library, Duke University.*

Hitchcock, George (and *kayak*): *Kayak Collection. The Poetry Collection, University at Buffalo.*

Justice, Donald: *Donald Justice Papers. Special Collections, University of Delaware Library.*

Plymell, Charles: *David Ray Papers. Special Collections, University of Chicago.*

Solotaroff, Theodore: *Ted Solotaroff Papers. Manuscripts and Archives Division, the New York Public Library. Astor, Lenox, and Tilden Foundations.*

Stafford, William: *William E. Stafford Archives. Special Collections and Archives, Lewis & Clark College.*

The Massachusetts Review: *Massachusetts Review Records. Robert S. Cox Special Collections & University Archives Research Center, UMass Amherst Libraries.*

Vogelpohl, Fr. Herbert: *Subiaco Abbey Archives.*

The remaining correspondence by Stanford and images appear from the following institutions and individuals, to which or whom grateful acknowledgment is here made:

The letters to Ralph Adamo, Irv Broughton, Cheryl Campbell (now Cheryl E. Ross), John McKernan, and Bill Willett are from these individuals' respective private collections.

The June 20, 1977, letter to Louis Gallo is from the private collection of Ralph Adamo.

The letters to Donald L. Kemp, Fr. Jerome Kodell, Robert T. Motter Jr., and Fred Overstreet; the Donald Justice letter inscribed in *Open Places*, no. 11; the 1977 letters to C. D. Wright, John Stoss, Ralph Adamo, John S. Morris, John McKernan, and Irv Broughton; the two 1977 letters to Ellen Gilchrist (one of which is also to Ralph Adamo, Louis Gallo, and Everette Maddox); a copy of the May 30, 1977, letter to Adamo; and the June 2, 1978, photograph of Stanford by Frederick Kullman are from the Frank Stanford Papers, Yale Collection of American Literature, Beinecke Rare Book & Manuscript Library.

The letters to Leonard Randolph and Philip H. Robins are from Lost Roads Publishers Records, Yale Collection of American Literature, Beinecke Rare Book & Manuscript Library.

The 1978 letter to Ellen Gilchrist; the late summer or early fall 1977 letter to John McKernan; the letters to Dorothy Stanford and Carolyn Gilbert; the 1978 letters to Ginny Stanford and C. D. Wright, including Stanford's will; a copy of the April 1, 1974, letter to David Walker; the 1973 photograph by Ginny Stanford of Stanford at the White River Lodge house; and the cover photo by Ginny Stanford are from the Ginny Crouch Stanford Collection of Frank Stanford, Yale Collection of American Literature, Beinecke Rare Book & Manuscript Library.

The letters to Allen Ginsberg and Lawrence Ferlinghetti are from the Allen Ginsberg Papers, Special Collections, Stanford University.

The mid-August 1972 book inscription to Richard Eberhart and the letter to Karl Elder are from Jeff and Susan Hirsch and Amir Naghib, booksellers.

The mid-August 1972 book inscription to James Babij, the fall 1972 letter and book inscription to Eleanor Bender, the winter 1974 typescript publication history sheet sent to David Walker, the May 1969 Christ of the Ozarks photo, and the September 1970 photo of Stanford and Linda Mencin are from the private collection of A. P. Walton.

The January 1973 letter to Carolyn Gilbert is from the private collection of Carrie Rogers Prysock.

The February 12, 1974, letter to David Walker and December 30, 1974, letter to Michael Cuddihy are from preexisting transcriptions. Both appeared in a now-discontinued online literary journal, *The Alsop Review*, accessed in February 2008; the latter appeared in *Ironwood* 17 (1981).

Excerpts from correspondence to Frank Stanford (including the letter from Stanley Kunitz to Alan Dugan, the letter from Dugan to the Academy of American Poets, and Judith Shahn's writings to Stanford) are from the Frank Stanford Papers and the Ginny Crouch Stanford Collection of Frank Stanford, Yale Collection of American Literature, Beinecke Rare Book & Manuscript Library—except for the December 18, 1972, letter from Dugan to Stanford (annotated by Stanford and returned to Dugan), which is from the Alan Dugan Papers, 1861–2003, Stuart A. Rose Manuscript, Archives, and Rare Book Library, Emory University; the correspondence from Cheryl Campbell to Stanford, which is from Cheryl E. Ross's private collection; and the correspondence from Malcolm Cowley to Stanford (and to Irv Broughton), which is from the Malcolm Cowley Papers, Newberry Library.

The excerpt from Dorothy Stanford's correspondence to Michael Cuddihy is from the Michael Cuddihy Papers and Ironwood Press Records, 1932–2000, University of Arizona, Special Collections.

The memo from Richard Howard to Theodore Solotaroff is from the American Review Records, 1967–1977, University of Michigan, Bentley Historical Library. Excerpts from Linda Stanford's correspondence to Alan Dugan and William L. Fox are, respectively, from the Alan Dugan Papers, 1861–2003, Stuart A. Rose Manuscript, Archives, and Rare Book Library, Emory University, and the West Coast Poetry Review Records, John Hay Library, Brown University. Grateful acknowledgment is here made to the authors or their estates for this book's reproduction of their words herein.

INDEX

Contents of letters or notes directly related to a letter recipient are shown under the recipient's name. Contents of letters related to other topics are shown as main headings or subheadings under those topics. Named Stanford works include their respective genre or other allocation, named characters include their respective author or source, and named films include their respective director. The page numbers for illustrations are italicized. Frank Stanford is referred to by his initials ("FS").

C

D

E